taking command

CONTRIBUTORS

Colonel Samuel H. Hays

Lieutenant Colonel William N. Thomas

Lieutenant Colonel William J. Livsey, Jr.

Lieutenant Colonel Thomas A. Rehm

Lieutenant Colonel Robert T. Zargan

Lieutenant Colonel Warren H. Eisenhart

Major Daniel J. Tobin

Major Robert H. Marcrum

Major Quay C. Snyder

Major James C. Burris

Major Raymond M. Macedonia

Major Charles R. Russell

Major Ernest B. Wilson

Major Vernon B. Sones

Captain Fred Luthans

STACKPOLE BOOKS

Edited by

COLONEL SAMUEL H. HAYS
Director Military Psychology and Leadership
United States Military Academy

and

LIEUTENANT COLONEL WILLIAM N. THOMAS
Assistant Professor of Leadership
United States Military Academy

THE ART AND SCIENCE OF MILITARY LEADERSHIP

TAKING COMMAND

Contents

Preface

THE STUDY of leadership has assumed ever more critical importance over the last half-century. The rapid growth in size and complexity of our organizational structures has created a mounting requirement for increased skill and sophistication on the part of those in leadership positions. This demand for skilled leaders creates in turn a need for expanded basic knowledge of the processes and techniques of leadership and for ways to identify, educate, and develop potential leaders. To meet this demand, increased attention has been devoted in recent years to research in the academic disciplines of psychology, sociology, anthropology, political science, education, and management. This interdisciplinary approach has substantially modified traditional concepts. The resulting fund of knowledge has fostered the development of courses in leadership, management, and executive development in military, business, and education schools.

Recognizing the requirement and the need to equip future officers with the best and most recent knowledge in the field, the United States Military Academy in 1946 created the Office of Military Psychology and Leadership. Beginning with the state of the art as it was then conceived, this office has tried over the last twenty years to assemble and present to its students the best possible mix of theoretical knowledge, practical experience, and managerial methods. Many officers with wide command experience and extensive academic backgrounds in the behavioral sciences have devoted their talents and abilities to the task of developing this course. The field of study both as to content and method of presentation still lies on the frontier of human endeavor. We are still far from satisfied with either the extent of our knowledge or the proper proportions of empirically supported data and conventional wisdom. The authors felt, however, that the current demand for instructional material in military leadership was sufficient to warrant a crystallization of current thought on the subject. By making this thought available, they hope to stimulate additional study and attract suggestions and criticism which will promote additional progress in the field.

Students in Universities, Service Academies, Officer Candidate Schools, and Noncommissioned Officer Schools across the land are preparing themselves to lead soldiers, sailors, and airmen in the Armed Forces. The responsibilities of this leadership in a rapidly changing environment present many awesome yet potentially satisfying challenges. This book is designed to assist students of

7

leadership whether enrolled in schools or engaging in self-study to a fuller understanding of, and a greater sensitivity for, the fundamental issues, problems, concepts and techniques involved in leading, influencing, and directing others. If, in some way, this book contributes to better equipping future leaders to meet their challenges with understanding, the effort will be justified.

The editors, S. H. Hays, Director of Military Psychology and Leadership, USMA, and William N. Thomas, Assistant Professor of Leadership, USMA, assume full responsibility for the contents of this book. They have accepted, revised or rejected the contributions of their associates in accordance with their own judgment. They recognize that the complexities of the study of leadership, the number of academic disciplines that must be harmonized, and the divergence of professional views leave them open to errors in fact and interpretation as well as differences of expert opinion. For any unintentional delinquencies we ask indulgence from our expert readers.

The succeeding pages are the cumulative effort of many past and present members of the Office of Military Psychology and Leadership, USMA who have tried to gather and present the best in current thought on Military Leadership for the instruction of our future military leaders. No single chapter can be said to be the complete product of any one individual. Colonel S. H. Hays, Lieutenant Colonels William N. Thomas, William J. Livsey, Jr., Thomas A. Rehm, Robert T. Zargan, Warren H. Eisenhart, Majors Daniel J. Tobin, Robert H. Marcrum, Quay C. Snyder, James C. Burris, Raymond M. Macedonia, Charles R. Russell, Ernest B. Wilson, Vernon B. Sones and Captain Fred Luthans have all contributed to the initial preparation, rewriting, and editing of portions of this book. All opinions expressed herein are those of the authors and editors, writing as private individuals and do not necessarily represent the views of any governmental agency. They gratefully acknowledge their indebtedness to their predecessors in the Office as well as to their colleagues and outside experts whose views, advice, and suggestions were solicited. Although they go unnamed, their essential assistance is recognized and deeply appreciated.

West Point, New York

S. H. H.
W. N. T.

Introduction

The art of leading men has held a basic fascination for man throughout the ages. Historians, philosophers, and scholars, as well as men of affairs, have speculated endlessly about the qualities or conditions that have endowed some men with the accolade of successful leadership while denying it to others. Despite intense study, there has been little agreement. Theories of leadership range over a wide spectrum from Carlyle's theory that great men determine the course of history to Pareto's concept that situations permit a circulation of elites. Many have seen social factors as the controlling element. Others have recognized only the preponderant influence of heredity. Each theory has been based on observation of historical fact and has claimed its own partisans. None could successfully explain all of the facts in the case.

The truth of the matter is that the exercise of leadership, though complex, is an extremely common and natural behavioral phenomenon. It occurs whenever one man influences the behavior of others for a purpose. It is performed by the chairman of the board, the foreman on the line, the commanding general, and the squad leader. It is present even without the trappings of rank or position when a private soldier persuades his buddies to cover him as he crawls toward the enemy. It occurs when one student persuades others to co-operate in a laboratory experiment or to support him in a discussion. All concerted group effort involves leadership—that is, the actions of one or more persons in a group who can get the others to co-operate for a purpose. The very universality of the phenomenon, plus the wealth of the personality, group dynamics, and situational data available to describe it, have contributed to the complexity of the study.

BACKGROUND

The ravenous demands of the expanding organizations of our technological society have given increased impetus to the study of leadership. Larger and more complex structures involving more human and material resources are making the traditional methods of leader selection and training increasingly less adequate. The critical nature of the selection and preparation of those who must assume the responsibility for leading and directing others has been receiving ever increasing attention. Early advances in the behavioral sciences, the use of

9

empirical methods, and the growth of Frederick W. Taylor's "scientific management" movement in the 1890's provided the initial perspectives and tools with which to tackle the subject.

The mobilization for World War I provided the opportunity for psychologists to apply their discipline to leader evaluation, identification, and prediction. In 1915, Hugo Münsterberg and Walter Dill Scott had devised and introduced psychological selection tests. During the war, Yerkes and Bingham of the Committee on Psychology went on to administer intelligence tests to nearly 1,727,000 men providing valuable empirical data for later comparative study. The Committee on Classification of Personnel, formed under Walter Dill Scott, studied problems of assignment and methods of rating officers for appointment and promotion. His work in this area earned him the Distinguished Service Medal.

The period between the wars saw many changes in industry and management which challenged psychologists and sociologists. Progress was slow, however, causing some disenchantment with the promise of finding an easy solution to leadership problems. At this point, the classic work carried on by Elton Mayo at the Hawthorne plant reawakened interest by emphasizing a human relations approach. Meanwhile, the Taylor society and the Personnel Research Federation assisted by such men as Ordway Tead, W. V. Bingham, L. L. Thurstone, W. H. Tukey, and General M. B. Stewart (then USMA Superintendent) had kept alive the more promising aspects of the research done during World War I, that focused primarily on the individual leader, his abilities and traits.

With this background, students of leadership faced the massive demands of World War II. Mobilization again provided a promising opportunity for behavioral science research. The Personnel Research Section of the Army, established in 1940, was, like its other Service counterparts, almost immediately deluged with requirements. Although some material, notably by Meier and Jennings, appeared during the war, publication of the results of research was generally delayed. The research on situational aspects of leadership by the Office of Strategic Services and the work of Stouffer and his associates was not published until after the war.

Spurred on by the expanding requirements of the Armed Services, government, and industry, research on leadership continued to involve such governmental agencies as the Office of Naval Research and the Army Personnel Research Office as well as universities, management associations, and institutes. The work performed by such men as Bass, Fiedler, Guetzkow, Hemphill, Pelz, Stogdill, and Tannenbaum was rapidly absorbed into the mushrooming schools on management which blossomed in industry, college campuses, and in governmental agencies during the mid and late fifties. Because of their urgent requirement for leaders, the military services have continued to be instrumental in fostering this research, study and instruction in leadership.

The last fifteen years have witnessed the collection of a massive amount of data on leadership. Laboratory and statistical techniques have been devised to permit the analysis of interpersonal relationships in a more empirical manner.

The academic disciplines of political science, sociology anthropology, psychology, and education have all placed their special insights and techniques at the service of students of leadership. Although the development of a comprehensive and scientific theory of leadership is still some way off, substantial progress has been made. There is a general agreement in recent literature that the complex of human interrelationships that leads to effective leadership can best be approached through the study of the individual as a leader, the social psychology of groups, and the situational factors affecting this interaction.

SPECIAL REQUIREMENTS OF MILITARY LEADERSHIP

The problems faced and the skills and knowledge to be mastered in military leadership are similar in most respects to those required of civilian leaders. The conditions of military service and the nature of the environment in which the military leader must operate, however, create a number of conditions which are unique. Specifically, leadership in the services is institutional in nature and appointive in fact. Although seen by some as being totally authoritarian, such a gross characterization of military leadership is no longer valid, if it ever was. The effective military leader establishes his leadership authority with his group so that in time of crisis, or a hazardous situation, he is able to effectively influence their behavior. This is true whether exercising leadership in staff or line positions. Command roles in all services carry with them the sanctions of law and a scope of responsibility for both performance and group welfare that is rarely found in other leadership positions. The vital importance of combat leadership exists at all levels of organization. The squad or section leader in charge of a small group is frequently called upon to perform critical operations involving life or death that differ only in scope from those of major unit commanders.

In addition to the grave responsibilities of combat and training for it, the military leader must also exercise managerial skills and techniques common to business or industry. Service units, depots, and administrative agencies are very similar in nature to organizations in the industrial world. In many cases, even the personnel involved are a part of the civilian labor force, indistinguishable in most respects from those in industry or business. Such assignments require the leader to adapt his techniques and methods to the needs of the group and the environment. Despite the wide variations in situation, organizational structure, or nature of the personnel to be led, the fundamental requirements of leadership remain the same. Subordinates must be influenced, controlled, and directed toward designated goals. Individual problems must be solved and institutional standards and objectives achieved.

Leadership over large and small organizations has been exercised in the past with varying degrees of success. Many leaders, using traditional knowledge and rules of thumb, have displayed great skill and aptitude for the task. Others have not. Often poor leadership produces results, but at minimum levels and at an exorbitant expense in time, manpower, and money. The increasing scope and complexity of the problems facing military leaders today leave less leeway for error and require an increased probability of high quality performance. Knowing only how to perform in one leadership position is an inadequate basis for coping with the rapidly changing conditions and environment of military service today. To be properly equipped, today's leaders should possess a knowledge of the "why's" as well as of the "what's." Some knowledge *of* leadership can be acquired through experience and practice, but a knowledge *about* leadership is the essential element that permits the leader to generalize from his experiences, increase his scope, and adapt to changing circumstances.

THE CONTENT OF LEADERSHIP INSTRUCTION

The proper question is not can leadership be taught, but what must today's leader learn to prepare him for the tasks ahead. This alone is a question of some complexity. The combined efforts of the academic disciplines have yet to provide us with a comprehensive scientific theory with which we can isolate and evaluate all the complex factors which influence the exercise of leadership. Each presents us with specific facets and insights which go far to illuminate and extend the scope of the traditional knowledge of the art. Similarly the pragmatic experience in industry and the military services can contribute an understanding of techniques, methods, attitudes, and skills which have produced results.

The study of American military leadership must be firmly based on the spiritual and cultural heritage of our society, on the knowledge developed by the behavioral sciences, and on the practical experience and judgment of generations of military leaders. In order to fit into the existing environment, a student must be aware not only of the objective knowledge of leadership processes, but also of the cultural and doctrinal aspects of its exercise in the American Armed Forces. This approach is based on the premise that leadership can be learned through an understanding of the philosophical framework, scientific principles, and past practical experience in the art. It is a generalization and translation of leaders' experiences and of scientific knowledge into the current military environment. It does not offer pat solutions; nor does it substitute for practical experience. Rather, it attempts to present to the student knowledge which he needs if he is to be a successful practitioner of the art of leading men.

The organization of the book recognizes that it is practically impossible to divorce the elements that interact in any event calling for the influence of a leader on a group. For academic purposes, however, it is necessary to isolate what is known about each of these interacting elements in order to illustrate principles of general applicability. After describing a practical integrated concept of leadership, it examines his qualities, style, and skills. Attention is next directed toward the followers organized as a group with special consideration to group structure and processes. The final section of the book is devoted to a consideration of the specific situations that the military leader must face.

The selected content is somewhat arbitrary and by no means covers all areas or examines all facets of the leadership phenomenon. As the student of leadership proceeds through this book, he should bear in mind that leadership is learned rather than taught. The mastery of basic concepts, the development of sensitivity and an awareness of specific problem areas, the learning of specific techniques—these can assist him by helping him better understand the "why's" of leading. Knowledge can make him a better leader—if he applies it with discrimination and judgment. Academic or theoretical knowledge, however, is no substitute for practical experience. Based on a foundation of understanding the processes of influence, one learns to lead through leading.

I

A Usable
Concept Of Leadership

THE EXERCISE of leadership is a universal and exceedingly complex social phenomenon that has long defied exact scientific definition and measurement. The incessant demands of government and industry for increased ability to predict and to develop leadership skills have stimulated a rapid growth in behavioral science research. Scientists in many related academic disciplines are continuing to analyze the factors and variables that enter into the process. Across the entire spectrum of study they face the most complex variable of all—man himself. Both individually and in groups men display such diversity and versatility in response to situational challenges that each question, even partially answered by research, raises still further questions demanding answers. This expanding search for scientific knowledge renders the study of leadership a dynamic and challenging one. Yesterday's theories or hypotheses are continually being modified or questioned by later studies.

While the search for a viable scientific theory continues, it is necessary for the practical world to assemble what is known and put it to use. The various perspectives and insights must be organized into a conceptual framework that can serve as a guide for the student who must use this knowledge in practice. In analyzing the theoretical approaches to the process, three primary factors can be identified in any leadership act: the leader, his group of followers, and the environmental and situational aspects of their task surroundings. Each of these factors, in turn, can be studied through the isolation of major variables that have been identified through scientific investigation. The entire framework is bound together by a concept of dynamic interaction between these major factors.

LEADERSHIP DEFINED

The basis of a common concept depends upon an understanding of the term leadership. Specific definitions differ depending on the writer. Basically, however, leadership is the art of influencing men. This definition, although short, indicates a dynamic motivating process or activity involving a leader and other members of a group. It identifies leading as an act rather than as a static set of

15

characteristics inherent in an individual. For military use, however, this short definition is of restricted value because it lacks purpose and is not sufficiently inclusive. A military leader influences subordinates for specific reasons; he motivates men toward a common unit mission or goal within an environment. Consequently, a more appropriate definition for the soldier and this text is that *leadership is the art of influencing human behavior so as to accomplish a mission in the manner desired by the leader.*

Leadership, Management, and Command

Any definition of leadership raises semantical issues, as the terms leadership, management, and command overlap widely in military and civilian usage. To many military personnel the terms leadership and command are synonymous. Likewise, industry frequently makes little distinction between leadership and management. To many people both in and out of the service, command is frequently considered to be the military equivalent of what the civilian calls management.

In the military, the mission normally is designated by higher authority. When influencing and directing men, the leader inspires by obtaining the willingness, obedience, confidence, respect, loyalty, and co-operation of his men. On the other hand, management is considered as the science of employing men and material in the economical and effective accomplishment of a mission. It is a component of leadership, but frequently has a less dynamic and less spirited connotation than leadership. A leader must both manage and inspire. Some hesitate to accept this definition, insisting that management is an art that includes the inspiration of men. Industry uses this latter interpretation widely; however, it is necessary to have a common frame of reference for discussion purposes. For academic reasons, management is construed to be largely a science, a systematic application of techniques. Leadership, in the military, is an art greater in scope than systematic techniques.

While a successful commander must be a skillful manager, command competence includes much more than management techniques. Command is the lawful authority that a leader exerts over subordinates by virtue of his rank and assignment. Therefore, a commander is the appointed formal head of a unit. This headship normally includes a requirement for exercising leadership, but its nature depends on the ability, behavior, or mission of the individual commander. A captain may be designated a company commander; however, he must still effectively influence others to earn the right to be called a leader. Thus, command is a position of legal authority while leadership is an activity. Leadership is a generically broader term than command and includes not only the authority but also the ability to influence others. A commander will not be a leader if he does little to manage and inspire his subordinates. On the other hand, an officer holding a staff position such as operations officer may still exercise leadership by effectively influencing others although he has no duly sanctioned command. Actually, any member, regardless of rank, becomes an informal leader when he effectively influences others to achieve the common unit objectives.

LEADERS CLASSIFIED

Leaders may be classified into several different categories. One system of leader classification concerns the manner in which he achieves his leadership position within formal and informal groups. In informal groups, a leader may emerge spontaneously from the group because he asserts himself and is accepted by others as being capable of pointing the way. For example, ten boys may decide to play a short informal game of basketball in the gymnasium. One individual, probably because of his basketball prowess, initiates the choosing of sides and determines the rules of play. He may have to shout down some opposition, but he emerges as the one who influences others to get the game started. He is the accepted emergent leader. This is normal procedure for the achievement of recognized leadership within unorganized informal groups.

Quite similar to the emergent leader is the charismatic leader. He is the leader endowed with a mystical personal power that causes his followers to bestow the right of leadership upon him. The charismatic leader may or may not be the most technically competent member of the group. However, he is the one person to whom the group unhesitatingly looks for guidance. He has a permanence of leadership that the emergent leader only rarely achieves.

History provides many examples of magnetic personalities who have been able to capture a following through belief in their mystical, magical, divine, or simply extraordinary powers. Although most religious leaders have a charismatic quality about them, this classification extends to other forms of leadership as well. Some divine right monarchs, and national heroes such as Jeanne d'Arc, Abraham Lincoln, and Adolph Hitler possessed an aura of charisma in their exercise of leadership. In its most extreme form, charismatic leadership can result in a fanatical devotion to the leader over and above the cause for which the group is organized. Many times the death of this leader can also spell the death of the movement that he led. This explains why a military unit can be particularly demoralized upon the death of a greatly revered commander. Charismatic leaders may be found in either informal or formal groups. Generally, however, they first emerge as a leader in an informal group and then retain their leadership as the group becomes structured and formalized.

Within formally organized groups, or institutions, the process of waiting for the emergence of a leader is too haphazard. More orderly processes of leadership designation are required. Formal institutional leaders are elected or appointed. In democratic nations, political leaders are selected by election to fill many of the roles in government. In consequence, these officials usually see their duty as acting for the people who made the selection. In industry, and in the military, leaders are appointed by formally recognized superiors. Frequently the objectives of higher authority are not compatible with the personal motives of subordinate members. As the motivation of human behavior depends largely on the satisfaction of personal strivings of the individual, one can readily see that the appointed leader has a difficult problem. A military commander must achieve an acceptable compatibility between the unit's mission, that may at times be hazardous or distasteful, and the personal aims of individual members of the unit.

Leaders may also be classified in accordance with their physical closeness to the "doer" level. All leaders deal with some group in a face-to-face relationship. These immediate followers know the leader well, form relatively valid opinions concerning his personality and capabilities, and are directly and knowingly influenced by his actions. As an organizational hierarchy develops, however, leaders at successively higher echelons become less well known. Their personalities are perceived in an increasingly distorted manner, and their influence becomes increasingly modified by the more immediate influence of subordinate leaders.

It is possible to distinguish several general levels of leadership. In industry these are normally categorized as top management, middle management, and first-line supervisor. In the military, levels may be categorized as general officer, field grade officer, company grade officer, and noncommissioned officer. Each of these levels has specific problems of its own, yet each is similar in many respects to the other.

FOUNDATIONS OF LEADERSHIP STUDY

Historically, most attempts to subject the phenomenon of leadership to analysis have examined the fundamental bases of leadership. These earlier studies focused on philosophy and moral law as fundamental to its understanding.

The past few centuries have produced a vast amount of military-oriented leadership literature. The analytical views of Maurice de Saxe, Jomini, Clausewitz, and Ardant du Picq, among others, have proved valuable. Military historians have furnished us valuable, extensive, and detailed analyses of military leadership of the past. The introspective comments of successful combat leaders also provide a basis for the study of military leadership. Over the last half-century, the rapid growth of civilian business organizations stimulated considerable interest and research in "scientific management" in business and commercial circles. For similar reasons, the study of military business management is greatly accelerated. A tremendous amount of literature on scientific management, personnel management, and human relations is now available.

Unfortunately, however, much of the literature available on the subject of leadership is not practical leadership theory. Also, some of it is undoubtedly based on faulty observation, pure speculation, or one individual's unique experiences, and is, therefore, of questionable validity. Before useful leadership doctrine can be formulated, two major tasks must be accomplishd. First, that which is true about leadership must be divorced from that which is pure speculation; and second, the body of knowledge on the subject of leadership must be systematized into useful theory. Within the past three decades, the behavioral sciences, particularly psychology and sociology, have assisted in accomplishing both these tasks. Thus, the two earlier foundations of the leadership concept, philosophy and moral law, have been strengthened by the addition of a third: science.

Philosophy

Leadership has many theoretical roots. Many influential writers, from the time of Confucius to contemporary philosophers, have expressed their views on leaders or the leadership process. Writers today still quote the Chinese Sun Tzu (500 B.C.) in viewing the theories of leader-follower relationships. Socrates, in Plato's *Republic,* proposed that leadership of civil institutions be reserved for the especially trained philosopher-kings, rather than the ill-informed masses who were meant to be followers. Aristotle offered opinions of moral conduct and described desirable behavior for tyrants and kings, teachings that influenced Alexander the Great. Plutarch discussed the leader-follower problem by studying the lives of noble Grecians and Romans. Machiavelli described the cruelty, dishonesty, and brutality of leadership in his time in his famous book, *The Prince.*

Moral Law

Moral codes inevitably affect concepts of leadership. Epictetus and Marcus Aurelius discussed the moral responsibilities and ethical codes of leaders under the Roman Empire. Judeo-Christian teachings have emphasized the dignity of man and his importance as a human being, as well as the ultimate divine source of all authority, imposing on the leader the necessity for the highest ethical standards in the exercise of that authority. These ethical standards became the basis for the code of the knight, the medieval battle leader, with its emphasis on patriotism, honor, and chivalry. This code survives today in the profession of arms. The members of our own constitutional conventions, insisting in their belief that a Supreme Being governed the affairs of men, made moral law fundamental to our Constitution and the American way of life. Since General Washington, Americans have always judged their leaders largely on their moral and ethical standards.

Science

The scientific study of leadership differs from the moral and philosophical primarily in its method of analysis. It is a knowledge-making process characterized by controlled experiments and systematic natural observations. When relationships between data are consistently found, science integrates isolated data and hypotheses into broader statements that may be called scientific theories or principles. Thus, science grows by inductive reasoning, moving from mere hypotheses to more useful theories and principles. Further, from the theory itself, it is sometimes possible to deduce hypotheses and predictions that can make the science more powerful than generalizations from empirical data alone. The process of generalization from hypotheses to theories by scientific research results in more certitude and fewer intangibles to relate. Psychology and sociology, as behavioral sciences, provide broad, valid, generalized descriptions and explanations that are useful in analyzing the leadership phenomenon. The generalities gained from the scientific method afford a convenient means to categorize the many variables involved in the leadership process.

Therefore, the scientific method is an additional means of deriving leadership theory. It helps categorize the many complex variables involved in leadership into a meaningful framework. Science augments divine faith and human reason as a means of understanding human behavior.

Also, the experiences and thinking of military men throughout the years provide a tremendous source of knowledge for a general understanding of man. The behavioral sciences help us to understand more specifically why men behave as they do. Thus, any concept or combined theory of military leadership should be a product of moral, philosophical, and scientific foundations. The over-all concept should be a systematic framework to guide one in managing and inspiring men.

THEORETICAL APPROACHES

While there are many theories of leadership, these theories constitute generalizations or abstractions in a complex field. A broad concept provides a means for relating the many complex factors involved when one individual effectively influences others to accomplish a specific task. Many theories on leadership pertain to either the leader, his group, or the task and situational factors. Actually, leadership derives from all three of these. But, most importantly, it is a product of the interaction that takes place among them. Currently, many researchers are studying the intimate relationship between leadership and group effectiveness.

The Leader

Because of mankind's previously mentioned tendency to set his leaders aside as somehow different from the ordinary run of mortal, it was only natural that the study of leadership should initially concentrate on the leader himself. This approach to leadership is commonly known as the "Great Man" concept, based on the theory espoused by Thomas Carlyle that history could only be explained in terms of the great leaders who have brought about changes in the course of mankind (Carlyle, 1901). All leader-oriented theories postulate that leadership is some quality or characteristic residing in the personality of the leader. The major problem has been the identification of this quality so that it can form the basis for the selection and development of leaders.

One of the most prevalent concepts throughout history has been that leadership is hereditary, that leaders are born and not made. The problem is thus one of selecting rather than developing leaders. The hereditary philosophy was the basic rationalization for the feudalistic system, where leadership positions were passed down from father to eldest son. Since no others were permitted an opportunity for leadership, the system obviously justified itself. With the downfall of feudalism and the advent of democracy, however, it became apparent that heritage was not particularly critical. Leaders often emerged from the masses, and it appeared that leadership could be developed. As with all aspects of human behavior, heredity probably does play a partial role in leadership. Nevertheless, empirical research has shown that experience, learning, and environmental factors are of considerably greater importance in leadership development than heredity.

Most of the leader-oriented theories concern the personality of the leader. As such, they have encountered the same difficulties that the entire field of personality research has encountered. Human personality is a complex concept and difficult to measure objectively. Questions of how to develop personality or to explain personality differences have been a central concern of psychology for many years. Several theories, each with some evidence in its support, have developed. Each of these personality theories is also a theory of leadership, such as Freud's father figure, Jung's extrovert and introvert, and Sheldon's body types, to cite a few. The most prevalent of these theories and the one for which there appears to be some justification is the so-called trait theory.

In this theory the human personality is seen as composed of a large number of different characteristics or traits. Each individual differs from every other individual in the degree to which he displays each of these traits. The trait theory of leadership postulates that there are certain traits possessed by leaders that differentiate them from followers. When scientific research attempted to identify the traits of leadership, however, results were surprising in that few consistent trait patterns were uncovered. In spite of many well-designed scientific investigations, no evidence has been uncovered to indicate that there is any single trait that consistently differentiates leaders from followers. The best that can be said is that some trends have been found. For example, evidence indicates that the leader tends to be more intelligent than the follower. There are, however, exceptions. Some evidence indicates that if a leader is too much more intelligent than the followers, then his effectiveness as a leader is impaired.

The inability of research to identify specific leadership traits tends to cast doubt on the whole trait theory. Probably the major drawback to this approach concerns the basic technique of attempting to measure traits in isolation. Such an atomistic approach does not reflect adequately on how one characteristic interacts with another. The human personality is a dynamic and unified organization of physical and mental factors that must be considered as a whole. In some ways, it is analogous to a house. The quality of a house depends not only on the materials that go into it, but also on its architectural design—the pattern by which these materials are put together. Two houses constructed of identical materials can be completely different because of differences in design. Similarly, two personalities can have similar traits, yet be completely different in total effect.

Even though specific traits that differentiate leaders from nonleaders have not been found, this does not mean that the trait theory is not useful. Traits provide a means for communicating about personality. Though traits cannot describe anyone completely, still they provide the best means available today that are readily understandable to most people. Their use facilitates the analysis and development of leadership. Also, the inability to uncover any universal leadership traits does not mean that they do not exist. Scientific measuring devices may yet be too crude to ferret out some traits that do in fact differentiate leaders from nonleaders. Finally, it may be true that, though there are no universal traits, there are certain traits required by leaders of certain groups or in certain situations. In other groups or situations, these same traits may be less important than others for maximum leader effectiveness. For example, though intelligence is probably one of the most important traits of the scientific leader, it is probably much less important than physical prowess for the captain of an athletic team. Here arise new difficulties, for all scientists must be intelligent and all athletes must have high physical ability in their sport. This raises the possibility that leadership traits may not be those that differentiate the leader from the follower, but rather those that are shared by the followers. In other words, the leader may be the individual who has the most ideal combination of characteristics required of all members of his group.

It can be seen from the above that the trait approach of today does not provide an adequate explanation of the leadership phenomenon. Although trait examination is not sufficient in itself to identify leaders consistently, both human experience and scientific experiments indicate that some people tend to be leaders, regardless of changes in the situation or the group with which they deal. There is no dearth of examples of individuals who have shifted from one major field of endeavor to another and turned in high-quality leadership in both. The mere fact that, since the death of feudalism, high-level leadership has, in most cases, been earned, is also strong evidence for a "Great Man" theory. To attain a position justifying the accolade of "Great Man," it is necessary to demonstrate outstanding leadership at a lower level, with a different group and under different circumstances.

Two examples from the experimental literature lend some support to the "Great Man" theory. In one, individuals were rotated between groups, and in another, the same groups were assigned different tasks. The first experiment was conducted with U.S. Air Force enlisted personnel. A significant finding was that those individuals (leaders) who excel in popularity, task ability, and assertiveness tend to hold their leadership in groups of different composition with similar tasks. Indirect evidence also indicates that their groups are more productive and satisfied. (Borgatta, Bales, and Couch, 1954.)

The second study was conducted with Air Force OCS candidates. Candidates were formed into six-man teams that performed moderately dissimilar tasks. Each candidate was rated on leadership displayed during the tasks and on certain personality traits. Results did tend to confirm the "Great Man" theory to some extent; however, the study showed that the nature of the group and the situation also determined which men were leaders. The most discriminating traits appeared to be those that involve other people, such as social maturity and extroversion. Those traits with a more personal tendency such as orderliness and adaptability were statistically nonsignificant. Intelligence, however, was an exception to this generality and did discriminate at a significant level. (Borg and Tupes, 1958.)

Similar evidence further indicates that individual personality is an important aspect of leadership. Though it is not known what constitutes a "leadership personality," the traits required of the leader tend to fall into two broad categories. First are those of a social and moral orientation, such as integrity and maturity, that assist the leader in the establishment of the proper relationships with his followers. Second are those concerning his capacity to deal with the problems and tasks confronting his group, such as intelligence and judgment. In view of the inconsistency of experimental results, it appears quite probable that the appropriate quantity of each trait changes with differences in individuals, groups, and situations. Traits should be regarded as only one component of a complex relationship between individuals in varying situations. Another component in this relationship is the group. The second major approach to a leadership theory examines leadership as a function of group dynamics.

The Group

A systematic analysis of leadership must recognize factors external to the leader. The leader does not operate in a vacuum; he mingles continually with his followers. It becomes obvious that the complex social interaction between the leader and followers and interactions among the followers are vital factors of the leadership setting. As a result, many researchers insist that leadership be studied primarily from a follower-oriented or group dynamic approach.

Social psychology studies the interaction process within groups. Many of its exponents postulate that leadership is a product of this interaction, and is conferred on the leader by the group members because he is seen as the individual who can best provide for their individual needs and guide them toward the group goals. Thus, according to this theory, it makes little difference what personality traits a leader possesses, so long as the followers have faith in him. A group may contain one leader or several, and the leadership of the group will change from time to time as new needs arise and someone else is seen as more capable of providing for these new needs.

A soldier looks toward group members for the satisfaction of many of his personal needs. Most social needs in our culture are satisfied through interactions with other people. Because the unit commander is the institutional head of the unit, he is particularly important in these group interactional processes. The soldier seeks status, security, maintenance of his dignity, and spiritual satisfactions. In the leader-follower relationship, if the formal leader does not satisfy the soldier's needs, someone else will. Hence, the formal or institutional leader may be replaced in the eyes of the follower by an informal leader. Further, the appointed military leader is encumbered by the requirement that he orient the goals of the group so as to accomplish an externally assigned mission. This can bring him into direct conflict with the group, if he has permitted an informal leader to formulate goals more closely related to the individuals' desires. If he fails in this, he can motivate them only at the minimum level. Morale will be low, *esprit* absent, and teamwork difficult.

In understanding group processes, lateral relationships are equally as important as vertical ones. Within any group a dynamic interaction of individual purposes, attitudes, prejudices, and emotions takes place amongst the members. These become the binding force that holds the group together. Under the stress of combat, it becomes particularly essential that the members of a unit know, take care of, and draw strength from each other. Studies in World War II revealed that faith in God and faith in his fellow soldier were the two factors considered most important by the American soldier in keeping him going when things got tough (Stouffer, *et al.*, 1949b). In the prisoner-of-war camps of the Communists during the Korean Conflict, it became the first order of business of the Communists to break down these strong interpersonal bonds, to make each prisoner distrust his fellow prisoners. When this had been achieved, some prisoners became docile tools in the hands of their captors, unwilling to help each other in distress, and willing to co-operate with their captors for personal gain.

In recognition of the factor of human interaction, the military, like industry, emphasizes human relations. Human relations is both a philosophy of group behavior and a style by which a leader may deal with his subordinates. Its goals are the integration of the members of a group into an effective, co-operative team in such a way as to provide both for the accomplishment of the group purpose and for the satisfaction of the needs of the group members. Human relations is predicated on an appreciation of human dignity and promotion of individual initiative. It emphasizes that leadership is most effective when all members of the group identify with the group's goal and their higher order social needs are satisfied through its attainment.

Human relations in industry received its initial impetus as the result of a series of studies conducted by Elton Mayo, a Harvard sociologist, during the twenties and thirties. These studies, carried out in the Hawthorne plant of Western Electric over a period of some twelve years, represent probably the most extensive observations of men and women at work that have ever been conducted. It is difficult to summarize such extensive research in a few words, but a few of the key findings are particularly significant. For example, group processes appear to either increase or decrease production depending upon whether workers feel that higher management is sincerely interested in their welfare. When specific incentives offered by higher management are interpreted by the worker as expressions of sincere interest, production increases. When the motives of higher management are mistrusted, however, the group deliberately curtails production to what is considered by the workers to be a fair day's work; even though greater production by each individual worker would result in an increased monetary reward. By and large, the worker voluntarily abides by this group-imposed work standard, even though it is not in his own best self-interest. Evidently, maintaining the respect of his fellow worker is more important to him than increased personal gain. (Mayo, 1933.)

The Hawthorne Studies are important in that they point out the importance of group factors in production and the fact that it is not the specific act of the leader that determines production, but rather the manner in which that act is perceived by the worker. If they trust him, if they believe that he has their most sincere interests at heart, they will work for him willingly and efficiently. If however, they distrust him, they will produce at only the minimum level. These results point out the extreme danger of looking upon human relations techniques as a set of tools for the impersonal manipulation of subordinates. If the leader is not sincere in his efforts, if he does not truly believe in the dignity and worth of his subordinates, all his "logical" efforts to motivate them may well backfire on him.

The varied application of human relations in military situations can be seen. The size, structure, and composition of a military unit determine the appropriate techniques required by the leader. Every unit is different from every other because the followers as well as the commanders differ. Inspiration of trainees in basic combat training and a platoon of an airborne division require different leadership techniques. Further, human relations techniques within a single unit vary. One incentive such as a three-day pass may satisfy one person but not another. Thus, it is easy for a leader who attempts to practice human relations routinely to make many errors in the process. He requires more than mere common sense.

The human relations approach should never be so follower-oriented that organizational proficiency and mission accomplishment are impaired. A military leader has two basic responsibilities—accomplishment of his mission and welfare of his men. Normally they go hand in hand, supporting each other. In the event of conflict between these factors, however, the mission takes priority. Every personnel policy must be weighed from the standpoint of its value to the individual, to his unit, and to the Army as a whole. The practice of human relations does not imply mollycoddling. Such practices violate the human relations philosophy, for they imply a lack of faith in the maturity of the soldier. A commander should exercise sound human relations while maintaining firm discipline and flexibility of action.

Group loyalty is extremely important to the effectiveness of the combat soldier. Therefore, any study of leadership must encompass an understanding of the follower, as well as the dynamics of social interactions that exist within the unit. Social scientists have vigorously pursued this group approach to leadership. In industry and education, an appreciation of group dynamics is manifested by the recent stress placed on human relations. In the military, emphasis is placed upon human relations; and the importance of discipline, morale, and *esprit de corps* is accentuated.

The Situation

"It depends on the situation." This often-heard expression in the military implies that many situational factors external to the leader and his group influence his decisions and actions. One leads a platoon in combat by procedures differing from those used in an Army Headquarters staff which is planning in the Zone of Interior. A platoon leader's quick decisions in combat are probably more authoritarian than those made during training periods. There are on record many cases of individuals who were unrecognized as leaders in stateside training, but who, in times of stress or emergency, seized the initiative and led the group to success. Had the situation not arisen, these individuals might never have demonstrated their leadership ability. Leadership demands vary between types of assignments and between levels of command. A successful motor officer may not necessarily make a good company commander or battalion adjutant; similarly, some aggressive company commanders will never be able to command divisions. It is also possible that an aggressive commander may be a total failure as an advisor.

Military leadership itself, when compared to other forms of leadership, may be considered as situational. An officer's oath of office and commission bears heavy moral responsibilities. Any leader must continually set the highest standards of moral conduct. He must take care of detailed personal problems of his men under trying situations. These responsibilities are far greater than those found in industrial, business, or civic leadership situations.

The military leadership picture is affected by an infinite number of situational variables, including the mission, terrain, climate, enemy resistance, duration in combat, casualties, replacements, rest, state of training, and availability of equipment and supplies. It is not possible to predict all of the factors that could affect a leader in the accomplishment of his mission. Many of these variables, however, may be considered structured and controlled by sound leadership techniques.

If leadership were purely situational, a leader in one situation could not lead in another. This is obviously not true. A vast number of civilian leaders performed creditably in World War II as officers in the service. Many a good infantry commander can lead an armor unit. Senior military leaders have been successful as statesmen, educators, and business managers after retirement. Nevertheless, situational differences must be recognized. They mean that traits and principles must be applied differently from one problem area to another.

The Integrated Concept

The preceding discussion indicates that each of the three factors: the leader's traits, the group, and the situation, contribute to an understanding of the leadership process, yet, no one of them is sufficient to explain the phenomenon completely. The trait theory does not contribute directly toward the solution of problems. Traits and characteristics are relatively static; leadership is a dynamic activity. Nonetheless, desirable traits and characteristics have a strong influence on others, and they serve as excellent guide lines for the development of a leadership personality. The group dynamics theory must be accepted because the leader always operates in a leader-follower relationship. The follower is not a mere automaton carrying out the leader's desires to the best of his ability. He is a human being with motives and goals of his own, strong attachments to his fellow group members, and attitudes towards his leader and the group goal that may add or detract from goal accomplishment. The leader must recognize the existence of these individual and group factors and how they affect his ability to influence the group. Leadership situations in the military differ widely and should be recognized. The gamut of leadership styles appropriate for the many unique situations encountered by the military leader call for a high degree of versatility. Each situation influences the leader's role and his techniques.

Therefore, the most logical approach to the study of leadership process is an interrelational theory that considers the interaction of the leader, the group, and the situation. A synthesis of these three factors provides a foundation for understanding the tangible principles and techniques of influencing human behavior. Thus, in the integrated concept, leadership is a dynamic interaction process involving the leader (with his own personality), the group (with its particular characteristics and needs), and the situation (in which the leader and his group are operating). This concept is supported by the dominant trend in current leadership research (McGrath, 1964).

No systematized concept or formula gives an assurance of success. Systematized procedures and principles are merely some of the tools that a leader may use to cope with leadership problems. No concept of leadership can offer rigid rules of thumb. Each leadership problem is imbedded in diverse multi-dimensional and variable factors that require sound judgment and consideration for solution. The capable leader is one who knows how to capitalize on the potentialities inherent in his own personality, his men, and the situation.

SUMMARY

Leadership is the art of influencing human behavior so as to accomplish a mission in the manner desired by the leader. The leader himself may be an emergent leader, a charismatic leader, or an appointed leader. Leaders can also be classified as to the level at which they exercise their leadership in relation to those being led. The levels in the military that correspond to civilian industry's top, middle, and supervisory management are general officer, field grade officer, company grade officer, and noncommissioned officer. The leadership employed at these levels is a function of many variables that may be classified for study into three broad factors: personality traits, situational effects, and group dynamics.

Each of these factors represents an approach to leadership. In the trait approach, leadership is a characteristic embodied in the personality of the leader. In the group dynamics approach, it is conferred by the follower on the individual perceived as most capable of providing for the needs of the group. In the situational approach, it is a function of the skills of the leader to deal with specific environmental situations. Each of these approaches has some evidence in its support and some evidence in contradiction. Only by an integration of the three approaches is there an explanation for both the supports and the contradictions.

The integrated concept, therefore, embodies a balance of the three major approaches to leadership. In this concept, leadership is viewed as a dynamic interaction process involving a leader, his followers, and an environmental situation. This concept serves as a co-ordinating framework to assist in analyzing the leadership process, in solving specific leadership problems, and in developing leadership skills. Like any philosophical system, it attempts to organize a vast number of variables into some reasonably coherent arrangement which may serve as a guide for understanding—and for action.

Suggestions for Further Reading

Bass, Bernard M., *Leadership, Psychology, and Organizational Behavior*. New York: Harper & Bros., 1960.

Browne, C. G., and Cohn, Thomas S., (eds.), *The Study of Leadership*. Danville, Ill.: The Interstate Printers & Publishers, Inc., 1958.

Cartwright, D., and Zander, A., (eds.), *Group Dynamics*. 2d ed.; New York: Harper & Row Publishers, Inc., 1960.

McGrath, J. E., and Altman, I., *Small Group Research: A Synthesis and Critique of the Field*. New York: Holt, Rinehart, & Winston, Inc., 1966.

Petrullo, L., and Bass, B. M., (eds.), *Leadership and Interpersonal Behavior*. New York: Holt, Rinehart, & Winston, Inc., 1961.

Section I
THE LEADER

THE INITIAL factor in the leadership process is the leader. For many years it was assumed that he was the key to the entire process, and research tended to focus on his personality, characteristics, qualities, and traits. Although succeeding investigation tends to emphasize the fact that he is only one of the elements of the equation, he is still a very important one. While recognizing that his performance and effectiveness are interrelated with the group and their situation, it is academically desirable to study the leader's input, his qualities, style, and skills in a degree of isolation.

The role of the leader carries with it certain expectations on the part of both his superiors and subordinates. These expectations tend to define many of the actions and activities that the leader must undertake. He, in turn, brings to this role his own personal characteristics and qualities that influence the style or manner he uses in exerting his influence. Chapter II discusses the role of the leader, different styles of leadership, and their effect on the group.

The foundations of military leadership are based in the moral and ethical codes of American society and on professional military ethics. Chapter III, "Moral Aspects of Leadership" describes this moral basis for the exercise of leadership and some aspects of the ethics of the military profession. These ethical codes assist in defining the leadership role and provide guides that can assist the leader in responding to moral problems.

Chapter IV "Leader Selection and Development" discusses one of the important tests of leadership, the ability to select and develop leadership among subordinates. The measure of any leader can be taken in the quality and performance of his subordinates. While developing and improving his own techniques, the leader by necessity must develop his subordinate leaders' ability as well.

The very essence of leadership lies in the ability of the leader to communicate. Chapter V discusses the process of communication and the various blocks to effective communication that can occur. A leader, alert to the problems inherent in communications processes, can overcome them and enhance his own effectiveness.

29

30   TAKING COMMAND

While leadership is an art based on effective use of interpersonal relations, it has many aspects of a skill or technique based on experience. Modern organizations, including those of the military, create a specific environment in which the management skills of the leader are brought into play. His skills and techniques must be appropriate to the requirements of modern warfare. His managerial skill should reflect the principles developed through years of organizational experience in business and government as well as in the military services. Chapter VI, "Military Management," describes the leader's management function in the service and some of the new management techniques being developed. Chapter VII provides guidance in the functions of planning and the importance of creativity in a military organization. Chapter VIII, then, describes the processes of organizing and co-ordinating a task once it is planned. After planning, organizing, and co-ordinating his task, the leader must direct his subordinates in its accomplishment.

The final essential leader function is to control and guide his subordinates' efforts toward ultimate success. These last activities are discussed in Chapter IX. Both the conceptual base and the managerial skills need to be reinforced with practical application if they are to improve actual performance.

II

Leadership Behavior and Styles

THE CONCEPT of leadership developed in the opening chapter describes the leadership phenomenon as a dynamic interaction between a leader, group, and situation. This concept encompasses a wide variety of leadership personalities, many types of groups, and a multitude of situations. Each calls for a change in the leader's behavior and style. Leadership behavior concerns what the leader does, while his style is more related to the way he does it.

There is a strong tendency to evaluate the effectiveness of a leader's behavior and style in terms of his group's success. This is particularly true for military leaders. There are, however, many weaknesses in determining leader effectiveness solely on a criterion of success or failure. Occasionally, a group succeeds in spite of the appointed leader. Conversely, even the most effective leader can face such overwhelming odds that his group fails. In any event, the leader's behavior and style of leadership remain a major factor in the success equation.

LEADERSHIP BEHAVIOR

Leadership behavior consists of the acts and functions a leader must carry out in order to fulfill his responsibilities. To a large degree this behavior is dependent upon what he thinks others expect of him. Usually, he draws his perception of these expectations from his superiors and subordinates alike. This requires that he perform both a leader and a follower role, since he is a leader to his subordinates and a follower to his superior.

In "role theory" a role is the expected behavior of a person occupying a specific status position. A leader occupies a number of status positions and, because of this, fulfills a variety of roles. His status relationships might include those of son, husband, father, club member, bowling team member, and squad leader in Company "A". With each status position, there are certain norms to follow and specific role behaviors expected. In the case of leader roles, the better he fulfills the behavior others expect of him, the better they see him as a leader; the greater is his influence and leadership capability. Role behavior, then, offers an explanation and some insight into the many perspectives by

31

which others observe and evaluate a military leader. The roles normally filled by the military leader include those expected by his peer group, his military organization, and the military institution as a whole.

The Organizational Role

Organizational roles are quite often linked with or incorporated within institutional roles. Each soldier identifies with or belongs to an organization in which he works, reports to, and interacts with. This organization might be Company "B" of the 1st Battalion, or it might be a larger organization of battalion, brigade, or division size. To be a part of such an organization means that the member must adopt its customs, manner of dress, general character, and personality. Organizations impart a special role for their members to live by. Usually these roles are not distinct from institutional roles, but they do set the organization apart from other organizations, giving it a special nature and providing a specific identity for its members.

The Institutional Role

Institutional roles are generally professional in nature and center on the ideals and goals of expected behavior. Thus, one of the important institutional roles of the military leader stems from his service to his country. He works for the people, upholding the U.S. Constitution and providing defense and national security. His primary responsibility is the accomplishment of his assigned mission. In accomplishing this paramount institutional role, the military leader is often required to inflict death or injury on an enemy and to expose himself and his men to the same risk.

At the same time, however, the military leader also is charged with the responsibility for the welfare of his men. In most cases, these two responsibilities reinforce each other. By looking out for his men, the leader secures their willing co-operation and improves their capability to perform the mission. By accomplishing his mission, he is usually taking the best action to ensure the welfare of his men. For example, by properly accomplishing his training mission, the leader better prepares his men to survive the rigors of battle, the shock of an unforeseen emergency, and the chaos and confusion of a crisis. In combat, the leader who aggressively patrols his area of responsibility is usually effective in accomplishing both of his primary duties simultaneously. By aggressive patrolling, he prevents a surprise attack, and thereby reduces the likelihood of his men being unprepared when the battle begins. In addition, his aggressive patrolling enables him to obtain current information of the enemy, and ensures him a more secure base of action. At times, however, the leader may find his responsibilities in conflict. He may not be able to accomplish his mission unless he orders his men into an action which he knows will result in casualties. Should this happen, the leader must realize that his mission comes first.

Amitai Etzioni argues that the personality characteristics required for the mission accomplishment role are in complete opposition to those required for the troop welfare role. He writes that to ask one leader to perform both instrumental (task) functions and expressive (social interaction) functions is the same as asking him to be a "Great Man." In other words, according to

Etzioni, the two roles are incompatible; and, although they may be carried out by one man, they tend not to be (Etzioni, 1965, pp. 688-9). The dual leadership theory he proposes is an interesting one for military leaders, since it emphasizes the need for a clear understanding of priority for mission accomplishment. It also highlights one of the difficulties of a military leader's role.

In addition to assigning major responsibility for the accomplishment of the mission and the welfare of the men, the military institution expects many other things of its leaders. It expects that they will be an example to their men in the performance of duty, in the sharing of hardships and danger with the men, and, above all, in the high standards of moral and ethical behavior. They are expected to comply with the basic customs of the service, to be an example in dress and bearing, to participate in the social life of the unit and installation, and to perform various ceremonial duties in addition to their basic operational and training tasks. In other words, the military institution expects its leaders to possess certain permanent or inherent characteristics known as traits.

Bearing	Integrity
Courage (physical and moral)	Judgment
Decisiveness	Justice
Dependability	Knowledge
Endurance	Loyalty
Enthusiasm	Tact
Initiative	Unselfishness

Figure 2.1 Leadership Traits
As listed in FM 22-100, *Military Leadership*

In order to ensure that the serious responsibilities of military leadership are executed in a competent and professional manner, the U.S. Army (an institution) prescribes a number of leader traits. These traits serve as a standard or goal that all leaders and, for that matter, all soldiers strive to attain. These traits can be looked upon as values of the military profession that the individual adopts as standards of conduct. These values are dynamic and therefore are best interpreted as devices that the person consistently employs in interacting with his environment. Given a highly positive situation, the military proceeds on the assumption that the presence of these traits in the leader will result in a high degree of organizational success. On the other hand, in a negative situation, although the presence of these traits may reduce failure, we cannot say that their employment will necessarily prevent it. Douglas MacArthur's reversal at Bataan, and Robert E. Lee's eventual defeat in the Civil War were more likely due to overwhelming odds than to any lack of leader traits. In training men to become military leaders, it is necessary to emphasize these traits in their early career development. This improves socialization into the profession and ensures a high set of values commonly shared by leaders of the service. As a result, many of the junior leader courses are designed to emphasize the leadership traits.

The Follower Role

In addition to the behaviors demanded by organizational and institutional roles, the military leader must also adhere to the role behavior expected by his superior. Much of this behavior will be the same as the behavior implied by the institutional role, such as mission accomplishment, the welfare of the men, and the traits mentioned above. A superior's interpretation of an institutional role may vary somewhat from the subordinate's interpretation. When this occurs, the subordinate must adhere to the institutional norm which specifies loyalty to superiors.

The personality of the superior influences the role of his subordinate. A company commander who tends to oversupervise his platoon leaders obviously restricts the limits of the platoon leader's role, while another commander's permissive attitude may encourage wide latitude in the behavior he expects of his subordinate. Since no two personalities are ever exactly alike, the subordinate leader must repeatedly demonstrate the capability of understanding his role and of adjusting to his superior. This does not mean that the good leader is one who compromises himself, or reinterprets values, mores, and ethics to fit the situation simply to curry favor. There probably comes a time in every military leader's career when a fundamental disagreement with a superior exists. Here the institution expects the subordinate leader to have the moral courage (an example of a trait in action) to make his objection known to the superior. Adjusting to personality differences is a normal human reaction and does not imply compromise of principle.

The Leader Role

Finally, the leader has certain behavior that is expected of him by his subordinates. Most subordinates are aware of the leader's responsibility for mission accomplishment and recognize that their immediate superior is limited in the degree he can affect a given situation. Still, a group's assessment of their leader's behavior resides primarily with his ability to satisfy their particular goals. In a study by Donald C. Pelz, subordinates perceived the best leaders as the ones who had the most upward influence and exercised the highest degree of autonomy (Pelz, 1952). Thus, the leader who has a wide range of decision-making authority, considerable influence with his superiors, and observed power within the organization is seen as a better leader than an individual who serves only as a channel of communication in passing out orders. Pelz's study emphasizes the importance of delegating authority to subordinate leaders. This, in turn, lends substance and high status to the subordinate leader's role, resulting in greater influence over his followers.

An extensive study conducted during World War II by Samuel A. Stouffer and his associates indicates that willingness on the part of soldiers to serve under their company commanders was directly related to two leader behaviors. These were (1) the soldier's belief that his company commander "knew his stuff," and (2) the soldier's belief that the company commander took an interest in what the men were thinking. Men in high morale units and men in low morale units were asked about specific leadership practices of their officers. The results of this investigation indicated that the men in the high morale companies were more consistent than those in the low morale companies in stating that their officers adhered to the following leadership practices:

Showed an interest in the men
Understood the men's needs
Were helpful to the men
Recognized the men's abilities
Were willing to back up their men
Gave the men a fair share of off-duty time
Gave the men an opportunity to do their jobs
Made the best use of training time
Had a fair furlough and pass policy
Had a fair promotion policy
Made good selections of noncommissioned officers
Gave talks on the importance of the outfit's job
Gave personal talks on the men's progress
Gave the men an opportunity to know the "why" of things
Meted out punishment fairly

(Stouffer, *et al.*, 1949a, pp. 382-391.)

The Human Resources Research Organization (HumRRO) conducted several studies for the Army in which their goal was to examine the roots of effective leadership behavior in Army units. Carl J. Lange and his associates published a study, code-named OFFTRAIN II. They found that platoon leaders who were consistently rated high were differentiated from those rated low in that they:

Stressed high standards of performance and urged platoon members to perform well on the task
Showed personal involvement in good performance by the platoon
Showed personal competence in the performance of their own jobs
Frequently promised rewards and infrequently threatened punishment when assigning work
Rewarded good performance
Punished poor performance resulting from a motivation failure and used punishment instructively
Obtained information and suggestions from subordinates and demonstrated good judgment in accepting and rejecting suggestions
Took action to reduce the effects of disrupting influences

(Lange, *et al.*, 1958.)

In a subsequent study, OFFTRAIN III, the HumRRO group investigated the same behaviors in platoon leaders conducting basic training. The researchers found many similarities between the behavioral acts brought out in their new study and the results from OFFTRAIN II. There were a number of differences, however, between the specific behaviors expected of an operational or "line" unit platoon leader and those required of a basic training platoon leader. For example, in the basic training platoons, it was more important that the platoon leader define the situation for his subordinates, assist them with personal and on-the-job problems, back up his noncommissioned officers, be consistent, admit his mistakes, and avoid getting "shaken up" by unexpected situations. The researchers felt that most of these behavioral differences could be explained in terms of the difference between the operational and training situations of the two studies.

In summarizing the two studies, Lange and his associates felt that a leadership training program should have two goals: (1) to teach student leaders a repertoire of behaviors for use, as appropriate, in many situations, and (2) to teach them to recognize the demands of a situation in order to determine better the probable effects their choice of action will have on others. As to specific behaviors to be taught, the researchers felt that the following were indicated by both studies:

Defining at an instructive level. Basically, this involves clearly explaining to the followers what their mistakes were and what to do to improve the next performance.

Appropriate use of reward and punishment. This must be based on performance, with recognition of the difference between ability failure and motivational failure.

Handling disruptive influences. This primarily involves assisting the men with personal and work problems.

(Lange and Jacobs, 1960.)

Edwin P. Hollander and James W. Julian, in a study designed to determine the role dimensions of leader-follower relations, investigated the willingness of group members to accept a leader's influence attempts. They found that the group's willingness depended on:

The leader's competence
The leader's interest in participating in group activity
The leader's interest in the group members
The leader's source of authority (appointment or election).

(Hollander, et al., 1966.)

This would indicate that subordinates tend to prefer a leader who actively works with them in group activity. It does not imply, however, that the subordinates necessarily want their leader to be simply one of the group. This point was brought out by Fred E. Fiedler whose findings indicated that subordinates do not desire a close personal relationship with their leader. (Fiedler, 1957.)

In summarizing the leader's role, it seems clear that the group he is leading exercises an influence upon his behavior as well. Not only do subordinates recognize a leader's responsibility to the institution, but they also expect him to satisfy requirements the institution places on him. Subordinates, however, also expect a leader to be concerned with their needs, helpful to them in satisfying their personal goals, friendly in his approach toward them while maintaining some social distance, and to have a strong influence within the organization.

Dimensions of Leader Behavior

Role behavior opens up a number of perspectives about leadership behavior. It demonstrates that leaders themselves tend to be influenced; that what leaders do is largely dependent upon what they think is expected of them; and that leaders operate simultaneously from a number of frames of reference. There has been no differentiation in these various roles, however, in regard to the specific behaviors that fall under each of them. Each involves behavior expectations on the part of both followers and superiors.

Initiating Structure

A number of investigators have attempted to categorize these various leader behaviors. Their findings provide a significant contribution since their categories are closely associated with the primary responsibilities of the military leader.

In Andrew W. Halpin's study of aircraft crews, he classifies certain leadership acts as initiating structure and others as showing consideration (Halpin, 1954, pp. 19-22). He found that superior officers expected their subordinate aircraft commanders to score high in initiating structure. This dimension is task-oriented and relates primarily to getting the job done, organizing the group, assigning jobs, and supervising group effort. Behaviors related to this dimension involve the structuring of a situation in such a way that the job is accomplished. Initiating structure is the primary behavioral aspect of the leader's follower role.

Showing Consideration

The leader's technique in dealing with his subordinates is a second cluster of effective leader behaviors Halpin reported in his study. It involves the consideration shown by a leader toward the members of his unit. The showing of consideration indicates friendship, mutual trust, respect, and a certain warmth in interpersonal relationships. It also includes a number of practices that subordinates look for in their leader:

Rewarding good performance
Standing up for subordinates
Being approachable
Assisting in the solution of personal problems of subordinates
Keeping subordinates informed.

Carroll L. Shartle, in reporting on the Ohio State Leadership Studies, points out that these two principal dimensions of leader behaviors are complementary aspects of effective leadership. Both "initiating structure" and "showing consideration" are needed for the successful exercise of leadership. A possibility of conflict exists, however. As Shartle points out, while a leader knows his superiors expect him to produce; he may because of his concern for his subordinates, be reluctant to apply pressure on them (Shartle, 1956, pp. 125-6).

Leadership behavior can be categorized as those acts or activities in which a leader directs his efforts toward role fulfillment. It is quite possible to find natural leaders who are deficient in these behaviors. It takes training and experience to be able to handle effectively all of the leadership roles.

LEADERSHIP STYLES

A leader's style determines how he will lead, the manner and techniques he will employ, and the practices that set him apart from others. A leader's personality strongly influences his style and, of course, his personality tends to be a relatively fixed quantity in any given situation. It is a leader's style that usually draws the comment, debate, argument, and attention from historians and biographers. Two military leaders may both meet all the challenges of role behavior and still exhibit entirely different personality characteristics. Some, like Napoleon and George S. Patton, Jr., were strong central leaders who tended toward centralization of authority, close supervision of subordinates, and flamboyant displays of their rank and position. Others, such as Robert E. Lee and Omar N. Bradley, emphasized a decentralized military structure with wide latitude for decision-making delegated to their subordinates. Then, there is Ulysses S. Grant who, though extremely modest in his personal display of position (he wore the tunic of a private soldier), was a demanding taskmaster who did not hesitate to drive his army to the limits of its endurance. The popular belief that all military leaders are of a single stereotype holds no validity when a comparison of the personalities of the successful leaders of the past is made.

The military leader holds an appointed position in a formal organization. As such, the responsibility for decisions and subsequent action within his unit or command always rests with him, regardless of how the decision is reached. It follows, then, that the organization is his source of authority in making the decisions for which he is responsible. He may or may not delegate this authority to his subordinates according to the degree he has decentralized his tasks into subordinate tasks. A leader who makes all the decisions for tasks within his organization is taking a highly centralized or autocratic approach. This same leader probably consults few subordinates in arriving at these decisions and relies primarily on his own ability and experience. At the other extreme we find military leaders who conduct a highly decentralized operation, delegating much of their authority to subordinates and reserving to themselves authority for decision-making on those matters that affect the whole organization. The leader characterized by this latter type of behavior is more likely to consult subordinates on their views before making key decisions.

How a leader carries out his leadership duties has become a subject of considerable inquiry and study. Robert T. LaPierre lists two areas of authority in which a leader's style may vary from one extreme to another. These authority areas center around (1) the control of decision, and (2) the enforcement of decisions. In a sense, these represent two specific variables of leadership style. LaPierre treats the style a leader employs as an autocratic-democratic dichotomy. He considers leader styles as two separate behavioral tendencies. He suggests that these two styles include such techniques as:

Autocratic Control
    Intimidation—involves extremes of money fines or losses, coercion, threats, force, and even tyranny.
    Seduction—involves subtle trickery such as monetary rewards or bribes, promises, propaganda, and manipulation.
Democratic Control
    Persuasion—involves inducement of followers, ranging from "selling" an idea to a more "paternalistic" approach of demonstrating that the idea is "theirs" and is for their own good.
    Conversion—involves the convincing of followers that a certain course or policy is best.

(LaPierre, 1954.)

By using LaPierre's variables combined with ideas from Kornhauser in *The Politics of Mass Society,* and Blake in *The Managerial Grid,* it is possible to construct a leadership style diagram. This chart demonstrates the category of style a leader may employ and explains how a leader may be perceived based on his behavior, practices, and personality. It represents variables largely determined by the leader and his method of operating. It does not consider the variables derived from either the group being led, or from the situation.

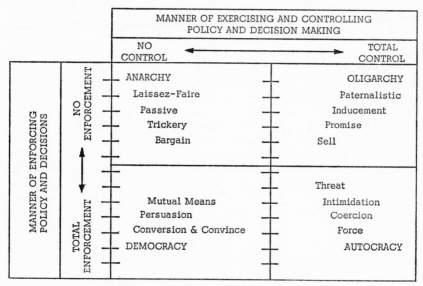

Figure 2.2 Diagram of Leadership Style

This diagram indicates that somewhere in the center of the continuum of both variables a leader may easily operate by a number of means and techniques.

Bernard Bass makes a strong argument that a leader's style and technique are largely dependent on whether he leads from a position of status (pure authority) or esteem. He then argues that, if a leader has both status and esteem, he can use any style he desires (Bass, 1960, pp. 277-300). Bass's theory is based on the principle that a leader must first attempt leadership, then he must achieve success as a leader in order to be effective. The leader, to achieve initial success, must be followed by the group. The group's response in following the leader strengthens the leader and encourages him to attempt leadership again. Successful leadership, then, reinforces the leader, while effective leadership depends on reinforcing the followers. The followers of a successful leader gain reward by satisfying their needs, or achieving goals. When they receive this reinforcement, they are more likely to want to follow. By wanting to follow, they are more likely to want to achieve the goals the leader sets. An effective leader achieves a position of esteem with his followers. If an esteemed leader is placed in a position of command, he can lead with great flexibility, employing persuasion when appropriate or coercion when necessary.

Autocratic Versus Democratic Leadership

Kurt Lewin, Ronald Lippitt, and R. K. White conducted a classic study of leadership in climates of autocratic leadership, democratic leadership, and laissez-faire leadership. Essentially their results show that the groups reacted favorably toward democratic leadership by displaying enjoyment, constructive work, and by continuing to function effectively even in the leader's absence. The autocratically led group, on the other hand, displayed more hostility, aggression, lower morale, and tended to fall apart during the leader's absence. However, the quality and quantity of work under the autocratic leader was better, while its leader was present, than it was under the democratic leader while he was present. Under the laissez-faire leadership style, the groups demonstrated very little except boredom, horseplay, and either apathy or hostility. (Lewin, Lippitt, and White, 1939.)

This famous laboratory experiment in social psychology was a significant spark that ignited much interest and many studies in leadership. Interest in the subject of leadership style has grown in recent years. Not all of the studies have come from laboratory experiments, however. Many are conducted in operating industrial or military settings. For example, the Coch and French studies on resistance to change took place in a pajama factory. These studies centered around the human tendency to resist change and the effect of this tendency on changing methods of work, job transfers, and production reward systems.

They found that resistance to change among both men and women is both individually induced and group influenced. Frustration and anxiety were keys to the individual person's resistance; but social pressure, peer group norms, and group conformity and cohesion were the forces of group resistance. Coch and French attempted to create a change by the method of group participation. By allowing the workers to participate in a decision concerning their work, change was effectively introduced and productivity generally increased (Coch and French, 1948). Their study lent substantial support to human relations theory, democratic leadership, and group dynamics theory. They also provided an impetus to the industrial leadership concepts referred to as "participative management," "participative decision-making," and "team-management."

From these two studies, then, a democratic style appears to be more desirable than an autocratic one in some situations as far as the subordinates are concerned. A democratic style is useful in guiding and co-ordinating a unit's thinking toward a group decision that ensures a high degree of commitment in the mission. The group, in a sense, rules itself and the leader is accepted as a part of the group. He accomplishes his objective by making the unit's mission coincide with the goals and interests of its members. This type of leadership has been practiced for centuries, from the time of political forum discussions during the days of Greeks and Romans, to the foundation of the United States and the expression of democratic principles incorporated in the Declaration of Independence.

AUTOCRATIC	COMBINATIONS	DEMOCRATIC
All authority rests with leader		Authority rests with the group
Leader rules by command		Leader accepted by the group
All decisions made by leader		Decisions made by group participation
Decisions arbitrary, based on task rather than needs of group		Leader accomplishes his goals by making them coincide with those of the group members

Figure 2.3 Spectrum of Leadership

From this diagram, the extreme autocratic leader is one who makes all decisions for his group because he is presumed to have superior knowledge or ability. He directs the group members in their activities toward the accomplishment of the group task. The leader determines the policies and dictates the tasks, and the subordinates follow. The leader is depicted as a rigid disciplinarian who is quick to punish any infraction of the rules but who rarely gives praise for a job well done. He is the hub of activity in the group. This type of leadership was inferred by Plato who felt that political leadership should be entrusted to the "elite." Down through the centuries other men of learning have adopted this philosophy; for example, Alexander Hamilton, an exponent of the able, and Thomas Carlyle with his "Great Man" doctrine. According to Douglas McGregor, autocratic leadership is based on a philosophy of human behavior that perceives the average man as inherently disliking work, avoiding responsibility, and desiring security above all else. McGregor called this the theory X of human assumptions about man's basic nature. He blamed this theory and all its false assumptions for creating an inadequate organization theory and ineffective leadership concepts. To compensate for the inadequacies of theory X, McGregor devised his own theory which he called theory Y. In this theory, he made the assumption that work is as natural to man as is play and rest; that he will work more willingly for objectives to which he is committed; and that he will not only accept responsibility but will seek it when given the opportunity. (McGregor, 1960.)

AUTOCRATIC-DEMOCRATIC CONTINUUM

Whether one agrees with McGregor that man is innately motivated to work or with those who feel he is inclined toward procrastination and laziness, the most practical style probably lies somewhere between the two extremes. Robert Tannenbaum and Warren H. Schmidt devised such an autocratic-democratic continuum (Tannenbaum, 1958, pp. 95-101). In this continuum, there are degrees of democratic style, just as there are degrees of autocratic style.

A continuum of styles such as this one suggests that a leader does not necessarily have to adopt completely one style or the other. An effective leader can vary along the continuum, adjusting his style to the demands of the situation. A company commander, for example, could permit his platoon leaders

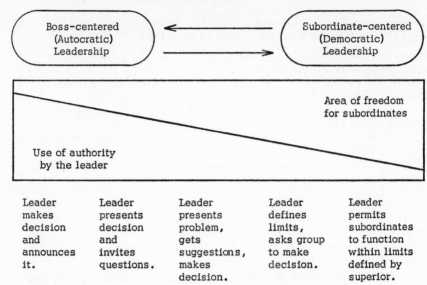

| Leader makes decision and announces it. | Leader presents decision and invites questions. | Leader presents problem, gets suggestions, makes decision. | Leader defines limits, asks group to make decision. | Leader permits subordinates to function within limits defined by superior. |

Figure 2.4 A Theoretical Continuum of Leadership Styles

Adapted from R. Tannenbaum and W. H. Schmidt, "How to Choose a Leadership Pattern," *Harvard Business Review,* March-April 1958, Vol. 36, No. 2, pp. 95-101.

complete freedom in discipline matters within their platoons. In the area of training, he might discuss his ideas with the platoon leaders and allow them to make suggestions. In preparing his company for an annual command maintenance inspection, he might feel he had the most experience, knew the best approach to the problem, and try to "sell" his ideas to the platoon leaders. In this same company on the battlefield the company commander, under the press of time and under fire, may make the decisions, announce them, and then forcefully see that they are carried out. Thus, one company commander might move along the full range of the continuum in exercising his leadership over the same group.

The question of whether a leader should be exacting or easy on his subordinates is not simple to answer. A democratic leader can be a tough taskmaster, and, for that matter, a purely autocratic leader can be very considerate. The style proposed by Tannenbaum and Schmidt considers only one variable, how a leader makes a decision. It does not include extremes of situation, organizational patterns, or the style of enforcing decisions. It provides, however, a vehicle for understanding leadership style and the degree of variety involved. A more comprehensive discussion of styles is developed by the managerial grid.

The Managerial Grid

In *The Managerial Grid,* Blake and Mouton propose a system of classifying managers on the basis of two variables. These variables are the manager's concern for people as measured against his concern for production. They are parallel to the two variables used to judge a military leader's style since he is similarly concerned with mission accomplishment and troop welfare.

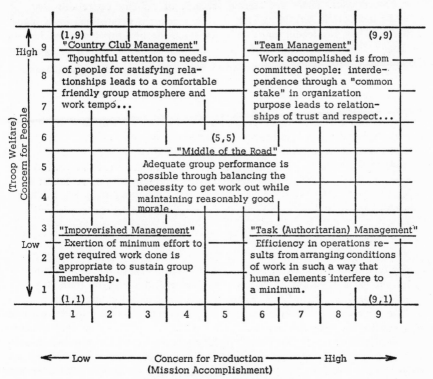

<——— Low ——————— Concern for Production ——————— High ———➤
(Mission Accomplishment)

Figure 2.5 The Managerial Grid

Adapted from *The Managerial Grid* by Robert R. Blake and Jane S. Mouton, Copyright 1964, Gulf Publishing Company.

The subject of leadership styles continues to be a popular area of investigation and interesting contributions are being made by such investigators as Fiedler (Fiedler, 1963 and 1966) and Hollander. The latter in a study of leadership styles, competence, and source of authority found competence to be more important in determining a leader's influence than was either his style or position (Hollander, *et al.,* 1966, pp. 8-10).

Leadership styles are patterns of authority relationships established by the leader within the group. They may range from extreme autocratic leadership, where the leader is the whole source of authority and makes all decisions, to extreme democratic leadership, where the leader guides the group to a group decision. Between these extremes are many variations. Whatever a leader's style, it varies in accordance with his own personality, the characteristics and needs of the followers (group), and, of course, with the demands of the situation.

Regardless of the many individual personality differences among military commanders, the military remains an institution built on executive authority. It is not democratic in the sense of the society it serves. Military commanders are not picked by ballot and the source of their legal authority is not derived from their subordinates. There are certain features of military operations that can never be democratic, primarily because the mission is determined by a higher authority. Thus, the leader cannot always make the unit mission coincide with the goals of the group. Rather, he must use his influence toward bringing the group to accept the unit mission as one of their own goals.

SUMMARY

Leadership involves highly generalized roles enacted with a group setting and with specific situations. The specific behaviors expected of the leader center around his dual responsibilities for mission accomplishment and providing for his followers. These two requirements involve initiating structure toward task performance and showing consideration for group members. A leader's behavior is largely directed by the expectations he perceives from his followers, his superior, the organization, and the over-all institution. In any conflict of roles, he will be judged according to his degree of success in guiding the group toward achieving the organizational objectives.

Leadership style or manner of performance specifically relates to the authority relationship the leader establishes between himself and his subordinates. Styles can be a function of decision-making, enforcement, or both. Style of leadership may also be a function of the concern shown for mission in relation to the concern shown for subordinates. One concept of leadership style consists of a continuum with extreme autocratic leadership at one end and extreme democratic leadership at the other. The relative position a leader adopts on such a scale is influenced by his personality, the nature of the group, and the situation in which they are involved. Regardless of style used, leader effectiveness is largely measured in terms of mission accomplishment.

Suggestions for Further Reading

Blau, Peter M., and Scott, W. Richard, *Formal Organizations.* San Francisco: Chandler Publishing Co., 1962.

Dubin, R., Homans, G. C., Mann, F. C., and Miller, D. C., *Leadership and Productivity.* San Francisco: Chandler Publishing Co., 1965.

Laird, Donald A., and Laird, Eleanor C., *The New Psychology for Leadership.* New York: McGraw-Hill Book Co., Inc., 1956.

Sayles, Leonard R., and Strauss, George, *Human Behavior in Organizations.* Englewood Cliffs, N. J.: Prentice-Hall, 1966.

Zaleznik, Abraham, *Human Dilemmas of Leadership.* New York: Harper & Row, Publishers, 1966.

III

Moral Aspects Of Leadership

THE EXERCISE of leadership inevitably involves moral and ethical considerations, regardless of the organizational level or type of organization. The very act of assuming responsibility for guiding, directing, or controlling others presupposes a moral responsibility for goals, missions, and methods. Even the act of counseling implies the assumption by the counselor of moral responsibility for the soundness of the goals he suggests as well as for the results of following his guidance. These responsibilities are inherent in the leader's role. He cannot escape them. The mantle of leadership carries with it a set of expectations on the part of both superiors and subordinates. Not only do they expect him to carry out the functions of a leader but also they expect him to perform them in a manner approved by society. His personal behavior, his value systems, his moral decisions are an integral part of his role and are reflected in the expectations of those he serves.

In addition, the status of leadership confers inescapable moral responsibility for setting the example for the group. The example the leader sets goes far toward determining the actual attitude and behaviors of the group, further, in fact, than verbal or written instructions. Thus the ethical and moral principles of the leaders are critical to the efficiency and effectiveness of an organization although their degree of importance and their impact on the structure may vary with the situation and the objectives sought.

MORAL CODES

Emmanuel Kant, in his *Perpetual Peace,* states, "Taken objectively, morality is in itself practical, being the totality of unconditionally mandatory laws according to which we ought to act" (as quoted in Ladd, 1957, p. 7). More recently, an anthropologist, in studying the moral code of the Navahos, said that, "A moral code is a collection of moral rules and principles relating what ought or ought not to be done—what is right or wrong. An ethic includes both the moral code and all the ethical conceptions and argumentation which are

45

associated with it." (Ladd, 1957, p. 9.) A moral code includes the fundamental rules of behavior necessary for that society's continued existence in its cultural environment. As Erich Fromm puts it, "The function of an ethical system in any given society is to sustain the life of that particular society." (Fromm, 1964, p. 241.) Moral codes establish a major portion of the framework and rationale in which leadership in a society is exercised.

Background

Ethical principles and moral codes have been in existence as long as man himself. The very existence of the societies in which men live is predicated upon the existence of established norms or rules of behavior. These ethical systems may gradually evolve within groups or culture, or be devised by a single law giver or philosopher. Some are attributed to and receive the sanction of Divine authority either as Natural Law or as the dogmas of specific religious faiths. Regardless of source, moral code provides the basic foundations for common law as well as the rules by which a society conducts its business.

For centuries thinking men have been concerned with the whys and wherefores of moral codes. Traditionally these matters were considered to be the proper study of priests or theologians. This accounts for much of the aura of sanctity and divine inspiration with which they are frequently clothed. In addition to religious leaders, philosophers also have considered morals and ethics a proper field of study, as their works from Plato and Aristotle to Josiah Royce and John Dewey testify. More recent scientific analyses verify that both primitive and modern societies face the same general questions of right and wrong. How should we behave? What are the rules?

For those of us raised in modern Western society, the historic Graeco-Roman philosophy and Judeo-Christian ethical system provide the basis for our moral code. Intertwined in the ethical history of Western man are concepts of virtuous behavior, the dignity of man, man's duty to man, and the concepts of freedom and equality. These have slowly evolved through the ages. As understood in the democratic society of today, they include the concepts of equal opportunity and social justice. These norms, and the ethical and moral concepts upon which they are based, provide the basic guideposts and limits for the conduct of the leaders of our society.

Military Code

Within the larger Western society many professional subgroups have ethical systems and moral rules that differ from those of the larger society by being more restrictive and more specific. A profession is an occupational field that, in general, requires specialized training in some abstract or practical body of knowledge. It accepts some degree of responsibility for the actions of its members and has sufficient corporate character to act as a body. Professions that wield extensive influence over the health or welfare of the members of society obviously require moral commandments in order to prevent the unscrupulous use of their power for the benefit of a few. Since the public is essentially at the mercy of the professional specialist, its primary protection lies in the professional's ethical code and the expectation that he will follow it.

The military, legal, educational, theological, and medical professions wield great influence over public welfare. Accordingly, they have developed the moral codes necessary to prescribe the ethical behavior of their members. The Hippocratic Oath of the medical profession has long guided the professional conduct of the doctor. The professional code of the warrior has an equally long history, extending from antiquity to modern times. Modern technology has greatly expanded the powers wielded by the professions. Therefore, far from reducing the requirement for these codes, the industrial conditions of modern society demand even stricter adherence to their rules.

Basis for Military Codes.   The military profession differs somewhat from the other professions in that for at least the past three centuries, it has been an arm of the state. It is highly organized on a hierarchical basis and normally controls a near monopoly over those weapons, men, and organizations which comprise the nation's coercive power. In the sixteenth and seventeenth centuries, the conditions resulting from the employment of mercenary soldiery made it clear that the professional military required rules of conduct. They further needed a greater degree of subordination to the governing political authorities. By the time of the American Revolution, the development of ethical and moral codes for the military profession was well under way. Understood as well was the principle that the military institution is subordinate to the guidance and control of the nation's political authorities.

The Army under George Washington carefully followed these inherited rules, as it has ever since. Washington scrupulously obeyed the desires of the Congress, even when it meant subordinating his military plans to the strategic desires of that body, which was not always in those days noted for its military expertise. The loyalty he exhibited toward the Congress, and to which he held the officers of his army, set the example and established the pattern for all American leaders who were to follow.

The fact that the nation entrusts its safety, wealth, and sons to a professional group is an indication of the special trust and confidence both the political leaders and the public at large must have in the military profession. Since Washington's day the power of the military profession has increased rather than diminished. Weapons have become more complex, specialized, and costly, as have the techniques and tactics of their employment. Larger proportions of the nation's manpower can be brought into service. Greater social control can be exerted over both the members of the military service and the public at large. Rapid communications and mass-destruction weapons, coupled with the requirements of international leadership, have forced military professionals into national policy-making circles.

Formal control over the military organizations of the United States is effected by law and administrative regulation. These laws, however, represent only the outward manifestation of the underlying professional ethical system and moral code that supports them. Fundamentally, the Army is controlled and self-regulated by its own informal ethical code. The code envelops all who exercise authority and leadership. It is at once an indication of the public faith in the Army's ability to uphold proper standards of conduct and at the same time a measure of the general expectation of performance by military leaders. This internal professional code establishes the atmosphere of mutual faith, security, and solidarity necessary to an organization in which each member must depend on his fellows for his success and, in combat, frequently his life.

Professional Solidarity. The leader's professional code supports him in his performance of duty. In turn, he contributes to the strength of the officer or noncommissioned officer corps by supporting the code. Any act of commission or omission made by a member of the group reflects either for or against the entire profession. Each leader must bear in mind that his conduct is not just his own business. It is the business of every other member of the profession as well. When an officer is arrested for speeding, it is not just John Doe who is arrested; it is Lieutenant or Sergeant John Doe, a member of a specific unit of the U.S. Army. Each member owes a moral obligation to the military profession as well as to the nation to ensure that the actions of its leaders conform to the highest traditions of the service and to its professional ethics and moral code.

Indoctrination. The indoctrination into this professional code begins with the leader's entry into the profession of arms. The concepts of higher loyalty, duty, honor, and country embodied in the code are exemplified by those leaders who have preceded him. Much of the code is taught in noncommissioned officer academies, in ROTC, in OCS, or in the service academies. Honor systems that demand integrity help to inculcate in each future leader the basic fundamentals of the code. They assist him in developing the moral courage required to make the hard moral decisions that he must make as a leader. The fact that these standards of the profession are more exacting than those of the general society makes this indoctrination a critical element in the development of military leadership in the service.

It is difficult, if not impossible, to express in writing the complex of ideas, attitudes, and injunctions that make up an ethical system or moral code. It is so interwoven into the fabric of our spiritual heritage and culture that only with great difficulty can one separate specific elements for analysis. For these reasons, ethics or moral codes are seldom completely expressed or defined in writing. Over the years they have been impressed on generations of soldiers through the examples of their predecessors, the customs of the service, and the traditions of the units in which they have served. Unit or organizational traditions are frequently exemplified in a motto or slogan which embellishes its crest, such as:

No mission too difficult, no sacrifice too great; duty first.
Unity is strength.
I'll try, sir.
Duty, Honor, Country.

Usually such mottos express some facet of the professional code. Duty, Honor, Country, the motto of the Military Academy, provides the most comprehensive basis for an examination of the component elements of the military moral code of the U.S. Army and the rationale for its ethical system.

DUTY

The first element in the military code is the concept of duty. Duty is a dedication to the service, its obligations, expressed or implied, coupled with loyalty to designated military and civilian authorities. This duty is first expressed in the words of the oath of office that state:

> I will support and defend the Constitution of the United
> States against all enemies foreign and domestic. . . . I will
> well and faithfully discharge the duties of the office. . . .
>
> (U.S.C. S16, 1958.)

Duty, then, for the military professional is service; service to country, to superiors, and to subordinates. The fundamental code considers that the leader is not working for himself, to advance his own fortunes, reputation, social status, or safety. Rather he is dedicating himself to the welfare of his unit, the support of his commander, and the execution of the responsibilities of his office in behalf of his country. That this element of the code has the sanction of law was shown in the words of the Commanding General, Sixth U.S. Army, in a reprimand to an officer found guilty of misbehavior in Korea:

> You have held personal safety and comfort above duty,
> honor, and country, and in so doing have deliberately vio-
> lated your oath . . . as an officer of the United States Army.
>
> (Hq., Sixth Army, 1956.)

Thus, under the concept of duty in the professional code, the military contract demands an almost unconditional subordination of individual interest, friends, or family to the performance of his duty and in fulfilling his responsibilities should such be required (Hackett, 1963).

Responsibility

Implicit in the concept of duty is a sense of responsiblity. The primary distinguishing characteristic of a commander's role stems from his assumption of responsibility for all that his unit does or fails to do. Many of the leader's responsibilities are prescribed in regulations, field manuals, and job descriptions. Some are required by Federal law. Others are issued as directives from various headquarters. The Code of Conduct is an example of an expression of the requirements of duty as they apply to prisoners of war. Over and above the detailed prescribed duties lies the leader's moral obligation to further the mission of his assigned organization and to co-operate with and assist others in accomplishing their missions. This is a part of his over-all moral responsibility to take all possible actions to enhance the security of the country through the use of his own talents, skills, or special knowledge.

Example. One of the foremost responsiblities of a leader is to serve as the example or model for his followers in everything that he does or is. The motto of the Infantry School, "Follow Me," clearly expresses the leader's duty of setting the example. Actually, the leader always sets an example, whether for good or bad. If group performance is to be good, the example set by the leader must be good. This is a moral obligation imposed by subordinates. They look to him for a model of what they ought to be. Not that they always reach the standard set if it is a high one, but many will be sure to outdo that standard if it is a low one. Both in his adherence to the professional code and in his personal conduct the effective leader must have the respect of his subordinates. Deviations from the strictest ethical behavior by an officer or leader are not easily forgotten or forgiven. The effectiveness of the leader is diminished by the degree of esteem he loses in the eyes of his followers.

Courage. One of the most dramatic ways a leader can lose esteem is to exhibit a lack of courage. The military profession places a high premium on this quality; it is a self-evident aspect of a leader's concept of duty. To lead a platoon in the attack, to fight off the advancing enemy even though outnumbered, this is the stuff of citations and decorations. Even leading or commanding a group of men with one's reputation and future hanging on their performance requires courage. The implicit demands of duty, that require an officer to place his responsibilities and mission above the call of self-interest or friendship, frequently require the exercise of courage beyond that called for in combat. This little-advertised aspect of moral courage is no less required than the physical type. It requires moral courage to stand up for an unpopular course of action when some of those opposed are one's seniors. It requires moral courage to take an unpopular action against one's subordinates when it has to be done. Yet duty requires just such decisions and just such courage of one's convictions. No effective military organization could exist were such courage lacking in its leaders.

Obedience

No organization can function effectively without the obedience of its members to the direction and will of the leader. One of the principal aspects of military character has always been the trait of habitual obedience to properly constituted authority. To be effective, this obedience must be prompt and willing; however, the responsiveness expected of the military professional is intelligent and discriminating rather than blind and unreasoning. The fast-moving situations of today put increased emphasis on knowing the reason and purpose behind orders and instructions. As much damage can result from exact compliance with instructions in inappropriate situations as from failing to take action at all.

Initiative. It is quite clear that the code expects much more of a leader than unquestioning obedience to orders. Situations change; unpredicted factors crop up. A leader must be able to analyze his orders in terms of the over-all mission, referring any question to his superiors, if possible, or making the decision himself, if not. The action taken must be a serious requirement, however, and must be what the individual believes would have been the action of his superior had he been present and known all the facts. The leader's proper performance of duty requires almost unlimited use of his initiative. Far from inhibiting individual initiative, the professional code establishes the expectation that a leader who sees that something must be done will take action, if necessary, on his own authority. The result of many a battle has hung on the thread of acceptance of individual responsibility and the exercise of initiative.

Loyalty to Man. Intelligent obedience requires steadfast loyalty to superiors, peers, and subordinates. The more critical the task of the unit, the more pressures that are brought to bear on decisions and performance, the more critical is the loyalty of the members of the team. Loyal support of a superior does not imply supine acquiescence in his every suggestion or proposal. The most effective loyalty is displayed by the officer who assists his superior in arriving at the best possible decision. He then accepts that decision as his own and loyally carries it out without passing the buck. Some have questioned whether this loyalty is to a man or to an office. In most instances it is to the man acting in his official capacity in the office. It is not just to the man himself or to the office by itself. Thus, loyalty is extended to the policies, attitudes, and desires of the man who is in the office rather than being limited to his official pronouncements. In turn, no leader achieves the wholehearted loyalty of his peers or subordinates without being loyal to them. In this instance, the demands of duty are that the leader protect the welfare and interests of his peers and subordinates to the same or even greater degree than he would his own—that is, to the extent that the mission and situation permit. Loyalty as an aspect of leadership is a three-way orientation. Ideally, it must exist mutually between superiors, subordinates, and peers.

HONOR

A fundamental component of the military professional code through the ages has been that of honor. A soldier without honor has always been a sad thing indeed, and in today's military profession he is nearly useless as well. Both the cohesion and the solidarity of the combat unit in battle and the reliable and effective performance of the staff or logistic organization in the rear rest heavily upon the honor of its leaders at all levels. Honor can be said to be made up of several components. The first of these is integrity.

Integrity

The quality of saying what one means and meaning what one says, of being upright, honest, and sincere is a vital component of honor in the military code. Soldiers throughout the centuries have depended upon others to support them as they risked their lives in combat. They have always had to depend upon the word of their subordinates and superiors, and the proud boast of an officer has long been that his word and signature are his bond. Lives, careers, battles, and the fate of nations have hung upon the ability of military leaders to state all the true facts to the best of their knowledge, regardless of what effect these facts might have on themselves or others. Today the battlefield requirements for integrity are still present. In addition, the complex requirements involved in the development and procurement of costly weapons systems and in the international political policy arena make the demand for integrity as great as ever. Subordinates must be able to trust their leaders implicitly. Nothing can disrupt the morale and effectiveness of an organization more quickly than an untrustworthy, quibbling, or temporizing leader. Cheating, violating a trust, sacrificing others for selfish interest, gaining unfair advantage; these are the cancers in a military society that must be rooted out wherever found, if that society is to retain its vitality and life. Personal integrity is an essential component of a successful leader's reputation.

Reputation. The influence and hence the effectiveness of a leader is largely determined by his reputation which, in part, is a reflection of his honor. His reputation with his superiors is critical to his career and determines the types of positions and missions he is given. His reputation with his associates and subordinates determines to a large extent his ability to get the job done. Reputation is the reflected image of his character and the standard of performance that others expect of him. It can be damaged by malicious gossip, hearsay evidence, or the unwitting ill-considered actions of the individual himself. For this reason, the professional code has always expected the leader to cherish his reputation and to do nothing that would tarnish its luster. Likewise, members of the profession are expected to avoid saying or doing anything that would unjustly reflect against the reputation of others. Weakening or tearing down the reputation of military leaders reflects against the profession as a whole, destroys the esteem in which it is held, and reduces its effectiveness.

Authority

The power of authority has a unique ability to corrupt and destroy the reputation of its holders. The temptations of authority and power are many: the use of power for its own sake, for enhancing individual ego, for furthering one's self-interests, for personal advancement, or for personal spite. All such corruptions of authority damage the honor of the leader and seriously weaken the military structure. The measured and proper use of authority is an integral part of leadership, closely related to a leader's honor.

Justice. The extensive authority that a military leader has over his subordinates makes his application of justice critical to the morale and welfare of the organization. Subordinates in a military organization expect to be treated fairly and impartially. Any hint of favoritism or misuse of authority quickly creates a lack of confidence in the leader and reduces his influence and his effectivenss. Hence, both reward and punishment must be meted out without bias and with absolute impartiality.

COUNTRY

Every citizen is expected to be loyal to his country. By entering the profession of arms and taking the oath of allegiance, however, the military leader undertakes a special obligation. The military leader is not only a member of a profession specifically designated to guard and protect the state, he is also a member of an organization that could do his country and its citizens the greatest amount of damage. Either by failing to live up to the professional code, and thus not performing as expected, or by taking actual steps to destroy or threaten its institutions, the military profession could violate its trust and become the enemy of the common good.

Loyalty to Country

The concept of patriotism and loyalty to country is easy to grasp. Every school child would probably say he knew what it meant. When the officer swears that "I will support and defend the Constitution of the United States against all enemies, foreign and domestic; and I will bear true faith and allegiance to the same," (U.S.C. S16, 1958), he has clearly established his primary loyalty. Nevertheless, questions of divided loyalty sometimes arise. In the natural course of events, loyalties tend to be strongest at the small-group level. Each individual belongs to several groups or organizations, some with strong ties of loyalty. The Civil War brought a specific problem of divided loyalties to the regular officers from the South. Many of these, including Robert E. Lee, found that their loyalties to their state or region were stronger than to the Federal government and the Constituion they had sworn to defend. They solved their problem through resignation. Yet, many people at the time considered them to be traitors, while other considered them heroes and honorable men.

Problems of divided loyalty may appear today in different forms. Domestic disturbances that take on a regional character could again raise the issue of loyalty to state before loyalty to country. Officers assigned to international agencies find that the clash of loyalties generated by conflicitng national and international interests can be troublesome. It is in our national interest that our officers be assigned to such agencies. Frequently, however, they have to ask themselves whether their highest loyalty is to their country or to the international agency to which they are assigned. This is a complicated problem for which there are few precedents and no general agreements. Louis B. Sohn, Professor of International Law at Harvard, has stated his opinion that:

> The officer who becomes a permanent employee of the United Nations owes basic allegiance to it rather than to his native country. This rule would not apply, of course, to contingents temporarily given to the United Nations for short-term tasks.

(As quoted in Reese, 1964, p. 37.)

Faced with a conflict of interest between the international authority and his national loyalty, an officer usually can ask for instructions. This does not always solve the problem, however. As international agencies and international command structures become more numerous, this area of conflicting loyalties can be expected to become more prominent.

Conflicting loyalties could occur in still another area, such as between the Constitution and some program of a specific administration. This problem has occurred rarely in this country, although it did happen in Nazi Germany when Hitler required his army to take an oath of allegiance to him rather than to the country or to the constitution. As we have seen, the military code requires loyalty to one's duly constituted authorities, while the oath of office requires that officers support and defend the Constitution and by implication the laws of the land. Were some future chief executive to give instructions to the Army that were in violation of law or the Constitution, a moral dilemma could arise. In such an instance, it would be the responsibility of the courts to establish the legality of the order. Pending that decision, the leader would remain obligated to obey the orders of his superior unless they clearly violated the Constitution or existing law.

Civil-Military Relationship. With support of the Constitution and its processes as a basis, the military professional must now work out his relationships with the civilian agencies of government. George Washington set the example and pattern for dealing with the legislative branch of the government. Subsequent military commanders have been equally careful in their loyal support of the civilian secretaries who represent the Administration in providing guidance for military policy. The principle of civilian control over the military establishment is so firmly established as to be unquestioned.

Taking a commission or warrant does not mean that a leader ceases to have a political point of view. The professional code prescribes that the leader in his official position, or in fact in any role which could affect his official position, should remain totally neutral with regard to political parties and issues. Privately, he should vote according to his beliefs and desires. Publicly, he has a moral obligation to the men he leads not to influence or sway them by word or deed to support one party or another. The authority and sanctions available to military leaders in the chain of command are too strong to permit their use to influence the political allegiance of their subordinates. Further, each military leader can expect to serve under a number of different administrations composed of members of different parties. As long as he remains in the military service, he must be as loyal to one as to another. The confidence in which the military organization is held by the members of the administration depends in good measure on its political neutrality.

While the professional military leader must be neutral toward political parties and issues and fully responsive to the policy guidance of civilian authority, he is not excused from having a complete knowledge of the principles and operation of our government, as well as of current public issues involved. If he is to support the Constitution intelligently, he must know in some detail just how our system of government operates. Secondly, the ideological struggle over the past half-century has made mandatory the education of all military personnel on our system of government and on the issues that it faces. As the reaction of our prisoners of war in Korea tended to show, only too often our men have been inadequately prepared to defend themselves against the propaganda and psychological stratagems of their captors. A leader has the moral obligation not only to prepare himself to understand and support our constitutional system, but also to train and prepare his men to do likewise.

Support of Policy. The military organization is a part of the executive branch of the government. As such, it is required to execute public policy as defined by the President and his policy representatives in the Department of Defense. Occasionally, some of these policies may be unpopular among some or all of the members of the military service. It is immaterial whether the individual leader likes or believes in the policy. So long as it is clearly not illegal or immoral, he is bound by the professional code and his oath of office to execute that policy to the best of his ability, and to support it wholeheartedly before his subordinates. As the servant of the nation, he must do the nation's bidding whether he likes the nation's bidding or not. Since the military leader represents himself not as an individual but as an official of the government, he may not publicly oppose or protest against established national policies or programs.

AREAS OF POSSIBLE DIFFICULTY

The preceding discussion of various elements of the professional code has touched upon a number of problem areas. Some specific problems of a moral nature that a leader must face repeatedly during a military career are examined more fully below.

Integrity

Reporting. Full and accurate presentation of all the facts in administrative or operational reports is essential in the military structure. Reports form the basis for individual administrative actions, for the procurement of personnel and equipment, for the formulation of public policy, and for the preparation of combat operational plans. Information on the status of individuals, on the status of equipment, on the location or actions of the enemy, on what occurred during a specific action or incident is reported from a variety of units. It is then consolidated, analyzed, and made the basis for high-level decisions involving millions of dollars and frequently thousands of lives. On some occasions, making an accurate report at a lower level might tend to cast the lower unit commander in an unfavorable light or suggest negligence or deficiency in accomplishing a mission expected of him. Many times it requires considerable moral courage to report facts which thus indicate poor performance by the maker of the report. It also requires considerable courage to report to a senior commander facts that he does not want to hear, even if they are true. Yet the issues are so critical that there must be no equivocating, quibbling, or evasion in the preparation of reports, verbal or written. Every inaccurate or untrue report weakens the military structure, damages its efficiency, and makes the system more susceptible to subsequent and even greater falsifications or inaccuracies.

Recommendations and Decisions. The necessity for making the best recommendations and decisions can challenge the moral courage of a leader. The military leader from corporal to general must make recommendations to his superiors on proposed actions or policies. Inevitably, moral issues arise. The leader faces the problem of weighing all of the considerations. Sometimes, the best recommendation may not be the most politic one. A practical and sound policy recommendation may be unpopular or contrary to his superior's stated preference. Occasionally, the leader faces the necessity of standing up for what he believes to be correct, even if it appears that he is bound to lose the decision and possibly the esteem of his superiors by doing so. Problems of this type become ever more critical as the leader increases in rank and responsibility. There is much pressure on the individual in this area and much rides on his decision. In the long run, the health of the military institution depends on each officer making his recommendations based on his own experience and professional knowledge. After carefully weighing the pros and cons, he should give his views objectively to his superiors, regardless of what he feels the views of others might be. If he is overruled, he should support the decision made. Until such a decision is made, he should support his own views as strongly as the merits of his particular position would indicate.

The superior's decision may still be unpopular. On these occasions the leader must avoid the easy way out by passing the buck of responsiblity for the directive on to higher authority. The code prescribes that he should issue the directive and enforce it as if it were his own. This requirement is soundly based in practical necessity. If the men see their leader enthusiastically supporting the directive, their own response is likely to be much more positive.

Occasionally, the leader must take unpopular action on his own authority. Commanders at all levels frequently come face to face with the necessity for making a decision that is unpopular with some or all of their subordinates. Here again, he must have the moral courage to make the correct decision despite the fact that, by so doing, he might gain the temporary or even permanent disfavor of his subordinates.

Avoiding Blame.   The leader frequently finds that some decision or action he took turns out poorly, often for reasons that he had not anticipated. In such cases, the natural instinct is to protect one's position or reputation by searching for some excuse or some way to transfer the blame to someone else. In fact, in some individuals this form of ego protection is almost automatic. For fairly obvious reasons, the military code expects a leader to assume full responsibility for his acts and decisions, even if they turn out to be mistaken or have undesirable results. Similarly, a commander is expected to assume responsibility for the failure of an individual or unit in his command, even though he himself was not directly involved in the act itself. The commander who shifts blame or censure on others for actions for which he is responsible will soon lose the respect of his subordinates and his effectiveness at a leader.

Expedience

Illegal or Immoral Orders.   Adherence to the professional ethic by all officers normally protects subordinates in the chain of command from being faced with illegal or immoral orders. Problems of this nature tend to occur primarily in the higher levels of command where the issues are more ambiguous and the interpretation of applicable law or policy more uncertain. On rare occasions, a leader may receive instructions that he knows in fact to be illegal. Such an occasion might occur as the result of ignorance, indifference, or misinterpretation of law at a higher headquarters. Both the law and the code hold that a leader is responsible for his acts, as is the superior who gave him the orders. No leader, then, should execute an illegal order. By doing so, he becomes personally responsible for violating the law.

Orders that tend to violate public or international morality can raise more difficult questions, since these moral standards are not clearly defined and at times appear to be subject to considerable variation. The International Military

Tribunal at Nuremberg tried accused Nazis for war crimes after World War II. It took the position that there was a recognized international morality and that a person could be found guilty of violating it, even though he was following the orders of constituted authority. Since that time, this concept has been expanded by efforts of the United Nations to codify these standards of international morality through international conventions, such as the one on Human Rights. The rapid expansion of weapons systems, particularly those involved in mass destruction, and the rise of revolutionary warfare and counterinsurgency raise problems revolving around the question of whether the ends justify the means. Faced with an enemy who employs torture, terrorism, blackmail, and subversion, there is a natural tendency to fight fire with fire and to employ similar methods to defeat him. It is all too easy to rationalize the situation by telling oneself that the end or objective is good; hence, one can be excused for unethical means in achieving it. The gaining of a short-run advantage, however, should not be allowed to compromise the long-run objective. The winning of a battle might mean the eventual loss of the peace. Unfortunately, in many cases, the moral outrage aroused by unethical behavior ends up by overshadowing or neutralizing any good there may have been in obtaining the objective. In other words, the ends sought cannot be separated from the means employed. The ends do not justify the means. Each action must stand on its own, regardless of how good the end result might be. Each leader issuing an order, or executing an order issued by a superior, is responsible for its morality as well as its legality, and should guide himself accordingly. If the action concerned is illegal, unethical, or immoral, it will stay that way even if the outcome sought might appear to be a positive gain for all. Countless years of experience shows that moral behavior produces the best results in the long run (Hazlitt, 1964, p. 354).

Situational Ethics. Today there is an increasing tendency, particularly on the part of youth, to belittle moral rules and to attempt to evaluate right and wrong based on the situation. Advocates of the so-called situational ethics claim that the inflexibility of existing moral rules tends to make them inapplicable and inappropriate in many cases. This situational approach has grave deficiencies when applied to the military ethic. The moral rules of the game create an expectation that members of the profession will behave in a specific way. Secondly, the moral acts of a military man have widespread implications. The individual who acts never knows how far these implications extend, how many people are affected, or what the end results might be. While these considerations apply to any moral code, they are particularly critical to the military profession with its extensive responsibilities.

Money Management. The military leader charged with money management responsibilities may not feel the code is realistically compatible with the business world of today. Occasionally, he may be tempted to renounce or modify the code for himself at the moment. The area of money management has always been fraught with great pressures and temptations. Where large sums of money are involved or business interests brought to bear, there is a possibility of conflict between the moral and ethical codes of the business world and those of the military profession. Club managers, officers in charge of various nonappropriated funds, and procurement officers are subject to these pressures and problems. All too often the unsuspecting officer finds himself in the position of being trapped into receiving favors from persons with whom he is doing business before he realizes that they fully expect something in return. What to them is a legitimate business expense in promoting the sale of their product, to the officer can be a concealed form of bribery that weakens his moral position of impartiality and objectivity in office. For this reason, the code, reinforced by law and regulation, protects the officer by requiring him not to place himself in the position of accepting personal favors from those with whom he is doing business or of allowing his personal interests to be involved or appear to be involved in these transactions. Frequently, the mere appearance of personal involvement can be as damaging to his position as actual involvement.

Concern for Property. The exigencies of the moment, both in combat and garrison, place many pressures and temptations on those in charge of the management of supplies and equipment. It is an easy matter for a leader to slight materiel management under the pressure of a crisis. Although the leader's primary problem is the influencing and managing of people, he also has a positive role in managing and using property. Moral issues arise even in materiel management. The professional leader, like the sentry on guard, takes charge of his post and all government property in view. In many cases he is actually charged with personal responsibility for it. There are many regulations and procedures prescribed for the care, safeguarding, procurement, and disposal of government property. These rules are established to provide for the most efficient use of the property, to enable it to be readily available when needed, and to be disposed of when not needed.

On some occasions the pressure to obtain results in an inspection or competition or to improve the welfare or efficiency of a unit tempts military personnel to violate prescribed procedures in procuring equipment or in disposing of it. Borrowing or expropriating the property of another unit, or hiding excess equipment in order to present an equipment status picture different from that which is actually the case are typical examples of violations. Such actions are more than mere violations of procedures; they are morally indefensible. First, they are dishonorable deceptions in that they tend to present a picture of good management and readiness that, in fact, is not the case. Secondly, such actions tend to enhance unjustly the reputation or effectiveness of one unit at the expense of another. In the third place, it is an improper and weak substitute for the proper supply action that will ultimately cause somebody else to pay for the poor administrative procedures of the unit in question.

Another problem area in this field is the conversion of government property to private or personal use. All government property, vehicles, tools, weapons, or bedding were procured for specific purposes and are expected to be used for them. Some leaders are tempted to use this equipment for their own personal advantage. This temptation should be resisted. Succumbing to it in one instance tends to make future violations easier and to corrupt the integrity or the reputation of the leader.

There are many other situations in which moral or ethical questions arise in the conduct of the daily business of being a leader in the military service. In each case, adhering to the moral code, even though more difficult, will strengthen the position and enhance the reputation of the leader. Violating the professional code and succumbing to temptation will destroy his reputation, weaken his moral courage, and ultimately destroy his value as a leader.

SUMMARY

Institutional leadership reflects the moral foundations upon which the institution is built. The American military institutions are built primarily upon the moral concepts of Western society and its Judeo-Christian ethics, together with the modern democratic norms as expressed in the American Constitution. On this foundation, the professional moral code of the military service, because of the responsibility and critical nature of the profession, emphasizes certain aspects and demands higher standards than those of the general society. In addition to the moral commandments incumbent upon any individual, a man accepting a position of leadership in the Armed Forces is bound by the formal and informal codes of his profession. His oath of office and commission dictate that he meet specific ethical standards of conduct. These standards impose restrictions on the leader's behavior. By assuming the responsibility of leadership, the military leader assumes moral responsibility for the means used and the ends sought. In the process, he must face many moral problems concerned with these means and ends. By accepting the professional military ethic as his own, the leader not only finds it easier to cope with moral problems, but also supports and is supported by these professional standards. If the military profession of the United States is to retain its effectiveness and the public trust that it has so proudly held, each member must continue to hold these standards high.

Suggestions for Further Reading

Hackett, Lt. Gen. Sir John Winthrop (Br.), *The Profession of Arms*. London: Times Publishing Company, 1963.
Janowitz, Morris, *The Professional Soldier*. Glencoe, Illinois: The Free Press, 1960.
Marshall, Gen. S. L. A., *The Officer as a Leader*. Harrisburg, Pa.: Stackpole Company, 1966.
Roskill, Capt. S. W. (RN), *The Art of Leadership*. Hamden, Conn.: Archon Books, 1965.

IV

Leader Selection and Development

AN ESSENTIAL qualification of a good leader is the ability to recognize, select, and develop his subordinate leaders. The question often arises as to which is the more important in producing effective leaders—the process of selection or that of development. Actually, both activities are directed toward many of the same goals. Since they are not mutually exclusive, a more practical approach might be to think in terms of their interrelationship. At one extreme, if all persons were perfectly modifiable through training and development programs, knowledge of personal variables would be unnecessary. Each could be trained to perform in the manner desired. At the other extreme, if all persons were unalterable through training and development, selection by personal variables would be the only way of assuring good leadership. Neither extreme is true. Both selection and development are necessary to produce effective leaders. The selection process serves to eliminate those who do not satisfy the minimum criteria. It predicts potential leadership ability. It is in the realization of this potential that the leader's development complements the selection process.

LEADER SELECTION

One of the military leader's most challenging tasks is the selection of subordinate leaders and the guiding of their development. In the previous chapter, some of the moral dilemmas that face a military leader were discussed. One area in which the leader must frequently demonstrate moral courage in making difficult decisions is in the selection of subordinate leaders. It is also an area in which he can greatly influence the organization's effectiveness. Although a commander normally does not have the prerogative of selecting or rejecting personnel assigned to his unit, he is given wide latitude over assigning tasks to personnel within his unit. Effective placement of subordinates within the organization and the selection of subordinates for leadership tasks is an ability that distinguishes the perceptive leader.

Each leader is responsible for choosing subordinates. The platoon leader must recommend men for promotion. He assists in determining who shall

61

assume a position of leadership or perform a mission within his unit, or who is the best selection to attend Noncommissioned Officer or Specialist Schools. In making these selections, he will, in effect, single out those men who have indicated leadership potential or who have exhibited leadership ability. At the next higher level, the company or battery commander determines which of his assigned lieutenants will lead platoons and serve in other unit-level capacities such as mess officer or supply officer.

In order to make the best selection, the leader should use something better than random procedures. He needs to analyze systematically each eligible man. The variables that distinguish leaders are dynamic and everchanging in relative importance. As pointed out in Chapter I, the trait approach falls short of the mark as a means of identifying leaders. Not even the leader's appearance helps. Although there might appear to be general agreement as to what a leader should look like, there is in fact no relation between the facial characteristics agreed upon and those possessed by actual leaders. (Masson, 1957.)

Inconsistent results also have been obtained with tests ostensibly designed to isolate the "leadership personality". In fact, quite a few people agree with William H. Whyte, Jr., that personality tests may actually eliminate good executive talent from consideration (Whyte, 1956). At the present state of the art of testing, it appears that tests are more effective in determining those unfitted for a particular job than in identifying those who will do quite well. The intriguing problem is to predetermine those personal variables that are the primary contributors to success as a leader. By being able to recognize variables in others, the leader improves the validity of his selection of subordinates.

The variables of criteria for the most effective leaders are related to the group that is being led. Also, the demands of the situation in which he is to function as a leader determine to a large extent the qualities, the characteristics, and skills required. There are certain variables, however, that seem to constitute that practically indefinable characteristic possessed by leaders. This characteristic permits some leaders to assume consistently the role of leader in almost every group and situation.

Leadership Variables

Ralph M. Stogdill in summarizing a survey of leadership literature concludes that there are six factors associated with leadership (Stogdill, 1948). They are Capacity, Achievement, Responsibility, Participation, Status, and Situation. They emerge as the primary factors indicative of leadership ability, and taken together may be considered to constitute the characteristic dimensions of a leader.

Capacity includes the one ability that correlates most consistently with leadership—mental ability. Intelligence tests are one of the most reliable predictors for leader selection. Some studies, however, indicate that the most effective leader is only slightly more intelligent than the group he is leading. In other words, there appears to be a possibility that a leader can be too intelligent for the group he is leading. One explanation might be that the differences in interests, goals, and activity patterns act as barriers to joint participation on the part of the leader and his group. As a general rule, the emergent leader's intellectual level and aptitude are slightly above the average of the group he is leading. The best indications of this quality available to the military leader are the General-Technical (GT) scores and the Armed Forces Qualification Test (AFQT) scores recorded in the personnel records of all enlisted men. For officers, this quality can only be inferred from educational accomplishments and through observation. Testing an individual's intelligence quotient (IQ) is rarely done in the service, and, when it is, the results are not normally available. The factor of capacity also calls for a subjective evaluation by the leader of the subordinate's alertness, verbal facility, originality, and judgment. These are overt indications of the individual's mental ability, and a proper evaluation of these qualities may prove more valid than test scores or educational levels. When possible, subjective evaluations should be verified by the individual judgment of another observer in order to increase their validity.

Achievement is usually one of the easier variables to measure because an individual's past accomplishments often are a matter of record. Such things as attained educational level, the possession of special skills, and athletic accomplishments should be considered in evaluating the individual's achievements. This information is available to the commander in the personnel records of the men he evaluates.

Responsibility either assigned or assumed by an officer is reflected on his Form 66 which lists the sequence of duties assigned to him. Typically, the responsibility a leader is given or assumes varies from job to job depending upon his immediate commander's style of leadership. The best measure of an individual's developed sense of responsibility is derived through an intimate knowledge of his actual performance. The qualities that appear to provide the best measurement of responsibility are dependability, initiative, persistence, aggressiveness, self-confidence, and the desire to excel.

Participation is another personal variable that is best measured subjectively through association with and knowlege of the individual. It is only in this manner that the leader can arrive at an evaluation of the subordinate's sociability, his adaptability, his spirit of co-operation, and his sense of humor.

The degree of his participation in social interaction is related to the individual's status in the organization. In a military organization this variable involves the relative ranks of the candidates being selected for leadership positions. Frequently a commander will consider this as the governing factor. It is by all odds the easiest to measure definitively and has the added advantage of being clearly understood by all the candidates. An individual's attained rank is an objective factor and, in the military hierarchy, relative rank is clearly established between individuals.

Stogdill lists the situation as a sixth variable affecting leadership. He includes the characteristics of the group being led as a part of the situation. Consideration must be given to the mental level, status, skills, needs, and interests of the followers. In addition, the objectives to be achieved should be considered. The significance of this factor is that the commander must determine which subordinate leader is best suited for a particular leadership task involving a certain group of people trying to accomplish a given mission.

The Selection Process

Only rarely, if ever, does a commander have the opportunity to collect all the supporting data he needs and then dispassionately select the best qualified leader. Realizing this limitation, the importance of obtaining optimum results by systematizing the selection process increases. Having determined criteria, the next action is to assign relative weights to each variable. These weights are a function of the mission to be accomplished and the characteristics of the group charged with its accomplishment. For example, in selecting a section chief for a Nike site in New York City, capacity and responsibility may be more important considerations than participation or status, and accordingly are more heavily weighted.

After the leader has satisfied himself as to the relative importance of the six variables, he should ensure that he considers sufficient candidates for the leadership position. The purpose of this action is to provide an adequate variation on the predictor variables. Enough candidates should be considered to allow reasonable range from the best to the poorest qualified candidate.

The leader should then rank-order the candidates on each of the six variables. The most valid basis for this rank-ordering is an extensive knowledge of the candidates under consideration including their actual job performance. The final step is to check to see if the prediction of the selected leader's ability correlated with actual job performance. If the evaluation shows the leader is not fulfilling expectations, then the rank-ordering of the variables should be reexamined rather than automatically selecting the second most qualified candidate for leadership. This evaluation of the leader's effectiveness is a continuous process. A point to be remembered here is that it is easier to appoint a man to a position of leadership than it is to remove him.

LEADERSHIP DEVELOPMENT

After the commander selects his leaders, he has a further responsibility to develop their leadership to the fullest. This benefits both the organization and the subordinate. Leader attrition in military organizations is high. As a result of casualties, transfers, special details, discharge, and retirement, commanders are constantly faced with the necessity of developing subordinate leaders. Leadership development is especially important in the military since almost all promotions are made from within the organization. In addition, the Army in peacetime must plan for partial or total mobilization; hence all of its members must be capable of filling leadership positions well above their present grades.

Objectives of Leadership Development

The success of a leader depends to a great extent upon his motivation to accept his role. It also depends on his ability to determine and satisfy his group's needs, and his ability to bring them to the accomplishment of their goal under the conditions they face. These are functions of the personal characteristics of the individual. A leadership development program cannot possibly include all group and situational factors. It can only concentrate on the potential leader. Hence, a program should have the specific objective of developing the attitudes and skills that will allow him to handle the group and situational factors he encounters.

A number of different measures are available to assess the effects of training on attitude change. These center largely around attitudes toward the "human problems" of leadership, seniors and subordinates, leadership methods, and the organization itself. Most of these are questionnaire-type measures. Normally, the military leader has to rely on his own evaluation of whether his development program produces an attitude change or not. One of the difficulties encountered in attitude changes is in demonstrating the relationship between an attitude change and a change in performance. A professed attitude change that does not result in improved performance indicates that the leader should re-examine the program.

The particular skills that the leader must develop can be roughly classified as task skills and social skills. Task skills are concerned with the accomplishment of the group mission. They vary according to the type of unit and the level of command. They include skill in the solution of technical and tactical problems and skill in the efficient employment of the group in the accomplishment of the mission. If the skills that the leader should develop are task skills rather than social skills, he must study on his own or seek schooling to provide him with the needed skills. Further, if he finds that he has become overspecialized in some area detrimental to his over-all development, he must seek more broadening assignments. All leaders, particularly junior leaders, must actively seek opportunities to broaden their experience. In the words of General Omar N. Bradley, "There is no better way to develop leadership than to give an individual a job involving responsibility and let him work it out." (Bradley, 1966, p. 53.) Junior leaders should learn as many leader jobs as possible within their unit. It is a basic axiom that the leader must know the technical, tactical, and administrative aspects of his assigned branch of service. The leader, however, must retain the over-all picture of how his job fits into the accomplishment of the mission. He cannot afford to become like the specialist who learns more and more about less and less until, eventually, he knows absolutely everything about nothing.

Social or human relations skills are concerned with the social interaction process within the group. They include the ability to motivate the unit to accept the mission as its own goal and to provide for the satisfaction of the individual needs of the group members. They also include the ability to solve the many human relations problems that arise in the group. These are the human skills of the leader, the real "art" of the art of leadership. Typically, they are more difficult to develop than the more mechanical task skills. They involve development of the ability to evaluate the reactions of others and to apply the knowledge thus gained to obtain the co-operation of the members of the group.

If his leadership deficiences are in the field of human relations, the officer must conscientiously try new behavior patterns in a social situation. If the new patterns are effective, they will be reinforced by better responses from others. Each reinforcement will make it easier to adopt the new patterns permanently.

Usually, there is a certain amount of experimentation required in this process. For this reason, it may be wise to try out the new behavior patterns away from one's actual subordinates. For example, an individual can try out new behaviors in his social contacts with his friends. He can join extracurricular groups. These often give excellent experience in practical leadership as well as again providing a chance to try out new behaviors. A technique sometimes used by industry is to send their executives away for a management development course conducted by some industrial or educational institution. Here, placed in a new group composed of his peers, the individual can often get an extremely frank evaluation of his behavior and an opportunity to try out new behavior patterns on this new group. Upon return, he can use these new patterns with some assurance.

Responsibility for Leadership Development

The leader and the subordinate share the responsibility for the subordinate's leadership development. The leader must take continuing action in the areas of formal and informal leadership training, evaluation and counseling, and decentralized operations. These areas are interrelated. For example, useful evaluation presupposes that subordinate leaders have wide latitude in the manner they perform their assigned tasks and are permitted to make mistakes. Further, the best leadership training results from allowing the subordinate to perform in an actual leadership role and then be individually counseled by his leader.

Within a unit that encourages practice and permits honest mistakes, the commander has many opportunities to train his subordinate leaders. He may simply counsel leadership performances as they occur; or he may conduct informal discussions with all of his subordinate leaders to review real or hypothetical leadership problems. Another technique for informal training includes rotation of assignments. Rotation may be temporary, such as declaring a leader a casualty during a field exercise in order to give his second-in-command experience. Distributing special projects and initiating the understudy of key positions are two additional techniques a commander may use. A vital part of these informal training techniques is the feedback the commander provides. A good performance must be promptly rewarded and a poor performance clearly acknowledged. Formal leadership training courses can complement the experience gained in a unit. These courses may be given in noncommissioned officer and officer schools or may be a part of a specialized program. Full command support should be given these courses so as to encourage subordinates to seek additional leadership training.

Each leader is responsible for the continual improvement of his own leadership capabilities. His responsibility for his own development is equal to his commander's. As he progresses through his military career, the responsibilities assumed by a leader become increasingly more comprehensive. His leadership ability must keep step with this increased responsibility. To fail to improve is to stagnate. Too often in past times of emergency, outstanding company and battalion leaders have been thrust into positions of high command, only to fall short of requirements because they had not prepared themselves for responsibilities beyond the lower levels of leadership.

The first step in self-development is self-evaluation. This is a difficult step to take because each individual habitually uses unconscious or partly conscious defense mechanisms to protect his own self-esteem. It is no easy task to brush away these defenses. It is particularly difficult to avoid the tendency to rationalize one's conduct, to seek excuses rather than reasons for behavior. The aid of some impartial evaluator is often necessary, and the most obvious source of such an evaluation is one's immediate superior.

Based on an evaluation of his own leadership ability, a leader must determine new behavior patterns for himself and then test these new patterns. To change is not easy, because a person's past behavior patterns are satisfying to him even though they interfere with his effective performance. The situation is similar to that of the "bolo" on the range. His coach, his officers, and probably many others tell him that he is jerking the trigger. Yet, he cannot overcome his natural fear of the recoil and noise of the weapon. Because he is trying, he tends to disbelieve the advice of others. But, if some convincing demonstration can show him that he can shoot well if he will only stop jerking, he will redouble his efforts and eventually manage to squeeze off a shot. Having once been truly surprised by the weapon's explosion and recoil, and having observed the good results, he will increase his efforts. He will be able to get off more and more squeezed shots and eventually will become a good marksman. But the demonstration that is crucial to this sequence cannot be gained by watching another person shoot. It must be a demonstration of the man's own firing behavior.

In leadership self-development, the leader must convince himself to make the necessary change of attitude or skill. He must aggressively determine new patterns to try out. The patterns may result from study of the subject of leadership, from participating in leadership development courses, or from watching others to see how they achieve effective leadership. He may systematically collect ideas and techniques, or he may simply ask himself what he would do in a leadership situation confronting some other leader. These observations should not lead to imitation, but rather to the assimilation of new ideas.

Leader Evaluation

The evaluation of leader performance constitutes a special area of concern. Not only is evaluation a continuous process, but it is also a very vital one to a leader's development through his career in the service. Evaluation provides an excellent source of feedback on performance and indicates areas for improvement. It is a challenging task for a leader to render a truly fair appraisal of the junior leader's ability and potential. It is just as unfair to the Army and to the individual subordinate to overrate his performance as it is to underrate him.

The leader in evaluating the performance of his subordinates, seeks to accomplish two objectives. First, to improve the performance of the individual and the unit. Second, to provide the basis for future personnel actions. Performance evaluation can serve as both a learning and a motivational device. Knowledge of results is an important aspect of learning. Without such knowledge, improvement is very slight. Thus, performance evaluation provides the individual with the necessary knowledge to correct his weaknesses as well as to build on his strengths. In addition, recognition of proper performance provides intrinsic motivation for still further improvement.

One's peers are a useful evaluation source. Others on the same level can evaluate a person with surprising accuracy. At the same time, however, they are often quite reluctant to criticize openly, even when frankly asked to do so. They may interpret such appeals for frankness as concealing a desire for reassurance. A more indirect approach is often necessary. For example, it may be possible to engage a fellow leader in a discussion of a particular problem encountered during the day and one's own solution of that problem. By thus placing the problem on a more theoretical level, it may be possible for the leader to gain an honest evaluation of the techniques he used for solving the problem.

A known and trusted senior not in the immediate chain of command can be a valuable source of evaluation. As a senior, he has a broader background against which to evaluate performance. Also, he may be less reluctant to criticize than a peer. It is often easier to discuss one's shortcomings freely with such persons rather than with an immediate superior.

It is normally inappropriate for a leader to obtain direct evaluation of his performance from his subordinates; however, his subordinate's behavior gives some indication of his effect on them. The leader should notice if they appear comfortable and at ease in his presence. Also, their attitude toward duty can be revealing. Whether they willingly put in extra hours when required, or are strictly duty-hour soldiers who resent any extra duty time is an indication of their motivation and response to his leadership. The nicknames they have for their leader are another indirect source of evaluation. Nicknames are often devastatingly accurate, as well as extremely difficult to overcome.

Learning theorists maintain that immediate feedback achieves the best results. To capitalize on this principle, the leader should informally counsel his subordinate as soon as possible following a particular performance rather than waiting for a scheduled counseling session. The leader should weight his performance counseling heavily in favor of encouragement to try again and to attempt new techniques. A further consideration is that the leader should select only the one or two most correctable performance deficiencies. Too much advice or criticism at any one time may lower a subordinate leader's self-esteem and retard his development.

Evaluation Systems

One of the earliest evaluation systems focused on the leader's traits. Little attention was paid to the performance of his organization. Figure 4.1, which is the earliest efficiency report on record, is an example of this approach. On 15 August 1813, a brigadier general of the U.S. Army sent a communication to higher military authority with his observations and opinions of officers serving in his regiment. Note the general's biases.

After World War I, the U.S. Army started the regular and systematic submission of efficiency reports on all officer personnel. Initially, these reports tended to be highly trait-oriented, but the trend has been toward performance evaluation. After World War II, a serious attempt was made to devise more

EXCERPTS FROM
THE ARMY'S FIRST RECORDED EFFICIENCY REPORT

Major Edward Towne *	An excellent officer.
Captain Cooper	A man of whom all unite in speaking ill. A knave despised by all.
Captain Jonathan Richards	An officer of capacity, but imprudent and a man of most violent passions.
1st Lt. Ebenezer Slater	Willing enough—has much to learn —with small capacity.
2nd Lt. Howard Jackson	A good officer but drinks hard and disgraces himself and the service.
2nd Lt. William More	An ignorant unoffending Irishman.
2nd Lt. Griffin	Raised from the ranks, ignorant, vulgar, and incompetent.
2nd Lt. Perry)	Come from the ranks, but behave
2nd Lt. Daniel Johnson)	well and promise to make excellent officers.
3rd Lt. Hanan)	All Irish, promoted from the ranks,
3rd Lt. Tamey)	low vulgar men, without any one
3rd Lt. O'Connor)	qualification to recommend them, more fit to carry the hod than the epaulette.
3rd Lt. Smith	The very dregs of the earth, unfit for anything under heaven. God only knows how the poor thing got an appointment.
Ensign Thos. Jones	From the ranks, a good young man who does well.

* All names are fictitious.

Figure 4.1

objective and valid rating techniques. Up to that time little had been done to determine whether the rated qualities were the ones truly displayed by a successful leader. The current evaluation systems use forms which are designed to have some predictive value. Several changes have been made in the forms since World War II. Each time, a widescale standardization effort to determine the basic reliability and validity of the form preceded the change.

Rating Errors

The major problems in the use of efficiency reports stem from the fact that the reports are essentially subjective. The form merely represents a device for recording one man's subjective evaluation of another. This fact introduces three human errors into the rating system: the halo effect, the constant error, and the generosity error.

The halo effect results from a tendency on the part of the rater to generalize from an over-all impression to specific traits of the ratee. For example, a good personal appearance may impress the rater that he is dealing with a generally "good man" who, consequently, is intelligent, honest, and a leader of men when, in fact, he is none of these. On the other hand, an over-all poor impression of an individual may induce a "reverse halo" or "horns" effect, wherein his real attributes are overlooked or disregarded.

The constant error stems from the fact that some raters tend to be lenient in their ratings, thereby giving subordinates high ratings. Others tend to be consistently tough and give low ratings. Unless a suitable correction is made for such tendencies, an equitable comparison between the men being rated cannot be made.

The generosity error is the major problem. Most raters have a tendency to rate high, making it difficult to discriminate among personnel. There appears to be three basic causes for this tendency. First is the desire to give the man the benefit of the doubt. Since the rater can never observe every performance of his subordinate, he rates only on observed performance. Second is a tendency to rate the individual in comparison with all those of his own rank plus all ranks below him. The basic thought process here is that since the individual is a leader, he must be superior. The higher his rank, the better he must be. As a leader advances in rank, his reports tend to improve. The third cause for inflated ratings appears to be the fear by the rater that if he gives his subordinate an average rating, he will in effect be giving him a low rating, comparatively, because of the existence of the generosity error. Thus, the generosity error becomes self-sustaining.

The practical result of these basic errors is that the over-all distribution of scores on officer efficiency ratings is highly skewed rather than normal, with the mode at the high end of the continuum. This is illustrated in Figure 4.2. Thus it appears that, like so many other psychological measuring devices, efficiency reports can discriminate failure better than success.

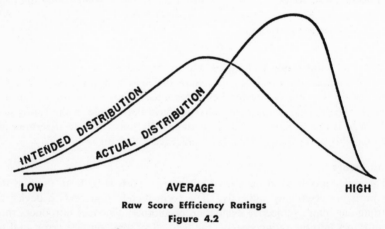

LOW   AVERAGE   HIGH

Raw Score Efficiency Ratings
Figure 4.2

The concepts of reliability and validity have specific meanings in performance evaluation. The reliability of ratings is the consistency of the ratings. A reliable rating instrument returns generally consistent results independent of time or the number of different raters. For example, a good leader who consistently performs well is rated high on successive rating periods. One who performs consistently poorly is rated low on successive periods. The validity of ratings is the degree to which they are truly indicative of the subordinate. The question that must be satisfied is whether the factors that appear on the report really measure what they are intended to measure, namely the man's leadership. This question can be at least partially answered through standardization procedures that determine coefficients of reliability and validity for the forms. In general, it can be said that those efficiency report forms developed since World War II have satisfactory reliability and validity, but they are short of being perfect. Consequently, there is a constant search for new and better means to evaluate the leaders of the Army. Since the leaders of tomorrow must come from the junior leaders of today, this is a subject of continuing importance.

TECHNIQUES OF LEADERSHIP DEVELOPMENT

Leadership development and training methods fall roughly into three categories: information presentation, simulation methods, and on-the-job practices (Campbell, 1966). The first is primarily educational, while the latter two place more stress on leadership practice and training. The techniques used most often in the military are information presentation and on-the-job practice.

Information presentation techniques have as their primary purpose teaching facts, concepts, and attitudes without necessarily requiring simulated or actual practice. This book is an example of this technique. Normally, opportunities for immediate application of the information are available as an important part of the technique.

The Lecture.   The lecture has limited application to leadership development; however, it is useful to present a great deal of information in a short period of time. It is also relatively economical in terms of men and material. Perhaps one of its chief advantages lies in the opportunity for a highly credible source to pass on his experiences and thoughts. This type of presentation may incorporate or consist of instructional television and motion pictures. The main difficulty is that it is a one-way technique with little chance for feedback or participation.

The Conference.   The conference emphasizes small group discussion with the leader providing guidance and feedback rather than instruction. Its major objectives are to develop problem-solving and decision-making capabilities and effective communications. The primary discussion group can be fragmented to form "buzz" groups. These smaller "buzz" groups consider some portion of the major question and report findings to the group as a whole. The case study is a useful vehicle for the conference technique. In this, the leader or a member of the group presents a hypothetical leadership case. The group then considers and discusses the many ramifications of various leadership acts. The conference technique is valuable in developing both the task and social skills a leader requires.

T-Groups or Sensitivity Training.   Sensitivity training is especially helpful in developing the social skills of a leader. The subject matter for discussion is the behavior of the individuals in the group; why they say what they do and why they react the way that they do. The effort may be directed toward the solution of some problem with the members examining their interpersonal skills in effecting a solution. T-group training is specialized, however, and should only be undertaken by a qualified trainer.

Systematic Observation.   This is a technique readily available to every military leader. The students in this development program learn by observing an experienced leader or group of leaders in action against various situational backgrounds. In this manner, they learn those practices that they wish to adopt as well as those they wish to avoid. Although the student is in a passive role, the realism presented serves as an effective motivational factor.

Simulation methods present the leader with a simulated or artificial representation of some aspect of the military organizational life. The leader then reacts to it as if it were the real thing. This technique involves varying degrees of realism; however, the actions of the student-leader have no effect on the operations of the actual organization. Thus, the leader does not ultimately have to face the responsibility for his decision.

Incident Method.   This method briefly outlines the problem to be solved, requiring the leader to determine what additional information he needs. It is up to the leader to obtain the pertinent information from the trainer. The leader then makes his decision. At the conclusion of the problem, the information the leader uses is compared with that available to indicate whether he considered all the relevant facts.

Role Playing.   This technique emphasizes the human relations aspect of leadership as the student-leader adopts a role specified in the case study. The success of this method depends upon how well the participants play their parts. The situation is left relatively unstructured so that it can develop naturally in accordance with the specific behaviors of the players. The major advantage of this method is that the student-leader experiences the difficulties and frustrations associated with the role and gains insight into realistic situations.

In-Basket Technique.   This method is related to role playing in the sense that the student-leader assumes a particular role, such as a company commander, and must solve the problems presented by his incoming correspondence. The major advantage to this method is that he is forced to make decisions. The discussions which follow provide evaluation and interpretation of his actions.

On-the-job training methods provide actual practice in doing the job. The major advantage to this method of training is that there is no transition needed from training to job performance. Realism supplies the incentive to learn. Obviously, mistakes the leader makes affect the efficiency of the organization. This method can be extended into job rotation. Here, the leader broadens his experience. He gains factual knowledge about the operations of different parts of the organization and practice in the different leadership skills required. Because this method is basically trial and error, the trainee's superior should provide some degree of guidance.

The development of the leader's social or human relations skills involves an attitude change on his part. To make a lasting change in an attitude, there must be ego involvement. Accordingly, the trend of training in attitude change is toward participative techniques. Since the Hawthorne experiments (Roethlisberger and Dickson, 1956), participation has received increasingly wide acceptance as a means to motivate people to a higher level of performance. The application of this principle in leadership development offers exciting possibilities but also poses many yet unanswered questions. Recent research indicates the durability of attitude shifts is related to two factors. First is the degree of reinforcement the trainee receives during his first attempts to apply his new leadership skill after his training course. Second is the extent to which the trainee becomes emotionally involved in the learning experience.

SUMMARY

The leader faces a responsible challenge in his selection of subordinate leaders. One of the marks of an effective military leader is his ability to "choose and use" subordinates. His authority to make selections carries with it an obligation to both the Army and the individual being considered. In order to satisfy these obligations and take best advantage of the actual and potential talent available, the leader must determine the relevant variables pertaining to the situation. These variables can be classed under the general headings of Capacity, Achievement, Responsibility, Participation, Status, and Situation. After the leader assigns weights to these variables in accordance with the situation, he rates the prospective candidates for leadership selection against these criteria in as objective a manner as possible. In order to do this, he must have an intimate knowledge of each of the candidates. Once the leader has made his selection, he must follow up and continually evaluate his selection.

Performance evaluation can serve not only as a validation of the leader's selection but it can provide the basis for future personnel actions. Most importantly, it serves as a means of feedback for the individual and thereby improves his job performance and adds to his leadership development.

It is incumbent upon the leader to recognize his responsibilities for the continual leadership development of his subordinates as well as for his own development. Leadership may be learned, although the point of departure for initiating this learning varies widely.

Leadership development programs may be either formal or informal. Evaluation and counseling are essential components of either training method. The two primary areas in leadership development are task skills and social, or human relations skills. The latter area necessitates attitude modifications that are best accomplished by using participative techniques.

Suggestions for Further Reading

Taylor, Jack W., *How to Select and Develop Leaders*. New York: McGraw-Hill, 1962.

Marshall, Samuel Lyman, *The Officer as a Leader*. Harrisburg, Pa.: Stackpole Books, 1966.

Freeman, G. L., and Taylor, E. K., *How to Pick Leaders*. New York: Funk & Wagnalls Company, 1950.

McGregor, Douglas, *Leadership and Motivation*. New Rochelle, N.Y.: Cambridge Press, 1966.

V

Interpersonal Communication

A PERVASIVE factor in influencing human behavior is the ability of the leader to communicate his desires to the group that is to carry them out. Regardless of his other attributes, if he is unable to communicate with his subordinates, he is ineffective as a leader. Communication is fundamental to leadership. In a broad sense, communication is essentially a leadership act. It is only through this transmission of information back and forth between the members of a group that the group is able to define the situation and determine what action the group must take to accomplish its goal. Through interpersonal communication, the leader helps the group define the situation and co-ordinate its actions.

If that ingenious primeval ancestor who first discovered how to make fire had been unable to communicate this knowledge to others, the secret would have died with him. Man would still be living in caves! Modern man communicates almost continuously with his fellows. When he is not actively speaking to another person, he is usually reading, watching television, listening to the radio, or watching a motion picture. All of these are examples of interpersonal communication.

THE CONCEPT OF COMMUNICATION

Interpersonal communication is the key to understanding others. For it is through communication that people are able to interact and relate to each other. The building of these interpersonal bonds is fundamental to the development of the group solidarity discussed in Chapter XI. Communication is also the means by which the leader is able to influence the group. The truth and frustration of this statement is felt every time a commander is separated from his unit and loses communication with them, although he is still communicating with them through his established policies and the discipline instilled in his unit.

Definition

Communication is the process of transmission and receipt of information

75

between two or more individuals. The information communicated is normally thought of as being ideas, knowledge, or factual data. In addition, however, much of our communication is emotional. A smile is an emotional communication reflecting our inner state of happiness, while a frown indicates anger or dislike. Emotional communication is usually quite easily understood and often induces a like emotional state in the receiver. This process can be very rapid in the case of extreme emotion. For example, the phenomenon of panic or unreasoned fear can spread swiftly through a group, particularly if the group is closely packed. Art, music, and much literature are emotional communications, wherein the originator transmits his feelings to his audience. Most communications contain some emotional content, in addition to the factual content which they intend to convey.

Communication takes a variety of forms. Basically, however, it consists of the transmission of symbols to which meaning is attached. Words are the most common form, whether written or spoken. There are many other symbols—for example, road signs and map symbols. Bodily actions such as facial expressions, gestures, movements—all communicate thought or feeling to the individual who views them. On the athletic field co-ordinated action is achieved through communication by movement. Each member of the team watches the movements of the other members and guides his own actions on the patterns of movement which develop.

A Leadership Act

In all interpersonal communication, a change in the communicator brings about a change in the recipient. The two parties to a communication are interdependent. This is the basic criterion which determines if communication actually occurs or not. This is also the crux of leadership. Leadership takes place when one person influences or effects a change in the other. In a very rudimentary form then, every communicative act is an influence or leadership act. The effectiveness of the leadership—whether the change is in the manner desired by the leader—is determined by how well the communication has been transmitted, received, and understood. This points up the basic importance of communication to the leader. If his communication is to be effective and influence the behavior of the recipient, he must ensure accurate transmission, receipt, and interpretation of his message. Unfortunately, many factors enter the communication picture which can, and often do, distort the message. The result is that the message is interpreted in an inaccurate manner. To understand how these distortions creep in, it is necessary to understand what occurs when a message is communicated.

THE PROCESS OF COMMUNICATION

It is difficult to explain exactly what takes place when one man communicates with another. Much of the process occurs within the nervous systems of the communicating parties. Interpersonal communications always involve at least two people—a communicator and a recipient. Both possess an information storehouse—the memory portion of the brain. Initially, the information to be transmitted is in the memory of the communicator. After the transmission is complete, the information is present in some form in the memory of the recipient. There may be little evidence of the change indicating that communication has in fact taken place. Although there are barriers which make the communication process appear unnecessarily complex, a rather mechanistic model is helpful in diagramming the process. This model is adapted from that developed by Claude E. Shannon (Shannon and Weaver, 1949). It is also based upon current knowledge of the human sensory motor and central nervous system, and on knowledge gained from scientific communication experiments.

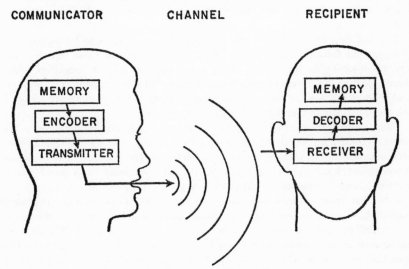

Figure 5.1 The Communication Process

A Communication Model

Essentially, the model contains three major elements—the communicator, the channel, and the recipient. The communicator is the originator or transmitter of the message. The message then travels by a medium or channel. The recipient receives the message. Although not strictly a part of the model, feedback is necessary for the communicator to gain some knowledge of the effect of his message on the recipient. The point might well be made that feedback is in itself a message transmitted back to the original communicator; however, the communicator cannot be satisfied that the process is complete until feedback occurs.

The Communicator. The communicating process originates in the communicator and may be described in three phases as the message travels from the memory to the encoder and then to the transmitter. The memory is the storehouse of all the communicator's past experiences. From this source, the communicator selects or formulates an idea. The idea may already be somewhat distorted from reality or its original form. Right here, in the selection, is the first chance for error in the communication process. If the wrong information is selected or if the information has been distorted, the wrong message is communicated.

Having selected the information for transmission, the communicator makes an estimate of the knowledge which is in the memory of the recipient and which the recipient may use in order to decode the message. For example, a soldier can describe a combat action to his buddy with little preliminary explanation. In writing to his wife about the same incident, however, he has to assume a different frame of reference and include many more explanatory details. All too frequently, the communication of information fails because the communicator assumes a level of knowledge on the part of the recipient which he does not have.

The last step in encoding is the selection of the symbols to be transmitted. Whatever the symbols may be—words, gestures, arm and hand signals—they have no meaning in themselves. They only serve to trigger meanings which already exist in the minds of the communicator and the recipient. The communicator dares not assume that the meanings existing in his memory are identical with those existing in the memory of the recipient.

Since words are the most frequent symbols used in communication, a few remarks concerning words are in order. Words are only symbols, and their value depends on the meanings that are attached to the symbols. The meanings of words are learned; they are not innate. The meaning of a word varies, therefore, from individual to individual. A glance through any dictionary will indicate that many words have multiple meanings. For example, the word "secure" has a double meaning. The most common definition of secure is "to make safe;" however, it also means "to get hold or possession of." The meaning can be critical to a commander when he is told to "secure" an objective. This raises the question of whether he is to both seize and defend the objective, or just seize it.

A seldom realized fact about words is that they carry emotion. Much of our language is emotionally "loaded." Consider such words as "courage," "enemy," "democracy," "racial," "peace." Each of these conveys a certain feeling in addition to a logical thought. The emotional aspects of words are learned, just as their objective meanings are learned. For example, if a child's parents habitually express contempt when referring to politicians, then the child learns that the word "politician" is a contemptuous word. Even such an apparently neutral word as "dog" has strong emotional effects on the individual who was severely bitten by a dog at some time in the past. The interpretation of a word in the symbol coding section of the brain includes the emotion as well as the logic attached to the word. In many cases, the emotion distorts the logic. The result is that messages containing many emotionally loaded words are interpreted more in terms of the emotion than in terms of the logic intended. Propagandists take advantage of this fact in order to tell the truth falsely.

From the above discussion, it is obvious that there are many factors that can cause the recipient to interpret words differently from the communicator. The choice of words or other symbols is one of the most important factors in a communication. It is never wise to assume that the recipient perceives the chosen symbols in exactly the manner that the communicator intended.

Having decided what information is to be communicated, the communicator next organizes his message. As an example, a patrol leader, during his debriefing by S-2, might report incidents occurring on the patrol in several ways. He could report them in chronological order, or he could organize the incidents into categories such as enemy activity, terrain, and miscellaneous information. He could relate the major items of information first and those of lesser importance later. There are innumerable ways in which any particular communication may be organized. An important point, however, is that the first and last parts of any long communication are remembered better than information which comes near the middle.

Upon completion of encoding, the message is transmitted. Transmission is accomplished through the motor nervous system of the body. This may be verbally, through writing, or through bodily action. Often when verbal communication is used the message is transmitted simultaneously through words and through such bodily actions as gestures and expressions. If the two reinforce each other, the message will be better understood, whereas the converse may cause confusion or disbelief.

The selection of a transmission means is usually not a difficult process—it is dictated by the situation. Oral communication is the simplest and most preferred. Normally it would seem somewhat absurd for two people who are face-to-face to write messages back and forth. Yet this happens frequently in offices or headquarters because a memorandum can be retained and read at a later time and acted on at the most convenient moment. The same information spoken may easily be forgotten. Actually, much information is better communicated through writing than speech. Tabulated data, sketches, diagrams—these and many other devices save thousands of words and ensure better retention and understanding on the part of the recipient.

The Channel. After transmission the message must pass through the intervening medium between the communicator and the recipient by means of some source of physical energy. Normally, this is sound or light. If impediments exist within the medium that interfere with the transmission of this energy, the message will arrive at the recipient weak and distorted, if at all. Such factors as distance, darkness, and intervening sound are examples of these barriers. When barriers exist, some form of a booster is necessary. This booster may be in the form of a messenger who carries the message over the intervening distance, or some mechanical device such as a television, telephone, radio, or other communication equipment. It should be kept in mind that these devices are not truly "communication" devices. They merely serve to increase the capability of the human motor system to transmit and the sensory system to receive the message. Many of the barriers in the channel are a product of the organization.

The Recipient. The recipient in the communication system has a detector, a decoder, and a memory section similar to the communicator. The detector is the human sensory system. Only through his senses can man receive any information concerning his environment. Most communications are received through the senses of hearing or vision. These two senses, however, are selective in nature. One can only look at a certain area at one time, and a signal that comes from a different direction is not detected. Similarly, a person is able to single out and concentrate on certain sounds in his environment. But, when he does, other sounds are frequently not noticed. Consequently, before a communication can be received, the appropriate sense must be attuned to the channel on which the communicator sends the message. Unfortunately, within the human psychological make-up there exists a little understood process which causes a periodic shift of attention from one factor in the environment to another. As a result, it is difficult for the recipient to maintain his attention for extended periods of time on any particular communication. For example, the soldier listening to a long lecture or reading a field manual may find his mind wandering. He is re-living last week-end or dreaming of his next leave, rather than acquiring the knowledge he should.

The incoming signals that are detected by the senses in the form of symbols are passed along to the decoding portion of the brain. Thus, decoding is an active, rather than a passive, process. Frequent use throughout most of our life has made us very familiar with a number of words, therefore the decoding of the symbols is normally a very rapid process; however, if the word is not well known, it may be necessary to do a great deal of searching through the memory to find its meaning. If the meaning was never learned, for example, in the case of a foreign language, the message stops at this point and no further comprehension can take place.

It is possible for the recipient to understand every word in the communication and yet not understand the idea transmitted. There is a second step in decoding wherein the separate symbols are organized into thoughts. This again is an active process involving much digging back into the memory to find past knowledge on which the incoming information can be based. For instance, an American reading an account of some event related to the passage of legislation in the Congress would find the account easily understandable because of his knowledge of American legislative procedures. A foreigner reading a translation of the same account may find it completely incomprehensible because he does not understand our governmental processes.

Each transmission has an emotional impact and a degree of correlation with the recipient's previous knowledge and experience. In addition, the message faces possible distortion through conflict with the recipient's attitudes. In a unit in which past experience (such as rash promises of additional privileges that could not be fulfilled) has fostered an attitude of disbelief, messages down through the chain of command will be critically analyzed and skeptically received by each man.

Feedback

An important though not inherent part of the communication process is feedback. Simply stated, feedback is knowledge of results. It is the process by which the communicator receives some indication of the effect of his message on the recipient. Feedback is achieved in many ways. In spoken conversation the communicator hears his own voice. He makes adjustments according to the feedback he receives of his own sounds. If he is in a face-to-face relationship with those with whom he is communicating, he may observe their facial expressions, gestures, and actions. For example, the instructor in a classroom constantly observes the reactions of his students. If he sees that they are nodding, some sleeping and others standing up, he knows that he is not maintaining attention. In a face-to-face relationship, the communicator may also achieve feedback by asking questions of the recipient, by requiring the recipient to report back to him what he has learned, or by allowing the recipient to ask questions about the communication.

Feedback may be blocked by many factors. Distance is a major blocking force. Without the face-to-face relationship, a time delay is entered in gaining feedback. The communicator, even though talking over a telephone or some other device designed to overcome the time delay factor, is unable to observe the facial expressions and actions of the recipient. As a general rule, the more complete and immediate the feedback, the better the communication.

BARRIERS TO COMMUNICATION

For purposes of discussion, barriers in the communication process fall into two categories. There are those barriers that arise in the channel between the communicator and the recipient, and those that are in the communicator and the recipient. Most of the barriers in the channel are physical barriers that produce noise in the channel, blocking or distorting the message; or they physically halt the transmission of the message between the communicator and recipient. The barriers in the communicating parties are more psychological in origin. Usually, both classes are present and the leader must consider their presence in his communication attempts.

Physical Barriers

The most obvious physical barrier blocking or distorting communication is distance. The closer two people are together, the more clearly and frequently they can communicate with each other. Conversely, the farther apart they are, the more difficult it is for them to communicate effectively. This distance is communication distance, not necessarily actual measured distance. For instance, the communicating distance from the motor park to the motor shop, a distance that must be covered on foot, can be greater than it is by telephone from the motor shop to the orderly room. Increased communication distance has three effects that tend to cut down on communication effectiveness: (1) it increases the physical exertion to accomplish the communication, resulting in fewer communications; (2) it introduces a time delay; and (3) it cuts down on feedback.

Another physical barrier is the size of the group itself. When many people are trying to communicate at once, this produces cross talk that can distort and even totally block out a message. As the size of the group increases, the complexity of possible interactions goes up geometrically. In a four-man group there are 25 possible interactions, and in a five-man group, such as a fire team, there are 90. It is easy to see that, as the group size increases, the sheer complexity of possible interactions increases to such an extent that co-ordinated group action may break down. The number of interactions may be computed with the formula $Y = \frac{3^n - 2^{n+1} + 1}{2}$ (Bass, 1960, p. 347). This results in great difficulty in controlling the communication within the unit. From the leader's point of view, the problem of increasing group size is one of spreading himself and his own influence over a wider number of people. This problem is commonly known as the "span of control" problem, and is discussed in Chapter VIII. Suffice it to say here that, as the group size increases, the leader has more difficulty in controlling the communication process within the group and in communicating with the other group members.

Too much communication is as dangerous as too little. All command posts have a variety of communication channels—upward, downward, and sideways. At critical points in an action, the volume of traffic on these nets frequently becomes so great that it exceeds the capacity of the commander and his staff to receive and digest. Over-communication can also result in the delay of important messages. Consequently, the leader must control the communication process into and within his organization to ensure that it is orderly. This includes the control of his own communication. The commander who issues too many orders leaves no time for his subordinates to execute them.

One solution to the span of control problem is to break the group down into subgroups, each with its own leader, and establish a higher leader over these subordinate leaders. The higher leader communicates with his subordinate leaders, and they in turn relay to their subordinates. This introduces new communication problems. At each echelon at which the message must be relayed, there is a delay; and there is a similar delay in feedback going back upwards. Each time a message is received it may be distorted, and these distortions become cumulative with further relay. Also, a message that is originally transmitted with a strong motivating tone is frequently watered down as it passes down the line, so that at the end it completely lacks force.

The selected medium may have inherent within it vulnerabilities to noise or distortion. For example, oral communication has the disadvantage of rapid distortion of the information in the memory of the recipient. Unless he takes complete notes, he may quickly forget many of the important factors in the message. Written communication has the advantage of more permanence, but it lacks the advantage of immediate feedback. The communicator cannot really be sure that his message is understood. Written communication also lacks the force that can be conveyed by a face-to-face oral directive, and takes more time to prepare.

The direction of the channel can constitute a physical barrier to effective communication. Within most formal organizations, the communication net is used primarily to transmit orders downward and to receive reports upward. Although this procedure is the primary purpose of a communication net in a formal organization, it can also become a barrier to effective communication because it tends to discourage communication for other purposes. The subordinate looks upon himself as merely the recipient and not the originator of communications. Those that he does originate are in response to some previous request for information. It also tends to fix attention of both parties on this vertical communication chain at the expense of any lateral communication. The general result is that communications downward are excellent but those upward tend to be poor, while lateral channels are frequently nonexistent. There tend to be few requests upward for clarification of orders, little reporting of information downward, and frequently poor feedback throughout the net.

Psychological Barriers

Psychological barriers to effective communication are present in both the communicator and the recipient. Even if the message could be transmitted perfectly through the channel, these are the factors which still produce distortion of the message. For convenience of classification, these factors can be divided into perceptual, conceptual, and cultural barriers to communication.

Perceptual barriers are those that arise primarily due to the different frames of reference of the communicator and the recipient. Both have experiences that shape their memories and prepare them to interpret the messages they send and receive. Obviously, no two people ever have identical experiences. Consequently, it is impossible for an idea brought from one memory to be relayed and perceived in exactly the same fashion in another. Based upon the experiences stored in his memory, the recipient will compare the information in order to gain comprehension. It is the similarity of the experiences in these storehouses that determines how accurately the recipient perceives the message transmitted by the communicator.

Another problem in the military leader's communicating is that his recipient's perception of a communication is often distorted by social distance. The disparity in status or rank within the Army is a source of perceptual difference. For example, the private sees things differently than does the sergeant who, in turn, perceives things in a different light from the captain. Their experiences are primarily at different levels and their perspectives slightly dissimilar. In addition to being a perceptual barrier to communication, social distance can hamper communication merely through a person's natural reluctance to cross this distance. The private finds it easier to communicate with the sergeant than with the lieutenant, and the lieutenant feels easier with the captain than the colonel.

The difference in perception of a message may be due to conceptual differences between the communicator and the recipient. Where the perceptual differences deal more with improper reception of the message, conceptual barriers are more concerned with differences in the memory itself. Thus, conceptual barriers are caused by differences in semantical frames of reference rather than perceptual reference frames. The same words or concepts do not have identical meanings for everyone. Some of the most comprehensive and meaningful research in this area has been done by Osgood, Suci, and Tannenbaum. Through use of the semantic differential, they obtain values that they plot on three-dimensional axes. These plots indicate relative positions of individual concepts. (Osgood, *et al.*, 1957.) How far apart these conceptual plots can be in semantic space is often illustrated when one attempts to communicate with a foreigner. A fluency in the other's language may indicate only that one understands the words, not that one comprehends the message.

Closely allied with the conceptual barriers to communication are the cultural barriers. These are barriers both to perception and to conceptual formation due to cultural differences between the communicator and the recipient. Rather than being due to individual differences, however, they are due to social group differences. Going deeper than mere language differences, cultural differences are rooted in the philosophy and traditions of a group of people. These barriers to communication can extend to gestures as well as words. For example, the American gesture of waving goodbye could be interpreted by a Vietnamese to mean to come closer. A discussion of the effect of these cultural barriers to communication and understanding is in Chapter XIX.

OVERCOMING BARRIERS TO COMMUNICATION

Difficult as these barriers to effective communication seem, the leader can still communicate effectively if he takes the trouble to do so. The physical barriers to effective communication suggest their own solution. Obviously, the best way to overcome the distance barrier is by moving, or by using some electronic or other device to reduce the communicating distance. The important point is that the leader must be constantly aware of the existence of physical barriers and their effect on his communication. There are three factors that can greatly increase a leader's effectiveness in overcoming the psychological barriers. These are: interpersonal trust, empathy, and listening. In order to improve his ability to communicate, the leader must develop these three areas. They are his greatest weapons in reducing the perceptual, conceptual, and cultural barriers distorting his effective communication with his followers.

One of the greatest aids to effective communication is the establishment of a climate of mutual trust and confidence between the leader and his subordinates. This is born out of a sense of sincerity and frankness between individuals. Successful leadership is dependent upon the resulting open and effective communication. For the leader's message to be fully understood, the subordinate must be ready to accept the communication. The factors of expertness and trustworthiness are essential to the credibility of the communicator. (Hovland, Janis, and Kelley, 1953.) Both of these are important in permitting the subordinate to have confidence in his leader and to feel that he can trust his leader. When these elements are lacking, communication becomes guarded or unnecessarily complex. The communicator consciously includes irrelevant detail, attempting to make his meaning clear. The recipient, in turn, is searching for hidden meanings, trying to divine the true intent of the communication. Often a leader's reputation has so affected his image that it speaks louder than his words do. This sad fact is illustrated by the alleged comment made by a fellow diplomat when informed of the death of Talleyrand, "Now I wonder what he could have meant by that?"

Although it is important for the subordinate to trust the leader, it is more important for the leader to have faith in his subordinates, and this is something over which the leader has more control. When the leader does not have confidence in his subordinates, he tends to conceal his attitudes about an issue. He may conceal them by evasive, compliant, or aggressive communications (Mellinger, 1956). The leader's greatest barrier to effective communication may be his assumptions that his subordinate is too stupid or incompetent to understand his directives. The leader also builds a barrier when his lack of truth causes him to make his communication overly detailed and involved. Chapter IX discusses this problem of overdirection.

For the leader to get his message across, he must be able to translate his communication into the reference frame of the recipient. This requires a certain amount of empathic ability on the part of the leader. He must attempt to structure the world as the recipient sees it. This strikes home with the realization that what the leader is saying is not what is really being communicated. The communication that is taking place is contained in what the recipient is thinking during the communication. The communication is perceived and interpreted by the recipient in terms of his own world and his own concepts. In composing his communication, the leader must make an honest effort to duplicate the recipient's semantical frame of reference. His feedback will indicate how successful he is. An interesting check on communications is to recall a conversation. The most vivid recollections are of the communicated thoughts rather than the received ones. The communicator should keep in mind that this is true of his recipient's recollections also.

Therefore, to overcome barriers to communication and to understand what the recipient is thinking, it is a good idea to listen to him when he communicates. Paradoxically, the best listener is the best communicator. For it is through listening that the communicator gains an appreciation of his recipient's perceptual, conceptual, and cultural reference frames. To listen well, the military leader should disregard symbols of authority. In themselves, they have nothing to do with the wisdom or foolishness of what is said.

There are three specific measures a leader can take to improve his listening ability. First, he should attempt to determine what the speaker means. Second, establish the speaker's credibility by examining his logic, proof, or evidence for his statements. Third, check to see what the speaker left out or failed to explain satisfactorily. (Van Dersal, 1962, p. 107.)

COMMUNICATION IN ORGANIZATIONS

Most of the leader's communicating is done with or to a group. Though he may communicate to the group through a subordinate group leader, the intended recipients of most of his communications are the individual group members. It is their concerted effort that results in goal accomplishment. And, it is only through organizational communication that the group members are able to co-ordinate their efforts.

Although men working together in an organization accomplish their tasks as individuals, the effort is not truly a group effort unless communication takes place among the members. Thus, communication is the primary group process. Communication is required to provide the information for the accomplishment of the group task. It is also necessary to the emotional life of the organization—the building of group attitudes, feelings, and *esprit,* which are the binding ties that make the strength of the group more than that of its individual members.

Formal Organizations

One of the distinguishing characteristics of a formal organization is that it is an established network of relationships based upon hierarchal positions. The structure of the formal organization also tends to prescribe a stable communication net. This net is the chain of command. As the name implies, it is also a chain of communication, with information passing successively from leader to subordinate. In his position, the leader is able to exercise a great amount of control over the flow of information into, out of, and within a group. An experiment conducted by Bavelas is interesting in this regard. Bavelas gave several groups of five men the task of solving problems from information distributed among the members of the groups. The groups were arranged into various communication nets so that freedom to communicate with other members was required in accordance with the nets. After solving the problems, the members of the groups were asked if any member was looked upon as a leader during the solution. Results showed that those individuals who were so placed in the nets that they could control the flow of information were looked upon as leaders, regardless of their individual personalities. (Bavelas, 1951.) These results indicate that, to some degree at least, the position makes the leader. Thus, the control of information in the formal organization reinforces the leader's power.

Upward Communication. The need for downward communication within a formal organization is usually rather obvious to a leader. Somewhat more obscure, however, is the matter of obtaining effective upward communication. Upward communication is necessary for the military leader to remain "in touch" with the men in his organization. He can use it as a means of maintaining effective control of the organization. Not only does it improve his over-all picture of the actual tasks that are being performed, but it also serves as an early warning of problems that may occur. It is the leader's means of keeping his finger on the pulse of the organization.

Through a channel of effective upward communication, the subordinate at the working level is able to contribute thoughts and ideas which improve efficiency and save time. This recognition by the leader that his men are a valuable source of information gives them a greater sense of participation in the group's task. Evidence of the leader's respect for their dignity thereby assists further communication by fostering a feeling of mutual trust and confidence. Also, this atmosphere aids the further acceptance of future downward communication. Upward communication, too, serves as a valuable indication of the effectiveness of the leader's communication. By this feedback, he has some idea of how imperfectly his message was received. Occasionally, an open upward communication channel merely serves as an opportunity for the release of pent-up emotional tensions and pressures. Although not directly helpful to the mission, this can often allow the subordinate to devote his full attention to the task at hand after having "gotten it off his chest."

Most commanders traditionally announce an "open door" policy to stimulate upward communication. This can be effective, if the leader recognizes that the same psychological and sociological barriers previously discussed are still at work in this situation. There is a great reluctance on the subordinate's part to enter the forbidding atmosphere of the leader's office. The leader can overcome this obstacle if he supplements his open door policy with frequent informal visits about the organization. In this way, he can talk with his men in surroundings more familiar to them. Another opportunity for more informal upward communication occurs at social gatherings of the organization. Here, in a more relaxed atmosphere, the leader can sample opinions, attitudes, and ideas.

One of the quickest ways a leader can stifle upward communication is by not acting on an idea or a complaint once he receives it. This only needs to happen a few times before the soldier adopts a "what's-the-use" attitude. The leader's attitude can be equally damaging to upward communication. Some leaders appear to believe that no news is good news. They go blithely on their way oblivious to the true condition of their unit. The leader must realize how difficult it is for the subordinate to go counter to tradition, authority, and prestige in his attempt to communicate upward. The leader cannot afford to ignore him. The leader must also realize that the subordinate is reluctant to report shortcomings and failures. Consequently, information he receives of this nature is likely to be filtered and distorted by the time the leader hears it. This tendency is especially significant because the military leader influences the subordinate's promotion and advancement. (Read, 1962.) Part of this distortion honestly may be due to the subordinate's frame of reference and unfamiliarity with the over-all mission as perceived by the leader. Hence, the subordinate's upward communication may omit details or implications the leader needs to know. He may be reluctant to reveal his ignorance on a matter he feels the leader may be better informed about than he is. Thus, he rationalizes that it is better to remain silent and appear a fool than to open his mouth and remove all doubt.

Informal Organizations

Grapevine. It is important to remember that formal organizations are composed of real people with individual personalities. Consequently, within a formal organization, any number of informal organizations may occur. These informal organizations become the bases for an informal chain of communication within the formal organization. It is over this channel of communication that rumors and other informal communications are transmitted. This fairly stable informal chain of communication is called the "grapevine." The term arose during the Civil War, and came from the manner in which bare telegraph lines, resembling grapevines, were strung from tree to tree. Where the lines crossed, the soldiers made a crude line tap. Hence, any rumor or unconfirmed communication was said to have come "from the grapevine."

The leader's first inclination is to consider the grapevine as a necessary evil. True, it does appear to subvert the goals of his formal communications. Many times, it seems to be irresponsible, uncontrollable, and totally unpredictable. This is due primarily to the grapevine's being predicated on the interests of the moment, but the leader must also recognize that the grapevine can be useful to him as well. Through it, he can gain a great deal of insight into his men's attitudes and their interests. In this way, he can best determine effective incentives for motivation.

The grapevine is amazingly accurate in the information it passes along. Experiments indicate that the grapevine is 80 to 90 per cent accurate in the transmission of information on noncontroversial issues (Walton, 1961). The very nature of the grapevine permits it to overcome some of the psychological blocks to accurate communication. In the first place, since the information is passed among friends, it is transmitted and received in an atmosphere of mutual trust and confidence. Also, this causes the information to be passed among peers who have more similar reference frames. Since the nature of the information is of immediate interest to the group, there exists an intent to communicate on the part of both the communicator and the recipient. The grapevine, through the recipient's selective retention, establishes a reputation for reliability and for providing information not normally available through formal communication channels. Thus, the recipient's attitude is one of acceptance and willingness to believe.

Through the grapevine, the leader can discover who are the leaders of the informal organization. The leader can then work through these informal leaders who do much to influence the group's opinions and attitudes. He can ensure that they are well informed so they, in turn, can supplement his directives and translate them into terms most readily understood by the group. Thus, the grapevine can be an aid to overcoming communication blocks.

For the grapevine to be useful, however, the leader must keep it supplied with facts. If he does not, it is perfectly capable of manufacturing its own facts. One of the primary reasons for its existence is to resolve the followers' uncertainties. Occasionally, this can lead to the transmission of information that, although false, is information the recipient wishes to be true—rumors.

Rumors. Rumors are unverified communications that members of the informal organization freely pass among themselves because they are believable and resolve uncertainty. They can be a problem to the leader because they generally spread unreliable information through the organization. Although they may subsequently become true, the rumor starts from a fabrication to supply missing information. So, it is a chance probability whether the information circulating in the form of rumor has any basis in fact. Missing information is the reason rumor starts. The unknown creates dissonance which rumors help reduce. As Gordon Allport states in his basic law of rumor, there are two ingredients required for rumors—ambiguity and importance. The amount of rumor in circulation is a function of importance times ambiguity (Allport, 1947, p. 33). This relationship holds an important message for the leader combatting rumors communicated through the informal organization. If either ambiguity or importance can be reduced to zero, there is no rumor (Allport, 1947, p. 34).

Since it is difficult for the leader to control what the individuals perceive to be important to them, the easier way to combat rumors is to reduce the ambiguity that spawns them. The leader should always attempt to keep the members of the group informed on those vital factors they consider important. If the group receives a mission that appears illogical, their reaction is to try to supply some reason so that it makes sense. This reason may be equally illogical or inconsistent with the actual facts. For example, the post commander's policy might change unexpectedly and require that line units periodically suspend training and rotate duty as the post police detail. The men in the unit may furnish the explanation that training has ceased because the unit is being deactivated and all the personnel are being reassigned as individual replacements.

Making information available can forestall many rumors' starting. A device that a leader might use to combat rumors once they have started is to acknowledge them and bring them out in the open for discussion and examination. This may be done by explaining the rumor through formal communication channels or merely posting the latest rumors on a rumor board. In the light of recognition, the faulty logic of rumors often becomes apparent. They can also serve as a morale boost. For instance, in Stalag IXb during World War II, a rumor clinic became part of the regular entertainment program (Allport, 1947, p. 32).

SUMMARY

Interpersonal communication is fundamental to the leader's exercise of leadership. It is the means whereby he is able to make known his desires to the group and perform his leadership role of co-ordinating their activities. The process he uses depends upon a shared channel of communication.

In his use of the process, the leader faces many barriers that can interfere with his communications. Aside from the obvious physical barriers, such as distance and size, psychological barriers also exist. The more common of these barriers are perceptual, conceptual, and cultural barriers between the communicator and the recipient. The leader's main aids in overcoming these barriers are the establishing of an atmosphere of mutual trust and confidence, while developing his empathic ability. He also improves his ability to communicate with the members of his organization by becoming a better listener.

Within groups, communication tends to become patterned with time, resulting in an organization. Formal organization gives the leader control over the communication process in the group. How he exercises his control determines how easily his subordinates can communicate upward in the formal organization. There is also within the group a lateral communication network. This informal organization arises within the formal organization as a result of the personalities of the individuals in the group. The communication network, or grapevine, in the informal organization serves to supplement information available to the group through the formal organization. While the leader can turn the attributes of the grapevine to his own advantage in improving his communication to the group, the grapevine can also serve to spread rumors through the organization. To ensure that the effect of his leadership is not diminished by rumors, the leader must recognize their existence and know how to combat them.

The leader's knowledge and ability to control the communication process is an essential prerequisite of effective leadership. For, leadership acts are basically communication acts. It is only through interpersonal communication that the leader is able to influence human behavior so as to accomplish a mission in the manner he desires.

Suggestions for Further Reading

Berlo, David K., *The Process of Communication.* New York: Holt, Rinehart & Winston, 1960.

Brennan, Lawrence D., *Modern Communication Effectiveness.* Englewood Cliffs, N.J.: Prentice-Hall, Inc., 1963.

Cherry, Colin, *On Human Communication.* New York: John Wiley & Sons, Inc., 1957.

Marting, Elizabeth, Finley, Robert E., and Ward, Ann, *Effective Communication on the Job.* New York: American Management Association, Inc., 1963.

Osgood, Charles E., Suci, George J., and Tannenhaum, Percy H., *The Measurement of Meaning.* Urbana, Ill.: University of Illinois Press, 1957.

VI

Military Management

MANAGEMENT is an essential component of the military leader's exercise of leadership. Military history usually records the more glamorous aspects of past wars. Often glossed over in the excitement of recorded battle is the leader's managerial ability, or lack of it, that influenced the outcome of these battles. As those in the military profession recognize, much preparation and many arrangements must be made before a leader can call, "Follow me" and sally forth with any hope of success. The successful leader is not only able to inspire and motivate men, he is also able systematically to organize their efforts. His ability to co-ordinate his available manpower and materiel resources so that they mutually reinforce each other is equally important. This ability requires skill in the management functions of planning, organizing, co-ordinating, directing, and controlling. Even the most inspired efforts require some measure of these five functions for success.

Effective management is achieved through judicious employment of the functions of management and the adaptation of new techniques. With or without these aids, management is the science of employing men and material in the economical and effective accomplishment of a mission. Thus, management interjects some of the stability of science into the art of leadership. Every leader is to some extent a manager.

ORIGINS OF MILITARY MANAGEMENT

The use of management practices by military commanders has its origin in the earliest recorded military history. Since the days of the Pharaohs, raising, equipping, supplying, training, maneuvering, and committing to battle the military force of a nation has demanded a high order of managerial skill. The industrial revolution of the eighteenth and nineteenth centuries merely emphasized the requirement.

The American Civil War should have been an eye opener to the War Department in this regard. There was much confusion in mobilizing and sustaining the forces of the North. Unfortunately, the immediate need of defeating the South, followed by the problems of reconstruction at the conclusion of this great conflict, overshadowed the need for reorganizing and changing operational techniques in the War Department. The Army was skeletonized and scattered all over the United States, primarily in the West.

For thirty-odd years, the Army continued in its cloistered existence. The nation waited until 1898 for the Spanish-American War to provide the much needed eye opener. When the battleship *Maine* went down in Havana Harbor, the Regular Army numbered some 28,000. Three months later the Regular Army plus the Volunteer Army numbered some 263,000. The confusion of the mobilization period was unbelievable. Authority to run the Army had been centralized to such a degree that the War Department was stymied in its attempt to direct every move from Washington, D.C. There was no General Staff to plan, organize, co-ordinate, direct, or control the diverse activities of the Army. The various subdivisions of the War Department and the Commanding General of the Army went their separate ways. There seemed to be no unity of purpose and certainly no unity of action.

The Port of Tampa, where troops were embarking for Cuba, was a scene of chaos. Theodore Roosevelt's testimony before the Dodge Commission paints a classic picture of the penalties of military mismanagement. Arriving troops commandeered railway coal cars to move out to the quays. On the quays, thousands of men milled about in confusion. Unit-size transports were assigned to two and three different units. Commanders pre-empted ships and facilities to ensure that their units got on board intact. (Senate Document, 1899, pp. 2257-8.)

Fortunately the war with Spain was a short one and resistance soon crumbled. The War Department was not severely tested in its ability for sustained operations on a wartime scale. On the other hand, the very brevity of the war had centered attention on the poor managerial practices in conducting the mobilization of forces and moving these forces to Cuba. A very active press had enlightened the nation on the conditions prevailing during the war. Accordingly, it would seem that the War Department would have been drastically reorganized immediately after cessation of hostilities, but such was not the case. Many individuals in the Army and Congress resisted any revamping of the War Department. The Congressmen were wary of any General Staff concept, fearing that such a device would breed an autocratic military caste that might eventually challenge Congressional control.

It appeared that the forces that "liked things pretty much as they were" would prevail and that the United States, as had happened after the Civil War, was destined not to heed the lessons learned in war. In 1899, a man of great vision arrived on the scene and prevented such a catastrophe. He was Elihu Root, appointed Secretary of War by President William McKinley. Secretary Root assumed office with an open mind. He studied the situation objectively, decided that reorganization was urgent, and campaigned vigorously for his beliefs. In 1902, he introduced a bill in Congress containing his concepts of the required General Staff. After a bitter battle, his bill was made law in 1903. Elihu Root can indeed take credit for giving the War Department a General Staff capable of managing its diverse and complex activities.

Evolution of Scientific Management

Parallel to the military's slow awakening to the need for effective management was the birth of the idea in civilian industry. Evidence exists that management practices were in use in China over fifteen centuries ago. Ancient

Rome and Mesopotamia both show evidence of an awareness of management problems and solutions. The innovations that began during the Industrial Revolution, were of such magnitude in their impact upon the economic, social, political and military fields, that their influence is still being felt to this day. The Industrial Revolution marked the beginning of centralized production and marketing, the demise of the guild system, the end of the craftsman's independence, and the inception of a new form of employer-employee relationship. The worker was removed from the family environment and placed in an organization that controlled the tools of production. The objectives of the organization and the worker were no longer synonymous. Ownership of the tools of production likewise placed upon the organization responsibilities that formerly had been shared severally by the proprietor-craftsmen. Concepts of equity in the subsequent division of responsibility and rewards due to this specialization of the productive process are still subject to social, legal, and economic interpretation and evolution. Finally, the Industrial Revolution marked the start of a technological revolution, the effects of which continue to be reflected in the changes in weapons, tactics, and organizations, as well as the national economic and social base from which the military draws both its men and material.

The earliest references to a scientific approach to a system of management are the writings of Charles Babbage. Babbage, an English mathematician, published a treatise in 1832 in which he described the methods used in a factory engaged in the production of pins. His emphasis was on the lack of scientific method in defining principles of management (Babbage, 1832).

More than eighty years ago, in 1885, an Army officer published a book called *The Cost of Manufactures and the Administration of Workshops, Public and Private* (Metcalfe, 1885). The book is still considered a classic in management. The officer was Captain Henry Metcalfe, West Point Class of 1868. Metcalfe was one of the first to propose that the administration and supervision of shops and offices is not an art, but a science which can be developed and learned. It is interesting to note that Metcalfe retired from the Army ten years before Frederick W. Taylor, the noted civilian authority, published his works.

In 1916, Henri Fayol of France wrote a classical monograph on *General and Industrial Management* (Fayol, 1949) that dealt with considerations of administrative management as viewed from the executive level. Fayol formulated principles of management that are still in use. These principles included such subjects as authority and responsibility, discipline, unity of command, morale, unity of direction, and *esprit de corps*.

Taylor, an American, is considered by many the founder of scientific management. His focus was at the operative level of management; and his two best known works, *Shop Management* (Taylor, 1911) and *The Principles of Scientific Management* (Taylor, 1919) are concerned with improving the tools and methods used by the worker. Taylor's experiments led him to develop concepts relative to production capacity, time and motion study, fatigue, worker durability, costs, and work measurement. Although Taylor's work emphasized the technical rather than the purely human side of management, he did point out the role of specific incentives in motivating workers and the value of specialization. Perhaps Taylor's greatest gift was his approach—attempting to apply the scientific method to industrial problems.

The military leader of tomorrow faces the proposition that the political, economic, industrial, and military fields are moving closer together. Although their respective areas of interest are increasingly overlapping, most of the current management literature is unfortunately directed toward the accomplishment of industrial goals. Despite this orientation, it would be a mistake for the military leader to consider such literature as incapable of transfer to the military environment. Advanced leaders in all fields are making use of ideas and techniques developed in other fields of endeavor. For example, leaders of industry, education, and the military, all attend and benefit from seminars conducted by each other. The use by industry of the principle of the military staff and the application of operations research in industrial organizations are examples of civilian use of military management innovations.

War and war preparedness have grown to be big business. During the past two decades technological improvements have been occurring with startling rapidity. Guided missiles, fire control instruments, air and land vehicles, communications, and armaments with all their complexities highlight the need for management in leadership. Troops cannot be led by any hit-or-miss proposition. Likewise in industry, management methods have frequently become a competitive factor probably as important as production techniques. Resources are critical, particularly during periods of national emergency. In warfare the effectiveness of all available men and equipment must be maximized. Hence leadership must be an orderly process. Without systematic means of managing men and resources under complex and diverse conditions, a leader is lost.

MANAGEMENT FUNCTIONS

Basically, a military leader employs his unit in accordance with its capabilities to accomplish some purpose. Management texts differ as to the number of specific management functions involved in this process and indeed even as to what they should be called. It is not critical if one author calls the issuing of orders the function of directing, and another the function of supervising. It is important, however, that a leader understand the activities involved in the management of an organization. These activities can be described as: planning, organizing, co-ordinating, directing, and controlling.

Planning—determining what is to be done, how it is to be done, where it is to be done, who is responsible for doing it or seeing that it is done, and when it is to be done.

Organizing—providing a structure that establishes relationships between men and materiel grouped together for a common purpose.

Co-ordinating—integrating all details necessary for the accomplishment of the mission.

Directing—the vital step between preparation and actual operation involving the issuance of orders and instructions to subordinates and others to indicate what is to be done.

Controlling—establishing and applying fully the necessary means to ensure that plans, orders, and policies are complied with in such a manner that the objective will be attained.

The above five management functions are tools that a leader may use to accomplish his mission. For example, a company has been assigned the mission of seizing a hill. The receipt of this mission initiates the use of the management functions by the company commander. Based upon his estimate of the situation, he reaches a decision as to how the company will accomplish this mission and prepares a workable *plan* to carry out the decision. He decides how he will *organize* the company—which weapons in his weapons platoon he will attach to his assault platoons, which he will keep under his own control, and what transportation and special equipment he will allocate to the various units. He *co-ordinates* with adjacent company commanders and with fire support units to ensure that his own actions are integrated with theirs, and he works out various co-ordination measures to ensure that his own unit functions as an integrated team. Upon completion of his planning, organizing, and co-ordinating, he prepares and issues an order that *directs* his subordinates to carry out the mission in accordance with his plan. But his work does not end here. Throughout the action, he is constantly checking on the execution of his plan so that he may either redirect any unit that deviates from the plan or else change the plan to meet changes in the situation. In other words, he *controls* the execution of the plan.

As the above example shows, all of the functions of management are involved in the execution of a tactical mission; however, these functions are not limited to tactical situations. They are equally applicable to tasks as diverse as cleaning a barracks, manufacturing automobiles, or placing a man on the moon. All of these tasks involve the use or expenditure of resources—men, materiel, money, and time—even though their ultimate objectives are vastly different. The functions of management are the tools that the leader applies to these resources in order to accomplish the mission effectively.

The functions of management—planning, organizing, co-ordinating, directing and controlling—occur at all levels in all types of group effort. It should be realized that different functions can and often do take place simultaneously at different levels of command. Thus, while the division general staff is co-ordinating, a brigade might well be in the planning stage of the same operation. In addition, in the military, as in other fields, more than one objective is often being pursued concurrently, so that it is possible to have more than one function taking place at a particular level of command at a particular time. Thus, while the commander is directing a current operation, members of his staff may be working on plans for future operations.

For ease of understanding, management functions are spoken of herein as though they existed in a pure form. That is to say, planning is often treated as being independent of organizing, co-ordinating, directing or controlling. In operation, it is more often the exception to find any one of these functions that is completely separated from the others.

MANAGEMENT TECHNIQUES

Today's rapidly changing technology greatly increases the complexity and scope of management problems while suggesting new techniques, ideas, and principles with which to solve them. The leader in his role as a manager, must be a planner, decision-maker, organizer, co-ordinator, and director; as well as the controller of his operation. His employment of men and materiel in the most economical and effective accomplishment of his mission requires him to understand the newest techniques and management aids. He must realize, however, that these techniques and aids merely provide assistance in analyzing and evaluating the information influencing the decisions for which he alone is responsible.

Project Management

One technique a leader can use to assist in solving one-time, complex projects is the appointment of a single project manager. Usually, he will also designate, or permit the project manager to choose, team members to work on the project. The leader retains the responsibility for identifying the mission or objective the project is to accomplish. He sets forth the resource allocations and limitations. As a control measure, he also directs a realistic and timely report control system.

Although retaining over-all responsibility, he delegates authority to the project manager to accomplish the project. Included in this delegation is the authorization to cut across functional organizational lines or cut "red tape" in getting the job done. The extent of this authorization, although usually quite broad, is specifically outlined. The project manager is expected to operate with a high degree of autonomy within the limits set down by the leader.

This delegation of authority places great emphasis on the project manager's leadership ability. His cutting across the organizational lines of authority can cause conflict with the other managers whom he, or members of his team contact. These functional managers have responsibilities both to their immediate superiors and to the project manager for the support of his project. Although the project manager does not have directive authority as the focal point through which all information flows, his input into the leader's decision process carries considerable weight. The project manager's unique position gives him superior knowledge about the project above that possessed by any contributing subsystem or subactivity.

While project management is a technique usually employed at higher echelons, it is occasionally used at Company and Battalion levels. An officer or noncommissioned officer, for example, may be designated by his battalion commander as the project manager to construct a battalion vehicle washrack. Several qualified assistants are temporarily assigned to the project team. The project manager is authorized to contact directly the battalion supply officer, all of the subordinate unit commanders, the local installation engineers, the salvage yard, and whatever other agencies are necessary to complete the project. Like other project managers, he must co-ordinate his contacts and activities carefully.

Perhaps the most famous project employing project management is the Manhattan Project that developed America's first atomic bomb. Other well-known project management programs are the ballistic missile program and the Polaris program. The Department of Defense has over one hundred weapon and support systems managed by project managers.

Program Evaluation and Review Technique

Program Evaluation and Review Technique (PERT) is another relatively recent development in management techniques. PERT was initially developed in 1959 to provide a planning and controlling vehicle for the Polaris weapon system. Since then, civilian industries, as well as military departments, have used the method in a multitude of management programs.

The basis of PERT is a graphic portrayal of the dependency and interrelationships between all elements of the project. The fundamental scale of this network representation is the estimated time for each event. Using this graphic portrayal, the leader can readily identify each step, determine material requirements, and predict performance time.

The PERT diagram serves to indicate the time phasing of various operations. It graphically represents the times for each activity to begin and end. To make this realistic estimate, the leader determines three times; the optimistic, pessimistic, and most likely time. The optimistic time, expected to occur on one occasion out of a hundred, is the expected time if everything goes just right. The pessimistic time, equally unrealistic, is based on an estimate of the time the activity will require if everything that logically could go wrong does. The most likely time is the estimate based on the leader's past experience and his forecast of expected circumstances. These three are combined mathematically to produce a realistic, fifty per cent probability estimate of the time between two events. These times for each activity are plotted and arranged into a graphic layout representing the entire project.

Analysis of the PERT diagram identifies the critical path. The critical path represents the sequence of activities that take the greatest amount of time to complete. The critical path serves as a control measure with which the leader can compare the actual progress. Also, he is able to foresee potential problem areas and arrange events to take advantage of any slack time in the program.

The path from event one to three to six is the critical path. Paths 1-2-4-6 and 1-2-5-6 each have less than the critical time. The first has two weeks slack time while the second has one week. The manager may decide to shift resources

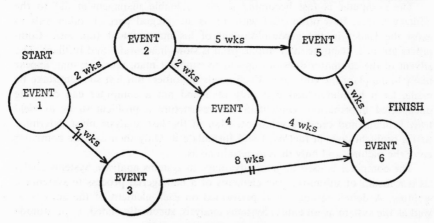

Figure 6.1 PERT Diagram

to the critical path from one of the paths with slack time in order to reduce the over-all completion time of the project.

Systems Simulation

A third relatively recent management technique is systems simulation. This is a means of solving a problem by developing a model of a real system. The model is then manipulated in such a manner as to draw conclusions about the real situation or system. Leaders can use systems simulations to predict results of contemplated actions, or to evaluate alternative courses of action. Simulations also can help define weaknesses in a presently operating system. Another popular use is as a training vehicle for leaders.

Computer models are the most versatile and widely used simulation models. Because computer systems operate on absolute data and are totally objective in their manipulations, one of the most significant problems encountered in the adaptation of manual systems to a computer model is the quantitative description of the variables employed. All variables must be precisely identified and assigned numerical values. The leader must possess a good appreciation of the interaction relationships between these variables in his design of the computer model. This presupposes an excellent awareness on his part of all aspects of the system as it presently exists.

There are some rather obvious limitations to systems simulation. The leader must realize that the results are predicated on the facts and assumptions he included in the model. Because of the assumptions involved, the accuracy of the model cannot be proven. None the less, if the simulation is to be of any value at all, the leader must have confidence in the results. Lastly, the most obvious limitation of a computerized simulation model is introduced by people. The interaction of the human variable is practically impossible to quantify and rarely can be adapted effectively to computer simulation.

MANAGEMENT AIDS

The computer is fast becoming a most valuable management aid to the military leader. It is often used with, or as an integral part of, other aids to assist the leader in the accomplishment of his management functions. Computers are fast, accurate, and stupid. Man is slow, inaccurate, and brilliant. The advent of the computer does not appear to supplant man, nor does man appear likely to supplant the computer. Each needs the other. But lest some mistake be made, let it be understood that only man and not a computer can correlate unexpected information. Only man can restructure a problem so as to yield truly brilliant and creative solutions. Man in the last analysis must determine that a problem does in fact exist and formulate it. Only then can the computer enter the picture, and only then in certain areas.

The computer is used to good advantage in systems analysis. Systems analysis is a means of submitting the elements of a managerial process to systematic scrutiny. A definitive analysis is performed on each element of the activity as well as the system as an entity. Systems analysis, succinctly stated, is an attitude or mental discipline toward the solution of a problem. Although it usually employs mathematical reasoning, its main characteristic is a combination of logic, judgment, and objective facts. Systems analysis requires that assumptions are precisely stated at every step in decision-making. It is a valuable means of arriving at quality decisions and more defensible solutions.

Automatic Data Processing Systems

The use of automatic data processing systems (ADPS) can achieve remarkable gains in managment effectiveness and efficiency in those situations where the parameters of problems can be determined and where either repetition or iteration are required.

Repetition involves the repeated use of certain information. Thus while it would be possible to figure one's own income tax on a computer, such an operation would be hardly economical, since it requires much more time to set up the program for the machine than it would to compute one or ten income tax forms. On the other hand, the Bureau of Internal Revenue can use such a program quite economically. Once the necessary information has been given to the machine, it can proceed automatically to check five or five million returns. This type of repetition is easy to recognize.

Iteration on the other hand is slightly different. In tracking satellites it is necessary to find the orbit which fits all the observations. A trial and error approach is used. Initially a guess and formula are both supplied to the machine. The machine improves the guess by means of the formula. As 5,000 to 10,000 observations might be involved, with each observation requiring as many as 100 iterations, it can be seen that while this, too, is repetition, it is of a different sort. The final solution is accurate despite the guess method.

When iteration or repetition or both can be used, the work is suitable for use on ADPS, provided that the instructions can be reduced to mathematical notation. Problems not capable of solution by hand and brain are no more capable of solution when placed on a machine. When the problem cannot be so formulated, ADPS today offers little help.

Supply operations, that include the maintenance, shipping, and replenishment of supplies, are ideally suited to ADPS equipment. For example, the Defense Supply Agency has the mission of providing clothing items for the three services. Electronic computers handle a large portion of the Agency's supply problems. A data processing center at Philadelphia, Pennsylvania, maintains a centralized inventory of textile supplies on hand in the entire depot system. The separate supply depots are connected by a transceiver network which obviates air and surface mail in requisitioning supplies. A field commander can presently transmit his order in minutes rather than days. Often the shipment goes out on the next available carrier. The ability of ADPS to provide up-to-the-minute information on the status of complex data, as in the case of supply inventories, holds out the promise of many tactical applications for this equipment. For example, it could be used to display intelligence data and our own troop dispositions and analyze the vulnerability of our forces to nuclear attack.

In addition to its ability to expedite solution and action on many problems,

ADPS has the potential for replacing many personnel currently required for administrative support organizations, thereby releasing more men for combat units. Two applications of ADPS that have already brought about manpower reductions in industry are automation and cybernetics. While the two terms have been used popularly without discrimination, a difference does exist. Where man has been eliminated from the production of certain kinds of work such as recording stock levels, the term automation has been applied to the use of ADPS. Where the system has been further altered to include the control function originally performed by man, this has more commonly been termed cybernetics. Thus, when the information of what has been shipped is automatically fed back into the stock control system and the system is modified to reorder new stock at certain minimum levels without further human control, the control function has been accomplished by cybernetics. While automation reduces the requirement for manpower in a system, cybernetics eliminates man from within the system.

Cybernetic units are used in abundance in the SAGE (Semi-Automatic Ground Environment) Air Defense System of the Air Force and the Missile Master System of the Army. Many types of computers are found in the fire control instruments of all the Services. From these one may predict that the use of cybernetics promises many rewarding future applications.

Operations Research

Operations Research (OR) is really a staff service performed by a group of specialists that provides the leader with a better basis for making a decision. The history of operations research began in England in World War II, centering around the use of radar, antisubmarine, and antiaircraft problems. During World War II, OR successfully provided leaders with information that increased the accuracy of aerial gunnery and bombing, the lethality of tank gunnery, the antipersonnel effect of artillery, and the location of V-II rocket launching sites, to cite a few of the better known endeavors.

The OR Team or staff is usually at higher operational command levels and is composed of scientists representing several disciplines. This permits a flexible approach to the solution of operational problems. The standard method of approach used by OR is the construction of a mathematical model of the system under consideration. The model is usually somewhat simplified by certain assumptions. By manipulation of the variables, certain information can be presented to the leader such as:

The importance of each of the factors under consideration.
The range of the parameters involved.
Whether or not all parameters are dependent upon one key factor.
Means for achieving greater effectiveness.
Estimates of probabilities involved.
The correct evaluation of success.

In receiving this information, the leader must consider the assumptions made and whether the effect of optimizing a particular operation will suboptimize another operation not presently under consideration. The work of OR in the area of aerial gunnery in World War II required only that new instructions be issued to bomber gunners to the effect that they should lead German planes "toward their own tail." This required neither money, material, nor additional men to implement and did not even require a change in plane formation. Here no other problem was suboptimized. This is not always the case. In a problem involving the transportation of recruits from several cities to reception centers, a solution that optimized economy dictated the movement of a few recruits from the East to the West Coast. The surprise solution offered by this minimum cost criteria, however, would not be satisfactory if the criteria were the assignment of recruits to training centers near their homes. If upon completion of training, 75 per cent of all recruits will be debarked from the East Coast for Europe, the solution for the economy criteria cited above might cost more in the long run. It can be seen that despite Operations Research, the leader must still make the decisions, if only on the validity of criteria or assumptions. That these decisions will be made upon a better basis than formerly is the main advantage provided by OR.

SUMMARY

Management is defined as the science of employing men and material in the effective and economical accomplishment of a mission. Management attains this end through the five functions of planning, organizing, co-ordinating, directing and controlling.

There has been a practice of management as far back as the beginning of recorded history, and probably before. The Industrial Revolution prompted the science of management, and this science has been expanding rapidly ever since. Poor management in the Spanish-American War and the appointment of Elihu Root as Secretary of War at the turn of the century eventually resulted in reorganization of the War Department and the institution of sounder managerial techniques in the Army.

This development of sound managerial techniques is exemplified today by the Army's use of project management, program evaluation and review techniques (PERT), and systems simulation. The computer is a great aid to military management. Its judicious use is invaluable in helping the leader in his decision-making process. An aid in itself, it also supports such other managerial aids as automatic data processing systems (ADPS), and operations research (OR).

Management techniques and aids do, however, pose a danger for the leader. He may become so dependent upon them for the solution of routine problems that the rationale of the procedures as well as the input data upon which the system operates are overlooked. New factors entering the considerations upon which the original model was designed could reduce the validity of the system and leave the organization incapable of adapting to the new environment. Arnold Toynbee attributes the downfall of many past civilizations to the fact that they became wedded to methods which initially proved highly satisfactory but which failed to adapt to environmental mutations. These historical failures should be grave reminders to our own civilization if we are to survive.

Today's solution to these challenges will not satisfy next year's requirements. Next year's solution will be inadequate two and three years hence. The only constants appear to be change and the absolute requirement for competent managers.

Suggestions for Further Reading

Johnson, Richard A., Kast, Fremont E., and Rosenzweig, James E., *The Theory and Management of Systems*. New York: McGraw-Hill Book Company, Inc., 1963.

Koontz, Harold, and O'Donnell, Cyril, *Principles of Management*. New York: McGraw-Hill Book Company, Inc., 1959.

Leeds, H. D., and Weinberg, G. M., *Computer Programming Fundamentals*. New York: McGraw-Hill Book Company, Inc., 1961.

McMillan, Claude, and Gonzalez, Richard F., *Systems Analysis*. Homewood Ill.: Richard D. Irwin, Inc., 1965.

Moder, Joseph J., and Phillips, Cecil R., *Project Management with CPM and PERT*. New York: Reinhold Publishing Corp., 1964.

VII

Planning

ALL MEANINGFUL activity within a military organization, regardless of level, is based upon some sort of plan. Whether planning involves nothing more than the thought process by which a squad leader determines what each of his squad members will do, or whether it involves highly complex and formalized planning such as that required by the Normandy invasion during World War II, it is an important function of leadership. Decisions are made during the planning process on the courses of action which will be followed to accomplish organizational objectives. In so doing, a framework is established on which the remainder of the leader's management functions can be based. The finished plan typically specifies the organization to be used, the co-ordination required, and the control measures to be employed. It also forms the basis for the directives issued to subordinate elements.

Planning is the means by which the organization is guided from the present into the future in order to accomplish a mission or objective. Upon receipt of a mission, subordinate leaders initiate their planning, seeking to identify *what* is to be done, *why* it is to be done, *where* it is to be done, *who* is responsible for doing it, and *when* it is to be done. The mission provides purpose to the planning process. Not as readily apparent is the need for planning in the absence of missions from higher authority. All leaders, including those at the lowest level, must habitually look to the future, and plan those activities over which they have direct control. For instance, leave schedules for members of a unit should be developed several months in advance to ensure that personnel are given the opportunity to take authorized leave at times that do not conflict with critical training or other unit activities. Finally, leaders must anticipate the next mission from higher authority and take those preliminary actions that will allow them to react quickly when such a mission is received. The activity associated with this anticipatory phase is generally known as forecasting. It is the first step in the sequence of planning actions.

103

STEPS IN PLANNING

The three steps in the planning function are forecasting, estimating, and plan preparation. Although these steps are sequential, they are so interrelated that they may appear to take place simultaneously. For example, information discovered in the estimating step may lead to a revision of the forecast before the final plan is prepared. The leader's understanding of these steps is fundamental to his ability to plan.

Forecasting

For our purposes, forecasting will be considered to be that phase of planning that occurs before the receipt of a specific mission or the formulation of an objective. This distinction is made to emphasize the fact that, although specific missions give direction to planning, the planning process should begin long before this time. The leader and his subordinates are constantly gathering information and evaluating trends in order to predict the situation which will exist at various times in the future. From this information the leader is able to foresee opportunities that may become available, the problems that may arise, and the areas in which decisions may have to be made. Obviously, effective forecasting requires a great deal of creative ability on the part of the forecaster in order to estimate the future effects of current events.

The more accurate the information on which the forecast is based, the better will be the predictions that are made. For example, a leader, knowing the dates of enlistment or induction of his men and their obligated terms of service, can predict quite accurately how many of those currently assigned to his organization will be due for discharge in three months. He may not be able to predict as accurately the number of new men to be assigned during the same period, since his only information on replacements may be much more restricted. Accuracy of information depends a great deal on the length of time in the future that one is trying to predict. The more distant the event, the less accurate the information and hence the prediction. The private soldier who, on the basis of several remarks passed in the barracks, forecasts that he will be eligible for a pass some 30 days hence, is likely to have a very low probability of accuracy. On the other hand, the division G3 can probably predict quite accurately that on the next day one brigade of the division will participate in a scheduled river crossing exercise under ideal river conditions.

Forecasting is a continuous process, regardless of the current mission. The leader and his assistants are always looking ahead to see what lies around the corner. The forecasting step is especially critical for an organization such as the U.S. Strike Command. This organization is responsible for planning the commitment of U.S. forces to practically any part of the world on extremely short notice. Such commitments may be made in response to requests for assistance from major U.S. military commands around the world or in other areas where a crisis has arisen that threatens U.S. interests. It is obvious that crisis situations cannot be accurately predicted. Therefore, a large number of contingency plans are developed that will allow operational forces to prepare plans for rapid implementation in response to arising emergencies. Planning for contingencies where a great number of realistic assumptions are required highlights the importance of the forecasting step. Based upon the assumptions and information determined in this step, planning then progresses to the next step—estimating.

Estimating

The estimating phase of planning begins with the designation of a mission. Whereas forecasting involves a general look into the future to see what might exist, estimating is specific and aimed at the solution of a particular problem. The estimate itself is a logical and analytical approach to the solution of a problem. Whatever the form used in making the estimate, it usually involves five basic actions.

The first action involves problem clarification or mission analysis. In the interest of giving a subordinate the maximum amount of freedom of action, missions may be stated in very broad terms. It is necessary then for the leader to analyze the mission to determine all the objectives, both explicit or implied. In his analysis, the leader must determine the primary, secondary, and collateral objectives important to mission accomplishment.

Primary objectives are those that are the *raison d'être* of the organization. In combat units the primary objective of the organization is frequently not specifically stated but rather is implied by the designation and assignment of the unit. For example, a mortar platoon assigned to an infantry battalion has the mission of providing fire support for that battalion, whether or not this has been stated.

Most primary objectives can be broken down into a number of intermediate objectives that when accomplished, facilitate or assure the achievement of the primary objective. From the point of view of a higher headquarters, the seizure of a hill in combat may well be an intermediate objective. From the point of view of the organization charged with the capture of the hill, this is a primary objective.

Secondary objectives are concerned with the efficiency and effectiveness with which primary objectives are attained. The research and development program of the Army is an example of a secondary objective. Through the development of better equipment, better techniques of employment, and better selection and training methods, it should be possible to produce an Army that can accomplish its primary objectives with greater efficiency and effectiveness. It should be pointed out that these last two terms are not synonymous. Efficiency refers to the accomplishment of the mission through a more frugal use of resources. Effectiveness, on the other hand, refers to a more complete accomplishment of the mission with current resources. Thus efficiency focuses on the resources, while effectiveness looks toward the objective.

A final classification of objectives includes those that are known as collateral objectives. These are certain programs that provide social or economic benefits to the members of the organization, the general public, or supporting organizations. Illustrative of collateral objectives are the Information and Education program, Special Services activities, "Open House" demonstrations, ceremonies for the general public, and works of good will such as the German-

American Clubs. The accomplishment of collateral objectives may require the use of men, material, and time needed for the accomplishment of primary objectives. Ignoring collateral objectives, however, may hamper efficiency in accomplishing the primary objectives. The untenable position in which the German Army found itself in the Ukraine in World War II because of the excesses of the SS Troops is an excellent example of a failure to consider collateral objectives.

As was indicated earlier, missions may be assigned by higher authority or they may be formulated by the leader himself. A mission assigned by higher headquarters may be quite specific, "Seize Hill 222," or quite general, i.e., "Conduct training in preparation for combat." In either case, it is necessary for the leader to analyze the mission to determine if any additional objectives are implied by the mission. For example, the mission to seize Hill 222 may imply that positions on this hill be used to bring fire on an enemy holding up an adjacent unit. The mission to train for combat would certainly imply the additional missions of preparing all equipment and personnel for combat service.

A leader at any time may formulate additional objectives himself, so long as they do not detract from assigned missions and are within the general policies and guidelines set down by higher authority. Frequently such objectives fall in the area of secondary or collateral objectives. For example, a commander may set an objective of improving the living facilities of his unit, increasing the tactical competence of his officers and noncommissioned officers, or winning the unit softball championship. It is quite obvious, however, that in those cases where resources are inadequate to accomplish all desired objectives, priority must be given to those derived from the assigned mission.

The second action in the estimating process is the compilation and consideration of all facts that have a bearing on the accomplishment of the desired objectives. A clear analysis of the mission will indicate what facts are needed for the plan. This information might include such matters as other missions that may affect the solution, the availability of resources, the authority of the leader in this case, and existing policies that might be applicable. It is often necessary to make realistic assumptions to fill in for facts that may not be readily available.

Armed with specific objectives, pertinent facts, and assumptions, the planner can now design possible courses of action in the third part of the estimating process. In considering various courses of action, the planner can, and should, be creative. It is obvious that consideration should be given to as many ways as possible to solve the problem. To do this, in actual practice, however, demands a conscientious effort on the part of the planner to overcome certain blocks to his creativity. The tendency to fall back on ways and methods that were successful in previous situations tends to inhibit discovering creative, and perhaps better, courses of action.

The fourth action in estimating leads naturally from the above. Now it is appropriate to analyze and compare these various courses of action. This is actually a two-part procedure. First, the leader analyzes each of the courses of action in order to predict their possible consequences. This step-by-step visualization of the planned operation or activity should allow the planner to predict with reasonable accuracy the probability of success of each alternative and its impact on the organization. Following this analysis, the leader compares the courses of action. Though there is no standard method for this comparison, it should normally lead to an enumeration of the advantages and disadvantages for each course. In doing this, however, the leader must exercise judgment. The practice of deciding the over-all merit of a particular course of action on the basis of the number of advantages versus disadvantages can be dangerous; since one disadvantage may far outweigh several others.

The leader's thoroughness in the preceding four parts of the estimating process determines how easily he can accomplish the fifth—decide on the best course of action. Within military organizations, the responsibility for making the decision rests solely on the commander. He may rely heavily on the recommendations of his subordinates and on decision-making techniques. Techniques that aid decision making are discussed in the preceding chapter; however, the commander's judgment, based on his knowledge and experience, plays an indispensable role in making the decision.

This estimating procedure is applicable to a wide range of problems and situations. In the Army a specific technique, the Estimate of the Situation, has been devised for the solution of tactical problems, while the Staff Study is frequently used for the solution of many other type problems. Other techniques are used in industry, scientific research, and for other purposes. Yet all generally include some variation of the above five actions. These can be used not only in the solution of tactical or technical problems, but equally as well in those problems where people are the most important single aspect.

In actual practice within the Army, particularly at higher levels, the estimating process followed in the planning of tactical operations involves the preparation of several estimates. In the first place, each of the commander's principal staff officers prepares an estimate covering the area of his own responsibility. Rather than the decision step, each estimate concludes with the staff officer's recommendation to the commander as to the best course of action. Having received each of the staff estimates, the commander then makes his own estimate, using information provided by the staff and his own judgment to arrive at the decision.

Plan Preparation

A plan is the means by which the decision is translated into action. In the Army, it is common for the leader to outline his concept of the operation at the time he makes his decision. The concept typically provides subordinates with some insight into how the leader visualizes the over-all implementation of his decision. The plan must include sufficient detail so that the leader's concept and his decision are clear. One method to ensure understanding is for the leader or his assistants to co-ordinate the plan with subordinates or adjacent elements during the preparation of the plan. In working out a more complex plan, it is frequently useful to begin with the objective sought and then work out successive actions required back to the present situation. This permits a realistic estimate of the time required for each phase; thus the leader has some idea of the time available for planning and preparation. Also, this permits him to prepare a time schedule to initiate successive parts of the plan.

The final plan must answer the questions of who, what, when, where, and, in some cases, why. Specifying in detail how subordinates should carry out their assigned tasks usurps the prerogatives of subordinates and should therefore, generally, be avoided. When the final plan has been completed and approved, it is published either as an order for execution or as a plan that may become an order at some future time. Distribution is made to all affected agencies, so that they may prepare their own implementing plans.

The further into the future the organization has planned its activities, the greater will be the need to review these plans continuously and the information on which they are based. Obviously, more accurate forecasts can be made as the time for execution approaches. Minor changes in the forecast may require only minor revisions to the estimate and plan. It sometimes occurs, however, that the original forecast is so out of line with developments that a new forecast is required. This in turn necessitates a new estimate, decision, and plan of action. Actually two forces are working in opposition. On the one hand, due to the uncertainty of long-range forecasting, the leader naturally desires to refrain from expending time and effort in the formulation of a plan until he is reasonably sure of the accuracy of his forecast. In opposition to this is the lead time required by subordinates to formulate plans for their own individual portions of a mission. Thus, the timing of decisions that must precede plans is one of the most critical aspects of the planning process. At no time, however, should a leader conserve his resources when such action could result in lower efficiency of the unit. The efficiency of the unit is the predominant consideration. In effect, this means that the leader and his assistants are often required to repeat the entire planning cycle to develop a new plan.

Continuous planning is essential regardless of whether the plans are implemented as written or not. Performing the detailed estimates, analyses, and comparisons required in the planning process play an important part in training the leader, his assistants, and subordinates. The types of problems foreseen, decisions made, co-ordination conducted, and orders prepared greatly assist in the solutions of future unforeseen problems, that will require similar processes and decisions.

CHARACTERISTICS OF PLANS

Regardless of the situation or the problem to which this planning sequence is applied, there are a number of characteristics which are generally applicable to all plans. The prime characteristic of a plan is that it is capable of accomplishing the mission. This sounds too obvious to mention. All too frequently, however, planning is accomplished without the planner fully understanding what is required. Objectivity should be the rule so that the completed plan is logical, factual, and realistic with respect to both the capabilities of the organization and the situational factors.

The plan must be simple yet comprehensive. On one hand, the plan must provide a concept which subordinate commanders can easily grasp and place in the context of the over-all scheme of things, with all elements reduced to their simplest form. But, additionally, it must be specific in pointing out the extent and direction of the part subordinate organizations play. Lacking either of these qualities, the plan loses its effectiveness, and the other functions of management are very difficult to implement. Too detailed a plan squelches the initiative of subordinates and reduces flexibility because of plan's rigidity. Too vague a plan leads to confusion. A cumbersome plan places those who implement it in an undesirable position if there are changes in the forecasted operating conditions.

Continuity is essential. In a plan covering long periods of time, the sequence of objectives is clearly identified and the desired manner of transition from objective to objective is indicated so that the entire plan becomes a meaningful whole.

A final characteristic of a plan is that it be economical—economical with respect to personnel, time, space, and material. The plan should yield, within an acceptable degree of risk, a maximum return for the effort expended. The degree to which the plan facilitates the other functions of management is a good test of economy.

There are many other characteristics that are desirable in good plans. The paramount characteristics, however, include mission accomplishment, simplicity, comprehensiveness, continuity, and economy.

CREATIVITY IN THE PLANNING PROCESS

Many critics allege that rigidity of thought is a characteristic of military planning. This is usually based on the misconception that the discipline and conformity necessary for concerted action will not permit creativity. Nothing could be further from the actual truth. In point of fact, creativity is an essential and necessary ingredient of military planning.

Philip with his Macedonian phalanx, Hannibal with his Carthaginian soldiers, and Rommel with his Afrika Corps are examples of military leaders who effectively used creative thinking in planning their campaigns. Recent technological discoveries and the need to keep Army doctrines and concepts abreast of the changes these achievements cause make it even more imperative for today's military leader to be creative. America's future military strength may well reside in the creative thought and actions of her military leaders. Creative thought is needed at all levels of organization.

Creative Thinking

Creativity is primarily an intellectual process, a process whereby one combines and recombines his past experiences to end up with a new combination, a new relationship that satisfies a solution to a problem. This sounds like ordinary problem-solving and it is, except for four requirements which the process must satisfy to be called creative.

First, the solution must be novel.

Second, the solution must be worthwhile.

Third, the solution must result in a tangible product, something one can see, feel, or react to—not just an idea—ideas are the starting point, not the complete act.

Fourth, the solution must be perceived by the group as being novel. This distinguishes it from recreative acts.

The ability to think creatively is universal. It is not the sole property of any particular social class, sex, or occupation. Industry and the military long ago recognized this fortunate fact and now actively seek and reward creative practical ideas from any source within their organizations. Anyone, leader or follower, can contribute a creative suggestion.

The Creative Process

A convenient way to study the creative process is to divide it into steps or phases. There can be many such divisions. Here, the process is divided into three phases. These are: The Awareness Phase; The Attack Phase; and The Selection Phase.

Awareness Phase: Creativity cannot occur unless one is aware that a problem does or may exist. It is important to understand that the creative person must first be able to sense a problem. Since he cannot simply set out to be creative, he must first be able to define some area that requires his creative effort. Mechanically, the first step then is to search the environment for problems. A leader's sensitivity to his surroundings will determine to a great extent how effective he will be in this important phase of the creative process.

Attack Phase: The essence of the Attack Phase is the high production of ideas, with the object of finding as many approaches, or alternatives, as possible. Various techniques have been developed to help stimulate creative thought. One of the most popular approaches is brainstorming, which is a procedure based on the principle of deliberate deferment of evaluation, while devising a variety of alternatives. This principle is important because making value judgments too early limits the quantity of ideas for consideration. It also hinders the possibility that an infeasible idea might trigger a creative idea. Although Alex F. Osborn originated this technique (Osborn, 1957) with groups of problem-solvers, its principles are just as applicable to the individual problem-solver. In fact, a combination of individual and group thought is perhaps the most effective technique for producing creative solutions. In the combined approach, each individual conducts his own personal brainstorming session before and after the group session. The individual session ensures that ideas will not be suppressed by critical group pressures. The group session produces new ideas by combining the ideas formed in the individual sessions (Taylor *et al.*, 1958).

Brainstorming requirements are:

1. An informal, permissive atmosphere.
2. A restriction on judicial thought and criticism.
3. A large quantity of ideas.
4. An effort to combine or modify previous ideas to produce additional ideas.

5. Complete freedom of expression.

Brainstorming is a difficult technique because many military men, by education and experience, tend to think judicially rather than creatively. As a result, there is a tendency to criticize an idea too soon. By deferring judgment, however, a leader can devise far more alternatives for consideration. Many otherwise good staff studies have resulted in failure merely because not all of the significant alternatives were considered.

Selection Phase: There are many examples that might justify an assumption that the creative act is characterized by a moment of insight that often is preceded by subconscious thinking. It appears essential in the creative selection phase to make conscious use of periods of incubation in which the subconscious can range freely through its stored data, sorting and rearranging until an illumination suggests and transmits a solution. Even in the selection phase, it is necessary to maintain an attitude of deferred judgment. Consequently, the output from the creative process is a list of possibilities ranging from the ridiculous at one end of the scale to the conservative at the other end. Therefore, the decision will require hard thinking, centered around an effective evaluation of alternatives, with a conscious awareness of the risk involved in selecting unproven and unusual courses of action.

Blocks to Creativity

Among the blocks to creative thinking are habit, emotion, and cultural restraints. As the result of both education and experience, one tends to become rigid in his thinking. The ability to withhold judgment until the end of the particular investigation is gradually reduced. As clues are revealed, that in the past have pointed to one cause-and-effect relationship, past experience points to quick conclusions. Such habit has been variously termed functional fixation, set, "problem-solving rigidity", mental mechanization, *einstellung,* and other terms, depending upon which aspect of the phenomenon is being considerd. The ability to approach each experience as a new entity without preconceptions is a vital portion of creative thinking.

Equally restrictive to creative effort are emotional blocks. Here the individual's apprehensive attitude toward the success of new ideas erodes his determination to evaluate its merits. Rather than risk failure, he files the thought in File 13. The degree of anxiety that the individual experiences affects his creativity. An individual who is preoccupied with threats from the immediate and mundane, whether real or imagined, is consumed by anxiety; and this anxiety interferes with his ability to think creatively. Contrariwise, the individual who is thoroughly secure may not be motivated to produce creative effort. Evidently, what is needed is enough uncertainty to motivate and enough security to offset the detrimental effects of anxiety that uncertainty produces.

Cultural blocks are those imposed by society and are reflected in the way one thinks one should think about things. These blocks represent the perceived values of society and are therefore very difficult to overcome.

While aware that creative effort is blocked by habit, emotional and cultural restrictions, the leader has an obligation to be creative. The leader must develop, to the degree possible, a climate for innovation and change that will stimulate creative people to produce ideas. The amount, extent, and depth of emphasis that the leader should place on developing the creative atmosphere will depend on the requirements of his unit for creative solutions. Each of his subordinates must be made to feel that his ideas and suggestions to solve problems or improve procedures are not only desired but actively sought.

Creativity in the Army

In the Army there are numerous opportunities for the application of creative thinking. Normal duties can be greatly improved if one applies creative thinking to his job. After developing experience in an assignment and learning the tools of the operation, it is possible to stand off, so to speak, and see how the operation or project can be improved by approaching it in a different way. This process quite naturally eliminates the "file cabinet" planning method and definitely encourages the new and radical ideas that may lead to better solutions. Particular advantage should be taken of creative thinking abilities during the estimate phase of an operation. At this time all avenues of approach to a solution should be explored and subordinates should feel able to think and speak freely in attempting a solution. Each new estimate should be approached in this same spirit.

Some years ago at the Army's Command and General Staff College, the Commandant, General Garrison H. Davidson, advanced the idea of "creative discontent." Quite independently, General James M. Gavin referred to this same idea as "intellectual nonconformity." Although referred to by different titles, both views recognize that intellectual advances are not limited to those who hold high command or staff positions, nor are they necessarily enhanced by an increased rank. The central point is that a leader should foster collective thinking to tap latent power inherent in the many original and worthwhile ideas that may be advanced by junior members of an organization. Although collective thinking is seldom thought of as a trademark of military organization, the successful leader obtains the best result from the minds of his assistants and still retains the requirement for discipline. Also, in the training of young leaders, it is well to remember that one day they will advance to positions of greater responsibility where originality will be required. If, in their junior years, this original attitude has been thwarted, originality for the Army of the future will be lacking. This fact underlies the requirements of the Army and points out the responsibilities of all leaders to develop and encourage creative thinking during the estimate phase of an operation. All men should understand that it is proper to question or even argue a point until the decision is reached by the leader. But, once the decision is made, everyone should adopt it as his own and follow it with loyalty and vigor. Additionally, there are many situations that arise during the execution of an operation which demand creative solutions. The innovation of a device by Sergeant Culin to aid tanks in breaking through the hedgerows of France is well covered by General Dwight D. Eisenhower in *Crusade in Europe* (Eisenhower, 1948), and illustrates the use of creativity to overcome an obstacle during execution. Mission type orders are particularly conducive to the development of creative thought in the execution phase.

SUMMARY

The final result of planning provides an answer as to what is to be done, how, where, by whom, and when. There are three steps in planning: (1) forecasting, in which the factors, forces, and effects that will prevail are predicted; (2) estimating, that culminates in the commander's decision; and (3) plan formulation, in which the detailed execution is spelled out. In solving planning problems, it is necessary to determine the objectives and the order in which they should be accomplished. Objectives are classified as primary objectives if they directly facilitate accomplishment of the primary unit mission. Secondary objectives facilitate the accomplishment of the primary objectives in terms of efficiency or effectiveness. Collateral objectives do not directly facilitate the primary unit mission, but provide values to individuals and groups both inside and outside the organization.

Good plan characteristics include mission accomplishment, simplicity, comprehensiveness, continuity, and economy.

Creative planning is essential to the continued effectiveness of the military. The three phases in the creative process are the Awareness Phase, the Attack Phase, and the Selection Phase. The desirability of creative planning is generally agreed upon. There are, however, certain blocks to creativity. These are habit, emotional, and cultural restrictions. Both the leader and his subordinates should attempt to maintain those positive attitudes and that favorable environment which foster the development of creative thought and action.

Suggestions for Further Reading

Hatch, Lt. Col. Kenneth M., "Creative Thinking and the Military Profession." *Military Review,* August 1966, pp. 78-86.

Maier, N. R. F., and Hayes, J. L., *Creative Management.* New York: John Wiley & Sons, 1962.

Terry, George R., *Principles of Management.* 3d ed.; Chapters 1-4, Homewood, Ill.: Richard D. Irwin, Inc., 1960.

U.S. Army Management School, *Army Management.* Fort Belvoir, Va.: 1963.

VIII

Organizing and Co-ordinating

EVERY LEADER must be, among other things, an organizer. He is repeatedly faced with the requirement of organizing his group or unit in a manner best adapted to the accomplishment of some task or mission. Since the personal characteristics and specialized skills of his subordinates vary greatly, he must assign tasks and responsibilities in a manner that achieves maximum group effectiveness. The pattern of relationships thus established is commonly referred to as an organization.

Organizing may be defined as the process of establishing relationships between functions, material, and men, grouped together for a common purpose. It is a management function essential to the effective and efficient performance of a mission. It is also an extremely popular subject for management theorists, and probably more has been written on this subject than on any of the other functions of management. This chapter will not attempt a complete survey of the field. Rather, it will focus on those aspects of organizing that are particularly applicable to the job of the leader.

Once the pattern of relationships is established in an organization, the activities of the individuals have to be co-ordinated if the organization is to accomplish the goal for which it was organized. Co-ordination is an especially important management function in the Armed Forces. Military operations, from the simplest fire and movement problem to the most complex air, sea, and ground attack of a heavily defended shore, are impossible without co-ordination. The direct result of a lack of co-ordination is confusion. Co-ordination achieves an orderly unification of group effort that provides singleness of action in the pursuit of a common purpose.

ORGANIZING

Purposes

Organizations are established to accomplish goals. Also, organizations are composed of people. As simple and obvious as these facts may appear, they pose somewhat of a dilemma for the military organizer. Since the nature of the

115

mission dictates the work that must be done, it is easier to organize for a single mission than to create an organizational structure capable of accomplishing a number of missions under varying conditions. Once a unit is manned, however, an informal organization is created; and the group bonds that thus develop between members of the organization are extremely important to the teamwork of the unit as a whole. As a result, the organization that is most desirable from a purely task point of view may prove less than satisfactory because it involves the breakup of a previously established network of formal and informal relationships.

In view of this dilemma, military organizers attempt to accomplish two purposes in the design of military units. On the one hand, they attempt to develop a permanent organization that is capable of performing a large portion of the missions that could normally be expected to fall to such a unit. This permanent unit becomes a "home" for the soldier in which he trains, lives, and builds group bonds. On the other hand, the organizers attempt to build into all permanent organizations a degree of flexibility that will allow tailoring the unit to the specific job with minimum disruption of the internal relationships within the unit.

The first part of the job, that of developing a permanent organization, is the more difficult task. It involves forecasting the many varied situations in which the organization may be called upon to perform and providing the necessary means within the organization to accomplish these tasks. These determinations are molded at Department of the Army level by experienced senior officers who have an appreciation of the tasks inherent in a myriad of missions, of the weapons, tactics, and logistics involved, and of the individual human capabilities and limitations involved in discharging the positions which are established. The final result of such effort, in the case of a unit such as a rifle company, is known as a Table of Organization and Equipment (TOE).

For the accomplishment of a particular mission, the TOE is frequently inadequate, and some changes of organization must be made. To facilitate the establishment of such temporary organizations, the military uses a building block technique that permits tailoring an organization for combat with minimum disturbance to the relationship within the blocks. An example of this can be seen in the flexible assignment of battalions in the division. Under this arrangement the commander of a particular battalion may well find that he is operating under a brigade commander and adjacent to other battalions with which he has not previously worked. But, within his own battalion, the normal working relationships have not been disturbed. This method of tailoring organizations for a job is commonly referred to in the Army as "organizing for combat."

Junior officers and noncommissioned officers develop organizations to accomplish specific tasks. Types of tasks may range from a combat patrol, through maintenance details, to charity drives. In these tasks, they use the building block principle and the TOE. Junior leaders are rarely involved in the development of TOEs for permanent organizations, though they may have to execute a change within their own unit that has been directed by a change in

TOE. Whether developing a permanent or a temporary organization, the process and principles are equally applicable.

The Process of Organizing

The process of organizing involves three primary steps: determining the tasks; establishing the structure; and allocating the resources. By determining the tasks, is meant the dividing of the over-all mission into specific tasks that are capable of being accomplished. This process was discussed in Chapter VII "Planning." The amount of detail required in this subdivision will depend on the working level; that is, the closer to the operating level, the more detailed will be the breakdown. To prevent overlaps or gaps from occurring between specific tasks, clear-cut delineation is made when subdividing the mission. As a final check, when the lists of tasks are added, the total of the efforts should enable the accomplishing of the assigned mission.

In the second step the structure is established. The list of tasks is analyzed and the specific duties and responsibilities of the individuals who will have these tasks are determined. At the same time, these individuals are grouped into units and subunits, according to the type of duties they will perform. While doing this, working relationships are established between each individual and each unit in the organization. This is done so that each person will know how to perform his own task within the assigned task of his particular unit, and so that all units, in turn, will work toward a common goal. The end result of this step is a pattern of relationships based on specific tasks to be performed by individuals, with the continuing purpose of integrating their efforts for the accomplishment of the over-all mission. As the final step in establishing the organization structure, the results are charted. This chart is known as an organization chart and includes a written description of the duties and responsibilities of each member of the organization.

After the framework for the organization has been worked out, personnel are then assigned to the tasks, provided with the necessary equipment, the space in which to work, and the time in which to carry out their duties. This is known as allocating resources.

Principles of Organizing

In addition to the process of organizing, it is necessary to consider some basic principles and characteristics that will influence this process when establishing an organization. There are differences of opinion as to how many principles of organization exist. Some say there are none, while others list as many as ninety-six. This is merely a matter of how detailed one categorizes. Four principles which adequately cover the field are: unity of command, span of control, homogeneity of tasks, and delegation of authority.

Unity of Command. Unity of command means that there is only one man responsible for each part of the organization. When this principle is applied, each man in the organization is responsible to only one superior. The net effect is that every person knows to whom he reports and whom he directs. This principle is frequently violated and the cause of much difficulty. (Raube, 1958.)

"Too many cooks spoil the broth" adequately expresses the confusion that results in organizations when this principle is violated. Consider for a moment the case of the late General Joseph W. Stilwell who, in World War II, was forced to wear many hats as a result of poorly defined command channels. As Deputy Supreme Allied Commander of the Burma Theater, General Stilwell was responsible to Admiral Lord Louis Mountbatten; as Chief of Staff to the Supreme Commander of the China Theater, his allegiance was to Generalissimo Chiang Kai-shek; and as Commanding General of the C.B.I. (American Land and Air Forces in China, Burma, and India), he was responsible to the U.S. Joint Chiefs of Staff. An undesirable situation such as General Stilwell experienced, in which he was responsible to more than one man for the same job, is known as multiple command.

The Tables of Organization and Equipment for combat units are set up to accomplish the combat mission. Combat units are also called upon to perform diverse noncombat tasks such as occupation duty, disaster relief, and administrative support tasks. Unfortunately, the TOEs of these units are not so flexible that unity of command can be tenaciously maintained through the established chain of command.

One means of attaining flexibility in the use of personnel and units is known as dual subordination. Dual subordination occurs when an individual has two commanders, but his responsibilities to each are clearly delineated. For example, a battalion has just received a large number of recruits who must be given basic training. The battalion commander decides that the best way to conduct some of the basic training is to use battalion committees. In this situation a platoon leader in one of the rifle companies can quite easily find himself with two commanders. As a member of a battalion training committee, he is commanded by the committee chief; and, of course, as a platoon leader he is commanded by his company commander. This situation of dual subordination does not hamper morale and does allow the mission to be accomplished. Indeed, it is often necessary, if the mission is to be accomplished at all. If the commander establishing dual subordination does not clearly delineate the responsibilities of the subordinate to his two superiors, or if the two superiors do not adhere to such delineation (which is more often the case), then dual subordination will not work, for it will become multiple command.

Span of Control. The second principle, span of control, is based on the recognition that there is a limit to the number of individuals one supervisor can manage effectively. Many authorities claim that no man can control more than seven subordinates and that he needs at least three to keep him busy. To state positively that three to seven subordinates are the limits of man's span of control is not entirely accurate. There are many variables which influence the number in individual cases, and three to seven should be only a guide. The basic problem here is the number of relationships with which a commander is involved. This problem is discussed in Chapter V—Interpersonal Communication. The general rule is that, as the number of subordinates increases arithmetically, the number of relationships increases by geometric progression (Suojanen, 1958). It can be seen why many authorities put such a low limit on span of control numbers.

> And Moses chose able men out of all Israel, and made them heads over the people, rulers of thousands, rulers of hundreds, rulers of fifties, and rulers of tens.
>
> (Exodus XVIII, 25.)

This Biblical example is an early illustration of the use of this principle in its flexible form and of the principle's persistence through the years (Beishline, 1950).

In applying the span of control principle to an actual situation, it is necessary to analyze the kind of work done by the subordinates. In cases where their work is identical and simple, it may be desirable to exceed the number seven. One man can control from ten to thirty men in a task that is highly repetitive. A sergeant with a detail of twenty trained men could be assigned the task of setting up tents for a battalion, and the span of control would not be too great. On the other hand, it would not be possible for a sergeant to control twenty men in a field artillery battalion headquarters. It would be beyond the capabilities of one man to control twenty men engaged in such diverse activities as fire direction, survey, intelligence, supply, transportation, and personnel.

Tasks that involve a high degree of interaction between members of the group and between the leader and subordinates require shorter span of control. Examples of such tasks are planning tasks and those that deal with changing conditions and methods. In such cases, it is necessary that all members of the group be kept constantly abreast of the situation and that the leader be readily available to resolve differences of opinion and to make decisions. Tasks that involve people with shallow backgrounds, training, and experience also tend to make shorter spans of control desirable, since understanding must be checked more closely and frequently, followed with further instruction by the commander. Therefore, the level of understanding of the task, need for interaction to accomplish the task, and the diversity and number of tasks being performed greatly influence the span of control.

A commander can supervise more activities if they are located in a centralized, concentrated area. The advent of nuclear weapons dictates a requirement for distance between units as well as dispersion within units. Both distance and dispersion tend to restrict the commander's ability to supervise activities of his subordinates. Modern means of transportation and communication, especially the helicopter and television, reduce some of the limitations imposed by distance and dispersion. Despite both of these modern advantages, however, certain geographical areas offer terrain or weather which largely negate the beneficial effects of modern transportation and communication. Jungle operations offer one such example.

Time, the third factor affecting span of control, refers to the time it takes to transmit orders through the chain of command, the time it takes to receive approval or decision from higher headquarters, and the time required to react in emergency situations. To reduce the time required to accomplish a task, it is desirable to keep the span of control short.

Three major factors are thus identified that influence the span of control of an organization: nature of tasks, distance, and time. Further, these three aspects of the span of control principle are interdependent. Therefore, to determine the "best" span of control of an organization, the leader must find a balance to satisfy the minimum requirements of these aspects.

Homogeneity of Tasks. Homogeneity of tasks applies to the grouping of like tasks and functions in the organization. Homogeneous means alike, similar, or allied. Similar or related jobs give rise to similar problems and require incumbents with levels of intelligence, experience, and training which are often quite similar. Certain economies in the training and background as well as the span of attention of the leader of such a group can be realized. For example, a leader may have two 8-man squads of mechanics, each made up of four men who maintain radios and four men who maintain helicopters. The leader of such a squad would be required to be trained in both fields, and his span of attention would be required to operate over both. The economy involved in an organization made up of one squad of helicopter mechanics and one squad of radio mechanics is apparent.

Homogeneity of tasks is the predominant principle by which jobs are grouped. Occasionally, however, rather than grouping similar functions, complementary functions are grouped to facilitate economy and effectiveness. Complementary functions are functions which, though dissimilar, are either related sequentially or are integral parts of some complex task. While most often complementary functions are the basis for procedures, these also become the basis for organizing in special situations. As an example, a section of a relatively high headquarters might be charged with the full-time production of intelligence summaries. Such an organization might well be composed of linguists, photo interpreters, a political scientist, an economist, and possibly other specialists; and headed by a senior officer. Nothing about these jobs is homogeneous, yet all are essential to the intelligence mission. Thus, while homogeneity of tasks is the basic principle, organizing is also conducted on the basis of complementary functions.

Delegation of Authority. Delegation of authority means that individuals are given authority in keeping with their responsibilities. When a man is made responsible for a job, he is given the "power" he needs to do it and sufficient freedom to use his own initiative in its execution. This principle can be violated in two directions—by underdelegating and overdelegating.

If a commander underdelegates, the subordinate is not given enough freedom to act. For each decision, he must get the commander's approval. This, of course, ties the commander to a mass of detail and keeps him from his own work. From the point of view of the subordinate, he may feel that the commander does not trust his judgment. It is impossible for the subordinate to do a good job, for he cannot act without first getting approval. If he should, the commander may not approve, and the subordinate will have to do the job over again. Another bad effect of underdelegation is that the organization may cease to function when the commander is away, since there is no one present to make decisions.

Equally as bad as underdelegation is overdelegation, or giving away too much authority. A commander who lacks self-confidence may overdelegate authority in an attempt to avoid making decisions himself. In so doing, he is delegating responsibilities that he must assume himself. Even though he makes subordinates responsible to him, the commander is still charged with 100 per cent of the original job. His job is to get unity of effort. To do this, he must personally exercise over-all control. (Raube, 1958.)

The amount of delegation depends to a great extent on the individual situation. A brigade commander sent off on a training mission to a remote area would be given more freedom and authority than the commander of a brigade close to division headquarters. Delegation of authority also depends to a great extent on the confidence the commander has in his subordinates. It may likewise be affected by the complexity of technical details, the number of subordinates, and the time available to accomplish a certain job. The over-all principle, however, is that subordinates should be given the authority necessary to do their jobs.

These four principles are not rigid laws to be blindly followed but rather are guidelines that assist in structuring the function of organizing. D. Ronald Daniel emphasizes this point by writing:

> The principles of organization, in short, are a double-edged sword. Employed with skill and with discretion, they can be useful in defining and refining an organization structure. Applied insistently and inflexibly, they can result in a rigid, bureaucratic organization structure poorly attuned to a company's unique needs.
>
> (Daniel, 1966, p. 97.)

The Military Organization

A commander at any level is responsible for all that his unit does or fails to do. It may at first appear that the commander must personally supervise every action or decision for which his unit is responsible. Due to the complexity of military jobs, this is physically impossible. If this were attempted, the commander would have little or no time to solve any other problems. In the first place, he would become bogged down in a mass of details. Secondly, he cannot be an expert in all the many specialties for which he, nevertheless, is responsible. The point here is clear. He needs assistance in his exercise of command. This introduces the organizational pattern which practically all military organizations follow, the line and staff.

Line and Staff. In the line and staff relationship, the term "line" is synonymous with the chain of command. It is the vertical hierarchy of commanders from the troops in the field to the highest military command. In the Army chain of command, the line runs from the individual soldier to his squad leader, platoon leader, company commander, and on up to the President of the United States. At any point in the chain, there is a commander who is responsible for the entire chain beneath him. Stated simply, it is a system of intermediate commanders between the Commander-in-Chief and the troops in the field.

A commander cannot possibly supervise personally all the actions of his command. At each level in the chain of command above the very lowest, the commander has a group of assistants or staff who advise and inform him on matters for which he is responsible.

The staff secures information and furnishes such advice as may be required by the commander, translates his decisions and plans into orders, and transmits orders to the troops. It informs the commander on matters that require his action, makes continuous estimates, and prepares tentative plans for possible future action for the commander's consideration. Louis A. Allen strikes the comparison between line and staff:

> Line refers to those positions and elements of the organization which have responsibility and authority and are accountable for accomplishment of primary objectives. Staff elements are those which have responsibility and authority for providing advice and service to the line in the attainment of objectives.

(Allen, 1958, pp. 225-6.)

In short, staff functions are an extension of the commander's functions, with the commander and his staff being viewed as a single entity.

A relatively recent concept of the staffs serving as an extension of the commander is the director staff. In addition to advising the commander in specific areas, directors are ". . . vested with authority to determine the actions to be taken by the command in specified fields—hence to direct those activities of the command which fall within their respective fields. A director may have authority to issue orders in his own name to carry out his assigned responsibilities and also has the co-ordinating functions of a general staff officer." (FM 101-5, 1960, p. 9.)

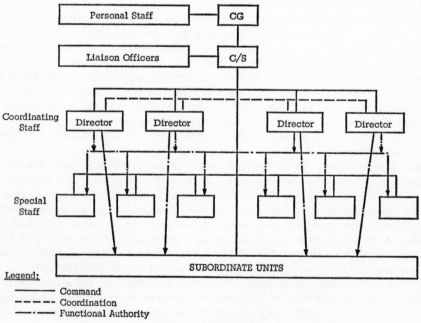

Figure 8.1 Director Staff

The practice of including sections within the staff at adjoining echelons that are charged with similar areas of responsibility is termed staff parallelism. A like performance of duties is accomplished at various levels of organization by the staff. For example, all organizations contain people, and hence all staffs require a section to co-ordinate the personnel matters of the organization. Where similar areas of responsibility are found grouped in like staff sections at adjoining levels, advantages accrue. The foremost of these is a quick, direct line of communication which facilitates co-operation and co-ordination. The S1 at brigade can go to the G1 at division or the S1 at battalion on personnel matters. Matters that are subject to rather routine handling in that they fall within the scope of general policy may be discharged through staff channels in the name of the commander. This simultaneously expedites the matter and removes such action from the commander's span of attention. The commander is notified of its accomplishment at the appropriate time. Staff parallelism, in addition, facilitates the two-way flow of information between echelons, since knowledge of one's own staff organization is the key to the location of the interested staff section at the next higher or lower headquarters. By virtue of staff parallelism, the interrelation of the areas of staff responsibility at any echelon remains relatively fixed, which also means that an extensive orientation period is not required by incumbents who move from one echelon of staff to the next. Disadvantages of staff parallelism stem more from the inappropriate use of a direct channel of communication than from any other source.

The primary mission of the staff is to facilitate the attainment of the objective by the line organization. To do this, the staff acts as an extension of the commander to facilitate the efficiency and effectiveness of the line units.

In discharging this function, the staff is governed by the exception principle. That is, only those things that deviate from the standard are brought to the attention of the commander. Thus, when there is no standard, as with a new mission that requires a new plan, the staff presents the new plan to the commander for his approval. In the course of operations, the commander is presented with only those areas which are exceptional, in that they either do not fall within the present policy, or they require an interpretation, as when two policies appear to dictate mutually exclusive courses of action.

Taylor's Functional Organization. F. W. Taylor, the father of scientific management, developed a unique line-staff organization. Although Taylor's concept of "functional organization" has not been wholly adopted by either industry or the military, some of his thinking is reflected in other type staffs. Taylor advocated not merely a change in staff, but a complete new organizational concept. Rather than divide the departments of an industrial organization into subordinate units, each with its own supervisor responsible for all that the unit did or failed to do, Taylor advocated that eight supervisors be established subordinate to the department manager. Each of them would be granted functional authority over all operations within the entire department that fell within his particular area of responsibility. For example, one of the supervisors would prepare the instructions for each worker on how to set up and operate his machine for the particular product that was being manufactured, another would maintain all the machinery for the department, and still another would handle all disciplinary problems. Half of the supervisors would work in a planning office where they doubled as a planning staff, while the other half would exercise directing and controlling functions on the floor of the shop. It can be seen that this organization placed the individual worker in the position of reporting to eight different supervisors for eight different functions. This represents a degree of dual subordination that is so extreme as to represent an absolute break with unity of command. It can also be seen that the elimination of intermediate line supervisors leaves an extremely large span of control for the plant manager. (Allen, 1958.)

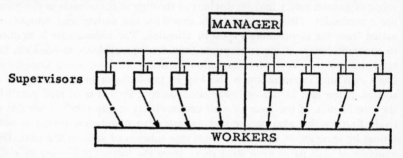

Legend:

—————— Command

- - - - - - Coordination

— • — Functional Authority

Figure 8.2 Taylor's Functional Organization

CO-ORDINATING

As a function of management, co-ordination seeks an integration of all details necessary for the accomplishment of a mission. It achieves effectiveness by bringing all agencies concerned with an undertaking into one blended action with a minimum of effort and friction. The following analogy very graphically describes the process of co-ordination:

> Harmony is a key word in understanding the meaning of co-ordination. Usually we hear it used in connection with music. The same is true of timing. The conductor of an orchestra has planned his program, decided on the numbers, organized the disposition of brasses, woodwinds, strings, and percussion instruments. Now he is ready to direct the performance. Regardless of how highly skilled each player may be, the concerted efforts can be completely ruined without effective co-ordination. If the first violin decides to play Bach when the others begin Debussy, it is impossible to

achieve harmony. It would be equally disastrous if the tuba came in on the gentle solo reserved for the flute. Each individual contribution must be perfectly timed.

(DA Pamphlet 41-D, 1957, p. 69.)

There are basically two types of co-ordination: the co-ordination of thought and the co-ordination of action. Co-ordination of thought requires a previous development of concepts, to include objectives, which are commonly understood by two or more parties. Thus, co-ordination of thought is accomplished between people. Such co-ordination precedes co-ordination of action, which involves the relation of physical activities, either with respect to time, or with respect to each other. The main contributors of co-ordination of action are timing and the sequence of performance of the phases of a project. These phases tend to become the specific steps in any task. Thus, to facilitate co-ordinated action, the plan states the steps to be taken in the execution of the project, their order, and usually the place of performance.

Co-ordination provides an excellent example of the lack of a clear distinction between the various functions of management. It is not possible to separate co-ordinating from planning. Co-ordination of thought takes place during the planning process in all three steps—forecasting, estimating, and plan preparation. The final plan is designed to produce co-ordination of action on the part of the organization as a whole. Thus, co-ordinating may be looked upon as both a technique for the accomplishment of planning and an objective to be achieved by planning. Organizing is undertaken so as to provide an optimum of co-ordinated action, and the control process frequently involves the co-ordination of thought so as to improve the co-ordination of action during the execution of the mission.

In co-ordinating, the leader has a double responsibility. Not only is he required to co-ordinate his own actions or contemplated actions with other interested agencies, but also he is obliged to ensure co-ordination of the activities of his subordinates. Thus, he maintains liaison with other units as well as guarantees the teamwork in his own unit.

Co-ordination in the Military

In general, co-ordination is accomplished between units by the commander or his representative, the liaison officer. Additionally, the executive officer or chief of staff is specifically charged with responsibility for co-ordination of the staff, and may co-ordinate activities of subordinate units when so authorized.

Command Co-ordination. Upon receiving an order for a mission, all commanders who have areas of common interest co-ordinate with each other to ensure that their operations mesh and that no gaps or overlaps in responsibility and authority will occur during the operation. Although initially such gaps or overlaps may not be apparent, the execution of a mission frequently reveals situations that present commanders with mutual problems. As an administrative example of such a problem, consider the case of maneuver damage in an area used by two organizations. A tactical example might arise from a shift in unit boundaries that places a stay-behind patrol in the zone of a unit other than its parent organization. At higher levels the commanders agree on the general course of action to be taken and the liaison officer or their staffs work out the details. Commanders must also notify other interested agencies of either the division of responsibility or its assumption by one commander or the other.

Liaison Co-ordination. The commander establishes liaison with another unit when he needs to keep abreast of developments in that unit. Supporting units habitually establish liaison with a supported unit. In addition, liaison is frequently established between higher and lower headquarters and between adjacent units on the line.

The main purpose of liaison, whether by a commander or his representative, is to ensure mutual understanding and unity of purpose. To accomplish this, a commander may dispatch one of his subordinates to another unit to maintain contact and represent him. This permits continuity in the exchange of information. Also, personal contact promotes co-operation and co-ordinating effort.

Staff Co-ordination. The staff often effects horizontal liaison with units at its own level and vertical co-ordination with units of higher or lower levels. Both horizontal and vertical co-ordination are facilitated by staff parallelism. Certain areas of co-ordination are normally reserved for the attention of the chief of section, while more routine co-ordination falls to his subordinates. Here again, one finds evidence of the exception principle. Routine co-ordination is conducted by staff subordinates, and exceptions as well as matters of interpretation are reserved for the chief of section. For example, an assistant battalion S3 spells out co-ordinating details for a night relief of one company by another. He includes such routine matters of co-ordination as whether telephone trunk lines will be removed and replaced or left intact, whether or not heavy weapons will be traded, and what disposition will be made of supplies and ammunition located on position. After co-ordination with the company commanders concerned, he notifies the S3 of the details for inclusion in the order.

Co-ordination Techniques

Conference. The face-to-face meeting, or conference, is a frequently used method of co-ordinating; however, it can be somewhat expensive in terms of time, particularly when the participants must travel any distance to join the conference. In recent years this limitation has been minimized by communicating devices such as the telephone, radio, teletype, and television. But, in the military, the problems of security and electronic countermeasures pose a hazard to electronic methods. Therefore, the face-to-face conference remains the best method of co-ordination.

Conference co-ordination provides several other advantages. First, expert knowledge and a wide range of experience and opinion can be easily sampled. This often results in a better course of action than that proposed by individual members. Second, bias and oversight of individuals can be negated. Third, lines of communication are shortened in large organizations. Fourth, from an educational viewpoint, each member's viewpoint is broadened, and he may gain an appreciation for the other members' problems as well as those of the entire organization. Finally, and certainly not least in importance, co-operation may be secured. Recent studies indicate that this feature may prove to be at least as important an advantage as the "combined judgment" feature of committees (Costello and Zalkind, 1963).

Individual Contact. By far the most common method of co-ordination is through individual contact. The average leader is involved in a great deal of face-to-face individual co-ordination, and this can become extremely time-consuming, especially if it is necessary to travel any distance. Consequently, the telephone is an extremely useful, timesaving device for co-ordination of minor details. If the co-ordination is extensive or complex, however, there is frequently no choice but to travel to all various agencies with which co-ordination must be effected.

In comparison with the conference, individual contact has both advantages and disadvantages. From the point of view of the leader effecting the co-ordination, the time-consuming aspect is a serious disadvantage. Further, it is not unusual for the leader to have to repeat his co-ordination with some agencies to iron out new details which have come up in subsequent co-ordination with other agencies. From the point of view of the other agencies with which co-ordination is effected, the fact that they do not have to leave their regular jobs to attend a conference is a definite advantage. Since the major disadvantage for the leader is one of time, he can save much of this by simply calling the other parties with whom he wishes to co-ordinate and arranging a time to see each. This is only common courtesy; it allows the other parties time to prepare for the visit, and it precludes the possibility of one of the other parties being absent when he arrives.

Correspondence. When conferences or personal contact are not possible or are not needed, co-ordination may be accomplished by written correspondence. This technique is generally quite slow and is not used for high priority matters. Each person can read, however, and take action on the co-ordinating correspondence at a time that is most convenient for him, and it is not necessary to call all members from their jobs nor for one man to go around to see all the others with whom co-ordination is necessary. Also, of course, a written document provides a permanent record and can be studied in depth. In larger headquarters most matters of routine nature are co-ordinated in this manner. Correspondence is often used in conjunction with the other techniques. For example, a written document may be circulated to all parties of a conference to read ahead of time, so that they may come better prepared to work out a solution. After the conference, a written summary may be circulated among the participants for their concurrence, just to make sure that when agreement was reached during the conference, all parties were on the same "frequency."

Overco-ordination

In co-ordinating the efforts of an organization, overco-ordination is equally as undesirable as underco-ordination. A point of diminishing returns is reached when the use of the precious time of others in effecting co-ordination of thought results in no real improvement in the functioning of the organization. Ideally, in an experienced unit, a great deal of the necessary co-ordination is accomplished by the staff and subordinate commanders as a matter of standing operating procedure, without anyone specifically having to direct its accomplishment for the particular task at hand.

There is also a real danger that the overco-ordination of action of subordinate units results in a violation of the need for simplicity in the plan. It is possible for a plan to so overco-ordinate the actions of subordinate units that the plan becomes too complex and leaves too little room for initiative on the part of the subordinate commanders. Regardless of the amount of co-ordination of thought necessary in its preparation, the plan should remain conceptually simple, specifying only those details that are necessary to ensure that the various activities occur at the proper time and that simultaneous activities mesh without mutual interferences. It is true that many times it is necessary to specify a great deal of co-ordinated action on the part of subordinate units, especially if the operation is complex. It should always be remembered, however, that, if the co-ordinating details become too complex, the whole purpose of co-ordination will be defeated because the plan is not understood by those who must execute it.

SUMMARY

Organizing is the process of establishing relationships between functions, material, and men grouped together for a common purpose. Sufficient flexibility is built into the structure of TOE units to permit the tailoring of temporary organizations to accomplish a particular mission.

Organizing is accomplished in three steps: determine the tasks, establish the structure, and allocate the resources. The principles by which these three steps are governed are unity of command, span of control, homogeneity of tasks, and delegation of authority. The final organization should be capable of effectively accomplishing the mission.

The line organization works directly to accomplish the primary objectives. Staff organization works to facilitate the operations of the line and to increase the attainment of secondary objectives in terms of economy and effectiveness of the line. The staff advises, recommends, and does those things a commander would do if he were many people. The chief of staff co-ordinates the staff, a job which is discharged by the executive officer at brigade and below. The director staff is similar to a general staff, except that greater authority is delegated to the staff chiefs to direct subordinate units within functional areas.

In the execution of its tasks, the staff uses the exception principle to reduce the commander's workload to manageable proportions and takes advantage of staff parallelism to facilitate the flow of information and co-ordination.

Co-ordination is the process of integrating the men, material, and actions of an organization on the basis of time or sequence of performance so that maximum effectiveness may result. Co-ordination is of two types—thought and action; with co-ordination of thought preceding co-ordination of action.

Suggestions for Further Reading

Allen, Louis A., *Management and Organization*. New York: McGraw-Hill Book Co., Inc., 1958.

Koontz, Harold, and O'Donnell, Cyril O., *Principles of Management*. New York: McGraw-Hill Book Co., Inc., 1959.

Newman, William H., and Summer, Charles E., Jr., *The Process of Management*. Englewood Cliffs, N.J.: Prentice-Hall, Inc., 1961.

Richards, Max D., and Nielander, William A., (eds.), *Readings in Management*. Cincinnati, Ohio: South-Western Publishing Co., 1958.

IX

Directing and Controlling

THE LEADERSHIP functions of directing and controlling logically follow in sequence the functions of planning, organizing, and co-ordinating. A plan is the end result of the planning process. It typically prescribes the manner in which the personnel and materiel will be organized, specifies the type and extent of co-ordination required between various elements of the organization, and, to some degree, has an influence on the way in which the operation will be directed and controlled. A plan is essentially a guide for action, however. It is only upon implementation of the plan that the functions of directing and controlling become significant. In brief, directing is the leader telling his subordinates what he wants done. Controlling is the means he uses to determine if his directives are being carried out. A plan is worthless unless subordinates are told their part in the operation and unless the commander ensures that each understands and performs his duties properly. In an address at the U.S. Army Command and General Staff College, General of the Army Omar N. Bradley related the following anecdote which serves to reinforce this point:

> General John J. Pershing, while inspecting during World War I, found a project that was not going too well, even though the officer in charge seemed to have a good plan. The general asked the lieutenant how much he received, and when the lieutenant replied: "$141.67 per month, sir," General Pershing said: "Just remember that you get $1.67 for making your plan and issuing the order, and $140.00 for seeing that it is carried out."
>
> (Bradley, 1966, p. 49.)

Within the Army, the leader initiates the directing function by issuing his plan as an order. But once his control means tell him that the operation is not going as planned, new directives are frequently issued. This need to direct and control alternately is a continuous process, ending only with mission accomplishment.

131

DIRECTING

The leader tells his subordinates what he wants done by issuing his instructions. These instructions serve to initiate action, to amplify or modify previous instructions, or to redirect the efforts of subordinates as required by the leader's view of changes in the situation. The key to effective directing lies in careful supervision of the execution of the plan. By so doing, the commander can determine the extent of additional guidance necessary and can select the appropriate means of communication to achieve the desired result.

There are a number of factors that affect the extent of direction necessary. For example, a reasonably static and repetitive operation requires less direction than a changing one. An assembly-line operation in industry, where the same product is being turned out day after day, is a vastly different matter from a combat situation with its continuously changing requirements. The size and complexity of the organization affects the extent of direction necessary. A greater directing effort is required as the organization becomes more complex, with various sub-elements geographically dispersed. The competence and level of experience of subordinates are other factors that influence the amount of direction required. More competent and experienced subordinates desire and need less direction from their leaders. This fact is especially important to subordinate development. Most subordinate managers will accept a greater responsibility for the operation when given greater freedom to direct their own activities. In turn, they will be less inclined to over-direct their own subordinates. A new organization may require considerable direction, but as the organization matures and develops standard procedures, the amount of direction from the top can be substantially reduced.

Directives

The communications a commander uses to transmit directions to subordinate leaders and elements are commonly termed "directives." Directive is a general term that is used to refer to all forms of oral and written orders and instructions. Directives may apply to the day-to-day functioning of the organization, as in the case of regulations, or they may be specifically applicable to the situation at hand, as in the case of operation orders and administrative orders. Standing operating procedures carry the same weight as orders and instructions and are included in the term directive.

Written directives are more accurate and more precise than oral directives and can serve as a lasting communication to the person receiving them. Written directives require time and effort to prepare, however, and, if written in too great detail, result in inflexibility. The quantity of written material a person will actually read is limited.

There are no firm rules as to when a directive should be oral or put in writing. Generally, oral orders are used (1) in time of emergency, (2) when the action to be performed is relatively simple, (3) to clarify a written order, or (4) in face-to-face leadership situations. On the other hand, written directives are used (1) to transmit orders over long distances, (2) when precise figures or complicated details are involved, (3) when the execution of the directive extends over a considerable period of time, (4) when a permanent record of the existence of the directive is necessary, or (5) when the sequence of operation needs to be followed exactly. The most effective way to communicate a directive is to transmit it both orally and in writing.

Characteristics of Directives

Clarity is the first essential of any directive. It is more important than technique or brevity. To obtain clarity there must be no ambiguity. Words must be carefully chosen; they must mean the same thing to the writer and the reader; and the use of unfamiliar abbreviations and highly technical language should be avoided if there is any danger of misunderstanding. Generally, short sentences are preferable, since they are more easily understood. There are formulas that give a relative measure of how the difficulty index, or "fog factor," rises with long sentences and polysyllabic words (Flesch, 1946, p. 58). In the Civil War, General John Sedgwick allegedly kept one officer on his VI Corps staff who was not particularly noted for his keen intelligence. This officer was required to read each order published by the headquarters. If he could understand it, the order was dispatched. Clarity is particularly important in written directives because of the reduced feedback in such cases.

A directive should also be complete and concise. The individual receiving the directive must know how much initiative he is allowed and the range of his authority and responsibility. There should be no doubt in his mind as to what is to be done and the quality and quantity of performance that will be considered satisfactory. Furthermore, the time allowed for performance should be indicated. In giving missions to subordinate units, the commander should prescribe only those details or methods of execution necessary to ensure that the actions of each subordinate unit will conform to the plan of operation for the force as a whole. The more urgent the situation, the greater is the need for conciseness in the directives. Any statement of reasons for measures adopted should be limited to what is necessary to obtain intelligent co-operation from subordinates.

An important characteristic of a directive is that it should be realistic. There is much wisdom contained in the Department of the Army leadership principle which states, "employ your command in accordance with its capabilities." The wise leader keeps this principle in mind when issuing directives. If an individual or unit is unable to comply with a directive, the directive must of necessity be disobeyed or modified. For example, if an order to swim a river is issued to a man who cannot swim, obviously he cannot comply with the order. In determining whether the directive can be accomplished, the leader should consider whether the man who will receive it has the necessary authority, experience, and ability to perform it satisfactorily. The leader should consider whether time, equipment, personnel, external conditions, and other aspects of the total situation permit the man to comply, if he uses a reasonable amount of effort and ability.

Effectiveness of Directives

Closely allied with realism is the fact that a directive should be timely. In ensuring the timeliness of an order, a leader must take into account that directives are normally issued through a chain of command and take considerable time to reach the man who must execute them. As indicated earlier, by-passing normal channels is resorted to only in urgent situations. The habitual use of the chain of command, on the other hand, indicates respect for subordinates and ensures that all affected by the order are kept informed. Thus, a leader strengthens his chain of command by using it to disseminate all directives and other items of interest.

Orders should be disseminated in time to give subordinates the maximum time to estimate their own situation, prepare plans, organize, issue their orders, and prepare their own subordinates for the contemplated operation. Commanders must anticipate the delays involved in the successive dissemination of orders. When detailed orders cannot be issued, essential details should be issued in fragmentary form. Often it is desirable to issue warning orders of impending operations in order to gain time for preparatory measures and to conserve the energy of troops.

The timing of an order in relation to other activities is also very important. An attempt should be made to choose a period of reduced activity in current operations when issuing directives for future operations. For example, it would not be timely for a battalion commander to conduct detailed briefings on the next month's activities on a day that companies are taking their annual Army Training Test.

Overdirecting

Overdirecting restricts initiative and should be avoided. A directive should not unwarrantedly trespass upon the province of a subordinate. It should contain only that information that a subordinate must know to carry out his mission intelligently and to further the mission of the next higher unit. As a general rule, a directive tells the subordinate what to do but not how to do it. It may be necessary, in some instances, to indicate the methods to be used in order to co-ordinate the force as a whole. For example, a tank unit commander on the march may prescribe detailed procedures for his subordinate units at refueling halts in order to expedite the refueling and prevent a pile-up of following units at this point. Such details in directives should be the exception rather than the rule, and are normally covered by standing operating procedures.

The excellent means of communication available today greatly ease the problem of direction. By the same token, they create problems of overdirecting. Many a harassed commander has rued the day the telephone was invented. Television offers great possibilities in the field of direction, if leaders learn when to "keep their fingers out of the pie."

Overdirecting restricts initiative because of too much "how" rather than too much "why." In issuing directives, it is usually possible to explain why the order is given. The American soldier likes to be kept informed. Directives should always leave some of the detailed planning to the person receiving them, for often unanticipated conditions arise that require the use of initiative. If the person receiving the directive understands why it was originally issued, he is better able to adapt his actions to the over-all purpose. Explaining why also contributes to morale and co-operation.

The following are examples of a field artillery battery commander issuing instructions to his executive officer. In one case there is little latitude for thought or initiative. The other, however, permits over-all understanding of the mission and elicits co-operation.

"Lieutenant Jones, take one of your howitzer sections down to the gun park this afternoon. Have them remove the tube from the carriage and carry it fifty yards away from the carriage. Then time the crew, and see how long it takes them to move the tube back on the carriage and have the howitzer ready for firing. Do this four times, average the individual times, and give me the results at 1600 hours this afternoon."

"Lieutenant Jones, our battery has been selected to participate in a helicopter air movement demonstration next week. The helicopters we will use cannot carry a complete howitzer because of weight limitations. Therefore, it will be necessary to use two helicopters to transport one howitzer. The carriage will be suspended by sling beneath one helicopter and the tube will be suspended beneath the second helicopter. Because the helicopters will be landing simultaneously, the pilots will land their howitzer loads approximately fifty yards apart. I want an accurate time figure for my planning purposes on how long it will take to assemble a howitzer and have it ready for firing. The time in question should start from the time the helicopters have landed the two loads. Give me the computed time by 1600 hours today. What are your questions?"

An excellent historical example of avoiding overdirection is the following directive from the Combined Chiefs of Staff to General Dwight D. Eisenhower during World War II.

"You are hereby designated as Supreme Allied Commander of the forces placed under your orders for operations for liberation of Europe from the Germans. Your title will be Supreme Commander Allied Expeditionary Forces.

"You will enter the continent of Europe and, in conjunction with the other United Nations, undertake operations aimed at the heart of Germany and the destruction of her armed forces." (Eisenhower, 1945, pp. vi-vii.)

Although orders issued to lower level commanders allow much less latitude than provided General Eisenhower, all directives require some degree of interpretation. This can be accomplished most easily within a sound framework of announced policies.

People are different in many other respects than just the manner in which they interpret directives. This fact should not be ignored by the commander when issuing orders. The better the follower is understood and his probable reaction to an order predicted, the better can be the direction.

If direction is to be effective, it must generate followership—a desire to obey. Far more success is possible if the follower intrinsically desires to accomplish a task because the job is pleasing in itself or he gains self-satisfaction from its accomplishment. The American does not enjoy being "bossed around" without exercising some thinking or participation on his part. A direct order, although essential at times, leaves little room for follower participation. In order to gain the desired results, there are numerous ways in which an order can be issued, depending on the circumstances.

A direct order is one that leaves little or no choice on the part of the receiver. It is often required for short-run emergency situations, to stop waste or delay, for correcting disobedient, careless, or indifferent men, or for clarification of instructions. Although frequently necessary for short-run effectiveness, direct orders provide for no long-term growth of the subordinate.

In routine duties, most competent subordinates, particularly officers and key noncommissioned officers, require little more than a pointed suggestion. Although military tradition holds that a suggestion by a commander carries the weight of a command, its use generally implies a particularly high degree of confidence in the subordinates.

CONTROLLING

As General John J. Pershing pointed out to the lieutenant, once the leader has earned one per cent of his pay by issuing the order, he must next see that it is carried out to deserve the remaining 99 per cent. The function of controlling is primarily a matter of ensuring that directives are carried out in the manner intended by the leader. The three basic steps in controlling are: establishing standards, comparing results with the standards, and taking corrective action.

Before the leader can assess how well subordinates accomplish their assigned tasks, he must establish standards against which to evaluate the results. A standard is a model, criterion, or rule of measurement. Thus, a pair of superbly polished jump boots might serve as the leader's standard of shined boots and shoes for his men. The specifications given to manufacturers of military equipment are standards. Thus, the specifications for an item of clothing or transportation or a weapon all become standards for the acceptance or rejection of these items.

Standards of performance also are established to determine the ability of individuals and units to perform effectively. Unit performance is evaluated through Army Training Tests (ATTs). Standards for the ATT are based on whether or not the unit possesses the skills to perform successfully in combat. Individual performance standards include the scores that must be achieved in weapons firing to qualify as an expert, sharpshooter, or marksman, as well as the degree of proficiency in a military skill required for the award of a proficiency rating. Indeed, without standards of performance it is difficult to imagine how performance could be evaluated. The standard serves as a yardstick which is available to take the measure of the individual or organization in terms of quality, quantity, and expense of whatever resources are required.

Standards must be consistent with the ultimate objectives of the organization. Many problems can arise when they are not. It is obviously impractical to set the same standards of appearance for personnel of a combat unit in Vietnam as those maintained at Officer Candidate School because the objectives of the two organizations differ. Yet, it is not uncommon for commanders to concentrate on comparing results against standards that are only indirectly related to the objective, at the expense of more important standards. Among the more frequent examples of this practice are the placing of emphasis on the method of performance rather than on the results attained, and overemphasizing the so-called morale indices while disregarding over-all combat efficiency.

In expressing standards it is desirable to use basic units of measure. A basic unit of measure is not subject to fluctuation in value because of factors external to the job. For example, a standard expressed in number of parachutes packed per eight-hour day by one rigger is expressed in basic units. So long as the type of parachute remains the same and is packed under the same conditions, this standard can be used over a period of time. Should a monetary standard be established for this task, however, changes in the value of the monetary unit or the prevailing wage rates will cause the "standard" cost of packing parachutes to vary. Therefore, standards should be expressed in stable units of measure such as man-hours or items per unit of time.

In the determination of standards, a logical procedure is followed. First, the operation is subjected to a complete study to determine that it is necessary and that, as presently constituted, it represents the most efficient method to achieve its ultimate purpose. From this point on, performance is evaluated in terms of quantity and quality. In determining the standard, the conditions of operation and equipment are held constant and stated. Allowances for fatigue and delay are included when the standard is expressed as a rate. Such a standard might be the distance an infantryman can cover in an eight-hour day.

The second step in the controlling process is comparing results with standards. To this end, the leader personally observes the execution of the plan or receives reports on its progress. Observations and reports are compared with the standards previously set in order to determine the degree to which actual performance coincides with the plan. Where the performance and plan do not coincide, the leader must determine the net effect on the mission. Here, corrective action may be required.

In this step, the exception principle is especially applicable. The commander's span of attention is conserved by the staff. The commander is told that all is going according to plan with the exception of significant items that are not. The possible effects of any such deviations are pointed out and a course of action is proposed to overcome these effects. The delay of a unit in arriving at its attack position might dictate change in the time of the attack and further coordination with the other units concerned.

Finally, the commander must concentrate on critical control points. It is impossible for him to check the performance of activities under his control against all possible standards. The time and effort required to do so would be staggering. This is especially true in higher levels of command. Consequently, commanders concentrate on certain points in the operation that, it is hoped, will indicate how well a considerable number of standards are being observed. Observation posts, release points, and communication centers are good examples.

The comparison of results with the standards set calls for a subjective evaluation by the leader. In his evaluation, it is tempting for him to concentrate on those obvious aspects capable of objective measurement. Often during an operation the methods are more obvious than is progress toward the accomplishment of the larger mission. As a general rule, however, evaluation should be based on results rather than methods. For example, if a soldier is firing expert on the range, he should not be criticized for using a firing position that is not identical with that prescribed in the field manual. There are times, however, when it is necessary to evaluate methods because these are important for reasons of safety or economy, or in order to determine why the results themselves are not up to the standards. For example, the evaluation of the performance of a driver would involve not only his driving ability but whether he also operated his vehicle in an economical and safe manner. If a man fails to qualify on the range, it is necessary to evaluate his firing position, among other factors, since this may be the cause of his failure.

The evaluation of the performance of office workers is a particularly difficult task. The variety of tasks which they perform—typing, filing, reproduction, research, checking, answering the phone, and acting as receptionists—makes it difficult for an objective evaluation of their work and also makes it somewhat easy for them to work at less than maximum capacity. Thus, in this case, it is often necessary to evaluate methods. A technique recently developed to train supervisors to evaluate the work of clerical personnel involves the use of films. The trainees observe films depicting people at work in an office and evaluate the efficiency of their work. After a period of training in this method, it has been found that much agreement can be reached among evaluators as to how efficiently the force is working. Such a technique may be further developed in the future to assist in training people to evaluate many other aspects of performance that are primarily qualitative rather than quantitative.

A method frequently used in the Army for evaluating performance of individuals and units is the training test. Army Training Tests (ATT) are administered to individuals upon completion of Basic Combat and Advanced Individual Training and to units upon completion of the various phases of unit training. Though not perfectly valid, these tests probably are the best predictors of actual combat performance in the particular skills being tested. Testing is also being used today in order to determine the qualification of enlisted personnel to receive proficiency pay in their particular skills. Tests, however, cannot be used as the sole method for evaluating performance. Because they tend to be conducted on an annual basis, they provide little evidence of quality of performance a few weeks before or after the test. It is possible to work hard to prepare for a test, pass it, and then promptly forget all that was learned. Consequently, most performance evaluations must be based on close and fairly continuous personal observation, evaluating the qualitative aspects of the job, supplemented wherever possible by tests and quantitative data.

In the military it is difficult to come up with objective figures that are related to the primary purpose of the organization. Consequently, an attempt is made to gain quantitative data on just about everything that can be reduced to such figures, in the hopes that a composite of such data can provide an estimate of the effectiveness of the organization in its over-all job. Normally included are such factors as AWOL, venereal disease, delinquency, court-martial, accident and re-enlistment rates, scores achieved on weapons qualification and on Army Training Tests, and, where possible, cost data, such as maintenance costs and the over-all value of equipment lost, damaged, or destroyed.

In order to compare actual performance with established standards, the commander must first get the facts in the case and then analyze or evaluate these facts. The problem of getting the facts is an important one, and one that becomes more difficult as the organization grows in size and complexity. As was mentioned earlier, the gathering of facts is usually accomplished by personal observation and reports.

Personal observation may be made during formal inspection or informal visits. In this connection it should be remembered that the primary purpose of inspections and inspecting agencies is to ascertain the manner of performance and the state of affairs within a unit. It is not to take punitive action. There is no completely satisfactory substitute for direct observation and personal contact; however, this method of obtaining facts is time-consuming. It is physically impossible for commanders of large units to inspect personally the operations or even the results at all control points. Consequently, they must rely on reports, either from subordinate commanders or from members of their staffs, concerning performance on many aspects of the mission. It cannot be overemphasized that reports do not replace visits or inspections made personally by commanders and their staffs.

Reports vary in their means of transmission, required frequency, and detail. Three important characteristics of reports are timeliness, accuracy, and brevity. The exigencies of the tactical situation place high values on all three. The administrative situation places no less regard on these but may define them slightly differently. In the administrative situation, the report of the number of pieces of laundry processed might well be considered timely if reported thirty days after the fact. In combat, however, more current information is required, such as the number of casualties suffered or rounds expended for the previous twenty-four hours.

In any situation, reports should be prepared in terms of how they will be used. The use of graphic presentation of such information permits the individual who is comparing the actual performance with the planned performance to do so quickly. This is especially true of information reducible to numerical form. Examples of such graphic presentations of information are currently seen in presentation of incident rates, performance and logistical levels. Generally, such information is not sufficient to base corrective action upon but merely points out the need for more information upon which corrective action may be based.

Even though the first two basic steps of controlling have been properly performed and the responsibility and cause of deviations from standards are known, no control will result unless some corrective action is taken. The taking of corrective action is the third step in the controlling process. This step illustrates the interrelationship between directing and controlling. Often the corrective action consists of issuing a new directive that, in turn, requires controlling, and so forth. In this way, the leader's concept of successful mission accomplishment is finely defined.

Corrective action is of two types—immediate corrective action to ensure that the objective is gained, and administrative corrective action to prevent recurrence. Corrective action, designed to ensure immediate mission accomplishment, often involves methods identical to those aimed at administrative corrective action. Only the objectives differ. Administrative corrective action involves further investigation, especially in the case of recurring difficulties, to determine the nature of the factors responsible; disciplinary action, if the investigation reveals such is warranted; planning, to prevent recurrence of the situation; and initiation of such other measures as are approved by the commander. It is more important that corrective action be directed toward discovering and rectifying the cause of a failure in order to prevent recurrence than attempting to fix responsibility as a basis for punitive action or finding a scapegoat.

Failure to achieve desired results is often caused by conditions somewhat beyond the control of the immediate subordinate commander. These conditions may be weather, loss and breakdown of old equipment, lack of re-supply, and other unexpected obstacles in the operating situation. When such nonforecasted influences cause serious deviations from the plan, the commander must take some action to reduce their effect. To accomplish this, he may expedite supporting logistical activities such as maintenance and supply, or he may furnish additional combat support to the subordinate commander. For example, a division commander may attach an additional tank battalion to a brigade in order to compensate for unforeseen enemy armor activity in the area of that brigade.

The furnishing of additional support to a subordinate may not be adequate to compensate for unforeseen conditions. Unexpectedly strong enemy resistance, an enemy atomic or airborne strike, the failure of an adjacent unit to accomplish its mission, or the failure of a subordinate unit, due to internal conditions, to accomplish its own mission, all may necessitate a major revision of plans for the entire command. Such revision of plans is an essential part of corrective action. At the same time, it regenerates the entire cycle of planning, organizing, co-ordinating, directing, and controlling.

In many instances the failure to attain desired goals may be the result of an unclear directive. In such cases, the commander should clarify what is desired. He should also examine more closely his future directives to ensure that they convey his desires clearly. In other instances the failure may be due to more than a misunderstanding of instructions. The individual who failed may lack the necessary training and experience for the job. If this is the case, the subordinate must be given additional training. In some cases, the situation may dictate that he be replaced by a more competent individual.

Military organizations are made up of human beings, and, regardless of how well the basic functions of management are performed, the organization will be successful only to the extent that the individuals comprising the organization are willing to put forth effort to accomplish their assigned tasks. Somehow, someway, there must be developed in each individual a desire to execute his duties effectively. The task of the leader is to stimulate this desire.

Control Illustrated

The three steps of controlling—establishing standards, comparing actual performance with standards, and taking corrective action—may be likened to the actions of a thermostat. The thermostat of a heating unit is set at seventy degrees. This setting is what is expected, the standard desired. The thermostat constantly monitors the temperature in the room to determine whether this standard is being met. If the temperature is greater or less than seventy degrees, the thermostat generates a "negative feedback" signal, that is, a signal that directs the heating unit to take action to change the temperature in the opposite direction. If the temperature is too low, the signal will turn on the heating unit to increase the temperature; while if the temperature is too high, the signal will turn off the heating unit to decrease the temperature. In the controlling process, corrective action is the negative feedback signal.

Exercise of Control

The general rule is that the person who issues an order (establishes a standard) is the one who exercises control over its execution. For example, if the squad leader directs a soldier to dig a foxhole in a particular location, then the squad leader checks to see that the hole is dug in that spot, and makes corrections, if necessary. The platoon leader, having given the squad leader orders to cover a particular section, checks and corrects the squad leader on whether his squad does cover that sector. It will be noted that the man responsible for performing the task is not delegated responsibility for controlling that task. The soldier has not been delegated authority to be the sole determinant of whether or not he has complied with such authority with reference to the platoon leader's orders. Neither would the man who sells stamps in the unit post office be delegated authority to audit his own books, for such an arrangement courts embezzlement. This concept—that authority to control a particular activity is not delegated to the person who is responsible for performing that activity—is known as the concept of noncoincidence of responsibility and control. Under this concept, control normally resides one echelon above the level that is responsible for execution. That is, control resides at the level that directs.

The practical aspects of the principle of noncoincidence of responsibility and control can be seen when one considers the great amount of time and effort involved in controlling. It may be relatively simple for a commander to sit back in his command post and, on the basis of the information he receives through his communication channels, prepare plans and issue orders. When he issues the orders, however, he cannot delegate authority to his subordinates to supervise and control their own execution. He must get out of his command post to see what is happening. If he should insist on issuing all the orders, it is obvious that it would be physically impossible for him and his staff to do all the necessary controlling. There is only one way out of this dilemma. He must delegate to his subordinates the authority to issue orders in their own right. Thereby the subordinate becomes responsible for controlling the execution of his own orders. If the platoon leader insists on designating the foxhole location of every man in the platoon, he would be responsible for seeing that every man is in his position. If, however, he assigns sectors to his squad leaders and delegates responsibility to them to emplace the men, then they become responsible for controlling the actions of their own men. The platoon leader's job has been considerably simplified, not only in planning and directing, but also in controlling.

To the degree that authority and responsibility are retained at the higher echelon, an organization is said to be centralized. When authority and responsibility are delegated to lower echelons, the organization is decentralized. An organization may centralize certain areas of responsibility and authority, such as the authority to convene a general court-martial, and decentralize other areas, such as the authority to administer punishment under Article 15 of the *Uniform Code of Military Justice* (UCMJ). Various indices have been used to portray the degree of centralization or decentralization of an organization. A common index in commercial organizations is the level at which authority has been delegated to expend a given sum of money. In the normal day-to-day operations of an organization, the degree of centralization or decentralization is not so much a matter of the specific manner in which the commander has organized his subordinate units as it is a matter of the policies that he has established to guide the daily operation of the unit as a whole. Thus, there may exist two identically organized units, one highly centralized and the other highly decentralized in its operations, due to the different policies pursued by the two commanders.

One manner in which the commander does influence the degree of centralization within the organization, and consequently the control authority of his subordinates, is through the organizational relationships he establishes and the missions he assigns his subordinates. This is particularly true in combat. For example, the engineer battalion of a division may be assigned tactical missions that require that the separate companies of the battalion be employed in a variety of roles, each involving a different degree of control of the engineer effort within the division. When an engineer company is attached to a brigade, the division commander has decentralized part of his engineer capability by granting authority for the employment of the company to the brigade commander. The company thus performs tasks designated by the brigade commander in furtherance of the brigade mission. On the other hand, when the division commander keeps all his engineer companies under the control of the engineer battalion commander, he has centralized his engineer support, and the companies are employed on tasks in furtherance of the division mission. Military organizations have long appreciated the requirement for flexibility in control and have developed gradations in the delegation of responsibility and authority that influence the degree of control exercised by the commander over his subordinates.

The span of control is another key factor in determining centralization of control. A broad span of control by its very nature requires decentralization, while a narrow span almost inherently results in centralized control. But aside from the purely task and organizational factors involved, decentralized organizations do have certain advantages in terms of the impact of delegation on both the higher commander and his subordinate leaders. James C. Worthy lists some of the benefits of decentralization as developing a greater sense of responsibility and initiative as well as creativity in leaders. It also provides a larger pool of promotable leaders (Worthy, 1950).

Delegation to subordinates requires a great deal of patience and self-control on the part of the leader himself. It is easier to give someone the answer than to take the time to guide him to a sound solution that he will feel is his own, thereby gaining more confidence and seeking more responsibility. To stand aside while observing mistakes is a frustrating experience. Yet a person learns from his mistakes. Control that is too tight inhibits the development of subordinates. If a person is denied his method of finishing a task, he probably will go to his grave thinking that his method was right and would have worked better had he been allowed to use it. Most people discover their own mistakes before severe damage occurs. In this case a real lesson is learned.

There are psychological barriers to delegation, many of which reside in the personality of the leader. First, a lack of faith in subordinates, the feeling that no one can do the job as well as he, can be a real stumbling block. Second, there may be a feeling of insecurity on the part of the leader. He may be haunted by a fear that, if he delegates too much authority, the subordinates may outshine him. The fear of lowering the importance of one's position is also a strong motivating force. The leader may reason that if he delegates too much authority, his superiors may conclude that his position is not vital and therefore eliminate it. The environment which a commander creates will therefore influence the activities of his subordinates, and a strong commander is required to provide the situational environment that will be most conducive in effecting the orderly development of his subordinates.

There are risks involved in delegation. The subordinate who has been delegated authority may fail, and his failure will reflect on the leader himself. These risks can be easily exaggerated. Paradoxically, the more successful leaders appear to be those who permit as much decentralization as their subordinates can handle (Katz and Kahn, 1951). The unit pride and spirit of competition that develop as a consequence of delegation not only lessen the risks but also contribute to the effectiveness of the larger unit to a degree not possible under centralization. Thus, in an effective organization, the sum of the parts is greater than the whole.

Delegation is vital to the controlling function. In this complex age, it is axiomatic that the leader must use assistants to control his organization. The axiom is clear, but the human problem of decentralization is clouded.

A degree of decentralization is essential for the functioning of any organization. How much and how far down the organizational structure it is accomplished for most effective performance is a function of the leader's competence and ability to tolerate the stress to which delegation subjects him, the follower's ability to accept the responsibility, and the demands of the situation in which both leader and follower exist.

SUMMARY

Directing is the vital step between preparation and actual operations, but it is also important after the operation is under way. Directing puts the show on the road. It is the means by which the commander tells his subordinates what actions he desires them to take, and corrects those problems which his control means uncover.

When issuing orders or instructions for the completion of a task, the leader must ensure that his orders are clear, complete, concise, realistic, and timely, in order to gain the proper results. He avoids overly detailed orders that tend to impair interest, reduce a desire to co-operate, and stifle initiative. The capable leader issues only the minimum number of orders to cover the situation adequately. In his desire to give effective direction, the leader must realize that the danger of overdirecting is always present.

Controlling is the constraining and regulating of execution to ensure mission accomplishment. It is the action taken by a commander to ensure that plans, ideas, directives, and policies are being complied with in such a manner as to ensure that the objective is obtained. The possibility of an error in one of the other functions or of a failure in execution by subordinates dictates that control be exercised over the execution of the plan.

The work accomplished during organization affects the function of control in two ways. First, the noncoincidence of responsibility and control established in organizing provides a framework for a check on the discharge of responsibility. Second, the location of authority and responsibility determines the location of the control functions as well as who will be engaged in this process. When authority and responsibility are delegated, certain benefits accrue. Such benefits include both the development of subordinates and the fostering of a sense of accomplishment among subordinates.

Controlling is performed in three steps: establishing the standards, comparing the actual performance with the established standards, and taking corrective action.

Standards may relate to policy, SOP, physical attributes, personnel, or performance. Such standards should be consistent with the organization's ultimate objectives. While standards may be expressed in either terms of quality or quantity, basic units should be used. Where standards are not directly measurable, judgmental opinion or relative measures are employed.

In comparing actual performances with established standards, it is a prerequisite that the standards be known before the fact and that responsibility for meeting these be fixed. Due to the large number of standards in effect, the commander must get the facts by use of observation at critical points and reliance upon reports for less critical areas.

When performance and standards do not agree, corrective action is required. Corrective action may be of an immediate type that seeks to ensure mission accomplishment or of an administrative, or longer range, type which seeks to prevent recurrence.

Suggestions for Further Reading

Koontz, Harold, and O'Donnell, Cyril, *Principles of Management.* 2d ed.; New York: McGraw-Hill, 1959.

Newman, W. H., and Summer, C. E., Jr., *The Process of Management.* (Parts Five and Six) Englewood Cliffs, N.J.: Prentice-Hall, 1961.

U.S. Army Management School, *Army Management.* Fort Belvoir, Va., 1963.

P O C D C

Section II
THE GROUP

Leadership cannot be exercised without followers—a group to be led. Great feats of leadership imply great feats of followership. Leadership, as a phenomenon of group interaction, can only be studied in conjunction with the characteristics of the groups that are led. The study of social psychology and group dynamics has progressed rapidly in recent years. While it has been recognized at least since Aristotle that men were essentially group-oriented, it has not been until recently that man has attempted scientifically to measure and to evaluate the interactions and dynamics within a group. Every leader participates in a number of important ways as a member of the group he leads. In order to lead it effectively, he needs to understand the significance of the group to its members as well as those characteristics typical of group action.

No man lives entirely outside of a group. He both contributes to and absorbs satisfaction from the group of which he is a member. The group assists him in achieving identity and in defining his role. In turn, he contributes something of his personality and characteristics to the composite personality of the group. Chapter X "The Individual and the Group" discusses group attraction and functions, describes a concept of group interaction and processes, and analyzes the influence of the group on the individual.

Military groups, because of the high degree of stress they must be able to withstand, require a high degree of solidarity and *esprit*. Field conditions and combat require substantial group interdependence, mutual confidence, and a high degree of identification with the group or unit. Chapter XI discusses group solidarity and *esprit* and the measures the leader should take to develop them in his unit.

A unit can have a high degree of group solidarity without being highly motivated toward performing its mission. Conflicts between institutional and group goals can result in low motivation and poor morale. An important task of every leader is to maintain the morale of the men in his unit and to develop a high degree of motivation toward their assigned goals. Chapter XII outlines problems involved and techniques by which the leader can maintain "Motivation and Morale."

145

The key word that describes an effective military unit is Discipline. Supported by a high degree of group solidarity and *esprit*, armed with a high motivation to perform its mission, a group needs only the trained response of discipline to convert it into an effective unit. The temptations, confusions, and pressures of combat place severe stress on military units that can be overcome only by discipline. Chapter XIII discusses the means by which a leader can inculcate and maintain discipline in his unit.

Military groups are hierarchical in nature with each man occupying a specific position within the rank structure of the organization. Thus, individual interaction, particularly between the leader and the group, involve senior-subordinate relations. To the young leader newly appointed to a position of responsibility, his relations with both his superiors and subordinates can be a matter of some concern. Chapter XIV discusses these problems and provides some guidance to assist the leader in solving them.

The military leadership role involves senior-subordinate relations that in turn inevitably require counseling. The leader is counseled by his superiors and must counsel his subordinates. Counseling is a very complex form of interaction that requires considerable skill to be performed successfully. The individual being counseled must accept the corrections or advice as part of his own thinking before he can improve. Chapter XV describes the counseling process and provides guide lines that the leader can use in counseling his subordinates.

The process of leadership is essentially a product of group interaction. The leader, as a member of the group, must understand its characteristics and processes. It is only through mastering the techniques and skills of building *esprit*, developing motivation, and instilling discipline in his unit that he can display the qualities of a true leader.

X

The Individual and
The Group

EFFECTIVE LEADERSHIP can only be based on a thorough understanding of men. Each man, however, is a system composed of a fantastic array of biological systems and subsystems. For a leader fully to understand psychological man, requires more than a knowledge of these biological subsystems. It requires a knowledge of how these systems affect each other, and an appreciation for the totality of their relationship. The same is true of man's social systems. He not only brings his biological make-up into his social systems but also his psychological differences. The fact that a number of individuals like himself compose his social system further complicates analysis.

Man is born into social systems. An individual, for example, is first a member of a family group, that is, in most cases, part of a neighborhood, town, or city. Later, he joins other groups such as schools, the Army, or civic organizations. All of these are forms of systems in which man lives, works, plays, governs himself, obtains and distributes goods and services, and provides himself with protection on a collective basis. Some of these are formally organized, and some are quite informal and loosely structured. Some exist only as a frame of reference. Why man finds it necessary to form, join, and maintain groups and organizations has caused endless debate over the years. But, essentially, it seems that man is attracted to groups because they offer him satisfactions he could not obtain otherwise.

GROUP FORMATION

Man has many needs. As discussed in Chapter XII, Abraham Maslow uses needs as the basis for his theory of personality. He categorizes them into a need hierarchy. The higher needs in his hierarchy are socially oriented and infer that man has a strong preference for living in groups. (Maslow, 1943.)

Status Groups. George Homans, in *The Human Group*, states, "Civilizations, governments, and institutions come and go but the small group has remained as the persistent form of social organization. Its survival affirms that small groups satisfy important human needs which no other form of organiza-

147

tion can supply." (Homans, 1950, p. 468.) Robert T. LaPierre bases his theory of social control on the face-to-face relations of people in small groups. He calls these "status groups." He uses status to explain how people perceive their place in the world. By drawing influence from and making reference to their various status groups, people are able to gauge their own opinions, check and compare their own interpretations of experience, and maintain identity with reality. In other words, groups apparently satisfy the individual's need for a standard by which he can check himself. (LaPierre, 1954.)

Group Function

Informal Groups. Groups provide satisfactions individuals cannot obtain alone. This is one of the basic tenets of organization theory explaining why individuals form groups. For example, in the military service, a new "recruit" becomes acquainted with his immediate bunkmates in the same barracks. They eat together in the same mess hall, they march together, train together, and essentially share all the new and strange experiences together. It is not long before they find themselves sharing their coffee breaks, attending movies, or exploring the local town together. They essentially learn to support one another and find that their new and strange experience is easier to cope with when in the company of a buddy or a group of buddies. This loose type of an association is referred to as an informal group.

Groups depend on individual members for co-operative effort and personal contribution toward reaching group goals. Individuals, in turn, are dependent on their groups for certain needs that only group participation can satisfy. (Zaleznik and Moment, 1964, p. 6.) This means, then, that an individual both gains and contributes by his group affiliation. He probably has ambivalent feelings about his group because of this. For, any person who participates as a member of a group has both affection and disaffection for it. He interacts with the group in an atmosphere of dependency. He cannot always get his way, and his feelings both for and against the other members vary greatly. There will be ups and downs in the group's activities, for they will sometimes achieve their purpose, sometimes not. So, the individual sometimes satisfies his needs and gains his goals, but other times he achieves no satisfaction and may lose rather than gain. (Festinger, 1957, p. 132.)

The Group Concept

Definition. Any collection of people, who are related to each other by some common interest or attachment, is a group. Small groups may be defined as groups in a more limited sense, such as people in face-to-face relationships, who interact frequently in a fairly regular manner, or who interact continuously in an irregular manner. Whatever the definition, there are a number of types of groups, and many concepts to explain them.

Primary Group. Each of these concepts offers a number of illustrations that provide good insights into the group behavior phenomenon. One such concept is the "primary group" theory proposed many years ago by Charles Cooley. It is Cooley's belief that the primary group serves as the primary influence on the individual. As a child, the primary group may be his parents, family, siblings, then change to neighborhood peers, school buddies, and, finally, in adulthood, his work group or contemporaries. According to Cooley, the primary group is that membership group from which an individual derives most of his pleasure, influence, and expectations. As a corollary to the primary group, a person also has secondary groups that influence his behavior. These are usually large-scale associations such as a church organization, business corporation, or some other institution. Whereas the primary group is usually small enough to permit frequent member interaction, considerable intimacy, and participation, the secondary group may be merely one a person draws references from or makes reference to. (Cooley, 1924.)

Peer and Reference Groups. Two other popular concepts are the "peer group" and the "reference group." The peer group concept holds that individuals are more directly influenced by their peers than by other elements of their environment. An individual perceives his peers' attitudes and derives his own largely from them. The exact peer attitude may not be known by the person but he will tend to expect or anticipate what this peer attitude is. Examples of peer groups might be: juvenile gangs, members of a football team, noncommissioned officers in the same company or battalion, army captains in the same battalion, or cadets of one class in the same ROTC regiment. The concept of the reference group, on the other hand, goes somewhat beyond the peer group approach. This is the theory based on the idea of a "frame of reference" concept and is concerned with the source of an individual's inferences about various aspects of his world. A person draws ideas, perception, and motives from his reference group. This reference group may be an actual one in which the person is a member, it may be one that he aspires to join, identifies with, holds in high esteem, or one to which he feels dedicated or obligated. In the latter case, a person could draw his basic ideas and perception from a nonexistent or imaginary group. Examples of such imaginary groups might be: "ancestors" for the Oriental, the "Founding Fathers," or the "classless Utopian society" that the Communist Party refers to in their ideal life for a yet-unborn generation. (Shibutani, 1963, p. 101.)

GROUP PROCESSES

Theodore Newcomb (Newcomb *et al.*, 1965) and Abraham Zaleznik (Zaleznik and Moment, 1964) describe the group process in action as a group social system. For example, a small group is a social system in which the process of development establishes patterns of influence within a group. The process follows a sequence. Initially the individual members find it important that they establish some group identity. This provides the members with a set of limits by which they can compare their perception of events and their feelings toward other members. As a group takes on a task, it derives issues about which all can agree, such as the way to work, and the way to talk and communicate. Identity and purpose provide the group members with a definition of each situation that arises, consistency of ideas and attitudes within the group, dependability upon one another, and expectations about new situations and the group's future.

Structure

As a group develops in its ability to solve problems, accomplish tasks, or achieve its purpose, the members become rapidly acquainted with ideas, attitudes, and special abilities of each member. A group finds success by trial and error. Leaders who emerge and influence the group usually continue to do so unless the group fails in its purpose or does not succeed in attaining its goals. Unsuccessful leaders lose their influence while successful ones gain in influence. As a result, the power in the group shifts. The effect of all these procedures is the growth and development of group structure. Members arrange themselves in the form of a ranking, a communication net, or a group chain of command.

As groups structure themselves on the basis of ability or influence, they confer status on their members. Status refers to an individual's position in the group in relation to other group members. Status needs are satisfied through actual hierarchal rank in the group or through conferred rank, the latter resulting from the accomplishment of some function valued by the group. Satisfaction of status needs results in a feeling of power or sense of prestige. Each individual achieves satisfaction in these areas in ways that are unique to him. Satisfaction normally requires the response of others; although, on occasion, it may be experienced solely within the individual himself. The point here is that every man desires recognition. He wants to be regarded as a leader or a loyal follower. He seeks respect for his virtues, talents, and accomplishments.

A desire for status in one form or another is ever present in an individual. The satisfaction that a person may derive from increasing his prestige and esteem knows no limits. A wise leader cannot overlook the possibilities offered in this area. An individual should be made to feel that his prescribed assignment is vital to the objectives of the organization and that his manner of carrying out his duties is of concern to all members of the unit. The lowliest individual in the group wants to feel that he has a basic dignity and in some way has the regard and respect of his fellow group members and that he is making a valued contribution.

Frame of Reference. The more a group develops, the more firm these patterns of structure, status, and member relationships become. In turn, group standards develop as behavioral and attitudinal guides from member interaction and influence. These standards become a frame of reference for each member. If any group is to be enduring and accomplish its objectives, its members must have common purposes and attitudes. If a collection of individuals is to react as a group, it is necessary that the members' frames of reference be similar. This "shared frame of reference" is a group norm. Group norms serve as common bases for understanding, and simplify the establishment of rules and standards. As a corollary, they provide the basis for group solidarity, ease of communication, unit identification, and guidance for a group member's conduct.

When no previously established references exist, the group feels a need to establish them. The early American West provides an example of this. The gold rushes and land booms generated new communities, where previously there had been no organized towns, no courts, no clearly established rules of conduct. A brief look at the history of these times shows the development of social standards acceptable to the new group.

Group Norms.   A group norm implies something more than a group frame of reference; it refers to a behavior standard as well. For example, the Drill Instructor in an Army basic training center, with his wide-brimmed campaign hat, his erect posture, and authoritative command voice, is expected to be the epitome of a "soldier." These DIs are expected to be sharp, hard workers, knowledgeable, and set a tough and high standard for their recruits to live up to. Not only are the Drill Instructors treated this way, but also they act this way, and they check one another to make sure they are each keeping up to the standards. Thus, group norms serve as a common area of understanding, and provide a basis from which standards may be established. Members of any military unit have very different personalities and yet understand one another while working together because they interpret one another's behavior through common norms. Without norms, much of their behavior would not be understood.

Although the group leader is frequently the originator of many group standards and the exemplary exponent of most norms, experiments show that even a leader with high prestige will have difficulty changing individual group member's standards merely by changing his own. Kurt Lewin, the noted field theorist in psychology, felt that the most effective method of changing individual attitudes was to work on the group norm instead of on individual members (Lewin, 1951). Changing only one member's attitude results in his losing his position in the group because of his deviant behavior. Sensing the social pressure applied, he may revert to his old accepted attitude or mode of behavior. Deviation from the group norm in behavior normally will result in pressure from the other individuals in the group to bring the deviant back to the desired conduct. This may vary from simple censure to complete rejection and denial of membership to the offending individual. Thus, the absence of proper dress at a formal dance at the country club may simply result in questioning glances and some quasi-official comment from a representative of the group. But, a violation of sleeping on duty by a combat sentry may bring down wrath not merely from his group for jeopardizing their safety, but may result in a court-martial by the formal organization as well.

Group norms have an important place in military organizations. They can assist the commander in maintaining order and discipline. Strong norms provide group cohesiveness and the power of unit solidarity. Group norms consistent with the goals of the organization ease the task of the leader. They allow him to be absent from the group with the full assurance that it will maintain itself while he is gone. George Homans put it succinctly when he said:

> A norm . . . is an idea in the minds of the members of a group, an idea that can be put in the form of a statement specifying what the members or other men should do, ought to do, are expected to do, under given circumstances. . . .
> A statement of the kind described is a norm only if any departure behavior from the norm is followed by some punishment.
>
> (Homans, 1950, p. 123.)

Individual Roles.   Closely related to group norms are individual norms. This is discussed at length in Chapter II, under role behavior. A role is a norm that applies to a specific person. It is a pattern of behavior expected of an individual occupying a certain position within the group. The value of an individual to a group depends not only upon the position which he occupies in the group structure, but also upon the manner in which he plays the part expected of him in that position. The group itself defines certain behavior patterns that are acceptable and appropriate for members in the various positions of the social organization.

With each specific status goes a certain prestige—the respect accorded an individual because of the position held in the formal organization. But, how well the individual meets the group expectations and needs, that is, how well he fulfills his role, will determine the degree of esteem accorded him. In other words, role is the dynamic aspect of status.

In addition to the leader, each member of an organization has a particular role to play. The formal structure of the organization and the other members assign his role to him. The manner in which he behaves in his prescribed role in both his own eyes and those of other members of the organization influences the degree of status and security that group membership offers him. Within the limits of his own personality, he enacts the role assigned by the organization (squad leader, rifleman, etc.) as well as other members (unit intellectual, buffoon, goldbrick, etc.). These are referred to as his "formal" and "informal" roles, respectively. Both the formal and informal roles are enacted simultaneously, and the relative success with which he assumes the roles is measured by his conformity with group norms.

Group Character. There are proponents for a "group mind" theory, and, indeed, there is considerable evidence from some studies to indicate that such a phenomenon exists. There has been a feeling from students of Group Dynamics and Gestalt Psychology that a group is more than the sum of its parts. A group's behavior is not just a product of the goals, interests, attitudes, and personality makeup of the individual members; it is also a resultant effect of all these members interacting with one another. The "togetherness" of the behavior of a group of individuals is due largely to the reciprocal reaction in which there is a self-intensification by each member of his own excitement as he finds it also reflected in others.

Another aspect of this phenomenon is observed in military units that have a continuous existence as a group. Although individuals may rotate in and out of the unit, it tends to display a remarkable consistency in group attitudes and behavior over time. Changes in group norms and attitudes can be effected by the leader only with great difficulty and very slowly. This leads one to believe that the consistent behavior of such a group is more than just the product of the interaction of its members at any one time. It tends to retain and demonstrate an inherited residue of attitudes, norms, and behavior patterns developed by the interaction of previous members which dissipate only with time, changed environment, or substantially redirected effort.

This phenomenon of distinguishable group characteristics has considerable significance for the leader who must influence the group. It provides the continuity and predictability of group action that is an important ingredient of solidarity. He should be aware of the nature of these norms and attitudes; using them where appropriate and redirecting them where they are inappropriate.

Influences on the Individual

Roles. A group does not suddenly establish informal roles for its members. As their group interaction continues over time, roles develop based on external situations and the present and past role experiences of individuals. The formal roles, as defined by the organization, are effective for a new member as soon as he joins the group. These formal roles are based on the group authority structure and correspond directly with formal status positions. Formal roles outline the behavioral limitations for the group's system of superior-subordinate structure.

Informal roles are not necessarily authority-oriented and are usually related to individual and group goals, as well as to an equalitarian or peer structure. The informal group goals evolve through the process of interaction and group "oneness" as the group social system assimilates the members.

Influence. The group influences an individual through its structure, norms, roles, and continuous processes of interaction. An individual's participation, however, is related to his position in the group's hierarchy. Those with greater personal influence and authority initiate interaction and are interacted with to a greater degree than those with no authority or little influence. (Zaleznik and Moment, 1964, p. 72.) Although a person of relatively low status and influence participates less than the members of higher status, this is not essential to his obtaining satisfaction through the group. Nor, is it a necessary condition for his acceptance of a group decision. His satisfaction with the group is directly related, however, to his opportunity to express support of that group decision. (Hoffman *et al.*, 1965.) In exchange, the group receives reinforcement by the individual's expression of agreement, and his feelings of satisfaction. Both are reciprocally influenced. (Newcomb *et al.*, 1965.) For, even though the visible effects in the exchange of interaction are heavily one-sided, there is also an exchange of influence.

As previously stated, norms essentially establish a standard of expected behavior to which a person is expected to conform. Similarly, role applies to the expected behavior of a specific person. It is an expression of the behavior expected of him in his position. He is expected to comply with the role as defined by the group; however, a person may comply with the group's demands even though he may not necessarily agree with them. If he merely wants a favorable reaction from certain members, or the group itself, without either accepting or believing in the group norms and his roles, he is merely complying to avoid censure. (Kelman, 1961, pp. 57-8.)

When members of a group disagree with one another, an imbalance occurs. Members will talk to try to eliminate the imbalance. Communication that leads to awareness of the disagreement results in further communication aimed at influencing the deviant attitude. (Newcomb *et al.*, 1965, pp. 129-136.) The amount of communication directed toward the deviant member increases up to a point. If the communication proves fruitless and the deviant behavior continues, the deviate may voluntarily leave the group or be forced to leave it. The more an individual identifies with a group, the more likely he is to be responsive to group pressure toward conformity to group norms. This identification normally is initiated and is strongest at the lowest unit level. Before an individual can genuinely identify with a larger organization, such as a division, he must first be loyal to the small segments of this organization. Therefore, we cannot expect the soldier to have division or battalion spirit unless he first identifies himself with his squad, platoon, and company. This emotional attachment of identification with its attendant loyalties is extremely strong. Studies of combat examples in World War II reveals that group loyalty was one of the most powerful factors responsible for keeping the combat soldier fighting (Stouffer et al., 1949b). In a military organization, it is incumbent upon every link in the chain of command to stress unit identification.

Adaptation

Individuals continually face the problem of adaptation. In an interaction situation, an individual simultaneously must adapt not only to his own need imbalances but also to the demands made on him by his group and the situation (Newcomb et al., 1965, p. 273). The individual is a product of constant adaptation and adjustment. He has a lifetime of experiences and from these experiences, he has developed expectancies for each new situation. His attitudes, for example, can generalize from past experience to new experience. Suppose a soldier has developed a negative attitude toward a particular racial group. This attitude influences his actions in situations where he deals with people of that race. Even though published evidence refutes his attitude, the soldier may still cling to it. This old attitude is satisfying to him. Consequently, it distorts the way he sees, and evaluates, things.

Individual Preferences. Each individual has his own needs, personal preferences, abilities, and attitudes that he has acquired over the years, as well as habits of perception that are peculiar to him. He uses whatever he needs with each new group and insofar as he considers them relevant to a situation. One of the strong factors influencing him at the outset of joining any new group, or facing any new situation, is his preference for consistency and balance (Newcomb et al., 1965, p. 273). In other words, the individual wants to know where he stands, with whom he stands, and he would prefer it to be on familiar ground that he knows and understands. Individuals resist change.

Other persons in the group also have preferences, needs, attitudes, abilities, and their own history of experiences that govern their perceptual habits. Although a group is usually regarded as a unit, this does not mean that it has a mind of its own.

Changing Situations. The environment in which a group and its individual members interact influences group members individually and all of them collectively (Newcomb et al., 1965). An unfamiliar environment can produce unsettling situations. The group then must change its attitudes and adopt new norms consistent with the requirements of the situation. For example, a submarine crew shipwrecked on a hostile shore would have to restructure its norms and members' roles to cope with the altered situation. In time, however, groups adapt themselves to the requirements of a new situation. The submarine crewmen would perform poorly as ground combat soldiers in their initial baptism of fire, but as they remained in the situation, they would improve. With a little experience, they would soon adapt to their ground combat role. The need for survival alone would cause them to re-evaluate their structure, readjust their standards, and adapt to whatever was necessary to handle the over-all environment.

Group Change. The primary effect of situational demands is change. Group adaptation to meet the change in a situation creates change in the group. Everyone must change a little, for the individual cannot become a part of the group and remain purely himself. While at the same time, the group must change a little in order to allow him to join. Once he is a member, the assignment of roles and tasks, the shaping of norms and status patterns, and the processes of interaction continue to change. These changes occur largely as a result of changing situations and the requirements for adaptation on the part of the group and its individual members. They must adapt to each other and each situation. As they do, the group itself changes. Thus, it is an ongoing process of action, reaction, and interaction. Situational changes require adjustment. This creates new changes which, in turn, have to be reaccounted for by a repeating of the cycle. It is a dynamic process; for, in effect, a group is a social system that never stands still.

SUMMARY

Every soldier, sailor, marine, or airman, whether he is a leader or a follower, is an individual within a group and in a particular situation. As an individual, he brings to this situation certain attitudes, frames of reference, and a unique personality, that are the result of past learning. All his past experiences cause him to perceive his social and physical environment in a particular way. These perceptual patterns lead to the arousal of certain needs that motivate him to action. His particular response to a situation is in accordance with the sum total of his unique characteristics as he interacts with his group in their environment. As he interacts with the group, he gains a sense of belonging, acquires importance through his status, and attains goals he could not otherwise obtain. The individual identifies closely with the group and attains a sense of solidarity and "oneness." In turn for these benefits, however, the group demands that the individual comply with group norms, fulfill both formal and informal roles that the group prescribes, and contribute toward attainment of the group goals.

As groups develop, they learn characteristic ways of handling varying situations. The interaction of group members determines the influence, communication, and friendship nets. The patterns of interaction, individual member characteristics, and goal orientation determine the direction and extent of task performance. Analysis of a specific group over a long period of time shows that informal group properties are factors that cannot be disregarded by the formal organization.

Whether an individual becomes an effective leader in any group depends in part on his clear understanding of the group and its members. To gain such an understanding requires a considerable study of the personality of each individual group member with his motives and past experience, the peculiar characteristics of the group as a whole, and the situation in which both exist.

Suggestions for Further Reading

Blau, Peter M., and Scott, Richard W., *Formal Organizations*. San Francisco: Chandler Publishing Co., 1962.

Cartwright, Dorwin, and Zander, Alvin, (eds.) *Group Dynamics*. 2d ed.; New York: Harper & Row Publishers, Inc., 1960.

McGrath, Joseph E., *Social Psychology*, New York: Holt, Rinehart & Winston, Inc., 1964.

Newcomb, Theodore M., Turner, Ralph H., and Converse, Philip E., *Social Psychology*. New York: Holt, Rinehart & Winston, Inc., 1965.

XI

Group Solidarity and *Esprit*

THERE ARE many examples in American military history in which group spirit was one of the deciding factors in combatting overwhelming odds. The group spirit or *esprit* built up in a unit is an important component of its fighting strength. It can provide the *élan* to achieve ultimate victory or the determination to stave off ignominious defeat. The two factors essential to *esprit*—group solidarity and identification—can occur over time or they can result from the crisis of the moment. For instance, a critical situation can occur wherein the group closes ranks to meet the threat of outside forces and is sparked by an incident of self-identification which culminates in valor. The band of American colonists who held Breed's Hill; the group who held out against insuperable odds at the Alamo; and the "Battered Bastards of Bastogne" fought with increased combat power because of their solidarity and identification with each other.

Esprit in a top military unit is like the team spirit in a winning football team. The emphasis is on the outfit not upon the leader or any one man. It is a contagious thing that spreads throughout a unit like the flash of an electrical storm. It can encompass every man in the unit including the most recent arrival. There is a dynamism about *esprit,* for it can become a substance of vitality that fosters faith, loyalty, pride, confidence, unity, fraternity, and even a feeling of invincibility. The feeling of "one-ness" that is born out of group solidarity and *esprit* can be summed up by these words from Stephen Crane:

> He was welded into a common personality which was dominated by a single desire. For some moments he could not flee, no more than a little finger can commit a revolution from a hand. . . . There was a consciousness always of the presence of his comrades about him. He felt the subtle battle brotherhood more potent even than the cause for which they were fighting. It was a mysterious fraternity born of the smoke and danger of death. . . . He suddenly lost concern for himself, and forgot to look at a menacing fate. He became not a man but a member.
>
> (Crane, 1895.)

157

GROUP SOLIDARITY

Being accepted by his fellow man is very important to every individual. He needs to feel that he is a member of a group that he values. When the individual gains this feeling of acceptance from his group, it becomes highly satisfying to him. Like Stephen Crane's soldier, he becomes "not a man but a member". If he fails to gain acceptance, however, he feels lonely and insecure, particularly when under stress and exposed to danger. For example, the combat soldier may have to hit the ground owing to incoming artillery and suddenly he can no longer see anyone else in his squad. He finds himself alone and feels he is facing the entire strength of the enemy by himself. He is not likely to advance in such a situation, and, if the enemy should advance on him, he will probably want to escape as soon and as fast as he can. What he needs is assurance that others are there with him. Not only does he want to see the fellow members of his squad, but also, and probably even more importantly, he wants to hear their voices. What they say isn't important, but the noise and the chatter they make builds confidence. In *Men Against Fire*, S. L. A. Marshall cited the observation that the enemy troops were generally noisy, whereas American troops were trained to be silent, to avoid detection, and not attract hostile fire. This lack of noise and chatter was considered by Marshall to be detrimental to the American troops' confidence and to the feeling that they were part of a team. Hearing a fellow squad member provides psychological support and assures the soldier he is not alone.

Group solidarity is an interpersonal phenomenon involving emotional bonds among men. It is the positive feelings individuals have for their group and for the other individuals in it. The individual knows and likes the other individuals and they support and protect one another. Liking and being liked are important aspects of the group's attractiveness to an individual member. A recent study indicated that liking another and being liked was more important in the respect of group attractiveness than was attitude similarity (Aronson and Worchel, 1966). So it is with subgroups and buddy relationships in the combat units of the army. For, as Roger W. Little found in the Korean Conflict, every soldier had at least one buddy and just as often had more than one. The soldiers, although restricted in their buddy choices by the structure of the organization, chose their buddies largely on the basis of mutual loyalty and reciprocal liking. (Little, 1964.)

Group Solidarity and Unit Effectiveness

Alone, group solidarity is not a substitute for training and skill. Under certain circumstances, however, group solidarity can add to the effectiveness of a trained and skilled unit. It can raise an organization to levels of performance above its previously attained skill, or it can become the difference between two equally skilled units. For group solidarity to influence effectiveness the group task must be one involving teamwork. The greater the teamwork, the greater will be the effect that group solidarity has on group effectiveness. On the other hand, if the task is primarily one involving individual skills with little interaction among the members of the group, then group solidarity may have little if any effect on group performance. R. M. Stogdill of Ohio State University, described group solidarity as an ability of the group to maintain its structure and continue to function under stress (Stogdill, 1959). This is an essential aspect of military organizations, for they must be able to continue to function under the most severe stress. Therefore, in tasks that are highly stressful, group solidarity is extremely important to success, possibly even more important than skill and training. Skill cannot be applied by a group that has already disintegrated.

Because of the great necessity for teamwork in the military, and even more because of the highly stressful nature of combat, the military is probably the most outstanding example of an activity that is highly dependent on group solidarity for success. Group solidarity may be important to the success of an industrial concern, a business office, or a college faculty, but in an Army combat unit, it is fully as essential as training and skill to the success of the unit.

Group solidarity can also have adverse effects on an organization. Roger Little found that solidarity often created a set of norms contrary to the goals of the military organization. This resulted from the fact that the buddy relations were based on mutual risk and the norms were to minimize that risk. A buddy, for example, would not volunteer for an extra tour of combat patrol, for this would mean that his buddy would be expected to volunteer also and share the risk. By his heroics of volunteering and subjecting his buddy to this extra risk, the soldier was deviating from the norm. But, the norms were strong and this would mean social pressure in the form of ridicule, ostracism, and possibly even isolation from the group. No one wanted to be the buddy of an ambitious individual who took unnecessary risks. Consequently, there was a formal group solidarity, but it was based on an informal group goal, which was simply to survive. (Little, 1964, pp. 218-9.)

In an experiment on the disruption and cohesion of groups, John R. P. French reported that the most serious factors leading to the breakdown of organizational integration resulted from differences between subgroups or individuals as to the best course of action to achieve their group goal (French, 1949). This can lead to splitting a group into opposing factions, completely destroying unity until some settlement of the dispute is reached. In democratic groups, these situations usually come out into the open and can be freely discussed. In autocratic groups, disagreements are often covert or buried, leading to friction within the group and little or no commitment to the decided course of action. A similar situation occurs when the members of a group seek different goals, or when parts of a group seek their own goal and disregard the others. This is similar to the commander who is solely interested in his unit's mission, and attempts to achieve it at the expense of the other units in the organization. He thereby seriously disrupts the solidarity of the organization as a whole. When the military commander looks upon the mission as the only goal, while the troops look upon maximum well-being as their primary goal, a schism can occur. This can cut off the formal hierarchy from the lowest ranks. An example of this is expressed in the following excerpt from Stephen Vincent Benét's *John Brown's Body:*

160   TAKING COMMAND

If you take a flat map
And move wooden blocks upon it strategically,
The thing looks well, the blocks behave as they should.
The science of war is moving live men like blocks.
And getting the blocks into place at a fixed moment.
But it takes time to mold your men into blocks
And flat maps turn into country where creeks and gullies
Hamper your wooden squares. They stick in the brush,
They are tired and rest, they straggle after ripe blackberries,
And you cannot lift them up in your hand and move them.

(Benét, 1927, p. 91.)

Group Solidarity and the Individual

When a military unit is preparing for combat, one of the most important problems facing the commander is the necessity to establish strong unit identity and group solidarity. If the leader is able to induce successfully each soldier to identify with the unit and take pride in it, he can go a long way toward arousing in each and every man a strong feeling of "we-ness" (Coleman, 1964, p. 173). This feeling will give the men a better ability to withstand stress and to excel in adversity. A lack of this feeling can have the reverse effect, for it may generate insecurity, and cause individuals to think they are isolated or standing alone. When this happens, confidence in the unit decreases, optimism in the future drops, and the increased levels of anxiety and tension reduce an individual's ability to cope with fear. On the other hand, if the individual soldier feels he is part of a good outfit and he perceives that other soldiers in the unit feel this way too, a group spirit is likely to catch on. A group spirit such as this can spur individuals toward an intensity of action far beyond their normal expectations. The reason for this derives basically from the strength of the norms that a highly cohesive group establishes. Adherence to norms is more strongly valued in solid groups (Thibaut and Kelley, 1959, p. 133). When these norms are aligned with organizational achievement, the individuals often surpass their individual capacity, and the group as a whole may be inclined to tackle the impossible.

One effect of group solidarity is the strong ties to the other members that a single individual develops. This comes out in the form of loyalty and an intense desire "not to let the other guys down." So strong is the effect of this loyalty, that it has been credited as being the single most important factor in enabling soldiers to endure the violence of combat. In a study conducted by Sobel during World War II, the soldiers who suffered eventual breakdowns were found to use five defensive layers that protected them, or at least delayed their breakdown. The battle stress was highly traumatic and was, of course, harder on some than others. After a period of exposure to the stress, such things as "distant ideals," "hatred of the enemy," and "short-term military objectives" tended to wear thin. These defenses were given up progressively. Then, as the battle stress wore on, or got too severe, the person tended to lose pride in himself. This was not just a loss of pride in how he appeared to others, but loss of pride of his self, to himself. Finally, when he had lost all other defenses to protect himself from the stress, he had his buddies. This was his last resort. His loyalty to the group was the last thing to go, for it was sufficiently strong enough that essentially it kept many men from becoming neuropsychiatric casualties. (Sobel, 1949.)

Development of Group Solidarity

Close Association. The first factor in the development of group solidarity is the simple matter of close association among men. An individual cannot develop strong emotional ties to other men without knowing them well. People who grow up in the same neighborhood, go to school together, work together in the same shop, or live together in the same barracks, get to know each other well and, in time, usually develop affective bonds for each other. From their association with these other people whom they know, they gain their major social satisfactions. They go to each other with their problems and help each other in difficulties. All other factors being equal, the longer and more continuous these associations, the stronger will be the bonds. LaPierre cites the test of time in closely associating groups as one of the determinants of group solidarity (LaPierre, 1954, pp. 190-1).

Fergusson provides an example of this close association over time in *The Black Watch and the King's Enemies:*

> The members of an established group tend to evaluate current adversity in terms of their tradition; it trains its incoming members, usually but not always informally, in myths and legends about the group as well as in the rights and obligations of membership. Often the training in the traditions of the group is accomplished without much intent through stories told, perhaps boastfully, about the accomplishments of the group's great men.
>
> (Fergusson, 1950, p. 141.)

Group Purpose. Close association alone is not enough to develop strong bonds among men. An airline passenger may ride the same plane with a group of fellow passengers several times a month and not even get to know them. A common purpose requiring teamwork is necessary to crystallize the interpersonal bonds of the group. If the plane should be forced down in uninhabited territory and the former passengers were faced with the problem of survival, teamwork would be essential to the achievement of this goal. Consequently, strong group solidarity would undoubtedly grow among the members of this group, for they would have to work together for the survival of all. Therefore, group purpose and teamwork are essential factors in the development of group solidarity.

Common Experiences. Common unique experiences give a group a sense of its own history and help to develop solidarity. It is desirable that these experiences are those of success and victory rather than failure or defeat. Success breeds confidence. The more rigorous, difficult, or dangerous the successful common experience, the more it is able to build the solidarity of the group and the respect of its members for each other. It is not absolutely essential, however, that the group be completely successful in a rigorous experience in order for it to build solidarity. Any external threat by itself generates some solidarity, regardless of the action taken. Further, if the members of the group feel that they themselves performed well under the threat, but that the external conditions were too great to overcome, they can still feel pride in their accomplishments. Thus, a team of only mediocre ability may take great pride in a close game in which they lost to a big team of much superior ability. This is a moral victory. At the same time, a unit attacked by a much superior force may take great pride in the fact that it held back the attack for several hours before being forced to withdraw. The important point here seems to be the manner in which the members can rationalize their failure. If they can blame the failure on something external to the group, group solidarity will not suffer.

Competition. Another method used to build solidarity within groups that make up an organization is through competition between the groups. Experimental studies show that competition between groups results in greater solidarity and greater performance than does competition between individuals (Deutsch, 1949). In fact, competition between individuals often leads to a lessening of group bonds. Competition between groups requires that the members of each group subordinate themselves to group success and derive their satisfactions from such success.

In an interesting study on the effects of competition in building group solidarity, A. E. Myers of the Group Effectiveness Research Laboratory, at the University of Illinois, compared rifle teams in various types of competition. Among rifle teams that competed against each other, success was accompanied by an increase in esteem among the members of the team for their teammates, but failure was not accompanied by a loss of esteem. Among teams that merely attempted to achieve or exceed some standard score, it was again found that success was accompanied by an increase in esteem for teammates, but this was less than in the case of success in competition against other teams. When a team firing against a standard score consistently failed, however, this was accompanied by a significant loss in esteem for teammates. (Myers, 1961.) These results tie in with the observations previously mentioned concerning the reasons that a group can give for its failures. When a group loses in a competition against other groups, it can always blame the other groups for being too good for them. But when a group fails to achieve some standard that others can achieve, it cannot blame these other groups, it can only blame itself for the failure.

Competition does not necessarily destroy intragroup co-operation. Groups compete for certain goals and co-operate for other goals. When solidarity exists within the subunits and the subunits see that their goals can best be achieved by co-operating, they will co-operate. Competition usually leads to a healthy respect for the other units, and, out of this respect, a healthy co-operation can grow. The commander, however, must ensure that the competition does not get out of hand and lead to "cutthroat" tactics that increase resentment between the groups. If this sort of practice occurs, he may have to discontinue the use of competition and concentrate on goals requiring co-operation.

Group Solidarity and Interpersonal Communication

Considering all the factors that tend to build up and break down group solidarity, it is somewhat difficult to determine which will be primary in a particular situation. Nevertheless, there does appear to be one overriding factor that is the key to understanding all the others. This is interpersonal communication. Men cannot build up interpersonal bonds unless they know and understand each other, and this requires communication. The passengers on an airline fail to develop solidarity simply because each withdraws into his own little world and does not communicate with the others. All the factors which tend to build up solidarity—associating men together, giving them a common purpose, requiring teamwork in the achievement of their purpose—are all factors which increase the communication among the members of the group. Groups fail to develop solidarity when there is no communication, and groups with established solidarity begin to disintegrate when communication breaks down.

Differences among men interfere with communication, both because people just do not attempt to communicate with those whom they perceive as different, and also because when they do communicate they do not understand each other. They speak from different frames of reference. Yet, when they associate frequently and when the urgency of the goal requires that they do communicate, they find a way. In so doing, they broaden their own frames of reference to include those of the others. They gain an understanding of each other, prejudice breaks down, and group solidarity develops. When disagreements arise concerning what goal to pursue or what course of action to follow to achieve the goal, the only way to resolve these disagreements so as to maintain the solidarity of the group is through adequate communication of all parties with each other. Silence will certainly not solve the problem, but rather will drive the rival groups farther apart.

It can thus be seen that a major job of the commander in building unit solidarity is that of maintaining communication among the members. Further, he must include himself in these communications if he is to be perceived as a member of the group. Otherwise, group solidarity may develop without him.

ESPRIT

Esprit, or *esprit de corps* as the term is sometimes expressed, is not synonymous with group solidarity. *Esprit* is more than group solidarity, for it not only includes solidarity and cohesion, it also necessitates a strong identification with the formal organization. Without this identification, the norms of the group can develop counter to the wishes or goals of the formal organization. Roger Little found this to be true in his study of buddy relationships in front line rifle companies in Korea. Zagona and Zurcher observed a similar effect in their study of groups whose members scored low in dogmatism and who were oriented toward themselves as a group (Zagona and Zurcher, 1964). Among peer groups, this normative behavior, counter to organizational goals and standards, becomes much greater when the organization maintains little or no surveillance over the group (Zander and Curtis, 1965). This study is important to the military leader, for it not only emphasizes the importance of identity with the major unit, but also the importance of the leader's checking his subordinates.

Developing *Esprit* Through Identification

Since *esprit* consists of both group solidarity and identification with the formal organization, it is, therefore, important to examine the means a leader can use to build this identity in his troops. First of all, this identification must be with the unit, the organization, and the institution. The institutions, like the U.S. Army and the U.S. Marine Corps, for example, do a lot for the leader even before he arrives in the organization. They provide a history, heritage, tradition, and offer an opportunity for awards, advancement, recognition, and prestige. These are effective tools to aid the leader in achieving *esprit* in his unit. They are not sufficient by themselves; for *esprit* requires that everyone identify with the unit, not be awed by it.

Individuals identify with something when they find it satisfying to their needs to do so. If an individual finds that a group satisfies his needs for affiliation and status, he will identify with it. The informal group provides many satisfactions of social needs, and it is easy for the soldier to identify with the informal group when it accepts him. The formal group can also provide many satisfactions, both to the individual and the group. If the formal organization fails to provide such satisfactions, the soldier retreats to the security of his informal group with which he closely identifies. *Esprit de corps* will be nonexistent, and response to the formal organization will be at the minimum level. If, however, both the individual and the group perceive the formal organization as a major source of need satisfaction, they will identify strongly with the formal organization and with its goals.

The Formal Organization.   An initial step in the development of identification with the formal organization is that of helping the soldier to perceive his unit as the most important group in his military life. Unity of command and respect for the chain of command enter very strongly into this process. For example, a soldier lives in barracks next to his squad mates, and many of the orders that he receives concerning the way he will maintain his quarters and equipment come from his squad leader. Many also come directly from his platoon sergeant. When he goes to training, his squad is frequently broken up because the company is short on men (off on detail, pass, etc.). He is put in some other squad, or other men are put in his. When he goes on guard, he comes under a squad leader from another platoon; and the other members of his relief are not from his squad. When he goes on K.P. or detail, he again comes under the direction of noncommissioned officers other than his squad leader and works with men who are not in his squad. In such a situation, it is too much to expect this soldier to identify closely with his squad. The only time it really exists for him is when he goes on maneuvers or into combat. Although the above example is somewhat overdrawn, it occurs all too frequently. If the soldier is to perceive the formal organization as the most important group in his military life, it is important that he live, receive his orders, and perform his duties habitually within the framework of that organization. There are considerable administrative difficulties involved in the continual employment of military units as units. But, if the leader desires to build up real identification with the formal organization, this must be accomplished. So, as a technique, the leader must maintain unit integrity in all possible activities, and within all possible tasks. The only way to do this is to insist upon it. The duty roster will sometimes interfere with this, so will fatigue details, guard rosters, and other tasks requiring only a few men at a time. These problems must be overcome, however, for unit integrity is necessary for the development of *esprit*.

Goals. A key factor in building identification with the formal organization is the role that the unit plays in providing concrete and worthwhile goals. The unit can be the catalyst in building solidarity merely because it gives the formal structure real missions to accomplish. When the goal or mission is given to the soldier's group, he may not care about the goal himself, but he does not want his group to look bad or do poorly. When the soldier clearly perceives the mission as not only important to the organization, but also important to "his group," then the pride the individuals have in "their group" works for the leader and helps to achieve the mission. Much of this is a problem of communication. The leader's role is to ensure that the missions and goals are understood and clarified as to their importance. He must ensure that the individuals know their roles in the over-all effort.

Symbols. Symbols are an important means of getting individual soldiers to identify with the formal organization. Groups often adopt symbols on their own when no others exist. Such symbols may be a motto, a name, a battle cry, flags, insignia, a special uniform, and even a mascot. Once such symbols are adopted, newcomers to the group are expected to identify with them as well as with the organization. The wearing of the shoulder patch immediately brands the new man as a member of the organization and helps him feel he has been accepted. Special badges and tabs serve an even more significant means of identification for those units requiring a special skill. When a formal organization adopts such symbols, however, and prescribes that all members of the organization wear the uniform or insignia or pay homage to the other symbols, this does not necessarily ensure that the members of the organization will identify with the symbols and the organization for which they stand. Rather, the reverse appears to be true. When the individual identifies with the organization, then he will identify with the symbols which stand for it.

There is probably no symbol that more surely stands for the organization in the eyes of its members than the leader himself. He is a symbol who can actually cause identification with the formal organization. If he is a man whom the followers respect, is solicitous of their welfare, and brings them success, then they identify with him, and, consequently, with the organization he represents. He can then build *esprit de corps*. But if the followers cannot respect their leader, if he fails to provide for their welfare and bring them success, the followers cannot identify with him or with that part of the formal organization that he represents. He can prevent the growth of *esprit de corps,* or he can, with time, gradually destroy a high level of *esprit* built up in the past. But true *esprit,* once achieved, has marvelous staying power; and it can often survive within the formal organization in spite of the presence of an incompetent formal leader. If the goal of the formal organization is still worthwhile, if there still exist leaders at higher or lower echelons with whom the men can identify, this informal organization will carry on to bring the unit to the accomplishment of its goals. But such *esprit* must first be built, and this is a job that can only be accomplished by competent leadership.

Esprit Through Identification

During World War II while in the Sicilian Campaign, General Omar N. Bradley was confronted by his 9th Infantry Division Commander, Major General Manton S. Eddy, with the problem of finding a colonel to command the 39th Infantry Regiment. According to General Eddy, the 39th had been doing poorly, and was "showing signs of sluggishness." It was just not carrying its load compared to the other regiments. "What we need in the 39th is a character," General Eddy said.

General Bradley sent Colonel Harry A. Flint to the 39th. Shortly after "Paddy" Flint arrived in the 39th, he began showing up in the forward combat areas stripped to the waist (for easy identification), wearing a black scarf, carrying a rifle, and wearing a helmet with "AAA-O" stencilled on both sides. He would snarl at the enemy, and, while single-handedly rolling a cigarette, he would talk to the troops huddled in their foxholes, telling them, "The Krauts couldn't shoot in the last war and they can't shoot in this one." Not many days passed before his officers and men of the 39th began inquiring as to what this AAA-O on his helmet was supposed to mean. "My personal trademark," was his reply. He went on to tell the officers that it meant "Anything, Anytime, Anywhere, Bar Nothing," but a person had to live up to it and mean it. His officers asked, "Can we stencil it on our helmets?" But Paddy Flint was reluctant. He told them that it was a sort of sacred thing to him and he didn't want to see it plastered all over. "If a man means it, he can use it," was Paddy Flint's standard.

Not long thereafter, AAA-O began popping up on other helmets, on jeeps, rifles, howitzers, and soon it was everywhere in the 39th. It became the symbol of the 39th Infantry. It ignited a spark in the troops and gave them an identification unique in the U.S. Army. The spirit that ensued lasted throughout the war and resulted in the 39th becoming one of the fightingest regiments in the European Theater.

Paddy Flint died of a sniper's bullet in Normandy. But his spirit lived on. Even today, the 39th Infantry introduces its new recruits to Paddy Flint, and to the meaning of AAA-O. They wear it everywhere, for he gave them the identity that they so sorely needed. (Bradley, 1951, pp. 152-4.)

SUMMARY

Esprit de corps consists of group solidarity and strong identification with the formal organization. It involves pride in the unit and loyalty to it. It is enthusiasm that the members show for their unit. Group solidarity is the sense of unity that binds a group together and provides the strength to withstand stress. It is largely a product of the reciprocal feelings that the members of a group feel for each other and for their group as a whole. Group solidarity alone is not a substitute for skill and training, but it can add immensely to a skilled group's effectiveness, especially in situations of stress where teamwork is essential. In a ground combat unit, it is fully as important as skill and training.

Factors that assist in the development of group solidarity include close association among the members of the group, a common purpose requiring teamwork among the members, common unique experiences, and competition with other groups. Factors tending to retard or break down group solidarity include unaccepted differences among the members, rapid changeover of membership, disagreements among the members over the best course of action to achieve their goals, and pursuit of different goals by different parts of the organization. The factors that tend to build solidarity may be used to overcome those that break it down. The main requirement is that good communication exist among the members of the group.

To build identification with the formal organization, it is first necessary that the soldier perceive his unit as the most important group in his military life. The habitual employment of military units as units is the major means by which this is accomplished. A key factor in building identification is the provision of clear, worthwhile goals through the formal organizational channels. Symbols such as unit insignia and unit mottoes help the members feel they are accepted members of the organization. But the most important symbol of the formal organization is the leader himself. If the members of the group can identify with him, they can identify with the formal organization, and *esprit de corps* results.

Suggestions for Further Reading

Janowitz, M., *Sociology and the Military Establishment*. Rev. ed.; New York: Russell Sage Foundation, 1965.

Little, Roger W., "Buddy Relations and Combat Performance", in *The New Military*, M. Janowitz (ed.). New York: Russell Sage Foundation, 1964.

Marshall, S. L. A., *Men Against Fire*. New York: William Morrow Co., 1947.

Sayles, L. R., and Strauss, G., *Human Behavior in Organizations*, Englewood Cliffs, N.J.: Prentice-Hall, 1966.

Shils, E. A., and Janowitz, M., "Primary Groups in the German Army", in Broom and Selznick, *Sociology*. New York: Harper & Row, 1963.

XII

Motivation and Morale

ONE CHARACTERISTIC that is common to all successful leaders is the ability to motivate followers to work toward the accomplishment of organizational goals. The subject matter of each chapter in this book relates, in one way or another, to motivation. The adoption of a particular leadership style as discussed in Chapter II is based to a large extent on how effective the style might be in motivating the followers in the situation at hand. The motivation of subordinates is enhanced when the leader is successful in establishing effective communications with them (Chapter V). The next chapter on discipline covers, among other things, the motivational aspects of reward and punishment.

The leader with an understanding of the basic concepts of motivation, a knowledge of motivation theory, and some insight into how these theories can be applied to his own situation is better prepared to fill his leadership role.

THE MOTIVATING SITUATION

The leader is concerned with what will motivate rather than how or why it acts as it does. The promise of promotion is highly sought after by some, while others treat it with indifference or rejection. Public praise is the highest form of reward for some, while for others it is a source of embarrassment.

In order to understand the nature of the motivating situation, it is necessary to understand the relationship between need and incentive. A need is a deficit, while an incentive is that which will satisfy a particular need. The need for food produces a tension of hunger. The incentive that reduces hunger, however, depends to a great extent on a particular individual's past associations with reducing hunger. Thus, snails and spiders might reduce hunger quite well in some areas in the world but would rarely suffice in our own culture.

MOTIVATING NEEDS

There are various ways to classify needs. A simple but significant one is (1) basic physiological or primary needs, and (2) social or acquired needs, called

169

secondary needs. Some of the primary needs are hunger, thirst, sex, sleep, air, and satisfactory temperature. These needs arise out of the basic physiology of life and are important to the survival of the species. They are universal to all people, but they exist in different intensities. In some areas of the world, satisfaction of these needs dominate people's daily activities, while in others they are taken for granted.

Secondary needs are just as real and intense as the primary needs and, may at times, override satisfaction of primary needs. For example, clerical celibacy or dieting can become dominant needs.

Social needs are learned. The need for achievement, for recognition, affiliation, self-esteem, and status are but a few of the acquired or learned needs. Social needs develop in a larger sense from the cultural surroundings, from one's peers, and, most importantly, from the family. Different cultures stress different values. Hence, it is not surprising to find some cultures where the need for achievement, responsibility, competition, and male dominance—all highly prized in our culture—are highly discouraged. Similarly, the need for recognition, aggressiveness, and authority might be greatly influenced by one's peers while growing up. The need for belonging, being one of the gang, can have a profound effect on one's future behavior.

Probably the most important influence on the acquisition of needs is the family group. Like father-like son and chip off the old block, refer to similar values between father and son. The family who places a high value on achievement and competition very likely shares a high need for achievement, recognition, and symbols representing such achievement.

Thus, there are countless differences in what will act as an incentive or motivate different men even in our own culture. It becomes obvious folly to say that all men want to do well because of the promise of time off, or because of a raise in salary, or because of a pat on the back. The value of these incentives depends upon the degree of need in each individual.

Need Hierarchy

Since acquired needs stem from past experiences, it follows then that people differ in the needs which are important to them. It is easy for people to understand behaviors that satisfy needs which they, themselves, respect and with which they are familiar. But it is frequently difficult to understand behavior oriented toward the satisfaction of needs they do not appreciate or which have a different priority than their own. For example, a private may have a higher need to remain one of his group than to seek greater responsibility.

There are many eminent behavioral scientists investigating motivation as a result of need satisfaction. One of these is Abraham H. Maslow who has classified needs in a hierarchy of prepotency.

Physiological Needs. The classification that is the foundation of Maslow's hierarchy is the physiological needs. These are the needs related to the body's attempt to achieve homeostasis. These are considered to be the most prepotent of all of man's needs. It is not until man has satisfied to a reasonable degree these physiological needs for food, water, oxygen, sex, activity, etc., that other, higher needs emerge and influence man's behavior.

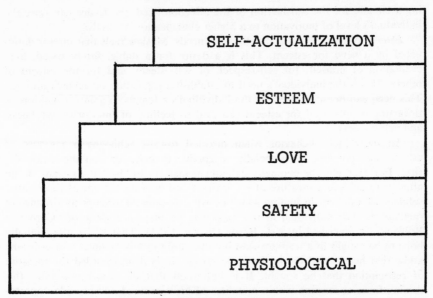

Figure 12.1 Maslow's Hierarchy of Needs

Safety Needs. Once the needs at the physiological level are relatively well gratified, a new classification of needs emerge. When man is no longer truly hungry, his next concern is with protection from bodily harm. Man's behavior is directed toward reducing or eliminating threats which impinge on his personal safety and well being. It is in the satisfaction of these needs that the military leader can be most effective. Men are very strongly motivated to follow a leader whom they feel has their personal interests at heart. Troops feel they can place their confidence in a leader who does not take foolhardy chances with their lives. The military leader in the American army is normally capable of ensuring that the men's basic physiological needs are reasonably well satisfied. By virtue of the very nature of their combat mission, however, their safety needs are threatened. Effective motivation in this case is the result of all the leader's previous association with the men, as well as his current actions that must inspire in his followers confidence that their safety needs will be satisfied by carrying out the mission in the manner directed by the leader.

Love Needs. When man's physical well being is no longer threatened, that is, his physiological and his safety needs are fairly well gratified, a higher classification of needs dominates his behavior. These are the individual's needs for love, affection, and belonging. Inadequate satisfaction of these needs can be the basis for some of the most common cases of maladjustment and psychopathology. These are the needs of the individual both to give and receive affection. The military leader can foster a spirit of togetherness or belonging within the unit. Although this may not completely satisfy the individual's needs for affection, this feeling of group solidarity can help prevent an individual's going absent without leave to obtain satisfaction of his need for love or belonging. By providing a climate for the satisfaction of the affection need, the leader can raise the individual's level of motivation to a higher classification of needs.

Esteem Needs. Next above the love needs, Maslow feels that man is dominated by a need for esteem. This is a desire for a stable, firmly based, high evaluation of himself, for self-respect, or self-esteem, and for the esteem of others. This is the individual's need to establish a reputation or achieve prestige. This need can manifest itself by the individual's attempts to gain recognition. A thwarting of this need for esteem can lead to feelings of inferiority, weakness, and helplessness.

An individual's behavior when directed toward achieving a measure of esteem may not always be socially acceptable or behavior that the leader desires. For example, the company delinquent may try to "beat the system" in an attempt to achieve a measure of recognition and gain the esteem of those other soldiers who delight in finding someone with the guts to attempt to circumvent regulations. The individual in this case may be playing a game of "Cops and Robbers" as described by Eric Berne (Berne, 1964). That is, he may actually hope to be caught in a transgression because, only in this manner, will everyone know that he violated the institutional norm. He is then accorded the measure of recognition that he sought. It is important that the leader recognize this driving force as existing within members of his command and provide opportunities for the satisfaction of individual needs that are more in keeping with the goal of the unit.

Self-Actualization. The pinnacle of Maslow's hierarchy of needs is occupied by the need for self-actualization. This is the classification of needs that can occur when all of the other needs have been reasonably well satisfied. These are the needs for realizing one's own potentialities, for becoming everything that one is capable of becoming. Although expression of this need is found most often in creative artists such as painters, poets, and musicians, it is not necessarily a creative urge. The specific form that these needs take will vary greatly from one person to another. In one person it can take the form of becoming the ideal commander wisely accomplishing his mission with due regard for his troops' welfare; in another it may be expressed athletically, yet another will be driven by this need in his efforts to write the "great novel."

Since this is the highest need in the hierarchy, Maslow feels that people who are satisfied in these needs are basically satisfied people and from them mankind can expect the fullest and healthiest creativity. These are the people whose behavior is motivated by nothing more base than to reach a goal in life for the sheer satisfaction of showing themselves that they were capable of attaining it.

Maslow does not view these as independent steps, each of which must be completed before an individual can progress to a higher level of needs. He suggests that the levels of needs are overlapping and interdependent with each higher need level emerging before the lower needs have been fully satisfied. For illustrative purposes, Maslow estimates that the average person is 85 per cent satisfied in his physiological needs, 70 per cent satisfied in his safety needs, 50 per cent in his belonging needs, 40 per cent in his esteem needs, and 10 per cent in his self-actualization needs (Maslow, 1943).

Cases of extreme deprivation of the basic necessities of life are not the usual problem of the leader. To be sure, a hot meal and dry socks can serve as a very effective reward to battle-weary troops, inspiring them to renewed efforts, but this is an exceptional occasion. In most cases, the military commander's concern is aiding his troops in the satisfaction of their higher needs.

Satisfiers and Dissatisfiers

Research conducted by F. Herzberg (Herzberg et al., 1959) indicates that the factors that influence man's attitude toward his work can be placed in two categories. Rather than visualizing the needs that motivate man's behavior as being arranged in a hierarchy as did Maslow, they feel that there exist two different and distinct continua of variables. One class of variables acts to satisfy the individual's need for self-actualization. These variables are called the satisfiers or motivator variables. The motivator variables are those factors that lead to positive job attitudes and that motivate men to realize their potential. The other class of variables cannot in themselves provide positive motivation, but their improvement can remove impediments to positive job attitudes. This class of variables is referred to as hygiene variables or the dissatisfiers. These are called factors of hygiene because they operate to remove health hazards from the environment of man. They are unidirectional in that, while they cannot in and of themselves promote positive attitudes toward work, they can produce dissatisfaction if they fall below an acceptable level.

Motivator Variables. The motivator variables are such factors as task responsibility, the opportunities for achievement, advancement, and recognition, as well as the satisfying nature of the work itself. A military commander in the exercise of his leadership does have considerable control over the variables that motivate his followers. Many times the leader must have the moral courage to permit his subordinates to make mistakes as they develop in their capacity for achievement. One of the greatest spurs to a subordinate's motivation is for the leader to assign task responsibility to him with only general guidance as to the requirements that he must meet. In contrast to providing specific limiting instructions as to how a task is to be accomplished, an emphasis on the more positive side of these motivator variables can cause the work to be much more intrinsically satisfying to the individual.

For these to continue to be motivators for the individual, the leader must also provide some form of recognition for the individual. Recognition is a basic social motive, and a soldier's performance can be acknowledged in many ways. A very easy, yet quite effective way to acknowledge performance is the simple, but sincere, verbal note of approval, the "pat on the back" indicating that the leader recognizes that the follower has performed well. Most men like to hear their names linked to good efforts and to success of the unit. A leader should go out of his way to let men know he recognizes and appreciates their efforts. To do so costs so little, yet is so very fruitful. For example, public information releases to local or hometown news agencies highlighting promotions, school graduations, and similar events require minimal cost and effort. Yet, they may mean much to the officer or enlisted man cited. This does not imply that one should receive unwarranted publicity or recognition. Men are quick to detect insincere or exaggerated comments. It does mean giving credit where credit is due.

Hygiene Variables. The dissatisfiers or hygiene variables are concerned more with the job environment or context in which the job is performed. Examples of hygiene variables are such things as unit policies, pass and leave schedules, interpersonal relations, supervision, and working conditions. These are similar to the type of factors listed by M. Scott Myers as maintenance needs (Myers, 1964). These are factors that are peripheral to the job. These dissatisfiers can decrease motivation, but according to Herzberg, improvement or elimination of the source of dissatisfaction will not alone spur the soldier on to greater effort. This theory of the dissatisfiers helps to explain why all of the effort in American industry directed toward making the worker happy did not always result in increased productivity. For years, as Myers puts it, emphasis was expensively and erroneously placed on maintenance rather than motivational factors.

For Myers, motivational factors consist of growth, achievement, responsibility, and recognition. In the military, this would include awards and decorations, service medals and badges, proficiency pay, unit recognition, utilized apitudes, goal setting, promotions, responsible assignments, and education.

The leader's job is twofold. He must provide conditions of motivation and satisfy maintenance needs. Conditions of motivation are task-centered; they depend on the leader's skill in planning and organizing work. Ideally, the planning and organizing of work begin at the top, to provide members at each succeeding organizational level with responsibilities. These, in turn, can be subdivided into meaningful portions that challenge capabilities and satisfy aspirations. Matching jobs with people requires a knowledge and control of the task, as well as an understanding of individual aptitudes and aspirations.

In terms of day-to-day behavior patterns, the role of the competent leader in satisfying motivation needs, includes providing each individual with the requisite job information and maintaining high performance expectations. Other contributing factors are encouraging goal setting and the exercise of independent judgment, providing recognition and rewards commensurate with achievements, and maintaining an atmosphere of approval in which failure is a basis for growth rather than recrimination.

Myers describes the maintenance needs as:

Security (fairness, seniority rights, grievance procedure)
Orientation (job instruction, work rules, bulletin boards)
Status (job classification, title, company status)
Social (work groups, coffee groups, organizational parties)
Physical (work layout, job demands, equipment, rest rooms)
Economic (wages and salaries, retirement, hospitalization, paid leave)

The leader's influence in satisfying the security and orientation needs is apparent. Feelings of security are largely influenced by the leader and determine whether the individual will assert himself in a constructive motivation-seeking manner, or will fall back on maintenance-seeking behavior. The satisfaction of orientation needs requires the ability and willingness of leaders to dispense information when requested and meets a need seldom satisfied by handbooks, regulations, or written policies alone. These needs become increasingly important to the soldier's attitude toward his job as the opportunities for meaningful achievement are eliminated and he becomes more sensitized to his environment and finds fault or gripes.

More recent research questions the dichotomous nature of hygiene and motivator variables (Malinovsky and Barry, 1965), (Burke, 1966). It appears that these are not two separate, independent dimensions, but rather that they do tend to interact in their effect on the individual's attitude toward his job. These later studies suggest that blue-collar workers respond to both hygiene and motivator variables, whereas higher level occupational groups respond primarily to the motivator variables. In other words, it is a foolish commander who believes in the old Army dictum: "troops are only happy when they are griping." Even the most dedicated soldiers can have their motivation decreased when their leaders are inadequately prepared to cope with and overcome avoidable frustrations, or when their leaders are negligent in looking after their welfare. The leader must understand and recognize the differences in needs among individuals and treat each person in accordance with his needs.

MORALE

Robert M. Guion defines morale as the extent to which an individual's needs are satisfied and the extent to which the individual sees satisfaction as stemming from his job (Guion, 1961, pp. 59-61). It follows then that a discussion of motivation is closely allied to any discussion of morale. Morale may be further defined as an individual's state of mind, prevailing temper, or spirit. It is dependent upon his attitude toward everything that affects him. Morale, work attitudes, and motivation are all closely interrelated. Morale involves more than external incentives. It is a satisfying internal emotional state built on self-confidence and self-esteem. Effective motivation should foster in the soldier a sense of responsibility, pride in job, confidence, and self-reliance that serve to support the individual's morale.

Evaluation of Morale

If motivation is contingent upon good morale, and if morale involves feelings and attitudes, then a basic question arises as to how the state of morale can be ascertained—that is, can morale be measured or appraised. By its very nature, morale defies exact quantification and numerical measurement. Morale can be evaluated with a fair degree of accuracy, however, by appropriately employing —singly or in combination—several different general methods: attitude survey, study of morale indicators, and over-all subjective evaluation.

Attitude Surveys. Attitude surveys are usually formal in nature, but they can be carried out in an informal manner. In using the latter method, a military commander seeks to learn his subordinates' prevailing attitudes by the use of questioning, observation, and careful listening during his inspections, casual conversations, and informal interviews.

Formal attitude surveys involve the use of carefully prepared questionnaires and formal interviews, both administered to statistically sound samples of the particular military population in which there is special interest. Within the Army establishment, these formal surveys are normally carried out by Department of the Army research agencies that are equipped with both personnel and facilities to conduct and interpret such surveys on a scientific basis. In general, it is not recommended that small unit commanders themselves attempt to structure and conduct any such surveys. Nevertheless, they should avail themselves of the data and the findings that Department of the Army furnishes to the field as a result of its own formal surveys.

Morale Indicators. There are a number of things, the condition and status of which serve as indicators of the state of morale. Some of these are statistical in nature; for example: requests for transfer, non-judicial punishment rates, number of men absent without leave, sick call attendance, venereal rate, self-inflicted wounds, lost property, stragglers, equipment deadline reports, and re-enlistment rates. Others, that are also recommended by Department of the Army include: appearance, personal conduct, standards of military courtesy, personal hygiene, use of recreational facilities, excessive quarreling, harmful or irresponsible rumors, condition of mess and quarters, care of equipment, response to orders and directives, and job proficiency (FM 22-100, 1965).

As Beishline cautions, indicators of morale considered individually and separately seldom are very meaningful. They are better evaluated as a group (Beishline, 1950). Even when viewed as a group, however, these morale indicators—and, in particular, objective statistics—should be interpreted very judiciously, because of the tendency to establish "morale rates." The use of such rates can be dangerous. First, these rates may be established arbitrarily. Also, rates in themselves do not explain causes. Then, too, rates can produce a detrimental effect if and when they are published by higher commanders for emphasis.

Subjective Evaluation. Finally, the commander may employ an over-all subjective evaluation, in which he views morale as a complete and separate entity and bases his evaluation on the assumption that he knows his men sufficiently well to be able to give an over-all estimation of their morale. More often than not the commander uses a combination of these three general methods: conducting informal attitude surveys, taking cognizance of critical morale indicators, and then making an over-all subjective evaluation.

To appraise morale by examining statistical indicators and by ascertaining attitudes is one thing. To determine the bases for these statistics and the causes of these attitudes is something else. In other words, to improve morale, the leader must do more than discover the symptoms. He must learn the causes and deal with them, not with the symptoms. Morale evaluation, then, is merely an aid to improving morale and does not in itself achieve this improvement.

SUMMARY

A leader influences his followers to accomplish a mission in the manner he desires. To do this, he requires a knowledge of human motivation. The satisfaction of human needs sets the stage for motivation. Needs are classified generally into the primary or physiological needs and the secondary or learned needs. Incentives satisfy a particular need and, to a large extent, depend upon what has successfully reduced the need in the past. The learned needs, and the incentives which satisfy them, differ with each individual depending upon the influence of his culture, his peers, and his family environment.

Maslow's theory categorizes human needs into a hierarchy, starting with man's basic physiological needs. When his more basic needs for safety, love, and esteem have been adequately satisfied, his need for self-actualization, to become all that he is capable of becoming, is dominant.

Another classification of needs places the factors that influence an individual's attitudes towards his work on two continua of motivator and hygiene variables. The motivator variables are those that drive a man in his attempts toward self-actualization. The hygiene variables are concerned with the job environment. While not positive, they can serve to impede or block motivation. More recent research indicates that these two variables are not separate and distinct but that they interact.

Motivation is contingent upon good morale; hence, the leader must be able to evaluate, diagnose, and correct causes of poor morale. The leader must be concerned with his subordinates' morale and with motivating them to produce the best performance.

Suggestions for Further Reading

Herzberg, Frederick, Mausner, Bernard, and Snyderman, Barbara B., *The Motivation to Work*. New York: John Wiley & Sons, Inc., 1959.

Maslow, Abraham H., "A Theory of Human Motivation," *Psychological Review*, 1943, 50, pp. 370-396.

McGregor, D. M., "The Human Side of Enterprise." New York: McGraw-Hill, 1960.

Meyers, M. Scott, "Who are Your Motivated Workers," *Harvard Business Review*, 1964, 42, pp. 73-88.

Vroom, Victor H., *Work and Motivation*. New York: John Wiley & Sons, Inc., 1964.

XIII

Discipline

ONE OF THE primary tasks of the military leader is to maintain the discipline of his unit. The factors discussed in the preceding two chapters on Group Solidarity and *Esprit,* and Motivation and Morale are fundamental to helping him maintain discipline. In addition to these, the leader must understand the part that reward and punishment play in developing discipline in individuals and within his unit. Thus, discipline is an attitude that is formed and maintained through reward and punishment, group processes and proper motivation. It is a vital ingredient of that social cement that binds the individuals of a group into a smooth functioning, dependable team. A football team, police force or military organization would be ineffective without the element of discipline. The military version of discipline is "the individual or group attitude that ensures prompt obedience to orders and initiation of appropriate action in the absence of orders. Discipline is a state of mind that produces a readiness for willing and intelligent obedience and appropriate conduct. Discipline within a unit insures stability under stress; it is a prerequisite of predictable performance." (FM 22-100, 1965, p. 27.)

Organizations that are subject to heavy stress and in which members must place substantial reliance on the predictable performance of their fellows are particularly dependent on discipline. The greater the stress and degree of interdependence, the greater is the need for group discipline. Military organizations that must depend upon individuals and small groups to withstand great stress, even the risk of death in the shock of battle, must have a higher degree of discipline. Such discipline does not just happen. It is carefully nurtured both in training and individual conduct on and off duty as a part of the everyday life of the group. To be effective in binding the unit together, discipline must become an almost instinctive reaction of both the individual and his group.

There are numerous indications of the degree of discipline that a unit or an individual possesses. Conduct on and off duty, standards of dress, bearing, cleanliness, and alert response all indicate the state of discipline in the organization. They are outward manifestations of that group solidarity built on *esprit,* morale, and thorough training. They portray those qualities of pride, initiative,

179

self-reliance, self-control, and dependability that assist in creating an effective unit.

DISCIPLINARY PROCESSES

Instilling discipline in a military unit is a complex social process, the principles of which have changed very little through the years. It represents the ultimate product of effective leadership in developing group solidarity, *esprit*, motivation, and skillful performance. Major General John M. Schofield provided a guide in his address to cadets at the United States Military Academy on 11 August, 1879:

> The discipline which makes the soldiers of a free country reliable in battle is not to be gained by harsh or tyrannical treatment. On the contrary, such treatment is far more likely to destroy than to make an army. It is possible to impart instruction and to give commands in such manner and such a tone of voice to inspire in the soldier no feeling but an intense desire to obey, while the opposite manner and tone of voice cannot fail to excite strong resentment and a desire to disobey. The one mode or the other of dealing with subordinates springs from a corresponding spirit in the breast of the commander. He who feels the respect which is due to others cannot fail to inspire in them regard for himself, while he who feels, and hence manifests, disrespect toward others, especially his inferiors, cannot fail to inspire hatred against himself.

As General Schofield implies, the development of discipline involves the entire scope of interaction between the leader and his subordinates. Mutual respect, adherence to ethical standards, fulfillment of expectations, the discharge of individual and group responsibility—all play a part in the process. Nevertheless, the most immediate means by which a leader can influence the discipline of his unit lie in his use of reward and punishment. Contrary to popular belief, punishment is not synonymous with discipline. It is only one of the means by which a leader can influence the motivation of his followers. Reward is an equally powerful motivating factor when properly employed.

In spite of their opposite nature, both reward and punishment are incentives that are used for the same two purposes: to aid learning, and to motivate performance that has already been mastered. As an aid to learning, reward provides a positive reinforcement for proper behavior. As in a race, the prize or reward at the end stimulates movement in the desired direction while fences (punishment) deter the racer from leaving the track. In addition to their reinforcing effect on the performance of the learner, reward and punishment also provide positive stimulation to others in the group who observe the acts that are rewarded and those that are punished. The use of reward and punishment to instill and maintain discipline must be considered as a group process that influences all members of the group even those members not specifically being rewarded or punished.

For greatest over-all effectiveness, a combination of rewards and punishments is necessary. Maximum motivation can be achieved by rewarding those who perform in a conspicuous manner and punishing those who perform in an unsatisfactory manner. For greatest effectiveness in the use of rewards and punishment, however, it is necessary to follow certain basic principles in their application.

REWARDS

Basically a reward consists of something of value that the learner or performer may obtain as a result of his performance. There are a large number of specific rewards that are available to leaders, including verbal approval, training holidays and passes, monetary rewards, trophies, badges, and combat decorations. For the reward to be of value, it must be something that either satisfies a basic motive or can be used to gain some satisfaction. For example, a decoration for valor is of direct value because it increases the status of the recipient. On the other hand, a training holiday has value only in that the time may be used to satisfy some other need, such as rest.

In comparison with punishment, reward has certain advantages. Psychological research indicates that as a general rule, reward results in better learning, both in that it occurs more rapidly and is more lasting (Sarason, 1957). Reward shows specifically what to do by reinforcing exactly that behavior which is to be learned. As a motivational device, it has the advantage of having a positive attraction. If the soldier really wants the reward, he will be willing to expend a great deal of effort to get it. Further, the use of reward usually results in higher morale and a desire to continue to do well in the future.

There are disadvantages inherent in the rewarding process, however. It may foster the use of dishonest methods in order to gain the reward without meeting the required standard of performance. Cheating in school is one example. In this case, the dishonest person is attempting to gain the reward—a passing grade—without meeting the standard of performance, knowing the subject. In the Army the falsification of range scores constitutes another example. Again, the overuse of rewards can take on the aspects of a bribe. "If you reward me, I will do as you ask." This unhealthy situation may well lead to reduced effort when no further rewarding takes place. The concept of periodic reinforcement is particularly applicable here. Psychological studies show that learning is extinguished more slowly if the learner is rewarded only occasionally during the learning process rather than every time he performs satisfactorily (Jenkins and Stanley, 1950). In practical terms, this would seem to indicate that only exceptional behavior should be rewarded consistently. Behavior that just meets the standard deserves only occasional reward.

Promised Reward

The technique of promising a reward for good performance can be an effective means of achieving increased effort on that task. But, it may have little if any effect on performance in the future. If overdone, it can actually result in poor performance in the future when no such promise is made. Before making such a promise, the leader must know that he can deliver. If a promise is made and the performance meets that standard, but the promise cannot be fulfilled, the result is a loss of faith in the leader. His followers will tend to place less faith in his promises. In this respect, it is not even wise to promise to "try to get" a reward for good performance. In spite of the qualifying nature of such statements, they are perceived as actual promises by the subordinates; and the same loss of faith occurs if the reward cannot be obtained. The leader must have a realistic concept of his power to produce on his promises. He undermines his influence whenever he attempts to do more for his men than he can reasonably hope to accomplish (Pelz, 1952).

In order to motivate, a promised reward must be something that is desired by those to whom it is offered. It must represent a worthwhile gain. A promise of tickets to a concert would probably motivate few American soldiers. But, a promise of football tickets might be a popular incentive. A promise of an hour off from training might stir only a few men, while most would try for a day off. The standards of performance to achieve the reward must be clear and known to all. Also, they must be attainable. For example, a reward offered to those who achieve a perfect score on the physical efficiency test will only motivate a very small number of men in an organization, if any at all.

During the actual performance, it is necessary to make a thorough and honest evaluation to determine who deserves the reward. In order to achieve it, the performance must have clearly met the standard; and all who attain the standard must be rewarded. Further, the reward must be all that was promised. To promise a three-day pass but only grant a two-day pass is equivalent to going back on a promise. The leader must be alert to detect dishonest attempts to gain the reward without actually performing up to the standard. There must be no playing of favorites and no backing down on the promised reward. To present an award to someone who clearly does not meet a previously announced standard may motivate the recipient; but it also creates strong resentment from those who know the reward was not earned. This resentment will be compounded if others attain the standard but do not receive the reward.

Unpromised Rewards

It is not necessary to promise a reward before giving one. Good work deserves recognition. When an individual or unit has performed in an exceptional manner, they have earned some reward. The purpose of a reward of this nature is to motivate future good performance both by the person rewarded and by others who observe that he has been rewarded. Actually, the leader has a great deal more flexibility in a reward of this nature. A pat on the back, a word of praise, or an expression of thanks is often an excellent form of reward in a case of this nature; yet, surprisingly, a promise of such a reward may be looked upon as hardly worth striving for. Decorations fall in this category. It is doubtful that more than a tiny fraction of Americans ever fought well in combat simply to earn a decoration, yet, most men deeply appreciate recognition of their acts. Contrary to the situation in which a reward is promised before performance, it is not inappropriate to promise to "try to get" a reward for performance after it has occurred. After a soldier performs an act of valor, it is perfectly proper for his leader to tell him that he is recommending him for the Silver Star. If higher authority eventually decides that the Bronze Star is a more appropriate award, the soldier does not feel that his commander has gone back on his promise.

Except in the case of a private word of thanks or praise, a reward granted after performance must be for performance which is clearly exceptional. Since no previous standards are established, it becomes increasingly necessary that the performance is perceived as clearly deserving of recognition by all who do not achieve the reward. Otherwise, the commander may be accused of playing favorites. Because of the halo effect, there is a tendency to perceive good performance on the part of those men who have performed well in the past, when in fact their current performance is not so deserving.

Presentation of Rewards

As a general rule, when a reward is rendered, it deserves public recognition. In this way, it not only adds to the status of the individual being rewarded, but it also aids in the teaching and motivation of others by showing what behaviors are worthy of reward. Public recognition may be accomplished by presenting the reward at a ceremony, by publishing it in the newspaper or in official orders, or by merely praising the individual in front of the group. The word " public", however, probably requires some clarification. The reward should be public to those who perceive it as worthy. A combat decoration for valor deserves the widest public recognition, but commendations for good work in other fields may prove embarrassing to the individual recipient if public recognition is made before a group that does not appreciate the work. For example, if a rifle company commander should publicly praise his orderly room clerk in front of a company formation, he may find that he has done considerably more harm than good. The combat troops in the company may subject the clerk to considerable ridicule. Yet, if the clerk's work has been clearly deserving of reward, it should at least be so recognized by the commander and the others in the orderly room who can appreciate the reward.

Group rewards build solidarity and *esprit* providing that the group works together as a team to achieve the reward. Group reward is normally more effective than individual awards in competitions between groups. It is interesting to note that competitions of this nature can build solidarity even in groups that do not receive the reward, although there is a danger in group rewards that some members may be singled out as scapegoats if the group fails to achieve the reward.

An example of an activity that may be applicable for group reward would be a squad Army Training Test. The success of the entire group depends on the degree to which each member performs his own duty, as well as on the way they interact in the group performance. Since the group is relatively small, each member knows what the other member is doing. Therefore, there can be some control of individual behavior by the group.

PUNISHMENT

Normally punishment is considered as the diametric opposite of reward. It consists of some unpleasant penalty imposed upon the learner or performer because of behavior that fails to meet the desired standard. Training involves the correction of errors.

Punishment is one method of achieving discipline, because it indicates errors to avoid and provides motivation to avoid them.

In the use of punishment for either learning or motivational purposes, the basic guiding concept is that of justice. There are some serious disadvantages to punishment. If it is to accomplish its purpose and avoid unsatisfactory consequences, the followers must perceive the punishment as basically just. Consequently, the first principle in the administration of punishment is that the standards of punishable behavior are known beforehand. That is, not only should the soldier know what the standard is, but he should also know that behavior that fails to meet the standard will probably be punished. Although, legally, ignorance of the law is no excuse, it certainly is considered unjust by the soldier to be punished for an act that he did not know was wrong.

Behaviors that may be punishable are set forth by law and regulation and in the policies and direct orders of the commander. To ensure that the soldier is aware of those that are set forth by law, the Articles of the Uniform Code of Military Justice are read periodically to all troops. The leader also has a responsibility to bring other regulations and policies to the soldier's attention. This does not necessarily mean that each unit must prepare a detailed set of instructions outlining punishable behaviors. Many standards are learned in basic training, and the soldier should be aware thereafter that a violation of these standards can lead to punishment. For example, the soldier learns in training that a failure to salute may lead to a verbal reprimand. He need not be periodically reminded of this. Nor is it necessary to point out that behavior that is generally socially disapproved, such as fighting, will be punished. In any case wherein there is a possibility that the soldier does not know that a particular act will be punished, however, he should be informed of this fact.

At times, it is appropriate for the leader to promise before a particular performance that those who fail in that performance will be punished. The purpose of such an act is to motivate to a minimum acceptable level, but it will seldom lead to performance much above this minimum level. An example of such a threatened use of punishment might be the warning that all who fail to pass a particular inspection will have to stand a second inspection on Saturday afternoon. Since such a punishment would occur at a specific time during which the soldier may have made previous plans, it is more just to announce this ahead of time than to wait until after the failure occurs. But, the constant use of threat every time a new task arises is an unhealthy device. As a general rule, it is better to establish general standards of punishable behavior and to ensure periodically that these standards are understood. As in the use of rewards, the extent of promised punishment should not exceed the leader's authority. For example, his ability to lead effectively is jeopardized if he threatens to reduce a man in rank and the reducing authority does not concur in the punishment.

When an act occurs that may lead to punishment, it is important that the leader make a thorough and impartial investigation to determine the cause of the individual's failure. Research by the Human Relations Research Office (HumRRO) reports that one characteristic of the effective platoon leader is his ability to differentiate between motivational failures and ability failures (Lange et al., 1958 and 1960). Motivational failures should be punished, but ability failures should not. In other words, if the soldier fails because he simply does not try hard enough or just does not care, the men perceive his punishment as just. But, if he fails because he lacks ability or because of other factors beyond his control, his punishment appears unjust. Thus, some form of investigation into the cause is essential. In the conduct of this investigation, if there is a possibility that the offense may lead to a court-martial, it is important to remember the rights of the accused and to protect these rights from the very beginning.

There is a certain danger in the term disciplinary action because it leads to the thought that discipline is gained solely through the use of punishment. Basically, good discipline is the product of good over-all leadership in an organization. When a commander must resort to a great deal of punishment, this is an indication that discipline has already broken down. The further use of punishment may be the least appropriate method of restoring it.

Because of the basic American values of the freedom of the individual and the rule of law, the exact nature and authorized limits of punishments that a leader may impose are much more closely spelled out by law and regulation than is true of rewards. There are still a very large number and variety of punishments that he can impose. At the least severe level, the failure to achieve a reward is "punishing" to the individual who fails. With increasing severity, punishments range up to verbal disapproval, reprimand, loss of privileges, extra duty, restriction, or reduction in rank. They continue on to those that may only be imposed by court-martial—loss of pay and allowance, confinement, dishonorable discharge, and even death. Although court-martial offenses may occur with any group of soldiers, the small unit commander is primarily interested in those less severe punishments that increase learning and motivate performance.

In comparison with rewards, punishments also have certain advantages. Generally, they are easier to administer in the sense that it is easier to discriminate behaviors that are worthy of punishment than those that are worthy of reward. It is easier to select a punishment that most men would wish to avoid than a reward that most would seek to achieve. It is probably for these reasons that punishment tends to be used more frequently than reward as a motivating device in the Army. Punishment does show behaviors to be avoided, and at times this may be highly important. For example, careless behavior that could lead to a safety violation must be avoided, and punishment can teach avoidance of such acts. Punishment is considered just and necessary when behavior is substantially out of line with expected standards. A failure to punish in such cases may well lead to considerable dissatisfaction on the part of the other members of the group who are complying with the standards. Further, both the potential to administer and the occasional use of some form of punishment is often necessary if the unit is to function at all. Otherwise, some persons may easily divert the group from the task.

Punishment does, however, have some serious inherent disadvantages. It is a poor learning technique in that it is based on fear, and the emotion may well interfere with learning. Although it shows what not to do, it does not show what to do. Thus, it is a highly inefficient method of learning because mistakes of a completely different nature may still occur after punishment. Many will search for loopholes—and find them—so that the leader finds himself constantly refining his rules until the discriminations become so minute that no one can understand them. In some cases punishment backfires, resulting in a stereotyped repetition of the same error. This occurs either because the anxiety associated with the punishment prevents logical thinking, or because the punishment has angered the recipient to the extent that he stubbornly refuses to comply.

Because of its unpleasant nature, punishment can lead to a dislike of everything connected with it, to include both the activity and the punishing person. For example, a soldier punished for some action taking place on the firing range may grow to dislike all aspects of weapons firing. He may actively seek to avoid future firing and make little effort to do well on the range. The punishing person is usually resented, even when the punishment is just. This resentment may lead to derogatory remarks about the leader and possibly to displaced aggression upon some innocent party. In a unit that leans heavily on punishment, there is often much bickering and fighting among members, which destroys *esprit*. Finally, punishment is somewhat unpleasant for the leader to administer. In spite of its unpleasantness and its possible bad effects, the leader should not hesitate to punish when the situation calls for it. If he is wise and just in his use of punishment, he can avoid many of the disadvantages of this form of motivation.

Rendering Punishment

In punishing offenses the leader must take into consideration the effect of the punishment on the offender, as well as on the group as a whole. Its purpose is threefold—to prevent a repetition of the offense by the offender, to deter a similar offense by another individual, and to maintain group standards of discipline.

Any punishment must, of course, be within the authority of the leader to administer. It should be appropriate to the offense and to the individual being punished. Although the general rule is that the commander should be consistent in his punishment, there are factors that militate against the assignment of the exact same penalty every time the same offense is committed. For one thing, the standards upon which punishment is based shift upward as the soldier becomes better trained. For example, the soldier who fails to salute during his first few days in basic training probably receives a correction. But, if he has been in the service for several months and still fails to salute, he deserves more severe punishment. The number of the soldier's previous offenses has an effect on the severity of the punishment meted out by the commander. The commander also considers extenuating circumstances or matters in mitigation in deciding on the exact punishment. Basically, he must be consistent in that all failures to meet the required standards are noted, investigated, and some action taken to correct them. Whether this action involves mere correction, retraining, or some degree of punishment, are all matters which depend on the facts uncovered in the investigation.

If punishment is to be of any value, it must be informative. The soldier punished must know what he is being punished for so he will know what to avoid in the future. Punishment in the form of censure of the individual is normally administered in private so as to avoid embarrassing the soldier in front of others. It may on occasions be necessary to make a public on-the-spot correction. This is embarrassing and thus a punishment in the eyes of the soldier. Also, the announcement of other punishments to the individual is usually private. Even punishment in private aids learning on the part of others. Troops usually know when a soldier commits an offense that results in his being called into the commander's presence. Further, when the punishment involves more than mere reprimand, the serving of the punishment is public.

It is especially important that the leader administers punishment with dignity and that he respects the dignity of the soldier. The leader must avoid displays of anger or personal animosity toward the punished person. He should convey the impression that the soldier is being punished because of improper behavior and not because the soldier is basically bad. The soldier should leave the interview with the impression that he can, and is expected to, perform better in the future.

One of the hardest things for a leader to learn and practice is that when a man has undergone punishment, he then becomes a member in good standing in the organization. One may have lingering or lasting doubts as to the man's judgment or attitude, but the leader must scrupulously avoid further penalty for an atoned offense. Other members of the organization perceiving any extension of a punishment may become incensed and resentful, even to the point of condoning or minimizing the offense that led to the punishment.

As a general rule, punishment should be meted out to specific violators rather than the entire group. It can be extremely discouraging to a soldier to strive hard personally but still get punished because someone else did not. Such a situation is equivalent to punishing a man for an ability failure. Although adequately motivated, he is punished because of his inability to control the behavior of the others in the group. Thus, unless rarely used, group punishment may lead to a "what's-the-use" attitude on the part of the initially motivated soldier. There are times, however, when group punishment may be in order to increase the sense of responsibility among group members for each other's behavior.

The authors of *The American Soldier* studies, noting the strong American tradition of team sports, wondered that the Army used group reward so seldom as a motivating device during World War II. They noted also that very little experimental research had been done in the areas of both group reward and group punishment. Based on the results of several questionnaires administered to Army samples, they were able to draw up certain conditions that appear necessary for either group reward or group punishment to be effective motivating devices. Two key points are particularly applicable to both group reward and group punishment. These are: the men must know that all members of the group will win the reward or receive the punishment, and the group must be able to identify the potential violators and control their behavior (Stouffer *et al.*, 1949a).

A barracks inspection may be an appropriate situation for group punishment. Of course, it is necessary to announce ahead of time that the whole barracks will be restricted or receive some other punishment if it fails to pass. In this case, definite group pressure can be placed upon those individuals who do not take action to prepare for the inspection. The delinquency report rate of an organization is an example of a situation that would not be appropriate for either group reward or group punishment. The men have little if any control over the off-duty behavior of the other men in the group. This illustrates the point that group rewards and punishments are most effective in accomplishing their purposes of learning, motivation, and group solidarity when they are based on duty performances rather than any off-duty activity. *Esprit*, expressed in group norms and group sanctions, can often act to influence off-duty activity. This is a manifestation of the interaction between discipline and *esprit*.

SUMMARY

The maintenance of discipline is a primary task of a leader. Developing discipline is a complex social process that involves all levels of interaction between the leader and his subordinates. Discipline as a vital element of group solidarity in military units is closely related to *esprit,* morale, and motivation. The most direct means a leader has to influence motivation and discipline is the use of reward and punishment.

A military leader has exceptional reward and punishment powers granted him by law. These he uses to aid his men's learning, to motivate their performance, and to maintain discipline in his unit. Reward results in better learning, higher motivation, and higher morale, but may lead to dishonest practices. It may be perceived as a bribe if overdone. Punishment shows what not to do. It is deemed just when the punished behavior is considerably below the standard. Punishment is a poor learning technique because it is negative. It is inefficient and does not show what to do. It may lead to stereotyped behavior, a search for loopholes, and a dislike for the punished activity. A combination of reward and punishment generally produces best results.

In promising rewards in order to motivate performance, the leader must be certain that he can deliver on his promise. The reward must be something that the soldier desires to achieve. The standards of performance to achieve it must be clear, attainable, and known to all. Rewards need not be promised beforehand; but, if the performance is outstanding, it should be rewarded. In general, a reward should be given public recognition before those who can appreciate it.

A guiding concept in the administration of punishment is that it be perceived as basically just by the group. Consequently, the soldier must know the standard of punishable behavior. A thorough and impartial investigation of any failure is necessary to discriminate failures that are due to a lack of ability and those that are due to a lack of motivation. In general, punishment should only be given in cases of a motivational failure.

Group rewards are generally appropriate and serve to build group solidarity. Group punishment is generally a poor policy, but may be appropriate at times. In either case, the group must know that all will receive the reward or punishment; and they must be able to identify potential violators and to control their behavior.

Suggestions for Further Reading

Department of the Army Field Manual 22-100, *Military Leadership*. Washington: Government Printing Office, 1965.

Sayles, Leonard R., and Strauss, George, *Human Behavior in Organizations*. Englewood Cliffs, N.J.: Prentice-Hall, 1966.

Secord, Paul F., and Backman, Carl W., *Social Psychology*. New York: McGraw-Hill, 1964.

XIV

Senior-Subordinate
Relations

THE HISTORY of civilization is replete with examples of obstacles to progress created by man's inability to develop and maintain a successful working relationship with his fellow men. In a leadership situation, the relationship between the senior and subordinate may determine whether a mission succeeds or fails. Mission accomplishment depends upon team performance. A winning team requires successful interaction among its members. Any interaction breakdown weakens the group and failure may result. Success serves the mutual interests of the group and the individual participants. If they succeed, they can expect to be rewarded. Therefore, the members of a team work co-operatively so their combined efforts will be productive.

Emerging from this team concept is the fact that a task-oriented group contains a leader and followers whose interaction becomes a senior-subordinate relationship. Whether the group is business, civic, religious, military or otherwise, the leader seeks to influence the actions of his subordinates. How successful the leader is depends upon the state of the interpersonal relations he shares with the members of the group. In point of fact, these senior-subordinate relations provide the atmosphere and constitute the medium for the exercise of his leadership. If the relationship is unsatisfactory, the leader creates unnecessary problems and will have difficulty achieving his goals.

HUMAN RELATIONS

By definition, senior-subordinate relations means an interaction between people, an interaction whose vitality depends upon understanding people. Everyone considers himself at least a potentially successful practitioner of getting along with people, but the hard facts of life demonstrate how frequently failure rather than success, occurs in this area.

From an impersonal point of view, human relations is concerned with successfully integrating the manpower resource into an effectively operating system. While this viewpoint is satisfactory in examining the purely operational system, it may underestimate another facet. The leader also must have frequent

191

contact with the people in the system and they will not tolerate impersonal treatment for long without some negative counter-action to the leader or the system.

A sensitivity to human relations should engender an appreciation of human dignity. This is the recognition that each person has the right to seek his own personal fulfillment in life and to be treated with respect as an individual. This view of the sanctity of the individual is a cherished American inheritance.

On the other hand, it is all too easy for a leader to exhibit a lack of respect for an individual through his rude or inconsiderate behavior. Some leaders fail to display an appreciation of human dignity because they erroneously associate impoliteness with manliness and forcefulness. A very few apparently believe that their subordinates expect them to be cold and impersonal. One common but contemptible expression of rudeness is the use of profanity. Profanity is not a mark of manliness or ability. Even men who use it themselves resent its being directed toward them. The soldier expects his leaders to be courageous, but not coarse; manly, but not mean; decisive, but not derisive; plain-spoken, but not profane.

Few organizational operations are performed simply to satisfy or accommodate the dignity of individuals. Nor should an organization be expected to solve everyone's personal problems. But, the sensible leader recognizes that human concerns must be taken into account in molding an effective team.

An organization's resource of people constitutes an aggregate of individuals brought together to accomplish some task. They differ due to factors in their heredity, maturation process, and environment. They develop different hopes and ambitions. They have different backgrounds and experiences. They respond to events in the world around them in an infinite number of ways. These things account for their wide range of behaviors. Some of the behaviors work in concert with the leader's goals, but sometimes they are in opposition.

An individual who is full of anxiety and frustration; who has personal problems, real or imagined, cannot do justice to his job. The leader must be prepared to recognize the telltale signs of discontent and act to relieve or correct it. Therefore, the leader who fosters good human relations, who tries to understand his followers and their significance to an effective organization, is more likely to be effective himself than is a leader who ignores the individuality of his subordinates.

Human relations suggest another corollary: mutual trust and understanding in the senior-subordinate relationship. The relationship thrives on trust and confidence. Suspicion can wreck it. It is incumbent upon the senior to understand and respect his subordinates. But this is not enough. Unless the subordinates respect the senior, trust him, and understand his intentions and efforts, the senior-subordinate relationship suffers. This relationship is bilateral, not unilateral. It is obvious that subordinates will have little respect for the senior and will place little trust in him if he fails to set the proper example in his performance of duty and in his personal conduct.

The application of human relation techniques requires skill and sensitivity. The leader can be successful, however, if he keeps one simple truth in mind:

people are naturally more happy and will work better if they think their superior is genuinely interested in them as individuals, and will look out for their welfare. This basic fact is well documented by the Hawthorne Studies (Roethlisberger and Dickson, 1956). Hence, one of the principal responsibilities of a military leader is to look out for the welfare of his men.

In studies made during World War II an attempt was made to determine the general attitudes of enlisted men toward their leaders. Questionnaires were distributed to U.S. soldiers all over the world. In this survey, about three-fifths of the men in one theater appended written comments to the questionnaire. Only one out of six criticisms dealt with incompetence. "The overwhelming majority of the criticisms dealt with special privileges of officers, their concern for their own prerogatives and welfare, and their indifference to the deprivations of enlisted men" (Stouffer et al., 1949a, p. 369).

The leader must perform some very careful introspection of himself. He must know his own strengths and weaknesses. He cannot permit personal problems and aggravations to interfere with the relationship he has with his people. He must resist the temptations for personal ambition and personal comfort at the expense of his people and organization. Subordinates expect normalcy and stability of action.

SOCIAL DISTANCE

Probably the deepest conflicts between the existing American culture and the military subculture lie in the areas of the visible class distinction between senior or subordinate and the corrective and punitive powers with which the senior is vested. These military "facts of life" seem to be directly contradictory to the basic American tenets of the equality of man. This conflict becomes particularly acute for the newly appointed leader. To him the conflict takes the form of a question, "How familiar should I be with my subordinates?" While familiarity may breed contempt, a leader can also become too distant from his subordinates.

What is involved in this apparent dilemma is the concept of social distance—a concept that is often referred to and discussed but without being accurately defined. Social distance can be viewed in terms of the intimacy, or the closeness, of association between individuals occupying positions at different hierarchial levels in the organization structure. In this case, "organization" is used in its generic sense, to include any type and size of military organization (e.g., squad, platoon, battery, battalion, corps, etc.), as well as the military viewed as a broad organization with hierarchy based on military rank.

Because of the complexity of the factors involved (e.g., the personality of the senior, the personality of the subordinates, the type of organization, and the nature of the situation), it is impractical to establish a hard, fast rule; however, two meaningful criteria are appropriate. They evolve from the basic purpose of good senior-subordinate relations, namely, to promote and facilitate the attainment of organization objectives and not merely to make men happy. The first criterion is the objectivity with which the senior can deal with his subordinates in evaluating their performance, making decisions regarding them, and issuing orders affecting them. The second criterion is the senior's ability to maintain effective contact with his subordinates. Without adequate contact, there can be little positive influence exerted and, hence, no strong leadership exercised. The leader must take into account these two criteria and maintain a social distance that keeps him in effective contact with his subordinates and yet permits him to maintain objectivity in dealing with these same subordinates.

F. E. Fiedler and his associates have studied basketball teams, surveying parties, open-hearth steel shops, bomber crews, tank crews, and general managers of business corporations. In summing up the results of these studies, they suggest that the main danger of overfamiliarity between superior and subordinate is not that it will breed contempt in the subordinate for the leader, but rather that it will break down the leader's objectivity in dealing with his subordinates (Fiedler, 1958).

The following guidelines should help the senior in establishing proper distance with his subordinates. He should not meddle unnecessarily in the affairs of subordinates. When they can, he should allow them to solve their problems, but be willing to help them if they cannot. The leader should know his subordinates sufficiently well to be able to evaluate them objectively, to praise them when they deserve it; but to criticize, correct, or punish them when they have not performed in accordance with their capabilities.

OFFICER-ENLISTED RELATIONS

Frederick the Great's classic instructions to his generals in 1747 contains this passage:

> The commander should practice kindness and severity, should appear friendly to the soldier, speak to them on the march, visit them while they are cooking, and alleviate their needs if they have any . . . they should not be treated in an overbearing manner.
>
> (Frederick the Great, 1951, p. 11.)

The reputation of the disciplined armies of Prussia is history, but, like Frederick the Great, successful leaders recognize that their leadership is directly dependent upon having someone to lead, to respond. The leader who has lost touch with his subordinates is left with only authority.

For the junior officer, officer-enlisted social distance is a critical subject. Because of his position in the organization, he has daily contact with enlisted personnel. It is at this level that the young officer develops his military expectations and experience. In turn, it is generally through the junior officer that the enlisted ranks gain their impression of the "brass."

Military rank is ascribed to the individual irrespective of his affiliation with any specific military organization. Thus, a captain who is a military chaplain is a senior or superior officer to all enlisted men just as is a captain in the infantry.

Noncommissioned Officer

Structurally, military organizations provide for an important intermediary between the officer and the private in the form of noncommissioned officers. These noncommissioned officers have demonstrated their professional competence as soldiers in progressive positions of authority. They are the "backbone" of the military establishment. In this role, the noncommissioned officer often becomes the catalyst for good senior-subordinate relations at all levels of the military hierarchy.

Both the officer and the noncommissioned officer have significant contributions to make to their relationship. Together, they can develop a mutually satisfying partnership and one advantageous to their common concern—their unit. This mutual dependence also helps answer problems raised by succession. Shortages of personnel in peacetime and casualties in combat often force an officer to operate with fewer noncommissioned officers than usual or places the noncommissioned officer in the position of commanding a unit without an officer. When officers and noncommissioned officers seek every opportunity to learn from and work with each other, they can confidently assume each other's responsibilities in an emergency.

Recognition of Potential Contribution

There are many factors that enter into the determination of why one individual is the senior and another the subordinate in any organization: personal desires, willingness to accept certain responsibilities, and general leadership ability—to mention a few. But this difference in organizational status represents a difference in position in the formal organization, not necessarily a difference in intellectual ability or general individual worth. Inherent in the higher hierarchial position is greater responsibility, but not greater intellectual ability. No one individual has a "patent on brains."

The subordinate can think, and he has knowledge and ideas—especially about his own job. The wise senior recognizes this fact, respects the subordinate's ideas and abilities, and takes full advantage of this knowledge and these ideas. He also realizes that respecting, accepting, and even inviting the ideas of subordinates, does not relieve him of his responsibility, nor deprive him of his right, to make decisions.

ASSUMPTION OF COMMAND

The initial impression that the leader makes can be a lasting one. He creates the environment for future actions of the unit, and he naturally desires that it be a good one. This occurs each time he assumes a new command, and, each time, different group dynamic and situational factors interact with his personality.

Some of the techniques of meeting with a new unit are worthy of consideration. Initially, the commander should arrange for the unit to be assembled in order that he may have an opportunity to talk with them. They are naturally interested in seeing him and knowing his policies. In this talk it is a good idea for the commander to take appropriate cognizance of the previous achievements and accomplishments of the unit and to express the pride and opportunity that this new command affords him. It is also well for him to chart for the unit his estimate of the missions and the specific tasks which lie ahead. He should avoid sweeping generalities that may be difficult to live up to or enforce subsequently.

In analyzing the command, the leader should make as complete and comprehensive an evaluation of the unit as is possible. In attempting to feel "the pulse" of the organization, he should check with members of the unit staff who have been in a position to officially observe and evaluate the organization. In assuming command, a leader will find that many people are willing to advise. Little reliance can be placed on informal talk by irresponsible individuals who know little about the organization or the factors for valid evaluation. While accepting information and evaluations from the former commander, the new commander must be cautious lest he pick up any biases that he may have. In other words, the new commander should listen, observe, read, and then make his own evaluation.

The new commander will have ample time and opportunity to affect the complexion and to influence the action of his organization without trying to make his mark upon the organization through arbitrary changes. Even some changes that at first seem essential may later prove unnecessary after a careful evaluation of pertinent factors. There may be times when a new commander must make immediate, and perhaps, drastic changes. But even then, his changes should be based on as thorough and as sound an appraisal as practical. His general guidance in this should be to make changes only when the requirement for change has been established as a result of his careful, thorough, and valid evaluation of his organization itself and the salient factors affecting his organization.

An important point for the new commander is to give special attention to the members of the chain of command—learn their names, become familiar with their jobs. The potential of these key individuals should be evaluated both for fulfillment of their present job and for future positions of greater responsibility. The leader should know, as a minimum, the individuals two echelons below him. The platoon leader should know well all the men in the platoon as early as possible. Even the company commander should attempt to know all the men in the entire company.

Immediate Senior

When an individual assumes command, he naturally and rightfully is interested in his relationships with his seniors. The policies of his immediate senior as well as the latter's personality have a bearing upon the command. The new arrival must become conversant with the policies of his commander and know how they apply to the unit and its operations. He should obtain the memorandums, training references, and other publications of the higher headquarters so that he knows what is policy and SOP for the unit. He should also attempt to learn as much as possible about the personality of his superior. He can readily obtain this from contemporaries and acquaintances who know the superior. One learns these idiosyncrasies in order to avoid any mistakes through lack of knowledge. This is not meant to imply that "bootlicking" or "apple polishing" is encouraged—on the contrary, a trusted subordinate status is one that is earned through display of ability.

The new commander should—as should any subordinate—treat prudently the comments that others make about his own new commander and other senior officers. There is a danger of forming a biased picture of the new commander before getting to know him. In particular, he should be careful of the comments made by disgruntled subordinates. No one is perfect, and sometimes things which are viewed by subordinates as shortcomings may well be seen by higher authority as commendable, and vice versa.

Initial Assignment

The young officer joining his first unit is naturally full of enthusiasm to assume his first command assignment. This enthusiasm is something that has been nurtured throughout the period of his pre-commissioned training. Yet, with all this enthusiasm and drive, there is a certain feeling of insecurity that might cloud his thoughts. This results from the feeling of undergoing a new experience—the responsibility of command and contact with enlisted personnel from a command position. This is a natural but uneasy sensation that everyone experiences to some degree. The solution for the newly commissioned officer is to realize its normalcy. This is readily accomplished by reflecting for a moment on the training and experience he has received prior to receipt of a commission. In this training, he has actually done many of the things that an officer is required to do without, however, acting under full responsibilities of command. His actions have been observed and evaluated, and his supervisors determined that he had the potential to be an officer. Paricularly important is the candidate's capability of directing and working with people. In addition, the tactical and technical instruction that he has received has developed his professional competence. In short, he should consider his potential and training, realize that an insecure feeling is normal and experienced by everyone, and determine that he will do the best job possible.

Subsequent Commands

The discussion about initial assumption of command applies as well to subsequent command assignments. Naturally, with years of experience, the feeling of insecurity vanishes. With each new and different type assignment, however, a certain feeling of apprehension reappears. This quickly subsides, though, as the leader undertakes his individual preparation for the assignment.

Group and situational factors may alter the approach used by the leader toward his command assignment. In combat, minimum opportunity exists for getting to meet and know the men of the unit before mission-type operations are undertaken. Here the process for assuming command is greatly accelerated and the responsibilities of the leader are increased—he has to establish his position of leadership in critical situations. As little opportunity may exist for a timely evaluation, hastily formed opinions will have to be made. This means greater reliance will be placed upon evaluations of others who have been in a position to observe. It also means the commander has a more pressing need to "know his stuff" so that he may earn his position of leadership and accomplish his mission.

This in no way relieves the commander of his responsibilities for announcement of policy or use of his chain of command.

Another situation that may occur is one in which a new commander is assigned to "clean up" a unit that is considered in bad shape. Normally, specific instructions are given to direct the efforts toward certain areas. Also, in this instance, time for improvement is reduced. In this circumstance, great reliance is placed upon guidance received from the higher commander and on available reports to assist in the evaluation. The problem requires action and quick results.

With each year of experience, the individual develops certain ideas toward job performance. These act as guides for operations, and he naturally clings to these methods which he knows work; however, they can be disadvantageous because they may lead to inflexibility. This "resistance to change" is a problem for older men of experience. Leaders must be able to retain objectivity in command and to recognize the abilities of performance and planning in others. It is well occasionally for the leader to reflect upon his job and his methods, particularly in assuming a command assignment some years after performance in a lower echelon of a similar command.

SUMMARY

Both the integrated concept of leadership and the functional definition of leadership (that leadership is the process of influencing human behavior so as to accomplish a mission in the manner desired by the leader) support the contention that senior-subordinate relations are logically the crux of any leadership situation.

The senior-subordinate relationship is based on the formal organization structure—that is, the relative positioning of individuals in the organization because of organizational responsibility and authority. In any organization, regardless of its nature or size, good senior-subordinate relations depend upon an understanding of human relations, an appreciation of individual dignity, and the existence of mutual respect, and understanding.

Because of the senior's responsibility for accomplishing the mission and the realization that this accomplishment of the mission is dependent upon the proficient performance of his subordinates, it is incumbent upon the senior to establish effective contact with his subordinates while remaining objective in his dealings with them. In other words, the senior must maintain a social distance that satisfies the two criteria of objectivity and effective contact.

In his relations with subordinates, the leader must realize that a difference in organizational position does not in itself represent a difference in intellectual ability or general individual worth. The individual soldier may have some very valuable ideas concerning his job and the military. The organizational status of the soldier in no way makes his needs, desires, feelings, and human dignity any less important than the leader's.

Of special concern to the commissioned officer is his relationship with the noncommissioned officers. The noncommissioned officer should be able to shoulder appropriate responsibilities, but to do this he needs commensurate authority and deserves proper prestige.

One of the most critical situations involving senior-subordinate relations is the assumption of command, because the relationship that is formed at this time largely determines the relationship that will exist later between the new commander and the subordinates. In all aspects of command assumption, careful and accurate initial evaluations by the new commander are required. The commander should guard against unfounded and inaccurate initial evaluations, since these can greatly undermine senior-subordinate relations.

Without depreciating individual ability, technical know-how, and certain nonpersonal factors, the effective accomplishment of any organization's mission is contingent upon good senior-subordinate relations in the organization.

Suggestions for Further Reading

Stouffer, S. A., *et al., The American Soldier: Adjustment During Army Life,* Vol. I. Princeton, N.J.: Princeton University Press, 1949.

Drucker, Peter F., *The New Society.* New York: Harper & Row, Publishers, 1962.

Wolf, William B., *The Management of Personnel,* San Francisco: Wadsworth Publishing Co., 1961.

Van Dersal, William R., *The Successful Supervisor in Government and Business.* New York: Harper & Bros., 1962.

XV

Counseling

EVERY LEADER is responsible for accomplishing his mission and providing for the welfare of his men. Perhaps not immediately apparent is the part that counseling plays in the accomplishment of these two tasks. The term "counseling" involves considerable semantic risk. First, a problem exists in distinguishing between counseling and psychotherapy (Farnsworth, 1966, pp. 79-80). Second, there are many definitions of "counseling." These definitions may be very general, or they may be quite specific, tied to and conceivably biased by certain counseling schools and theories. In this chapter, counseling is defined as the assistance the leader gives his men to help them adjust to the problems they encounter.

In doing his day-to-day job, the leader is concerned with both performance counseling and personal problem counseling. Performance appraisal or evaluation was discussed in Chapter IV. This chapter will deal with the methods and principles applied by a leader to assist an individual to solve personal problems or to improve his performance. Specifically involved are those cases in which the individual's performance is inadequate because of motivational, attitudinal, or emotional problems rather than simply a lack of skills or knowledge.

The leader as a counselor must draw on virtually all of the material presented in other chapters of this book. Of particular importance is the material on interpersonal communication, motivation and morale, and senior-subordinate relations.

THEORETICAL APPROACHES TO COUNSELING

There are many counseling theories. To provide the leader with a brief theoretical background, three broad classifications of theoretical approaches will be discussed: the directive, the nondirective, and the eclectic or mixed approach. The explanation will be brief and, to a degree, oversimplified. The approaches are not sharply differentiated. They overlap in several areas, and many professional counselors feel that, as knowledge and experience are gained in the field, the various philosophical and theoretical issues become blurred.

201

The Directive Approach

This is a rational approach to counseling where the counselor, through his experience and resources, helps a man solve his problems through rational or logical analysis. The term "directive" could be a misnomer in that the counselor does not assume an authoritarian judgmental attitude nor does he dictate solutions or actions. The practical use of the directive technique places heavy demands on the experience, knowledge, and objectivity of the counselor. In essence the directive approach could be looked upon as a short cut or economical approach to problem-solving. The counselor is a specialist possessing the necessary skills to separate the wheat from the chaff and to offer courses of action leading to problem solutions. The counselor, even in this directive approach, attempts to leave the decisions to his counselee, but he is much more direct in his guidance than is the nondirective counselor who will be discussed later. The directive counselor is definitely concerned with value systems. He attempts to influence the counselee regarding acceptable social behavior, outlooks, and other behavior patterns.

In summary, the directive counselor through his training and experience helps the counselee make a rational analysis of the problem situation. He does offer courses of action; he does help evaluate; he does attempt to influence, *but* his primary purpose is to attempt to structure the situation, leaving the final decision to the counselee.

The Nondirective Approach

The nondirective approach to counseling is also called the client-centered approach. This approach has a surface simplicity, but close scrutiny reveals this method of counseling has at its roots a "way of life" that stems directly from certain beliefs about the nature of man. This approach assumes that only the person concerned can solve his own problems, and that any change must come from within rather than from any direction or guidance from without. Thus the basic hypothesis of the nondirective approach is that every individual has the capacity to reorganize or to reorient himself so that he becomes the type of person he really wants to be.

The counselor is a vital instrument in this approach, not as an intellectual resource to help rationally analyze a problem, but as an understanding human being who can accept the counselee for what he is. It is the counselor's task to establish an atmosphere and a relationship with the counselee so that he can start to understand and reorganize himself. This atmosphere is one of total acceptance of the counselee, his behavior, and his values. The counselor does not guide, direct, or even advise. The counselor is not seen in a passive role, but in an active role of clarification of the client's feelings, of empathizing with the client, and of establishing a relationship of acceptance and confidence. This is not an easy task. The counselor must not only be able to see the world through the eyes of his client, but must be able to accept his feelings and behavior without value judgment. The nondirective counselor does not deny that the counselor will have a value impact on the counselee, but he avoids any direct impartation of his values to the counselee or criticism of the counselee's values.

The nondirective counselor will provide information to the counselee if the counselee desires this information in helping himself make a choice or decision.

The nondirective or client-centered approach places the responsibility of change and adjustment squarely on the counselee. The counselor attempts to set up a completely accepting atmosphere for the counselee to reorganize himself in a positive direction. The counselor clarifies his counselee's feelings by attempting to adopt his frame of reference and mirroring his feelings.

The Eclectic Approach

The eclectic counselor does not adhere to any one theoretical approach. He analyzes a given counselee's problem and selects the method or a combination of methods and approaches that he believes will lead to the best solution. He may use the directive approach in one case and the nondirective in another. This approach should not be considered to be trial and error counseling. The professional eclectic counselor must have as much as or more training than one who adheres to a single theory. He strives to select that which he finds best in the various theories and applies it based on the particular situation.

Evaluation of counseling theories leads one to suspect that it is not so much the accuracy of the theory used but rather the skill with which the theory is applied that produces results. The skills involved are similar in many ways. Except in some definitely psychotherapeutic approaches, such as psychoanalysis, it appears that there are some common procedures which are important. First, the attitude of the counselor is generally one of acceptance of his counselee. Second, the counselor attempts to empathize with the counselee, to adopt his frame of reference, to see the world through the counselee's eyes. And last, decisions and choices are, in the final analysis, left to the individual being counseled.

THE LEADER AS A COUNSELOR

At all echelons the leader is a busy man; he cannot be expected to become a sophisticated professional counselor, but he must be able to offer the assistance to his men that will help them in their personal adjustment. The Army has a number of agencies staffed with professionals who are trained in specific counseling procedures to help the leader and his subordinates with their counseling problems. These professionals can be particularly helpful with problems that fall outside of the leader's ability because of his lack of professional training, his lack of facilities, or the inordinate amount of time required. On a daily basis, however, the small unit leader is confronted with a multitude of counseling situations. At times, the leader himself initiates the counseling by discussing a subordinate's effectiveness, discipline, appearance, or some other matter which the leader has noticed. On other occasions, the subordinate will bring his problems to the leader. He may have problems ranging from dislike of his job to emotional family or financial problems. The soldier's problem can be completely personal or it can involve others to the point that an entire unit's morale and mission accomplishment is affected.

It is difficult to separate what may be considered normal day-to-day operations from real counseling situations. It appears that such an attempt is not very useful in a discussion of the military leader as a counselor. There will be times when a traditional counseling situation will exist, with the leader and his subordinate seated in a quiet room in a relaxed atmosphere. There will be other times when counseling, as defined in this chapter, takes place at a social event, on a field problem, on the sidelines of an athletic event, or as the leader and subordinate occupy the same foxhole while pinned down by enemy fire.

Role Conflict

At this point, the professional counselor might question whether the leader, burdened with his mission and his many responsibilities, which include the evaluation of his subordinates, can simultaneously be a successful counselor. It is true that the military leader faces different problems than does a professional counselor in a civilian college or the staff psychologist in a big industrial firm. He must, however, perform counseling functions. The role conflict, caused by his dual position as leader-counselor, is not desirable from a purely counseling point of view, although it is not unlike the role conflict of the parent, the teacher, or certain leaders in business and industry. Desirable or not, the military leader cannot be relieved of his responsibility to assist his men in making adjustments to the problems they face.

Objectives

In his counseling, the leader should attempt to accomplish four objectives. The first is to cause the subordinate or counselee to recognize and define his problem or his deficiencies. This calls for a great deal of patience and skill on the part of the counselor. It is usually because the counselee is incapable of doing this himself that he seeks or needs counseling help. Once the problem is defined, the leader can proceed to the next objective of having the counselee make a decision on the best course of action. The emphasis is on the counselee's making the decision. In order for the counselee to accomplish the third objective of actually taking appropriate action, he must have the commitment to the decision that comes from his participation in arriving at the decision. If these three objectives are met, the fourth objective is made easier. This last objective is for the counselee to assume full responsibility for his decisions and actions.

Although this discussion has stressed the part the counselee plays, the counselor's task is the more difficult of the two in accomplishing these objectives. He is the stimulus and the catalyst that make it possible for the counseling session to be successful. If the counselee could meet these objectives alone, he would not require counseling. This points up the importance of the techniques the leader-counselor employs in helping the counselee.

SPECIFIC CONSIDERATIONS AND TECHNIQUES

There are a number of considerations and techniques that can assist the leader. It should be evident at this point that the eclectic approach would be the most practical one for the leader. This does not imply that the leader is expected to be a professional eclectic counselor. It does mean that his approach and technique will depend on the leader's assessment of himself as a counselor, his knowledge of the person he is counseling, and the situation that exists at the time of the counseling.

The Leader's Image

It is a difficult thing for a leader to assess accurately the image that he projects to his subordinates. Without dealing in a multitude of personality traits, it is apparent that, if subordinates are going to bring problems to the leader and if counseling is to be effective, the leader must have projected previously a "satisfactory" image to his subordinates. Research indicates that the effective counselor is a person who is sincere, who is interested in his counselee as an individual, and who has respect for human dignity. The role conflict of evalu- ator-counselor is reduced if the leader is considered to be fair and impartial, and either relatively free of biases or capable of objective analysis. Too often leaders assume that subordinates will heed advice simply because it emanates from a person in a position of authority.

Preparation for Counseling

When possible, the leader should prepare for his counseling sessions. The physical setup can be important. In most planned counseling situations it is possible to have a comfortable room where the session can be conducted in a relaxed atmosphere. The session should be scheduled at a time when there will be no interruptions. Often the leader can obtain background information re- garding the individual he is counseling to help him conduct the session. Cer- tainly, if the session has been initiated by the leader, he can do some planning and organizing prior to the session. For example, in a session designed to give the subordinate assistance in career planning, his records could be screened prior to the session for previous assignments, educational level, and other perti- nent data.

Define the Problem

When the leader initiates the counseling session, he should outline the problem as he sees it. When the subordinate initiates the procedure, then the leader should ensure that the subordinate defines the problem. Frequently the subordinate finds it difficult to state his problem, or he gives a superficial statement that cloaks the basic issue. The counselor should be careful not to jump to conclusions about the nature of the problem and should, by skillful questioning, ensure that the counselee has defined his problem as best he can.

Learn to Listen

Most of the military leader's training is pointed toward rapid analysis of situations and decisive action. Often such training is a hindrance to effective counseling. The effective counselor must be a good listener—an active, inter- ested listener. But, to be a good listener, he must first get his counselee to talk—to express his feelings. It is not an easy task to get a subordinate to "open up." In keeping with acceptable military standards, the counselee should be encouraged to relax. The leader should capitalize on any effort the counselee makes in describing his problem. He should show interest and reflect the feelings expressed by the counselee. In many cases, the counselee, if encouraged by a skillful, interested listener, will talk through and solve his own problem.

Flexibility in the Selection of Counseling Techniques

The selection of the appropriate counseling technique is probably the most difficult part of the counseling process. The nondirective approach is effective many times when the counselee is having trouble expressing himself. At other times this technique may be inappropriate. It probably would not be the best method for a performance counseling session initiated by the leader, in which he is confident of the nature of his subordinate's problem and feels that the subordinate can improve his performance with some specific advice. This approach has been called in industry the "tell and sell" approach (Maier, 1958). This is not the only way to approach performance counseling. In fact, defensive reactions are quite common in performance counseling. A session that starts out to be a straightforward directive counseling session, initiated and, for the most part, conducted by the leader, may soon turn into a session where the leader is using many nondirective techniques to clarify the feelings of his subordinate and to cause him to accept his shortcomings. It is for this reason that even in performance counseling sessions some leaders prefer to use nondirective techniques to attempt to get the subordinate to appraise accurately his own performance and find solutions to his own problems.

One of the most successful ways to facilitate self-expression is to adopt the counselee's frame of reference, and look at his problem through his eyes. At times, this is doubly hard for the leader who must keep in mind the goals of his unit and the Army. Often what may be best for the individual is not best for the unit or the service. Most of the time, the skillful leader-counselor can be nondirective and at the same time control the session and guide it along lines that are consistent with policy.

Questioning Techniques

There are some questioning techniques that can be used, especially by the inexperienced counselor to help him keep the session under control, to help the counselee express his feelings, and to clarify the situation. The following questioning techniques are adapted from Department of the Army Pamphlet 611-1, *The Army Interview*. While there are other techniques and other classifications, these techniques facilitate the accomplishment of the counseling objectives and recognize the role conflict of the military leader-counselor.

W-questions: The W-questions, when coupled with "how," are a valuable tool for the counselor. The "What," "When," "Where," "Who," and "Why" type questions fit most counseling situations. They are brief, direct, and to the point, such as, "What did he say?", "When did you do that?", and "Where did that happen?". The W-questions are used to get detailed answers, to determine missing information, and to save time.

Leading questions: A leading question is one that is worded to encourage the counselee to give the answer he thinks the counselor wants. Leading questions may be used to open up a new line of inquiry or to make a suggestion or indicate a desirable answer. They may be used also to control the content of the session. Because of the nature of leading questions, they should be used with extreme care.

Probing questions: Probes are questions used to get information in addition to that given in response to a general question. Probing questions are of tremendous value in obtaining additional information about the underlying causes of a problem. These may be fundamental to the problem and of such nature that the counselee has refused to recognize them.

Probes may be short statements indicating understanding and interest, such as, "I see," "Tell me more about that," or, simply, "Uh-huh." Also useful are neutral questions, "How do you mean?", "Why do you say that?", "Anything else?". The counselor should not probe for information unless he considers it essential in helping to solve the problem.

"Yes"-"No" questions: In most counseling situations, it is essential that questions answerable by "Yes" or "No" be used sparingly. There are times when the "Yes"-"No" questions are of inestimable value to the counselor. They may be used to commit the counselee, or to close one phase of the session. Unless formulated with care and used with skill, "Yes"-"No" questions will extend the session, fail to elicit the data needed for accurate evaluation, and generally result in unsatisfactory counseling.

Alternative questions: The alternative question may be used to force a decision by the counselee, or for disposing of one topic and turning to another. Such questions as, "Which do you prefer?" or "If not, what will you do?" will serve to control the interview and focus attention upon the point at issue. Extensive use should be made of alternative questions in problem-solving situations, or where several possibilities for action are available to the individual. In such cases, the interviewer should, by a series of alternative questions, make sure that each possibility for action receives consideration.

The silent question: Silence for brief periods also has its place in counseling. It gives the counselee a chance to think and to evaluate what has been said so far. It can actually serve as a stimulant, encouraging the counselee to continue the conversation. It also gives him an opportunity to recall the information the counselor is seeking, to consider the question, and to be sure he understands it. Permitting a reasonable amount of occasional silence is a good technique. It gives the individual a chance to consider his attitudes and whatever feelings he may have regarding any aspect of his problem. Getting this information will enable the counselor to correct misunderstandings and help the individual to develop insight into his own interests and desires.

Situational questions: The primary purpose of the situational question is to encourage the individual to talk at length about hypothetical problems in order to reveal his knowledge and understanding of them. Simulated situations, related as nearly as possible to reality, may be presented to the individual for discussion. To be effective, situational questions must be derived from actual experience and must be put to the individual in such a manner that he will be able to comprehend their meaning and the several implications of the problem presented for solution. Situational questions are usually followed by questions such as "How?", "Why?", "To what extent?", and "Under what circumstances?". The counselor should guard against using questions intended solely to pin down a particular answer or to put the respondent "on the spot." The person being interviewed should be free to discuss the problem in his own manner but without evasion of the issue so that he may have full opportunity to reveal his probable response in an actual situation. The counselor should be discerning but not cunning.

Questions for clarification and reflection: This type of question is essentially a "mirroring" of the counselee's answers. Emphasis is on the feeling of what is being expressed rather than on specific content. The counselor captures and clarifies the essence of what the respondent says and reflects it. Judicious use of reflection and clarification will result in an increased feeling of acceptance by the respondent and in an elaboration on what he has been discussing. The counselor confines his reflection and clarification questioning to the individual's frame of reference and permits it to go only as far as the individual goes in his discussion. The counselor reflects only the immediately preceding statement and not something that was said much earlier or something that he anticipates well be said. In the reflection and clarification type of questioning, the feeling and intent of the counselee are reflected and clarified; it is his frame of reference that is used. Effective reflection and clarification call not only for accuracy of content, but also recognition of the proper intensity of feeling. An example follows: Counselee: "I like having responsibility best. I really enjoyed myself and felt alive when I had responsible things to do." Counselor: "You would be unhappy in a job without a lot of responsibility?"

Interpretation: In interpretation the counselor gives a reason for a feeling or action, connecting past and present behavior, feelings, and attitudes. Since interpretation often comes as a revelation to the counselee, it is essential for him to be ready to receive it. His readiness depends on the relationship with the counselor, the adequacy of personal adjustment, his degree of insight, and other aspects of personality. When the interpretation is correct, the counselee sees connections between memories of the past and his present attitudes and behavior. Effective use of interpretation requires insight and skill. Typical examples are: Counselee: "I am interested in going overseas because I can get a better job and earn more money." Counselor: "You mean that you could not do as well here in the States?" Counselee: "I have been well received. I do my work well, no complaints, but things could be much better in a way." Counselor: "You mean you are sort of left hanging?"

Summary questions: Summary questions are commonly used to close a counseling session; however, it may be advisable to summarize the several phases of an extended session. Typical summary questions are: "Have we covered the main points?" and "What conclusions have we reached?" The individual's ability to summarize is a test of the success of the session. A good summary will serve to indicate what has been accomplished or progress made.

Some Precautions

The good counselor must be patient. The counselee must not feel that he is being pressed or hurried. The counselor must guard against acting overly authoritative. Meaningful communication is easily lost if the counselee detects an authoritative tone or a patronizing attitude on the part of the counselor. If the leader is going to assist in solving his subordinate's problem, he must maintain a climate of mutual respect. Another common mistake is for the counselor to use psychological jargon or present a shrewd or clever attitude in dealing with his counselee. In counseling situations involving personal choice, the counselor should leave the decision to his counselee. Finally, the counselor must ensure that he does not commit himself or the Army to a promise or a position that he cannot keep.

AGENCIES TO ASSIST THE LEADER

The leader's limited resources, his limited counseling training, and the demand on his time make it impossible to assist fully all his men with their problems. For this reason, there are other agencies available to assist soldiers who have problems. The good leader-counselor realizes his limitations and refers his subordinate to an agency that has specially trained individuals to provide the services needed. Some of these agencies are discussed below.

The Chaplain

Chaplains are provided to Army installations and to troop units on the basis of troop strength. The distribution of Protestant, Catholic, and Jewish chaplains is generally in proportion to the distribution of these major faiths within the over-all American population. Chaplains minister to the religious and moral needs of military and civilian personnel and their dependents in the same manner as civilian ministers, priests, and rabbis minister to their congregations.

The particular type of problems which chaplains are most competent to deal with are those of a spiritual or moral nature. As a matter of practical fact, most problems of this nature are taken directly to the chaplain by the soldier; and rightly so, for all communications made to a chaplain in his capacity as a clergyman or spiritual confidant or as a formal act of religion are privileged communications. This privilege does not extend to the counseling relationship between a commander and his subordinates. Some individuals however, take problems directly to the chaplain that should have been brought to the commander instead. In such cases, the chaplain will normally refer the soldier back to his commander, though he may maintain an interest in the further development of the case. On the other hand, many cases brought to the attention of the commander, though not primarily religious or moral in nature, have religious or moral overtones. This is often true in cases involving family difficulties. If such religious or moral overtones do exist, it is advisable that the chaplain have an opportunity to talk with the soldier. A good working relationship between the chaplain and the commander will aid both in the accomplishment of their responsibilities.

Psychiatric Services

The Mental Hygiene Consultation Division provides out-patient psychiatric evaluations and treatment. Soldiers are referred to mental hygiene facilities from sick call, or by unit commanders or chaplains. The staff consists of officers who are psychiatrists, psychologists, and social workers, and enlisted specialists in psychology and social work. Evaluations are made for administrative discharges, or occasionally for courtsmartial. Treatment may consist of a series of interviews at the clinic with one of the members of the staff, or "field visits" by an enlisted specialist who visits the soldier's unit and commanders.

Officers and other troop leaders may also confer with members of the mental hygiene clinic staff without referring patients. Through the "Command Consultation Service," the staff provides advice and assistance to the commander. This service is especially valuable in promoting greater understanding and co-operation between the clinic staff and the commander. Staff members may be invited to the unit to conduct conferences with officers or noncommissioned officers on handling emotional problems. They are also helpful in suggesting ways to handle difficult family situations. The mental hygiene clinic is a valuable resource, but the commander retains the responsibility for final action.

The Legal Assistance Office

Department of the Army policy is to provide legal assistance to all service members and their dependents to the extent that personnel and facilities permit. This function is charged to the Judge Advocate General's Corps, and Legal Assistance Offices may be found at all major installations. These offices render advice on the meaning and effect of civil and military laws and regulations, provide assistance in the preparation of wills, powers of attorney, tax forms, bills of sale, and other legal documents, and refer cases to civilian agencies, where appropriate. The underlying purpose of the legal assistance program is to prevent personal legal difficulties that may contribute to a state of low morale and inefficiency, or result in problems requiring disciplinary action.

The American Red Cross

The Red Cross provides a variety of services both to individual members of the Armed Forces and to commanding officers. Red Cross representatives are found on every major military installation and also in all units of division size or greater overseas. Basically, the functions of the Red Cross that are of assistance to the commander in his counseling functions are those of providing information and furnishing financial assistance.

Because the Red Cross has field offices throughout the United States, it is an especially valuable communications source between the soldier and his home. Through this source it is possible for the soldier to gain information quickly about the health and welfare of his family. The Red Cross will provide confidential reports of home conditions for use by commanders in considering applications for emergency leave, morale leave, compassionate reassignment, deferment from overseas assignment and dependency or hardship discharge. It may furnish information on federal and state legislation and regulations on allotments, insurance, relief, and other benefits available to Army personnel and their dependents, and may aid in obtaining such benefits.

The Red Cross will provide assistance by loan or grant to Army personnel who need to return home on account of sickness, death, or other grave emergencies in the soldier's immediate family when the soldier is without the necessary funds. This help is given only with the approval of the commander and after the emergency condition has been verified by the Red Cross. Further financial assistance may be provided to Army personnel and their dependents for basic maintenance when allotments are delayed or interrupted, and for other emergency needs that may arise during a soldier's military service.

The Army Emergency Relief

The Army Emergency Relief is an agency established by the Department of the Army for the specific purpose of "taking care of its own." Its sole function is the provision of interest-free loans, or in some cases grants, to assist Army personnel in meeting emergency situations. AER offices are designated at every major Army installation, and annual drives are conducted throughout the Army to raise funds to support the program. Thus, it is a completely internally supported program. The AER provides financial assistance in needy cases where the Red Cross either cannot or will not provide such assistance because the case is outside their jurisdiction or no funds have been provided the Red Cross for that purpose. Regulations provide that any case must be cleared with the Red Cross first before it will be referred to the AER. Typical cases handled by the AER include the provision of loans or grants due to nonreceipt of pay, allotments, or allowances; loss of pay or other personal funds; emergency medical, dental, and hospital expenses; funeral expenses of dependents; travel expenses due to emergency leave and emergency transportation of dependents, to include expenses involved in meeting port calls; payment of initial rent or to avoid eviction; and other privations to dependents. In addition, AER handles confidential cases which, if otherwise handled, might be embarrassing to the individual or the command, or reveal security information. It should be pointed out, however, that AER is not a general loan agency and that they cannot make loans in cases that are not emergency in nature. For instance, they could not make a loan to assist a soldier in the purchase of a car.

An independent relief agency allied with the AER is the Army Relief Society, that provides financial assistance to the dependents of deceased Army personnel. Ten per cent of the funds raised during the annual AER drive is allotted to the ARS.

From the above discussion, it is obvious that there are many agencies available in the Army to assist the commander in the solution of his subordinates' personal problems. The commander, however, should avoid the concept of his own role as simply that of a router or dispatcher who listens to a subordinate's problems and then decides who else is best qualified to help him. There will be many times when the commander's function will be just that, but in a large number of cases he can provide the assistance needed himself. Further, even though the commander should refer a soldier to another agency for counseling or other assistance, he still retains responsibility for the soldier and his problem. Thus, he remains vitally interested in the assistance rendered to the soldier by the agency to which he is referred.

SUMMARY

The leader is responsible for accomplishing his mission and providing for the welfare of his men. His ability to accomplish these tasks to a great degree depends on his effectiveness as a counselor. Although there are many theoretical approaches to counseling, three convenient classifications are the directive, nondirective, and the eclectic. Of the three, the leader-counselor is more likely to employ an eclectic approach in his counseling of subordinates. In this way he can better tailor the counseling session to satisfy the needs of the organization and the individual. The conflict between the leader's role as a disciplinarian and problem counselor can be reduced through an awareness of the objectives to be accomplished and techniques available for use in counseling. Valuable assistance can be provided by outside agencies, such as the Chaplain, Mental Hygiene Consultation Division, and the American Red Cross. The leader's effectiveness as a counselor is determined by the image he projects to his men, his skillful use of counseling techniques, his ability to recognize his own limitations, and a genuine interest in his men based on a deep respect for the dignity of every individual.

Suggestions for Further Reading

Department of the Army Pamphlet 611-1, *The Army Interview*, 31 August 1965.

Harms, Ernest, and Schreiber, Paul, (eds.), *Handbook of Counseling Techniques*. New York: Pergamon Press, 1963.

Maier, Norman, R. F., *The Appraisal Interview*. New York: John Wiley & Sons, 1958.

Warters, Jane, *Techniques of Counseling*. New York: McGraw-Hill, 1964.

Section III
THE SITUATION

Behavioral science research indicates that the situation is one of the important dimensions affecting the leadership process. The same leader, leading the same group, might have to behave differently in different situations. For example, the style of leadership employed by the leader in a combat situation might be much more direct and positive than the style he might use in solving an administrative type problem. Situations, however, provide a very challenging area for behavioral scientists to explore. The difficulties in arranging valid experimental situations are extensive.

One of the bases for scientific interest in the situation stems from the phenomenon of emergent leadership. Groups appear to confer leadership on the person best qualified to solve the problem or situation of the moment. Leadership, from this point of view, is the interaction which takes place between the leader's skills and the situation. Many experiments have verified this tendency. Notable among these is the work done by Hemphill and others in the Ohio State University Leadership Studies; Fiedler and his associates at the Group Effectiveness Research Laboratory at the University of Illinois; and the scholars of the Survey Research Center, Institute for Social Research at the University of Michigan. The conclusions of the Office of Strategic Services (OSS) further emphasize the importance of this aspect of leadership. In studies during World War II, they noted that a leader's ability to fulfill his role is strongly dependent on the specific situation (OSS, 1948). A good summary of the situationists' position is in Alvin W. Gouldner's *Studies in Leadership* (Gouldner, 1950).

Even in a military organization in which leaders are appointed and not expected to emerge as a result of group interaction in response to a situation, there is a substantial requirement for group legitimation. The leader must be seen by the group as possessing the individual characteristics needed to resolve uncertainty and lead them to their objective. Thus, the military leader must be able to react to a wide variety of situations. Each situation has many interrelated facets making it difficult to link any one to a specific behavior of the leader. Physical environment, the duration of the situation, the frequency with which it occurs, the social structure of the group involved, the status of the

213

leader, the established leadership climate, the current value system, the degree of threat or urgency—all play an appreciable part in creating the over-all situation faced by the leader and his group. The many variations that these factors can assume make it most difficult to isolate any one as the determining factor upon which a leader could base a specific approach. Each must be considered in connection with the others.

The many leadership situations facing the military leader stem from his assignment in an American military organization. This assignment establishes certain basic conditions about the environment that influence the methods and techniques he may use. The characteristics of the American society as modified by the military establishment, the nature of the American soldier, the traditions and customs of the service—all establish certain expectations on the part of both leaders and subordinates. Some aspects of the American military environment and the nature of the American soldier are discussed in Chapter XVI, "The Soldier in American Society."

A high percentage of the time a leader in the Army is concerned with training. He must develop training programs, translate training programs into schedules and periods of instruction and finally instruct his unit. The effectiveness of the instruction and the quality of the leadership play a major part in the development of individual motivation, unit efficiency and group solidarity manifested in *esprit,* morale and discipline. Chapter XVII discusses some aspects of leadership of military units in training situations.

The ultimate purpose of military training is to develop combat effectiveness, but, combat situations introduce factors of urgency and stress, both on the leader and his group, which are not present during training. Some of these factors with which the leader must cope are discussed in Chapter XVIII, "Combat Leadership."

Leadership is exercised in staff and advisory roles as well as in the more direct role of the commander, although the attitudes, methods and techniques employed may be substantially different. Some of the situational factors and considerations that affect the exercise of leadership in such staff and advisor roles are considered in Chapter XIX, "The Military Advisor."

Each of these chapters presents general considerations and problems that apply to a certain type of environment. The leader, however, always faces a specific situation with a specific group in a specific environment. In order to assist the student leader in developing his ability to consider the many leadership variables and possible courses of action, Chapter XX presents a number of case studies for analysis. They incorporate one or more elements of the generalized situations of this section, as well as offering an opportunity to focus the concepts developed in Sections I and II on the specific problems of the military leader.

XVI

The Soldier
In American Society

THE MILITARY leader must operate within the environment created by the military establishment. The characteristics and qualities of the American military establishment are determined in large measure by the nature of American society and its culture. While many sociologists believe that modern technology is causing increasingly rapid social and cultural change, such change tends to be evolutionary in character. Cultural traits and characteristics tend to persist even though their expression might change. The leader should understand the nature of this military environment. He must know the men he is leading, not only as individuals but as products of their culture. Their shared heritage as American citizens is one of the strong bonds which fosters group solidarity. Each is an integral part of the larger population from which he is drawn. Both the leader and the men he leads are characteristically American soldiers, set apart from the larger society by their profession. As such, they are members of a group different from other national groups just as are New Yorkers, doctors, farmers, or any other large group of citizens with a shared identification.

In addition to being a member of a specific subculture in American society, the American soldier is a product of his times. In many respects, he is unlike any of his predecessors. As the soldier of World War I differed from those who fought in World War II, so today's soldier reflects the influences of this contemporary environment. A sociological sketch of the soldier necessarily reflects the current international situation, methods of recruitment and conscription, economic conditions, urbanization, reliance on technology, and many other culture determinants. There are, however, some enduring characteristics which have been true of the American soldier in the past and which, in all probability, he will continue to possess in the foreseeable future. The soldier embodies the cultural traits common to all Americans, as well as those specifically associated with his profession. Although stemming from the same fundamental outlook, there are significant distinctions created by the military subculture. The leader should be aware of both the basic characteristics and the differences created by the requirements of the military environment.

215

216 TAKING COMMAND

THE CITIZEN AND THE SOLDIER

Many of the similarities and differences between the soldier and the larger population can be observed in objective statistics. They provide a common foundation for interpretation and their use presents a picture of the American soldier with a minimum of narrative distortion.

Geographic Source. Due in great part to the effects of the nation-wide Selective Service System, the American soldier is a reasonable sample of geographic distribution in both officer and enlisted ranks. A slight over-representation exists in the southern states in which there has been a historic predisposition for entering military life. Local economic conditions and the location of several major Army installations may also be influencing factors.

	% of U.S. Population	By home of record % Officer	% EM
Western States	15	13	15
North Eastern States	25	25	21
North Central States	29	24	27
Southern States	31	38	37
	100	100	100

Figure 16.1 Geographical Distribution

Computed from SSO Report 43-65E as of 30 Nov 1964; Current Population Report, series P-25, No. 325, 8 Dec 1966

Religion. In religious affiliation the American soldier is also properly representative. Such differences as exist may be ascribed principally to the more recent immigrant status of the Catholic population. That is, the Army may be more attractive to groups attempting to better their position in life, and to whom the military is a particularly important symbol of national unity.

	% Protestant	% Catholic	% Jewish	% Other
Army	62	34.5	3.5	
U.S. (male, age 14+)	66	25.7	3.2	5.1

Figure 16.2 Religion

DOA, Office of the Chief of Chaplains, 27 January 1966, Basis for Appointment of Chaplains; Statistical Abstract of U.S. 1964, Table 43 (1957 data)

Minorities. In terms of minority groups, the Army is the most representative of all the services. In many respects, of course, the United States is a nation of immigrants. With time, however, the differences that set one group apart from another have generally been dissipated. One of the largest groups that is being successfully assimilated in the Army is the Negro. He participates equally with all other groups and is, in fact, not different in any way as a soldier from his fellows.

	% Caucasian	% Negro
U.S. Total	89.3	10.7
Ages 18-54, male		
Officer	95.7	4.3
Enlisted Man	85.1	14.9

Figure 16.3 Minority Groups

Data from A/Secretary for Manpower, DOD, as of 31 December 1964; computed from Current Population Report, series P-20, No. 145, December 27, 1965

Selectivity. These data point out the existing similarities between the American soldier and the population. Examination of other important areas, however, reflect the effect of selective processes at work in defining the American soldier. The selectivity of the Army in accepting individuals into its ranks is a function of the increasingly complex duties of the American soldier in a technological age. Because of this, disqualification rates for induction are relatively high.

Type Rejection	% of Total Examined
Administrative	3.9
Mental only	8.1
Trainability limited	6.9
Medical only	14.8
Both mental and physical	1.5
	35.2

Figure 16.4 Over-all Evaluation of Youths by Qualification for the Military Service

Health of the Army; result of the examination of youths for Military Service, July 1966, Office of the Surgeon General USA, Table 33 (1964)

Age. In addition to its predominately male composition, one of the most distinctive features of the military subculture is the relative youth of its members. Composition by age varies very little over time, as is shown in this table:

	1950	1952	1954	1956	1958	1960	1962	1964	1965
Median Age	23.6	22.9	22.7	23.0	23.8	24.5	24.2	24.0	23.9
Largest Age Group	20	21	21	20	20	20	20	21	21

Figure 16.5 Age Levels of Men Entering the Services, 1950-1965

Officer Sources. The sources from which the Army recruits the officer corps also show evidence of selectivity operating. Each of the sources below eliminates many candidates by various measures before commissioning.

	USMA	ROTC	OCS	Direct Appointment	Other
Composition of Army by Source of Commission 1965	7.8%	49.4%	22.5%	14.9%	5.6%
Sources of Army Officers 1961-1965	3.5%	69.9%	8.2%	4.3%	14.0%

Figure 16.6 Source of Officers

Sample Survey of Military Personnel (RCS-AG-366) as of 28 February 1965. Report of the DOA Board to review Army Officer Schools, Vol. II, February 1966, p. 157, Fig. 16 B-3-5

Education. One of the most revealing indicators is relative education. In a nation in which half the total population has completed high school, it is striking that the American soldier represents a significantly better educated individual. This difference can be attributed to the increasing technical expertise required of the military, and helps to explain the high mental rejection rate of the Selective Service.

	0-7	8-11	12	Some College	BA/BS	Graduate Work	
U.S. Total (Age 18-54, Male)	14.6	29.1	34.9	12.9	7.7	5.2	100%
Officer		.1	5.2	18.8	54.6	21.3	100%
Enlisted Man	3.9	15.9	64.4	13.6	2.1	.1	100%

Figure 16.7 Years of School Completed

OPOSS Report 41-66-E, as of 31 May 1966; Manpower Branch, OPO, OPD as of mid-month November 1965; Current Population Report # 158, 19 December, p. 7, as of March 1966, U.S. Department of Commerce. Report of DOA Board to review Army Officer Schools, February 1966, Vol. II, p. 273

Status. As a result of this selectivity, the reputation of the American soldier is a good one. Figure 16.8 gives some perspective of occupational prestige, i.e., the respect awarded to a position as opposed to the respect given to the specific individual in that position. One factor that may lead to misinterpretation of the table is that the Army ranks included are less than median ranks in a lifetime career, whereas the other entries represent career fields. Also, since the polls were taken in peacetime, they may reflect somewhat of a "Tommy Atkins" effect.

> Then it's Tommy this, an' Tommy that, an' Tommy,
> ' 'ow's yer soul?'
> But it's thin red line of ' 'eroes' when the drums begin
> to roll . . .
>
> Rudyard Kipling

SOCIETY AND THE SOLDIER

The American society from which the soldier comes has certain characteristics and trends that are difficult to portray statistically. These characteristics determine many of the attitudes, skills, and values that the soldier brings to his

Occupation	1947	1963
Physician	2	2
Scientist	8	3
College Professor	8	8
Lawyer	18	11
Diplomat	4	11
Priest	18	21
Instructor in Public Schools	34	27
Captain, RA	31	27
Owner of Factory of about 100 People	26	31
Author	31.5	34.5
Farm Owner and Operator	39	44
Radio Announcer	40	49
Carpenter	58	53
Plumber	59	59
Corporal, RA	64	65
Truck Driver	71	67
Lumberjack	73	72
Night Watchman	81	77
Shoeshiner (last)	90	90

Figure 16.8 Occupational Prestige

Selections from a list of 90 occupations ordered by prestige as rated by a national sample.

Extracts from Hodge, Siegel, and Rossi, "Occupational Prestige in the United States," *American Journal of Sociology,* May 1964; Opinion News, Vol. IX (1 September 1947), NORC

profession. An understanding of these characteristics is important in visualizing the relationships between the military and the general society.

Stratification

Every society tends to stratify in some way. That is, positions tend to fall into a system of graded ranks according to some criteria. This social phenomenon develops in part because of the universal need for a system of authority and in part because of the desirability of certain positions over other positions insofar as rewards of one kind or another are concerned.

Figure 16.8 shows a positioning of occupations by relative prestige, that is a form of stratification. But, whether a ranking is based on occupational prestige, wages, contribution to society, status, power, or something else, it differs from one society to another. It is sometimes more practical to lump finer gradations into ranked groups. Such stratified groupings may be called "classes," if they are based on economic criteria, or "status groups," if they are based on differences that portions of the population perceive in each other, e.g., education, politics, and kinship.

American society can be broken down in any number of ways. For example, upper, middle, and lower "class" are convenient categories of stratification based on income. There is a good deal of movement back and forth between these groups (mobility) in today's open society. The aspirations of individuals or groups are not generally frustrated by the knowledge that one can only improve his position within specified limits as might occur in India where a caste system operates.

Within the Army, status groups are the most obvious sign of stratification. The three basic divisions are enlisted men, noncommissioned officers, and officers. The criteria for this division are imposed by rules rather than by the natural give and take of competition and ability. Consequently, mobility is more directly controlled. In terms of quality, the mechanisms of stratification are designed to screen out the best qualified into the officer ranks. In terms of quantity, they restrict the size of each successive level. This partly explains the dissatisfaction that arises during periods of mobilization when otherwise qualified soldiers are restricted to a level below what they feel their actual potential to be.

The rigorous stratification of the Army (its visibility increased by the use of uniform and insignia) also serves to insulate members of one status group from those of another by reducing the personal element when difficult decisions have to be made. Thus, when a company commander must give an order, knowing full well that casualties will be suffered, his status affords a two-way buffer. On the one hand, it reduces the strain on him and, on the other, it eliminates the expectation of personal favor on the part of noncommissioned officers and enlisted men.

Technology and Specialization

With the increase of knowledge over time, society has become increasingly more involved with the problems of putting knowledge to practical use. All manner of fields of specialization have sprung up in order that concentration in a specific area of knowledge might allow for the best use of time and ability. It is no longer practicable to master large, diverse areas of knowledge, as did the Leonardo da Vincis and Benjamin Franklins of the past.

Today's society is highly specialized and is especially so at the practical level. The farmer, in colonial days, could exist almost without outside help. Now, he requires hybrid seed, chemical fertilizer, and bottled gas, as well as the services of mechanics, merchants, and lawyers. This is similarly true in other sectors of society.

The military is no exception to this trend. In fact, Lasswell has characterized military personnel as Managers (officers) and Technicians (noncommissioned officers and enlisted men) of violence. Figure 16.9 points out most clearly the trend toward specialization of the Army over the past century.

There are several results of this increase of specialization and the advance of technology. In its most general implications, it has led towards a faith in the rational and technical at the expense of emotional and human perspectives. It is currently popular to think of fighting wars with bombs and missiles rather than with men and sweat. Also, it is all too easy to allow managerial considerations of efficiency and change to override the stability of tradition and the total irrationality of courage in combat. This is not to say that it is bad or good, but that it is an observable trend.

Occupational Groups	Civil War %	Sp. Am. War %	World War I %	World War II %	Korean War %	1954 %
Civilian-type occupations:						
Technical, scientific;	0.2	0.5	3.7	10.1	10.7	14.5
Administrative, clerical;	0.7	3.1	8.0	14.6	19.2	17.5
Skilled mechanics,						
maintenance, etc.;	0.6	1.1	21.5	15.8	16.9	20.3
Service workers;	2.4	6.5	12.5	9.7	11.5	10.4
Operative, laborers.	2.9	2.2	20.2	13.6	8.6	8.4
Military-type occupations	93.2	86.6	34.1	36.2	33.1	28.8

Figure 16.9 Occupational Specialization in Army Enlisted Personnel, Civil War to 1954

(Janowitz, M., *The Professional Soldier*, 1960, p. 65.)

More specifically, it has led to changes in the structure of the Army. As Figure 16.9 shows, the relative number of combat soldiers has continually declined in favor of more technical specialities, even though they remain the reason for being of the rest. Furthermore, the similarity of many technical skills within the military to corresponding civilian skill fields undermines to a certain extent the solidarity of soldiers in their commitment to common military values. Radar technicians and riflemen become and remain career soldiers for different reasons. It has also led to changes in the grade structure of the Army. As

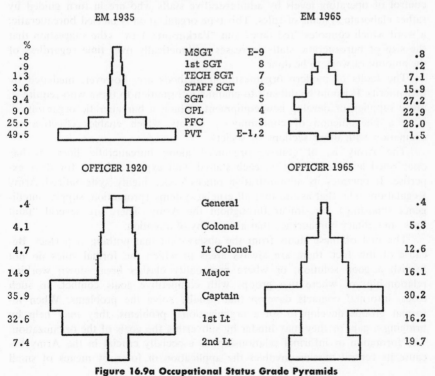

EM 1935				EM 1965
%				
.8	MSGT	E-9		.8
.9	1st SGT	8		.2
1.3	TECH SGT	7		7.1
3.6	STAFF SGT	6		15.9
9.4	SGT	5		27.2
9.0	CPL	4		22.9
25.5	PFC	3		28.0
49.5	PVT	E-1,2		1.5

OFFICER 1920		OFFICER 1965
.4	General	.4
4.1	Colonel	5.3
4.7	Lt Colonel	12.6
14.9	Major	16.1
35.9	Captain	30.2
32.6	1st Lt	16.2
7.4	2nd Lt	19.7

Figure 16.9a Occupational Status Grade Pyramids

technological (and managerial) skill requirements increase, the Army recognizes the advance by upgrading the rank for the job. The traditional rank pyramid approaches a diamond shape implying an increasing number of managerial (staff) and technical specialists (Figure 16.9a).

Finally, these technological advances have increased the amount of strain at all levels. Not only must the soldier work harder to attain and maintain the proper degree of efficiency in complex tasks, but he is under the continual pressure of crisis and changes in mission that stem from increased improvements in transportation, communication, and command control. Similarly, the officer must adapt to changing requirements at his level that stretch his ability and equanimity to the utmost.

Bureaucracy

Since specialization has developed as a mechanism for handling the complications of technology, mechanisms of control have had to become more sophisticated in order to direct and manage efficiently the complex life of the nation created by this diversity. Whereas the colonial farmer planted tobacco or corn to suit his pleasure and needs, the modern agriculturist must answer to a variety of organizations which assist him on the one hand, and, on the other, fit his efforts in with those of others to serve better the general need.

This increase in the complexity of society creates a requirement for organizations structured to handle the job efficiently. In contemporary life, this means control of operating levels by administrative staffs who are in turn guided by rather elaborate systems of rules. This type organization is labeled bureaucratic; a word which connotes "red tape" and "Parkinson's Law" (the suggestion that the size of bureaucratic staffs increases arithmetically over time regardless of the amount of work to be done).

The faults of modern organizational methods are, however, mediated by their merits. It would be difficult to channel information to those who require it, move supplies, or develop new equipment without a bureaucratic organization. It is a phenomenon of contemporary society which enables effective coordination with other sections of society.

The Army is, of course, organized along bureaucratic lines. It has established levels of authority, each staffed with experts selected for their expertise. It operates its administrative offices under highly systematized Army Regulations, etc. that assure that all crucial systems (promotion, supply, intelligence reporting) are similar throughout the Army. There are several "fault lines" in military bureaucracy that are worthy of attention.

The first of these stems from the observation that nothing is perfect. Because of this fact, there are always areas in which the formal rules do not furnish a good solution; or where personality clashes break down working relationship; or where two groups with competitive goals conflict. In such cases, informal contacts develop that usually solve the problems. When informal groups develop to solve organizational problems, they may help by bridging a gap; or they may hinder by subverting the goals of the organization. The formation of informal relationships is especially crucial in the Army because its central mission involves the application of force by means of small groups which are often together in stressful situations for long periods of time.

A second fault line develops where organizational authority and other authority converge on an individual. A principal area of contemporary concern is where the 'other' authority is professional. For example, a doctor, a technician, or an engineer is likely to be a trifle sensitive about the infringement of bureaucratic authority upon certain professional areas. If the authority of the bureaucracy tells him how to place a suture, a circuit, or a bridge abutment, he will insist on his own professional competence. As more soldiers develop a special area of expertise, or more professionals find a place in the military, the problem becomes more critical.

In both cases, the soldier is placed under a certain amount of strain to accept the military as it exists. Consequently, change tends to come from the top down. This is the nature of bureaucracy, but it has special consequences for the soldier who is often in the position of finding quick solutions to unique problems. This is true whether these are problems of the squad in the attack or problems of bridge construction. To offset built-in constraints in the solution of such problems and to ensure flexibility, it is essential that leaders at all levels know their units well and be aware of these fault lines.

Solidarity in Mass Society

Today's industrial society is characterized by the variety and impersonality of the contacts that an individual makes with others. Practically speaking, this means that there are many small groups of people with whom one associates on a day-to-day basis. Yet, individuals are not strongly committed to them and there is a reluctance to act together at this level. This trend is characterized as the 'atomization' of society.

This social trend leads to an increased commitment to secondary groups. These are groups of people with which one has some limited communality of interests, but the members of which rarely or never meet all together. As an illustration, the colonial farmer's life centered about such primary groups as his family and his immediate neighbors with whom he socialized, worked, traded, and politicked. A farmer now lives separated from his father's household in a smaller immediate family. His associations with others far transcend the immediate neighborhood. His social, economic, and political problems are handled through groups generally removed from those immediate friends whom he sees daily or frequently.

The American soldier lives in an environment that emphasizes primary group associations. At most times, but especially in combat, he is a member of a group in which he is more intimately and totally involved than if he were in a civilian environment. He lives and socializes with the same group with which he works. All his fortunes are more or less bound up in the same packet.

The reassignments inherent in Army life that make it difficult for him to link up with local communities also make it necessary for him to have military institutions to provide these social necessities. On-post housing and barracks life provide for this need, as do chaplains, service clubs, movies, Post Exchanges, etc. At the same time that those conditions bind soldiers together, they also restrict his associations with the civilian community. As a consequence, rapport with the civilian community at the local level is frequently somewhat less than perfect.

On balance, the American soldier benefits by the satisfactions of a close-knit integrated environment tailored to his needs. What he must give up to acquire this, of course, is a certain measure of choice, an alternative highly valued by American society as a whole.

SHARED UNDERSTANDINGS

Culture may be defined as a "system of shared understandings." As such, it includes the beliefs and values that are associated with social relationships.

While the majority of strongly valued beliefs held by the American soldier mesh with or include the beliefs of American society, there are areas wherein the Army is somewhat distinctive. Thus, the American soldier belongs to a subculture. Viewing the Army from such a frame of reference, certain significant differences in values stand out. Two such areas of difference are the concepts of authority and patriotism.

The Importance of Authority: Discipline and Democracy

The resistance of the colonies to an overbearing system of authority was one of the central factors leading to the American Revolution. Federalism in government is an outgrowth of that dislike for hierarchical authority. This particular facet of our society has been salient in the attitude of soldiers in all of the major wars in which the United States has engaged. It has been claimed that the illusion that enthusiasm could outfight discipline has been a consistent and unfortunate current in American thought since the Revolution. More recently, others have noted that one of the outstanding characteristics of the American worker is his sensitivity towards his rights. Federal employees feel strongly about the value of self-determination and react to the restrictions of government bureaucracy as detractions to federal occupation. Whatever point of view is brought to bear, the dislike of discipline and the distrust of higher authority appears as a foundation value in American culture.

On the other hand a strong system of authority—with equally strong sanctions justified in terms of the necessity for obedience in the face of danger—is fundamental in military organizations. Democracies at the governmental level are broadly tolerant of this aberration, accepting the fact that debate is at a premium in the heat of battle. The individual soldier may differ considerably from his leaders in his views on the value of strong authority.

One facet of the problem is the tendency of the military to use the existing network of authority to transmit routine matters that are legitimized in the name of the Army's combat mission. The citizen is used to defining some of these matters as "his business". In the U.S. Army, the problem is resolved by ensuring an understanding of the necessity of arbitrary authority and by effective leadership that does not lean unnecessarily on the "crutch" provided by a strongly authoritarian system.

The importance of authority to the leader is related directly to the responsibility inherent in his position. However more satisfactory leadership by persuasion may be, it is essential, on occasion, to rely on obedience to arbitrary decisions. In the contemporary American Army, this last resort is rarely called upon; especially at those levels of command above the platoon where orders are generally issued complete with some logical explanation. It is the platoon leader and the sergeant who are faced with the immediate crisis in combat and are supported by the authority of their position.

Pragmatism and Patriotism

American society as a whole is intensely patriotic; especially so because of its development as a nation of immigrants. Only in America, in recent history, have citizens become citizens as a matter of individual free choice; leaving their own country for another under their own free will. Consequently, Americans have always been intensely involved in the defense of democracy and freedom in the concrete as well as the abstract sense.

Because of the absence of any hereditary aristocracy in the United States, all sectors of society have a public service tradition. This takes in such things as Parent-Teacher Associations, Ambassadorships, and Military Service, in which duties are accepted without appropriate monetary incentive; but rather on the basis of principle. Military service, then, has always been a privilege as well as a duty.

It is certainly predictable that the American soldier would show a high degree of all-weather patriotism. All his training, all his goals have meaning beyond pure ambition only if they are interpreted in terms of love of country. It is this feeling carried a little further that makes the soldier especially conscious of national honor, for he is the ultimate defender of this standard. If the issue is passed over, it can be looked upon as a reflection on his ability.

The acceptance of patriotism by the American soldier as a black or white issue, that is with few gray areas between being "with us or agin' us," is fundamental. It serves as an indicator of personal dedication to duty, high *esprit*, and willingness to perform. The underlying patriotism of American troops has often been obscured by the attitudes of soldiers in combat who generally pass off "flag-waving" as hypocritical. It is expressed instead in terms of "not letting down my buddy;" a personal commitment to comrades, rather than abstract commitment to country. Without an underlying dedication, however, it is not likely that one's buddies would want to fight at all.

SUMMARY

The American soldier is a product of American society, and the Army is a microcosm of the population as a whole. Because of the nature of the Army's mission, the soldier is especially selected for physical and mental ability. He is, in this sense, an above-average citizen rather than an average one. The prestige of the soldier's job reflects this.

The American soldier is also affected by some of the differences between Army organization and civilian life. Especially important are the system of rank and the comradeship of life among fellow soldiers. On the other hand, the Army is following the same trends in bureaucratic organization and technological advancement as the country as a whole. The American soldier, however, differs from his national culture in his degree of acceptance of authority and patriotism.

Suggestions for Further Reading

Almond, G. A., and Verba, S., *The Civic Culture*. Boston: Little-Brown, 1965.
Janowitz, M., *The Professional Soldier*. Glencoe, Ill.: Free Press of Glencoe, 1960.
McClelland, D. C., *The Achieving Society*. Princeton, N.J.: Van Nostrand, 1961.
Whyte, W. H., *The Organization Man*. New York: Simon & Shuster, 1956.
Stouffer, S. A., *et. al.*, *The American Soldier*. Princeton, N.J.: Princeton University Press, 1949.

XVII

Leadership In Training

"In no other profession are the penalties for employing untrained personnel so appalling and so irrevocable as in the military." (MacArthur, 1933.) In this statement, General Douglas MacArthur presented the basic challenge of military training. The soldier trains for battle. With the advance of technology and modern weapons he can no longer count on having time to train after the conflict is joined. The modern world environment requires the maintenance of substantial forces in immediate readiness for deployment and combat operations. Thus, training to achieve and to maintain this combat readiness is intensive and continuous.

Training represents a major concentration of the Army. Most of the situations that the military leader must face involve some phase of training. From the time a recruit first enters the Army until the day he retires, he is trained, trains himself, and then trains others, rehearsing for that day when he might have to use his skill in battle. Well-organized and well-conducted training molds military units into smooth functioning fighting machines, builds group solidarity, unit *esprit* and discipline. By successfully training his men as a team, the leader establishes his position, creates mutual confidence, and develops the rapid skillful response required in combat.

No training situation is static. Despite the level of proficiency attained, training is never complete. New men are assigned while trained veterans depart. New operational missions replace the ones that the unit rehearsed. New weapons, vehicles or techniques replace those for which the men are trained. Maintaining operational readiness at the individual and unit level requires constant attention and the highest degree of skillful leadership.

The leader must instill in his men a sense of urgency and excitement in their training mission, set goals and high standards of performance. Using imagination, competition, and realistic situations, he must overcome the apathy and boredom that repetition frequently generates. His training management must overcome limitations of facilities, time, equipment, terrain, and weather. He must see that each man is challenged to do his best, praised and rewarded for success, critiqued and corrected for mistakes. When his unit reaches their peak

227

of performance, he must be prepared to repeat the process all over again with new replacements or on a different mission.

TRAINING PHILOSOPHY

The primary goal of the leader in training is the achievement by his unit of a high quality performance across the broad spectrum of its assigned and potential missions. This requires the mastery of individual skills and techniques by unit members and their integration into smooth, effective teamwork. As General Bruce C. Clarke has noted, the leader can greatly foster this process by adhering to established training principles (Clarke, 1963, p. 62).

Emphasize Fundamentals. The mark of a well-trained unit lies in the attention given to the individual development of each member. The fundamental military skills of marksmanship, communications, maintenance, and administration must all be mastered by each soldier to the degree that they apply to his job before the unit can be really proficient. A well-trained soldier is the only foundation upon which effective, combat ready teamwork can be built.

Employ Integrated Training. Integrated training in which many subjects are taught concurrently, is the key to accelerated and intensive combat training. Through integrating various training subjects, the men can apply all they know to all they do. For example, training in air defense, field fortifications, demolitions, first aid, sanitation, psychological warfare, escape, and evasion can all be integrated into a single tactical training exercise.

Inject Realism. The soldier performs in combat as he has been taught and rehearsed in training. Any weakness in training will be magnified many times in combat. Hence a leader should do his utmost to make each training situation as valid and realistic as time, facilities, and considerations of safety will permit. He should make every effort to duplicate the conditions, scenes, noises, and situations of the battlefield. Soldiers should picture as accurately as possible the combat situation in which they are being trained to perform. The leader must use imagination and ingenuity.

Cross Training. Cross training is vital to any organization. When personnel are trained in several jobs, the leader achieves the depth and capability that may spell the difference between success and failure in combat. Training individuals in duties other than their primary speciality increases the unit's peacetime efficency and potential combat effectiveness. Cross training increases each soldier's value to the Army, increases his pride and self-confidence, and may assist him in gaining promotion. The leader's foresight allows for flexibility and provides a replacement capability within his organization.

Chain of Command. An effective organization always has a smoothly functioning chain of command. A sound training program should emphasize the development of the chain of command. It is in training that the coordination, teamwork, and responsiveness of the chain of command should be brought to a peak of performance. The price of ineffectiveness in combat is too high to neglect the chain of command in training. Delegation of authority builds confidence and responsibility in subordinate leaders. Additionally, the leader's critique and corrections following a subordinate's mistakes in training reduce the number of similar mistakes in combat. The effective leader heeds his responsibility for training and developing his subordinate leaders.

Instill Self-Sufficiency and Confidence. Training should not only impart individual and unit skills, but it should also develop the confidence to practice these skills. Successful practice of these skills in realistic training situations instills this self-confidence. Rewards that recognize the individual's successes demonstrated by valid testing and evaluation build pride, confidence, and unit *esprit.*

The confidence to fight semi-independently under conditions of decentralized control is developed through training exercises. The leader in planning his training must ensure that adequate opportunity for independent action in training is given to his subordinate units.

PERSONNEL MANAGEMENT IN TRAINING

The training situation poses many personnel management problems. The assignment and motivation of cadre, assignment and adjustment of new personnel to the Army and the development of motivation, discipline, and *esprit* are examples of these problem areas.

Cadre

The cadre is the key group of experienced leaders around whom the unit is built. These are the men who must conduct the training effort. The assignment of these individuals to their particular jobs is an important consideration. Each member of the cadre comes to the new unit with many different abilities, capabilities, and interests. Sound assignment procedures satisfy three requirements. They place the individual in the job for which he is best qualified. They meet the needs of the unit. And, they attempt to satisfy the desires of the individual.

Ideally, every member of the cadre desires to establish the highest possible standards of discipline, training, appearance, and conduct. Their standards will be mirrored by the replacements.

Replacements

Every new recruit enters the Army with a certain amount of foreboding. He is entering a new environment in which he is unable to predict or anticipate fully what is to take place. The accounts of tough training, hard discipline, Spartan living conditions, and high standards only add to his uncertainty. The accounts that the recruit has heard could paint a bleak and insurmountable picture in his mind.

One of the primary tasks that needs to be undertaken by the leader is the reduction of this anxiety on the part of the new recruit. If the new soldier gets off on the right foot, he will tend to continue moving in the right direction. A good program of reception for these new men does much to speed their initial adjustment. The aims of the program should be to welcome the soldiers to the unit, explain the purpose of their being assigned to this unit, outline the procedures to be used in processing and issuing equipment, and provide a schedule of what activites will take place in the forthcoming weeks.

The training program itself aids and expedites the adjustment of new men to the Army. The training program provides concrete goals that normally will reduce the uncertainty in the mind of the new soldier as to what is to take place. The program aids the recruit in realizing that he is an important part of a unit. As the program progresses, the men develop pride in themselves and their unit as they progress from an unstructured group to a smoothly operating team.

During this adjustment period, the replacements normally have more personal problems than later when they are fully adjusted to the Army. These problems arise owing to the loss of emotional support provided by the individual's family. Liberal and effective counseling by the leader and key personnel within the unit helps to reduce these personal problems.

TRAINING MANAGEMENT

The leader charged with a training mission must take maximum advantage of available time, equipment, and facilities. To achieve his training objectives, he must take every opportunity to apply all of his management skills to the accomplishment of his mission.

Unit Training Cycle

The management of training begins with an assessment of the training situation, its requirements and objectives. Normally, this is controlled by the specific phase of training the unit has reached and future plans involving it.

The Life Cycle. A military unit, somewhat like an individual, passes through progressive changes that are frequently referred to as its life cycle. These stages consist of activation and organization, training, pre-embarkation and movement, overseas staging, combat, occupation, and inactivation. Such a cycle is normally found in units organized, trained, and committed to combat. Obviously, not all units pass through all of these stages during equivalent periods of time or even reach them in the normal sequence; however, each of the stages of a unit's life establish specific training requirements and objectives.

The Normal Training Cycle. Under peacetime conditions, most units undergo the normal training cycle. This cycle is usually adjusted to operational requirements, availability of training facilities, the climate, the nature of the terrain, and other factors. It frequently begins in the late summer or fall after summer maneuvers or administrative tasks are completed. It may begin upon receipt of a substantial number of replacements. Depending upon the status of the unit, the training may be conducted according to an Army Training Program (ATP) designed for a newly organized unit or under post cycle combat readiness training directives. ATP training initially transforms the recruit into a basic soldier. Then, it trains that soldier in a military occupational specialty so that he can perform a particular job within the unit. Upon the completion of individual and advanced individual training, the unit integrates these individual skills into organized teams. The formal ATP training cycle terminates with a field exercise and maneuver phase at battalion or higher level in which the unit learns to integrate its total effort in combined arms operations under simulated combat conditions.

The cycle for combat readiness training is generally similar to ATP training except that it normally begins with a relatively brief review of advanced individual training and proceeds from small unit training to combined arms maneuvers in a somewhat different manner. Its purpose is to maintain readiness and correct deficiencies. Since replacements are apt to be received throughout the year in a combat ready unit, individual training subjects and small unit training problems are repeated periodically throughout the year. Similarly, since the unit is considered combat ready at the beginning of the cycle, larger unit maneuvers and exercises may be interspersed throughout the training year in order to maintain large unit teamwork and to correct observed deficiencies.

Planning

The broad objectives of the training program are normally received from higher headquarters in the form of a directive. More specific objectives are designed at battalion or company levels to assist in planning and to focus priorities. For example, the broad objective assigned in a particular program might be: "Conduct cadre training during period X." The unit establishes specific objectives within this assigned mission, such as "Qualify all necessary cadre personnel as military instructors, qualify cadre instructors in their specific subject areas, bring all training equipment and facilities to a Command Maintenance Inspection status." These specific objectives clearly indicate what is to be accomplished.

Caution in setting objectives is essential. Unattainable objectives result in ineffective training, laxity, and a decline in morale. Objectives that are unnecessarily limited waste valuable training time and also result in lower morale. Realistic and well-balanced objectives are published in Army Training Programs for cycle training. The leader need only review these objectives to determine if the local situation warrants additional objectives or added emphasis on specific points. In any event, the objectives as finally determined should be disseminated. The American soldier works best when the purpose and goals for his training are clearly understood.

Time available for training is one of the most critical factors to be considered. Normally the directive assigning the unit its training mission specifies the time allotted for its accomplishment. The time allotted, however, is not all training time. In analyzing the local situation, all the demands on time should be considered. Certain operational tasks subtract from the time available for training. Preventive maintenance of equipment, holidays, and administrative requirements also cut into training time. The type unit, its mission, and its distance from training facilities all affect the amount of training time available.

Included in the leader's forecast is an estimate of the effects of administrative requirements. Administrative obstructions may result from a unit's requirement to supply fatigue, guard, and custodial details. These remove personnel from training and thus disrupt the training process. Although the administrative duties must be performed, the determination of the methods and personnel to perform them will affect training. For example, the integrity of the unit and the training sequence can be maintained when the complete unit is assigned administrative duties on a rotating basis.

The status of training facilities, training aids, and supporting equipment should be analyzed. This analysis is designed to determine the availability and serviceability of training areas, ranges, classrooms, and specific training aids. The number and type available in relation to the number of personnel to be trained poses the problem of how these facilities and aids can be most effectively used.

The analysis of these factors constitutes the estimate of the training situation. In arriving at the estimate, many decisions must be made to overcome problem areas and to achieve effective training. Among the more important decisions is the organization for training.

Organizing

Many factors in the local training situation are weighed in determining the type organization to be used. Basically, there are two training systems: centralized and decentralized.

Centralized training organization provides for all training to be given by committees of instructors. In this system, instructional groups specialize in teaching certain subjects. The centralized or committee system relieves subordinate units of much of the normal responsibility for training in those subjects. This centralized organization results in maximum standardization of training. It further provides for the most economical and effective utilization of qualified instructors, facilities, and training aids. The use of this system, however, results in only individual proficiency. Its use causes a loss in unit *esprit* and teamwork. Consequently, it is used primarily in individual rather than unit training.

Decentralized organization releases primary responsibility for detailed planning, direction, and conduct of training to company or platoon level. Only supervisory control and co-ordination is retained at higher level. This system is normally used in training line units. It encourages development of leadership qualities among the officers and noncommissioned officers since they have the responsibility to conduct and supervise the major portion of the training program. This type of training organization is more personal since only the members of the immediate unit are involved. This normally aids in developing morale, *esprit de corps,* and teamwork. Current Department of the Army policies emphasize the use of this system in all training where conditions permit. The resulting higher morale, improved *esprit*, increased motivation, and improved efficiency justify this type of training organization.

Analysis of the advantages and disadvantages of each system as it applies to the specific training situation will result in a decision as to the system to be used. In general practice, however, a compromise solution is often employed. A particular method is selected as the general organization for training with one or two critical areas employing the alternate system. For example, an artillery battalion would normally select a decentralized organization for its primary training organization. Critical areas such as radar specialists, vehicle mechanics, cooks, and radio operators would be trained in a centralized organization at higher headquarters. This method allows the advantage of both systems to be gained.

Co-ordinating

Regardless of which training organization is used, the training effort must be well co-ordinated. With a limited availability of space, time, money, men, and material, the leader must make a concerted effort to co-ordinate all aspects of training. There are few things more inimical to training motivation than for the troops to "hurry up and wait." This is the usual result when the leader fails to co-ordinate the many details necessary to the conduct of effective training. The right men and facilities must meet at the right time and place. Too often, it happens that a unit prepares to move to a particular location only to find that transportation has not been arranged. Someone failed to co-ordinate with the motorpool. Or, a unit deploys on a field exercise only to find the mess halls do not know they are to feed in the field, and the hot food arrives late and cold.

Co-ordinating is not an easy task. Every leader feels his own mission must have priority. Several units may try to occupy the same training area at the same time or decide to use certain facilities without checking to see if the facilities already might be assigned to some other unit. After co-ordination of the plan with all affected agencies, their actions are further co-ordinated through the dissemination of some form of training directive.

Directing

A directive is issued to implement the commander's concept as contained in the Training Plan. This directive is a Training Program. The normal format for this Training Program is a training memorandum which is disseminated to all subordinate commanders and other concerned personnel. Commonly included are such items as: the date the program is to be implemented, references to aid in understanding the over-all concept, the training objectives, the training records required, training policies, and a master training schedule.

Training policies are general guide lines on how training is to be accomplished. Frequently, these policies include guidance for the scheduling of classes, personnel to be used as instructors, and training areas to be used.

The master training schedule portion of the training program is probably the most explicit direction that the unit receives. It is designed to guide subordinate commanders in preparing their schedules. Commonly contained in these training schedules are the subjects to be taught, the number of hours to be devoted to each subject, and an outline of the general sequence of instruction. Examples of typical master training schedules are in Department of the Army Field Manual 21-5.

The success or failure of a training program is ultimately determined by the effectiveness of the instruction presented. Effective instruction depends on adequate preparation, and the training schedule can do much to aid instructors in their preparation. It should be issued early enough to allow subordinate units to plan their own training. References cited for each subject in the schedules, when specific and pertinent, save the instructors time and effort and ensure that correct material is prepared and presented. The time indicated for each subject should be realistic. This aids the instructor in preparing a logical presentation at a speed in keeping with the subject.

The planning, organizing, co-ordinating, and directing represented by the training program contribute to effective training. The ultimate effectiveness, however, depends largely on the subordinate's interpretation of the requirements as listed in the schedules and directives, and on their ability to do what is required. To ensure that the training activities are being conducted correctly and to co-ordinate changes as they occur, the leader must control them.

Controlling

Control of training is accomplished through the direct, immediate supervision of subordinates in the execution of their training tasks. This supervision is composed of three major phases—establishing standards of performance, checking performance, and taking corrective action whenever standards are not satisfactorily met.

The first phase, establishing standards of performance, is normally accomplished during the planning and directing stages of management. The published training program usually contains the basic standards or goals that the training unit must accomplish. Once the standards have been determined and disseminated, the leader checks the performance.

Since the leader cannot devote all of this time to supervising his unit's training activities, he must employ some logical procedure to gain the greatest benefit from the available time. An analysis of the time available, relative importance of the various phases of instruction, and known weaknesses indicate the priority of supervision. Normally, personal supervision proves to be the most effective method of evaluating the actual conduct of training. Although the commander will not be able to be present at all instructional periods, the junior officers and noncommissioned officers of the unit are expected to be present whenever their unit is undergoing training. This demonstrates their interest in the training and allows direct immediate control of the training effort at the lowest possible level.

While personal supervision and inspections are most effective for evaluating the conduct of training, the best method of evaluating what has actually been learned is some form of performance test. Army Training Tests have been designed specifically for this purpose and are normally administered annually. In addition, field training exercises of all types provide the leader an excellent opportunity to observe the effectiveness of the training of the men and the unit.

Evaluation alone is only one step in the supervision. The results of inspections and tests need to be analyzed to pinpoint deficiencies or weaknesses. The deficiencies that were noted and methods for improving training should be presented to the unit or individual concerned as administrative corrective action. Follow-up action ascertains that previous deficiencies have been corrected or are being corrected.

SUMMARY

The modern world environment emphasizes the importance of maintaining combat readiness through continuous and effective training. Established principles of emphasizing fundamentals, using integrated training, injecting realism, cross training, developing self-sufficiency and confidence substantially assist in this training process. Skillful employment of personnel management techniques in assigning and organizing the cadre and in receiving and orienting replacements creates a favorable training environment and minimizes personal problems.

Training management involves the determination of appropriate training objectives, the development of a training plan and training organization, followed by the co-ordination, direction, and controlling of the training effort. The successful employment of these management techniques to maintain operational readiness of a unit requires constant attention and the highest degree of skillful leadership.

Suggestions for Further Reading

Clarke, Bruce C., *Guidelines for the Leader and Commander,* Harrisburg, Pa.: The Stackpole Co., 1963.

Department of the Army Field Manual 21-5, *Military Training.* Washington: Government Printing Office, December 1964.

Ginzberg, Eli, *The Ineffective Soldier: The Lost Division.* New York: Columbia University Press, 1959.

Ginzberg, Eli, *The Ineffective Soldier: Patterns of Performance.* New York: Columbia University Press, 1959.

USCONARC Pamphlet, No. 350-11, *Training: Guide for Commanders of Company Size Units.* Fort Monroe, Virginia: Headquarters U.S. Continental Army Command, November 1966.

XVIII

Combat Leadership

COMBAT IS the ultimate test of military leadership. It places both the leader and his men under severe stress while offering them great challenges. Although equipment, men, and environment have changed through the ages, the fundamental leadership problems of combat are timeless.

The historian, Christopher Ward, recounts an episode that took place on 15 September 1776, at Kip's Bay (in the vicinity of what is now Lexington Avenue and Forty-second Street, New York City). British troops under General William Lord Howe had engaged Washington's Colonials with a fierce bayonet charge. The untrained, undisciplined, and inexperienced militia broke in wild flight before the "Redcoats."

> Washington tried to halt them, to rally them . . . but there was no controlling them. Washington's anger was spectacular. He dashed his hat upon the ground in a transport of rage, crying out, "Are these the men with whom I am to defend America?" He snapped a pistol at them. With his riding cane, he flogged not only private soldiers but officers as well; a colonel, even a brigadier general. But nothing would do . . . they broke . . . and ran.
>
> (Ward, 1952, pp. 242-243.)

Anxiety and the resultant stresses of combat always pose serious problems for the military leader. No army can expect to be spared their debilitating effects on both individuals and groups.

Combat is the culmination of every effort expended by the Army to procure, train, discipline, and perfect fighting units. It is in combat that the sweat of peacetime training finds its purpose. Combat challenges the individual soldier to perform his duty at the risk of injury or death. And, it is in combat the leader finds his ultimate challenge.

Combat presents problems in an environment that cannot be duplicated fully in training. One cannot synthesize the pervading fear of impending destruction that dominates so much of each individual's emotions in combat. The inertia and organizational friction, the confusion, the hysteria induced by fear,

237

the excitement and thrill of taking great risks; these cannot be successfully duplicated in training, although they play a great part in creating the unique atmosphere of combat.

HUMAN ASPECTS

The duties of a soldier in combat cannot be considered as just another undesirable phase of his over-all role, such as latrine duty, kitchen police, or the like. It is a duty that requires a sharp break with many moral prescriptions and routine experiences of peacetime society. This is true, not only for the civilian soldier, but for the professional as well, since he spends his life living within the codes established by his society. Whether the soldier joins the military voluntarily or not, he is committed to its goals. A unit in combat is extremely goal-oriented. At no time are the efforts and performances of the members of a unit so centrally focused on a single objective. Regardless of the nature of the mission, the phase of combat, or the degree of combat stress imposed upon the unit, it maintains its centralized direction against the enemy.

The enemy is both a reality and an intangible—difficult to see, hard to find, and, yet, present to oppose the unit's actions at all times. The enemy cannot be counted on to be where he is supposed to be, or to react in the manner expected of him. His only consistency is his deliberate and continuous opposition to the leader and the soldier in the accomplishment of their mission and other goals. This consistent uncertainty is a source of fear in the combat soldier.

Fear and Panic

The American society has provided the citizen and soldier an environment relatively free from fear. In combat, however, the normal state of the soldier is one of fear and fatigue. General George S. Patton, Jr., states in *War As I Knew It* that "No sane man is unafraid in battle . . ." (Patton, 1947, p. 336), and S. L. A. Marshall writes that, ". . . troops do not conquer their fear of death and wounds, . . ." (Marshall, 1947, p. 124). As a consequence, the soldier must live with continual conflicts between his desires to conquer the enemy and his fear of combat; his desire to escape the situation and his fear of being considered a poor soldier, or worse, a coward. The average American soldier can be expected to handle his fears in an acceptable manner and to generally display a positive and courageous attitude. Even when the going gets extremely rough, he often demonstrates unbelievable raw courage. Fear is ever-present, however. It is important for the combat leader to appreciate just how fear may affect the soldier.

Fear is an emotion involving the whole physiological pattern induced by the action of the sympathetic nervous system. The characteristics of fear are unpleasantness, fatigue, and a desire to escape. It involves such individual symptoms as violent pounding of the heart, a sinking feeling or sickness in the stomach, trembling, and, in extreme situations, a loss of control of the bowels and bladder.

Fear thrives upon frustrations, and it will persist and grow when the individual can do nothing to lessen the threat against himself. The soldier, beset by fear, vacillates between his desire to escape danger and his pride that makes him want to fight. In great fear, he may be captured by inertia—incapable of doing anything—either to satisfy his desire for safety or his motives to fight. The soldier in whom fear overrides all other emotions is an unwilling fighter, hesitant to advance against the enemy, inefficient to the point of uselessness and a detriment to his unit.

Intense fear may easily and quickly lead to panic. Panic results when individuals believe themselves incapable of overcoming a critical situation. The development of panic is usually characterized by the following three steps: first, there is a stress situation in which the individual is presented with factors that induce extreme states of fear. He desires to escape the situation. Second, there is some incident that occurs to the group or selected members of the group that arouses additional fear. This "trigger incident" could be an action that is correct and proper if fully understood, such as an ammunition party moving to the rear towards a company supply dump. Third, the fearful person interprets such an incident the wrong way. In this example, he might believe that the ammunition party was retreating from the battlefield. Action follows, usually running to the rear. Such actions "snowball." Other soldiers follow because they, too, are afraid and temporarily unreasoning, unintelligent, and forgetful of pride and discipline. Fear becomes so strong as to be a justification for action.

Combating Fear and Panic

Fear on the battlefield will be ever present, but it can be conquered by the emotionally stable and well-adjusted soldier who has been prepared to face it. Soldiers should be taught to expect fear and to recognize it as a psychological phenomenon common to all men in combat. Fear, in itself, is no enemy. It is only uncontrolled fear that becomes detrimental to the behavior of a soldier. The courageous man is not one without fear, but one who conquers his fear and performs in spite of it.

Besides recognizing fear, the soldier must be disciplined, trained, confident, and informed. He must be disciplined so that he will fight off the initial effects of fear; trained to protect himself in combat and to function as a member of a team; confident of the power of his unit and himself; and informed as to what the situation is and what can be expected in the immediate future. In this way, he keeps fear from becoming the major influence on his behavior in combat.

When the soldier himself cannot overcome the effects of fear, directed activity may do it for him. Many combat leaders have testified to the fact that they have been successful in overcoming fear in their men by making them do anything physical—moving from one position to another, even if not towards the enemy—assisting other men in carrying a piece of equipment—administering first aid to a comrade. Action appears to be a great steadying force and a successful cure for fear. In fact, the sensation of fear usually disappears entirely in the exhilaration and excitement of actual close combat.

Fear is not confined to the actual combat situation. It may become threatening to an individual in nonbattlefield situations such as a reserve area or rest

240 TAKING COMMAND

camp. The fear produced by anticipating combat, reliving combat experience, or the fear of being afraid may become just as real to the soldier as fear during combat. Accordingly, it can be just as important a problem to the leader. Activity, again, is a major cure for this condition. A busy soldier has little time to worry and brood. The factors mentioned in preceding paragraphs should be stressed. In addition, every measure should be taken to increase the soldier's sense of belonging to the unit. Increasing his identification with other men, who share his experiences, bolsters his confidence and pride. Through discussions and "bull sessions" with these contemporaries, he may be able to recognize that his emotions are not unique or different from those felt by the other members of the group. Sharing something in common with others, even fear, may give him comfort and a release from tension. It also allows him to evaluate objectively his own anxieties.

The avoidance of panic is accomplished by developing those same points that reduce fear. Maintenance of discipline, confidence in unit and leaders, knowledge of the situation, and *esprit de corps* all tend to minimize the possibilities that panic may occur. Should it occur, action must be taken to control the panic and prevent its spread. The leader must take immediate and decisive action at the first sign of panic. First, he must gain the attention of the panic-stricken individuals by some dramatic means. This may involve standing squarely in the path of the men as they flee and ordering them to stop and return. It may necessitate the use of physical force to stop them. Sometimes, only the leader's presence is required as a reassurance to the troops. If panic already exists before the leader is able to influence the activity, then it is necessary to direct the troops to some area where they may feel safe, be provided with factual information, and intelligently informed of their plight. They should then be reassembled in their organization assignments and have their confidence restored by a return to combat. If possible, they should be assigned easy and then progressively more difficult missions; thus, allowing them to rebuild their confidence with each successful accomplishment.

The best way to handle panic is for the leader to prevent its occurrence. Men should be trained to have confidence in themselves, their leaders, and their weapons. The leader should make every effort to eliminate the conditions which foster panic, such as hunger, fatigue, lack of confidence, and absence of information. He must build *esprit de corps* by teamwork and by insisting upon technical and tactical proficiency throughout the organization.

Rumor

Rumor is generally talk that is not based on definite knowledge but is mere gossip or hearsay. Rumors, like fear and panic, tend to develop in those periods when the individual is placed under stress. When soldiers lack concrete information, they tend to fabricate or repeat anything they hear that has some bearing on their situation. Rumors develop when individuals are living in a state of expectation or they are experiencing some discomfort, frustration, or boredom. Rumors, under these conditions, provide some release of tensions, even though such release may not always be very satisfying. An attempt to justify an existing state of fear can also start rumors (Festinger, 1957). For example, troops who have just come under a heavy mortar attack may start and believe a rumor that the enemy is launching an attack. Individuals sometimes tend to pass on rumors to satisfy their own importance or beliefs or to hurt others. Having and displaying knowledge, whether fact or fiction, does, in the opinion of some, increase their prestige. Others attempt to reduce their tension by spreading the rumor in the hope that someone will deny its truth. Rumor may take its toll of fighting men if allowed to flourish. It develops false hopes or fears that may undermine morale. Rumor can take its place in the influences which develop panic.

Fatigue

When a rifle company has been in combat for a period of time, one thing is certain about the unit—it is tired. The officers are tired, the noncommissioned officers are tired, and the men are tired. Physical and emotional fatigue is the common lot of the infantryman. And, depending on the circumstances of combat, this may become obvious within a matter of hours after entry into action. It may take a little longer to become evident, but it grows progressively worse as time in combat increases.

Physical fatigue is the result of many factors. During combat, the soldier is required to engage in considerable physical activity. Generally speaking, all his movement is done on foot; and normally he is loaded down with a pack, weapon, and ammunition, if not more. He lives with nature and, accordingly, must endure its extremes of heat and cold, most of the time with inadequate, if any, shelter. All of this becomes a drain on his physical resources. Seldom does he have an opportunity to recoup his strength. Sleep, when it is achieved, usually is in a foxhole or similar type fortification, with the soldier wearing the same clothing he has fought in.

A major contribution to the physical fatigue produced in combat is lack of adequate food. Although the combat ration is scientifically produced to provide the soldier the essentials of a proper diet, seldom will he have a chance or take the time to eat a complete meal. Upon many occasions, he will not be able to heat what he has due to a lack of time or immediate combat restrictions. Because of fatigue, he may just lack the energy to prepare a combat meal.

Fear, grief, horror, and like emotions, that soldiers continually experience in combat, also produce conditions of fatigue. The effects of this emotional type fatigue are physiologically identical to those resulting from physical exertion and, consequently, serve to aggravate what is already weakening the individual.

A tired soldier is not an efficient soldier. When a man's body is spent, he begins to lose control of his nervous system. He may become extremely emotional about minor events; yet, he may show almost no emotional reactions. He tends to be disinterested and his motor behavior is likely to become almost mechanical. Ostensibly "carrying on," he really is only occupying space and may contribute little to the unit's mission. Extreme fatigue leads to pessimism that destroys the unit and the self-confidence requisite to a soldier's combat motivation. Fatigue leads to carelessness, even to the extreme of neglect of self-preservation. The tired soldier often becomes a casualty because of his inattention to fundamental individual protective measures.

Individual and unit fatigue are problems that can best be prevented through proper management at higher echelons. Timely rotation of front line units to allow men to recuperate from the effects of fatigue is most important. Such action may not be possible, however, when battle is joined and the issues become critical. Accordingly, a small unit leader must be prepared to cope with fatigue within his unit—not only as it occurs but also in its prevention.

The solution is not simple since the situation, itself, precludes the obvious answer—relief from the lines. Maximum physical conditioning prior to combat is of paramount importance. Every effort should be expended, prior to a unit's entry into combat, to ensure that soldiers are at their peak of physical conditioning. Mental and moral strengths are also important in overcoming fatigue. A well-motivated soldier has the will to overcome much of his bodily weariness. Also, he has the drive to take care of himself in order to maintain his bodily strength.

Soldiers can be conditioned to withstand a great amount of fatigue. As combat progresses, however, and fatigue approaches, leaders must ensure that, within the realm of practicability, their men are not used for details that will cause a drain of their physical strength, i.e., water, ration, and ammunition carrying details. When the opportunity arises, men should be encouraged to eat, if not forced to do so. They should not be left to nibble because of a lack of sufficient energy to heat and consume a meal. Frequently, tired soldiers must be forced to maintain combat awareness. Weary soldiers do not like to dig in, are lax in maintaining camouflage discipline, and are negligent about their self-protective measures. Often, a verbal reminder may be sufficient to remedy their careless or lackadaisical attitudes. When fatigue weighs heavily on the soldier, though, direct orders and other authoritarian measures may be necessary to goad him to proper action. Under these conditions, the leader's example is of paramount importance and, in extended periods of combat, is one of the most, if not the most, difficult tasks a leader must face.

Combat Exhaustion

This discussion considers only temporary neuropsychiatric reactions to combat. Such reactions are typically those that may be relieved by rest at an aid station close to the battle area. Usually, the individual can return to his unit. These cases are officially classified by the Army as "combat exhaustion." Experience in World War II and Korea indicates an estimated 10 per cent or less of men in combat developed combat exhaustion (Coleman, 1964, p. 167). Among other reasons, the sporadic nature of the fighting in Vietnam has reduced psychiatric complaints to less than two per cent. There may have been more; however, those who received therapy at aid stations and returned to duty in a matter of hours were not made a matter of record.

The individual soldier who experiences combat exhaustion has reactions that vary with the severity and nature of the experience and his personality. The combat exhaustion point differs for each individual. Albert Glass has said:

> Certain single individual characteristics stand out from the mass of personal history data as pertinent to vulnerability or predisposition to combat stress; namely, (1) Age. The older combat soldier is more susceptible to psychiatric break-

down than his 18- to 21-year-old colleague. After 35 years, age becomes particularly significant in increasing vulnerability to combat stress which is due to lessened capacity for strenuous physical activity. Obviously, there are many exceptions, particularly among officers and noncommissioned officers. (2) Educational level. It would seem reasonable to believe that intellectual ability should be related to combat effectiveness. This hypothesis has not been substantiated because individuals with marked or severe degrees of mental retardation are generally rejected for military service. However, all studies agree that limited educational achievement of less than the eighth grade is significantly related with noneffective performance in both combat and noncombat assignments. No doubt, characteristics other than intelligence are involved in the level of schooling attained, such as capacity to conform and ability to work with others. (3) Other single criteria, such as race, religion, economic status, cultural origin, civilian occupation, and marital status, show no significant relationship with combat psychiatric breakdown.

(Glass, 1957, p. 194.)

As he is exposed to the constant pressure of combat situations, the soldier begins to exhibit certain symptoms which could be listed as indicators of this state. Generally, there is a state of irritability that is characterized by snappishness in attitude, overreaction, flare-ups, excessive use of profanity, and an inability to sleep. The common cause of this condition is a state of overwhelming anxiety. This produces symptoms which reflect, first, the disorganizing effects of anxiety; second, an unconscious device by which the individual tries to defend himself; and, third, the effects of fatigue. The continual threat of combat seems impossible to overcome or escape, and the normal adjustive reactions of the individual are relatively useless. He becomes completely ineffective and must be evacuated from the unit.

It has been theorized that, given enough time in combat, even the strongest soldier will become a casualty to combat exhaustion. The human being can stand only so much stress before something must give. As previously discussed, the well-adjusted, rested, and combat-oriented soldier will withstand stress to a great degree. Consequently, he will be less subject to combat exhaustion.

When it becomes apparent, however, that a soldier is showing the symptoms of combat exhaustion, the leader must evacuate him. To allow him to remain in combat will only aggravate the effects of this affliction. Extreme cases of combat exhaustion will seldom be cured to the degree that will permit a return to combat duty. On the other hand, less serious cases may be treated and cured by proper professional attention at medical units located relatively near to the front lines. Soldiers who have experienced only the initial symptoms of combat exhaustion may be successfully treated and returned to duty after a night or two of sound sleep, good food, and a relaxation from the tensions of combat. The maintenance of the psychological "self" in the face of these tensions is essential for both the individual and the leader. Certain intangibles and tangibles can provide each individual soldier with some supporting structures.

SUPPORTS

Ideals and Attitudes

History shows that men fight better for a cause in which they believe. It is part of the training of the American soldier to imbue in him the high ideals to which his country is dedicated and for which he may have to fight. Together with other ideals he has learned to value, the causes he fights for will sustain him through the abnormalities in life forced upon him by war. Strengthened by such convictions, the soldier is able to prepare for and approach combat. They support his motivation to fight and become a major factor in his life should he become a prisoner of war.

But in the cold, hard, reality of battle, when the soldier is faced with the immediate possibilities of death or wounding, those high ideals that have been paramount in his existence until then become much less important and are forced into the background or, possibly, fade completely from his awareness. Studies of combat experiences, and the conclusions of many combat leaders, indicate that more immediate goals and incentives leading toward self-preservation become the focal point of the soldier's behavior at this time.

The American Soldier study quotes a combat veteran, in answer to a question relative to what he was fighting for, as follows: "Ask any dogface on the line. You're fighting for your skin on the line. When I enlisted, I was patriotic as all hell. There's no patriotism on the line. A boy up there 60 days on the line is in danger every minute. He ain't fighting for patriotism." (Stouffer *et al.*, 1949b, p. 169.) Another source states that, "The combat soldier does not have an opportunity to think about patriotism and great causes. To him, the immediate questions are: What is the war to me? Will I be able to endure? Will I turn yellow? Can I take it?" (Kardiner and Spiegel, 1947, p. 33.) S. L. A. Marshall puts it in much stronger words, concluding that, "In battle you may draw a small circle around a soldier, including within it only those persons and objects that he sees or that he believes will influence his immediate fortunes." (Marshall, 1947, p. 154.)

This does not indicate that these attitudes of the soldier are a problem to the leader. He may well be sharing them. Nor does this discussion infer that the soldier is not patriotic. It only shows that the factors that determine his motivation under extreme stress temporarily shift in importance and strength.

Other attitudes of the soldier may be altered by his combat experiences. Few are of such nature that they will affect his performance. Of importance, however, particularly to the junior officer and noncommissioned officer, are the attitudes he holds about his leadership and fighting ability. Often, after initial combat or after actions that result in many casualties, junior leaders become overly critical of their own conduct in battle. They may feel that they are responsible for casualties taken within their unit; that more aggressiveness or tactical ability on their part would have saved lives. Obviously, thoughts of this nature can become depressing to the leader and affect his future performance.

Confidence

Confidence is perhaps the greatest source of emotional strength that a soldier can draw upon. With it, he willingly faces the enemy and withstands deprivations, minor setbacks, and extreme stresses, knowing that he and his unit are capable of succeeding. The infusion of confidence into an individual has its basis in his beliefs that the causes he is fighting for are morally right and worth sacrificing for. Believing so, he will have confidence in what lies ahead— in combat and his postwar life as well.

The soldier must be given confidence in the weapons of war that are employed against the enemy. This includes not only his rifle and other personal weapons, but the entire war strength of the nation. It is satisfying to know that one's rifle is more effective than the enemy soldier's. It is equally satisfying to know that there will not be a shortage of ammunition for that rifle or for the supporting artillery; that our country is producing more and better weapons; that our ships control the seas and our planes the skies.

The soldier's confidence that his leaders are tactically proficient and combat-wise, makes it much easier for him to advance toward the unknown. He is strengthened by the knowledge that, if he should become a casualty, his friends and leaders will come to his rescue; and that, once removed from the scene of battle, he will receive proper medical attention. Also, it is amazing how a unit's adherence to a policy of taking care of its dead will have a settling effect and a positive influence on the *esprit* of the unit.

Belief in his own abilities contributes to the confidence of the combat soldier. Many men can realize their abilities by objective evaluation of their own conduct in battle. Verbal approval or tangible evidence of combat achievement reassures others. Because of the confusion of battle, individual soldiers and units may not recognize that they did a satisfactory job. There have been instances of small combat units believing that they had lost a battle or were ineffective when, in the over-all scheme, their contribution was of major importance. Soldiers and units must be made aware of their successes. If they do not believe they have done well in one fight, their confidence for winning the next is at a minimum. Expectations of failure destroy morale. Confidence in victory ensures it.

Group Solidarity

The relationship between the soldier and the other men in his unit, as well as with the unit itself, is a factor of primary importance in a combat situation. Few men have the ability to live and fight alone. It is through the strength of the ties among the men of a group that unit cohesiveness and fighting ability are developed. S. L. A. Marshall holds that it is "one of the simplest truths of war that the thing which enables an infantry soldier to keep going is the near presence or the presumed presence of a comrade." (Marshall, 1947, p. 42.) The soldier's identification with his comrades and unit during combat is seldom, if ever, equalled during other phases of his life. Their successes are his, their problems are his, their failures are his. They become as much of his "self" as those persons and ideals which he previously held most dear in life.

The authors of *The American Soldier* quote a casualty of the North African campaign as follows: "The men in my squad were my special friends. My best friend was the sergeant of the squad. We bunked together, slept together, fought together, told each other where our money was pinned to our shirts. We write to each other now. Expect to get together when the war is over . . . If one man gets a letter from home over there, the whole company reads it. Whatever belongs to me belongs to the whole outfit." (Stouffer *et al.*, 1949b, p. 99.)

This feeling between men within a combat unit grows from mutual dependence in combat, where the action of the unit helps safeguard the individual who, in turn, helps preserve the unit. It goes much deeper than this, though, as indicated by another passage from *The American Soldier:* "Mutual dependence, however, was more than a matter of mere survival. Isolated as he was from contact with the rest of the world, the combat man was thrown back on his outfit to meet the various affectional needs for response, recognition, approval, and, in general, for appreciation as a significant person rather than a means— needs which he would normally satisfy in his relations with his family and with friends of his own choosing." (Stouffer *et al.*, 1949b, p. 98.)

Men within a combat unit identify with each other to the extent that there is a common feeling that they share a separate and unique destiny for which they will sacrifice to the extreme. The identification becomes so great that often a soldier will hesitate to fight with an unfamiliar group. S. L. A. Marshall attributes this too, ". . . the inherent unwillingness of the soldier to risk danger on behalf of men with whom he has no social identity. When a soldier is unknown to the men who are around him, he has relatively little reason to fear the loss of the one thing that he is likely to value more highly than life—his reputation as a man among other men." (Marshall, 1947, p. 153.) And, to him, these men are those in his squad, his platoon, and his company. This supports the importance of a casualty's being returned to combat duty with his old outfit. Rather than being an outsider to an already closely knit group, he is able to step right into a familiar role among the men he respects the most and who return the feeling.

Unit leaders must be alert to stifle anything that might introduce friction into the group and cause partial breakdowns of these relationships. Frictions may develop relatively easily, even among men who are so closely identified. Close group living has its disadvantages in the incessant demands and petty irritations it entails. When in combat, everybody is tense anyway as a result of multiple stresses, and the small frictions of interaction with one's fellows sometimes take on exaggerated importance. Effective leadership, however, can minimize these problems.

Decorations and Awards

Formal recognition of performance in combat improves both morale and *esprit*. Soldiers take great pride in identifying with a unit which is commended for its combat performance and will fight and sacrifice for that unit. In addition, soldiers must be individually commended for heroic conduct in combat. Individual decorations reward the soldier for his heroic performance, thus increasing his own self-confidence and sense of being appreciated by his superiors and country. In addition, individual awards recognize the soldier as an important part of his unit. This bolsters his self-respect among his contemporaries and, in turn, their respect for him is increased. Awards also serve as a motivating force for those who have not yet been in combat to emulate those who have.

When formal awards are not appropriate for combat action, informal commendation to both units and individuals is of great importance. A word of appreciation and approval by unit leaders at all levels increases the soldier's morale by recognizing that his performance is valued and that he and his unit are making an important contribution to the over-all effort.

Leaders must determine which of their men perform heroically. Seldom will they be personally aware of all acts of valor performed within their unit. Officers must seek such information from their subordinate leaders and other enlisted men who will readily discuss information of this nature about their buddies. Recommendations for decorations should be made as soon as possible after combat actions, and awards presented with appropriate ceremony.

MANAGEMENT IN COMBAT

The leader in combat will never have an inexhaustible reservoir of time, men, money, or materiel at his disposal. Resources are in just too short supply in the normally demanding situations of combat. Therefore, the prudent combat leader must be a combat manager. He must know and use "the science of employing men and material in the economical and effective accomplishment of a mission." He must make that definition function as a part of his mission. By this definition, it is obvious that systematic management is of paramount importance in combat. Under the stresses of battle, the application of the principles of management can easily be glossed over; however, the leader who does so only lowers his unit's effectiveness. Men and materials cannot be efficiently employed as the result of subjective evaluations and "off-the-cuff" decisions.

The circumstances forced upon the leader by combat rarely afford him the opportunity to prepare detailed and elaborate plans. The situation normally will compel him to make a brief estimate of the situation and develop a plan covering only the bare essentials necessary to ensure the accomplishment of the mission. The details of plans and operations of combat units must be taken care of through the use of "Standing Operating Procedures." These SOPs will usually be developed from basic procedures established by the leader prior to combat, modified, and enlarged as he gains combat experience. Events that, prior to combat, are irregular and unusual and require decisions of the leader may well become routines of combat when handled by SOP, thus freeing the leader for more critical duties. Forecasting becomes of increasing importance. As the leader develops combat "know-how," he will be able to develop more comprehensive plans and expanded SOPs that will be of sufficient flexibility to apply to the changing combat situation.

Modern combat demands that the leader be flexible enough to organize his unit to fit the situation. In his tailoring task forces, he must give due consideration to unity of command, span of control, and the allocation of resources. Rapidly changing conditions in combat require constant reorganization to facilitate future operations, replace casualties, or provide for the unexpected detachment of units. Special missions, such as helicopter operations, also tax the leader's organizational ability.

Due to the stresses affecting individuals in combat plus the confusion and noise accompanying battle, leaders must ensure that their directives are received and understood. This is particularly important within company level organizations, since orders are generally fragmentary and verbal. Co-ordination becomes a matter of concern for the same reasons, principally because communications become difficult between the leader and subordinate units and because key men become casualties.

A combat leader can be almost assured that, once he has issued a directive for his unit to carry out a mission, something will interfere with that operation —at some time and to some degree. If not the enemy, it might be the weather, the terrain, the frailties of human nature, or some other aspect of combat. Consequently, he must be continually "on top" of the situation in order to exert control and ensure that the mission will be accomplished. He must be in a position where he can be sure that his directives are being carried out and to inject corrective action into the operation of his unit when it becomes necessary.

Combat Replacements

In combat, the greatest need for new personnel is to replace casualties in combat units. The question is frequently raised as to the best way to effect such replacement. The two contrasting systems are individual replacements versus unit replacement.

There are merits to both systems. Individual rotation is simpler to accomplish, more economical in terms of money, and requires less over-all manpower. Fully trained, widely experienced veterans in the unit are capable of indoctrinating and integrating new blood. A new soldier can merely enter the fight, pick up equipment on hand, and go to work. Eventually, however, the unit efficiency wanes. In continuous combat, men can quickly get tired to the point of exhaustion, and need rest. Further, piecemeal assignments interfere with high morale and *esprit*.

Unit replacement has obvious advantages. The unit can be trained as a team before and during combat. Bonds of discipline and loyalty are made before actual combat is entered. Men become attached to their own leaders, companions, equipment, and characteristic ways of doing things. When they enter combat, they do so as a fresh unit. Nevertheless, unit replacement has drawbacks. The Army may not be able to man a unit replacement system. Such a system requires a tremendous number of units. Excessive reserves are a luxury. It is also costly to transfer whole units complete with all their equipment. A leader must weigh unit efficiency against expenditure of personnel and money in order to reach the best solution under existing conditions. As a generality, it is best to use an intact unit in combat when feasible.

The practicabilities of the combat situation may well preclude the desired replacement of combat units. This was true in World Wars I and II and in Korea, and will probably be true to a considerable extent in future wars. Consequently, the problems relating to the individual replacement bear careful scrutiny and understanding.

A combat replacement in World War II stated that, "Being a replacement is like being an orphan. You are away from anybody you know and feel lost and lonesome." (Stouffer *et al.*, 1949b, p. 273.) It is probably a psychological gain for the individual when he joins a combat unit for he has found a permanent home. In joining his unit, however, many doubts, fears, and uncertainties, previously dormant to a degree, become manifest in the soldier. Heading the list, of course, is impending combat and the soldier's natural fear of being wounded, captured or killed. He may be filled with anxiety as to whether or not he will be able to function properly as a member of the team. The team, in this case, consisting of veteran soldiers already wise in the ways of combat. As a larger aspect of this latter situation, he is faced with the processes of social integration—to become a liked and accepted member of the group. To the replacement, these are heavy problems, since the combat veteran is considered at the top rung of the status ladder. The new, nontested member of the group has grave doubts about his possibilities of ever being accepted by such a unique group of men.

This very situation, however, helps the soldier in his adjustment. Due to his attitude of respect toward the veteran, he is highly motivated to accept the authority of the veteran noncommissioned officers of the unit and the requirements they make upon him. He tends to model his actions after theirs. He listens to them and accepts their recommendations and advice. All of these factors help prepare him for the test ahead. Studies have shown that the veteran, himself, is motivated to impart his combat experience to the replacement. Eighty per cent of veterans of World War II, who were queried, testified to the fact that they usually tried to help out the replacement as much as they could in order to work him into the unit as quickly and completely as possible (Stouffer et al., 1949b, p. 278).

The groundwork for the replacement's adjustment to a combat unit must be laid immediately upon his joining the unit. A cold reception may prolong the period of adjustment, with an accompanying loss of combat effectiveness. The replacement should be welcomed by his immediate commanders, platoon, and company and, if possible, by his battalion commander. This helps him enlarge his identification with the unit. The veterans must make every effort to make the newly joined soldier a part of their informal groups. The leader should orient him on the unit's history, mission, and policies as soon as possible. The platoon leader must take a personal interest in the replacement, paying particular attention to any personal problems that he may have that might interfere with his adjustment and integration into the unit.

Obviously, the above discussion indicates that replacements should be assigned to a unit when it is in reserve or a rest area. The longer the period of noncombat time the replacement has with his unit, the better he will perform in combat. Every effort must be made to prevent assigning replacements to units while they are in actual combat. If such a situation occurs, not only is the replacement a stranger to the battlefield and the unit and possibly an ineffective soldier, but also these undesirable circumstances greatly multiply his chances of becoming a casualty.

Training in Combat

After his men have adequately rested in a rest area, the leader must turn to the necessity for appropriate training. His objectives at this time are to improve and sharpen his unit's efficiency, to maintain a peak of physical conditioning throughout his command, and to integrate replacements into the unit so as to make them competent working members of the organization.

When the situation allows, critiques of previous actions should be conducted and training directed toward improving areas where weaknesses have occurred. Reconditioned and new weapons should be zeroed in and, in the event new-type weapons have been introduced, all men should become familiar with them.

It is of paramount importance that the leader objectively evaluate this program to ensure that his schedule is sufficiently rigorous to maintain the battle spirit of his unit and yet does not overly train to the detriment of the morale of the men. The veteran recently off the lines may look at training at this time like closing the barn door after the horses are out. All men must be oriented toward the objectives and value of the training program and, above all, the leader must plan this training in detail and give it real meaning.

THE U.S. FIGHTING MAN'S CODE

In 1955, a special advisory committee, appointed by the President of the United States, drew up a set of standards designed to provide guidelines for the professional conduct of U.S. fighting men. As a result, on 17 August of the same year the President, by Executive Order 10631, proclaimed an official Code of Conduct for members of the U.S. Armed Forces.

A professional code, moral in nature, the Code of Conduct sets forth standards of conduct to be met by those men serving their country as members of the Armed Forces. It is, therefore, a basic philosophy of conduct common to all American military men.

The Code consists of these six declarations:

I.   I am an American fighting man. I serve in the forces which guard my country and our way of life. I am prepared to give my life in their defense.

II.   I will never surrender of my own free will. If in command, I will never surrender my men while they still have the means to resist.

III.   If I am captured, I will continue to resist by all means available. I will make every effort to escape and aid others to escape. I will accept neither parole nor special favors from the enemy.

IV.   If I become a prisoner of war, I will keep faith with my fellow prisoners. I will give no information nor take part in any action which might be harmful to my comrades. If I am senior, I will take command. If not, I will obey the lawful orders of those appointed over me and will back them up in every way.

V. When questioned, should I become a prisoner of war, I am bound to give only name, rank, service number, and date of birth. I will evade answering further questions to the utmost of my ability. I will make no oral or written statements disloyal to my country and its allies or harmful to their cause.

VI. I will never forget that I am an American fighting man, responsible for my actions, and dedicated to the principles which made my country free. I will trust in my God and in the United States of America.

As written, the Code is nothing new. It is merely an expression in writing of one segment of the professional code discussed in Chapter III. In the words of the advisory committee which drew up the Code: "We can find no basis for making recommendations other than on the principles and foundations which have made America strong and on the qualities which we associate with men of integrity and character." (Letter OSD, 1955.)

The primary objective of the Code is to increase unit fighting strength and to strengthen the individual's will to resist. The Code applies to all fighting men of the Armed Forces, whether in combat, captivity, or any other circumstance.

Like any soldier, every leader must adhere to the moral obligations prescribed by the Code. In addition, he is responsible for training his men to do likewise. He manages and inspires his subordinates in a manner that maximizes their opportunity to abide by the Code. Therefore, a leader must understand fully the details of the Code, its purposes, and underlying principles.

Code of Conduct Training

A leader must take care of his men. He starts with effective training. During basic training, all men are instructed in the fundamental thesis of the Code. This indoctrination continues during unit and combined arms training. The current Army regulation (AR 350-30) prescribes that Code of Conduct training centers on increasing unit strength and the soldier's will to resist. In addition, it prescribes that such training must assure men that:

a. Even as a prisoner of war, every man continues to be of special concern to the United States; he will not be forgotten.

b. Every available national means will be employed to establish contact with, to support, and to gain release of prisoners of war.

c. The laws of the United States provide for the support and care of the dependents of members of the Armed Forces including those who become prisoners of war and will continue to provide for their welfare.

(AR 350-30, 1964, p. 2.)

Among all issues, two factors appear to warrant major emphasis in training:

inculcation of high moral concepts, and development and maintenance of high standards of discipline and unit *esprit*.

The leader should integrate Code of Conduct training in all unit and combined arms exercises. Such instruction should be co-ordinated with related subjects such as tactical training, health and sanitation, patrolling, military law, intelligence, military discipline, and teamwork. Every soldier must know his rights and duties as prescribed by the Geneva Convention and other international agreements. The dispersion inherent in nuclear warfare and counter-insurgency requires that the men have the capability to resist despite isolation from other units. This can be developed in training through building confidence in the ability of the unit and its leaders to succeed.

Resisting Capture

The Code prescribes that a soldier does not surrender of his own free will. Likewise, a leader does not surrender his men while they still have the means to resist. This does not imply that one has to commit suicide in resisting. Some of our greatest soldiers became prisoners when all avenues of defense failed. But if means of resisting are available, then a commander continues resisting.

The term "free will" can stand clarification. Free will is a moral concept. One surrenders of his own free will when he does so voluntarily, in accordance with the way he views the situation. A leader must resist the enemy until all defense fails. When one believes that his unit can go on, it must. If it cannot, capture will be unavoidable. When and if capture occurs, the leader does not feel that he is quitting or giving up.

The story of John Paul Jones, captain of the *Bonhomme Richard,* and his fight with the British in 1779 is known to every American youth. When asked "Do you ask for quarter?" Captain Jones retorted, "I have not yet begun to fight." The subsequent victory of this hero is all part of American tradition. More recently, Brigadier General Anthony C. McAuliffe at Bastogne in World War II reflected the true fighting man spirit when he retorted to the German request for surrender with his now famous "NUTS!"

Military units must be able to hold off the enemy for a long period. Military history contains many heroic endeavors in this regard. Some notable achievements such as the Alamo ended with many casualties; others like Bataan ended in surrender. Many more like Bastogne saved not only time, but also ended in victory.

Incidents such as these reflect that, with inspiration by the commander and sound management of men and supplies, the battle is not easily lost. A commander does not surrender until the bitter end. Even then, when all defense fails, he should attempt to break out to friendly territory rather than submit to capture. The aggressive action may take the form of deeper penetration against lightly manned rear area forces. Barring a deeper penetration, the commander may choose to extricate his unit by infiltrating his forces to friendly lines, or he may combine escape and evasion with other methods of resistance and attack to return his troops to friendly forces.

Resisting After Capture

Regardless of all efforts to preclude capture, it is a fact of life that in any conflict some will become prisoners. Capture sometimes is unavoidable. Captured men still have the obligation to defend their country and oppose the enemy. Article IV of the Code states that a senior will take command and that lawful orders will be obeyed from seniors. Responsibilities and procedures are very similar to those in other leadership situations.

The senior officer must assume command and establish an organization. The authority to establish organizations within prisoner-of-war enclosures is clear. It has been provided for by the Geneva Convention of 1949. The senior officer organizes to ensure the spiritual, physical, and intellectual well-being of troops and to plan escapes. Officers and noncommissioned officers then continue to exercise authority equivalent to their rank before capture. When prisoners are collected as a group, the senior man, regardless of service, assumes command. If he becomes isolated from the unit or is unable to perform, the next senior man takes over. This is the first step to success; the leader must exercise command regardless of the circumstances. The leader must make an estimate of the situation and make plans for resisting, bettering living conditions, and escaping. He organizes personnel and assigns them specific duties for such activities as sanitation, first aid, procurement of supplementary food, housing, care of the wounded, and escape. Men are assigned jobs that match their qualified skills. For example, men with farming experiences can be assigned to the food procurement committee. Carpenters, plumbers, and masons can be employed in constructing or modifying facilities. There are always men interested in athletics who will establish recreational activities.

Obviously, all directed efforts must be co-ordinated and controlled. In this regard, formal communication channels are established and may be reinforced by a workable grapevine to keep all men informed. Execution of plans must be bold, skillful, and rapid. This is particularly true in the case of escapes. This is best accomplished by men working as organized team. All men must participate, each having a specific task. Everyone has a responsibility toward the group effort to succeed in returning to friendly forces.

Every effort must be expended to bring men to socialize with each other. There is no leadership by isolation. A soldier obtains mental and emotional support by his being a welcomed member of a tight, unified military group. This way his physiological deprivations and punishments are easier to take. "Give-up-itis" is usually traceable to the lack of spiritual or social satisfactions. Group unity will help to control fear in particular. The enemy can be expected to play on human emotions and maladaptive adjustment to daily problems. They will induce fear of the unknown and prisoner distrust for each other. This, of course, tends to split the unit wide open. The leader should encourage prisoners to share the deprivations and fight the enemy in unison.

All during his imprisonment, the leader plans escape. According to the Geneva Convention, a prisoner who makes an unsuccessful attempt to escape, or those who aid him to escape, may be subjected only to limited disciplinary punishment provided no one is hurt in the course of the escape. They cannot be severely beaten or subjected to inhuman treatment. Plans for escape should commence immediately after capture. Escape is easier at these early moments. Further plans for escape may be more deliberate with detailed organization, personnel assignments, supply procedures, deceptions, evasion maneuvers, and the like. Additionally, the leader should be alert to grab fleeting opportunities, such as enemy carelessness or confusion.

The key to resistance is sound management and dynamic inspiration. This means effective planning, organizing, co-ordinating, directing, and controlling. It necessitates full recognition of sound human relation practices, the motivation of men through group solidarity. In addition, it emphasizes the importance of morality as a fundamental factor of leadership. With these tools, a materialistic philosophy can be supplanted with the spirit of fighting men.

SUMMARY

The responsibilities of a leader during combat are no different from his responsibilities in any other situation, i.e., he must effectively lead his unit in the accomplishment of its mission. In combat, however, effective performance depends to a great degree on how well soldiers and units adjust to the multiple stresses imposed upon them by the circumstances of battle. It is to this problem that the leader must direct a major share of his leadership effort.

The predominating factor that influences the soldier's behavior in combat is his fear of impending destruction. Additionally, he is subject to the anxieties produced by the violence and confusion of combat while, at the same time, his energies are being drained by unusually demanding physical activity. Soldiers who are not emotionally and physically prepared to face combat will stand a good chance of becoming casualties to its effects.

A leader can provide positive support to the soldier's fight against the stresses of combat through positive leadership. Primarily, the leader must increase combat motivation by bolstering individual morale and unit *esprit*. Personal welfare of the troops is subordinate only to the limitations imposed upon the situation and the mission. Individual and unit confidence must be built up. Pride in achievement must be fostered and group solidarity cemented.

There is no greater challenge of tactical ability and leadership than a combat command. The leader, who has taken care that his men are well trained, have learned about combat and its effects, are well provided for, and are highly spirited, will successfully stand the test.

The Code of Conduct is a formalization of the unwritten creed that American fighting men have dedicated themselves to since the birth of our nation. It is a professional code of moral conduct based upon human freedoms and dignity. It establishes standards of performance for the soldier to live up to and provides guidelines to help him meet these expectations.

Besides giving the soldier an ultimate purpose as a fighting man, the Code sets forth specific guidelines for his conduct when capture may be threatening and for his behavior if he should become a prisoner of war. In either event, it is his duty to resist the enemy with every physical and moral means that he can bring to bear and to uphold the traditions and principles of his service and country. The Code of Conduct fits the very nature of a free man who holds firm convictions. As well as the soldier lives by the Code, it will serve him in turn.

Suggestions for Further Reading

Coleman, J. C., *Abnormal Psychology and Modern Life*. 3rd ed.; Chicago: Scott, Foresman & Company, 1964.

Janowitz, M., *The New Military*. New York: Russell Sage Foundation, 1964.

Marshall, S. L. A., *Men Against Fire*. Washington, D.C.: Infantry Journal, 1947.

Stouffer, S. A., *et al.*, *The American Soldier: Combat and Its Aftermath*, Vol. II. Princeton, N.J.: Princeton University Press, 1949.

XIX

The Military Advisor

A SIGNIFICANT aspect of the role of the American soldier in the second half of the twentieth century is his frequent service as a military advisor. The complexities of modern life, the prolonged Cold War, the rising expectations of newly emergent nations, the social and technical advances of modern man, and the intricacies of government and politics have resulted in assignments requiring the military leader to exercise leadership without the traditional tool of command authority. This is a challenge truly worthy of his best leadership talent. These advisory duties run the gamut from assignments with foreign armies and other military services to participation in joint military-civilian planning and coordinating committees. These assignments, although possessing certain novel features, are not entirely unique. The traditional role of the staff officer is one of an advisor to his commander and to the commander's subordinates. Similarly, mission accomplishment for the staff officer is largely dependent upon his ability to personally influence the commander and the line. The personal influence of the advisor like that of the staff officer stems from his professional competence and skill as a leader.

FOREIGN ADVISORY DUTY

An important factor in the accomplishment of the advisory mission is the impression individual advisors make on the local population. While in a foreign country, the advisor serves as a living example of America. He must ensure that his example is above reproach. All factions of the local population will be observing his actions and conduct. Derogatory propaganda often creates a false picture of Americans in the mind of the local populace. Normally, the advisor can correct this picture by strict adherence to such policies as the wearing of proper clothing, judicious spending of money, careful selection of associates and gentlemanly conduct on and off duty. Likewise, the host military expects the advisor to be highly professionally qualified. This follows from the very nature of his presence in the first place. An improperly assigned soldier in any unit is a serious mistake. An improperly assigned advisor can negate the entire

257

advisory effort. Local dissident factions are quick to exploit any improper conduct or lack of professional qualifications on the part of an advisor, in an attempt to discredit Americans in the eyes of the host nation.

Culture Conflict

Like any American in a foreign country, the military advisor may have some difficulty adjusting to the host country culture. He will, to some extent, experience "culture shock." The degree of difficulty encountered will vary depending both on the individual and the country to which he is assigned. As an example, from a cultural point of view, duty in Norway is probably somewhat easier than duty in Libya. Cultural differences have an impact on military doctrine and philosophy. The advisor must recognize that his advice and assistance must be offered within the framework of the host nation's culture. Often techniques that readily work in the U.S. Army are clumsy and inadequate when attempted by others. For example, American concepts of unit motor maintenance presuppose an easy familiarity of the soldier with motor vehicles. U.S. Army maintenance procedures may be incomprehensible to a soldier in a country largely dependent upon draft animals. Information and knowledge of a people is crucial to the efforts of an advisor.

Command relationships also reflect cultural differences. For example, Orientals place a great deal of emphasis on family ties not only in personal matters but also in public affairs. Thus, it may be inadvisable for an American advisor to advocate a promotion system which ignores this cultural aspect of advancement. The advisor can probably best adjust to these cultural differences by concentrating on long-range results and allowing the means, whenever possible, to be appropriate for the host culture.

The difficulties arising from cultural differences can be numerous. Edward C. Stewart states that U.S. Advisors' problems of communication and co-operation lie primarily in the disparity and conflict between the advisor's own cultural pattern and that of his foreign counterpart, and only secondarily in the strangeness of the foreign ways (Stewart, 1965, p. 4). A recent study (Chemers, et al., 1966) provides evidence that cultural training results in positive attitude changes toward foreign cultural patterns. As a broad generalization, training can help an advisor gain an appreciation of the people with whom he works and improve his relationships with them. Apparently, up to a point, familiarity dispels contempt. Gordon W. Allport also agrees that prejudice can be reduced by working together for a common goal as equals (Allport, 1958, p. 267).

In recent years, most individuals assigned to advisory type duties have received some language and cultural training prior to their departure for overseas. The training is becoming more sophisticated, and considerably improved over earlier techniques of merely acquainting individuals with a list of "dos" and "do nots". (Yamashita, 1965.) A recent study by the Behavioral Science Laboratory, Aerospace Medical Research Laboratories discusses techniques for training potential advisors. An interesting technique for cross-cultural interaction skill training is self-confrontation. The self-confrontation approach emphasizes the value of role playing and an immediate critique of the performance by the trainee himself. This is accomplished by using videotape replay of the role play situation. (Eachus, 1966.)

Military Assistance Advisory Groups (MAAG)

Most foreign advisory assignments are in the Military Assistance and Advisory Group (MAAG) program. Since the close of World War II, the United States has provided aid and assistance to many less well-endowed nations. This helps them to maintain their independence and resist overt and covert Communist aggression. The U.S. Army in providing the materiel support, advice, and training assistance to these forces, makes a substantial contribution to MAAG and Military Aid Missions. Over forty nations have requested, and are receiving, equipment and training to aid in the development of their defense forces. A current listing of MAAGs can be found in Army Regulation 341-50. The great majority of career soldiers will have the opportunity to serve in a MAAG at some period in their service.

MAAG advisors are faced with somewhat unique intermediate missions. These generally include such tasks as the supplying of suitable equipment to the host nation, training of their personnel in the use and maintenance of this equipment, assisting and advising the host country to develop their combat effectiveness and the development of respect and good will toward the U.S. Army and the United States in general. The MAAG advisor faces some extremely complex problem areas that generally are not major considerations for other type assignments. The MAAG advisor is the invited guest of a country. Being on an invitational basis, any adverse reactions could serve as a basis for being invited to leave. The situation is not too unlike the insurance salesman who is invited into a home to assist in the planning of an insurance program. Although the salesman may feel he knows what this particular family needs in the way of an insurance program, he cannot demand that they accept this program. He must sell the program step by step, considering the needs and desires of the individuals concerned. If he should become dogmatic or otherwise offensive, he would probably be shown the door and asked to leave. The MAAG advisor faces the same situation in accomplishing his mission. Some desirable qualities for individuals assigned as MAAG advisors are:

Loyalty. An advisor should be loyal to his country and to his counterpart. "Above all, the advisor must be sincere, honest, and forthright in his relations with his counterpart. He cannot bless them in public and damn them in private." (Hudlin, 1965, p. 96.)

Humility. It is best to allow the counterpart to adopt the advisor's ideas and implement them as his own (Denno, 1965, p. 29).

Physical Courage. The advisor should display courage in a professional rather than a theatrical manner. It is a good idea for the advisor to invite his counterpart or a member of the counterpart's staff to accompany him when he visits or inspects a unit (Denno, 1965, p. 29).

Patience. It is frustrating to have to react to insurgents and to wait for changes to be effected through a counterpart. Recommendation: compare the current state of the unit with its condition a few months previously (Denno, 1965, p. 30).

Empathy. "If an advisor can place himself in the shoes of his counterpart and truly understand and appreciate the counterpart's problems and frustrations, then he can assist in the alleviation of these problems and frustrations. Unfortunately, an advisor frequently arrives on the scene with preconceived ideas and charges full speed ahead without the slightest idea or care about the effect that it has on the counterpart." (Hudlin, 1965, p. 95.)

One of the major advisory tasks is to consider and resolve the needs for suitable equipment as seen by the host country and the MAAG. Most of the countries have suitable Tables of Organization and Equipment. From these, the advisor is normally able to obtain a realistic appraisal of the needed additional equipment. In the event the country does not have an appropriate organizational structure, the MAAG advisor assists and guides the planning and development of a suitable structure. It is of major importance in the development of an organizational structure that the MAAG member concerned not take a dictatorial position based on personal evaluation of what is desired. An organization that has proven to be highly effective for the United States may not be effective for another country. Whether or not the developed structure is similar to that of the U.S. Army is relatively immaterial as long as it fits local conditions and represents the desires of the host country. As soon as a suitable and effective organization is determined, the MAAG advisor can commence the programming of equipment.

Programming is a continual task and one of the more important in a MAAG assignment. Since each country operates on a yearly financial budget, it may not be possible for the advisor to obtain all of the desired equipment at a given time. To maintain effectiveness while remaining within the limitation of a budget requires determination or realistic priorities for the equipment needed. Depending upon the yearly appropriation to the country, equipment can be requisitioned in order of priority until the financial limitation is reached. As soon as the equipment is available, the MAAG leader can turn his attention to the training of the advised forces in the use and maintenance of this equipment.

The building of an effective unit training program is very similar to the development of a training program in the United States. The MAAG advisor employs the management principles discussed in Chapter VI. In evaluating the local training situation and developing the training plan and program, the advisor should give proper consideration to the personnel available, facilities, equipment, organization, and mission. Additional emphasis on the personnel aspects of the training problem is normally required. These people are the product of a different culture. To develop an effective training program, the advisor may have to deviate considerably from ideal American standards. The MAAG advisor should bear in mind, as he did during the development of the organizational structure, that for the program to be accepted by the advised unit, it must reflect the desires and wishes of his counterpart. As with the organizational structure, the advisor cannot force acceptance of a training program. The achievement of this objective must be accomplished through advising and assisting.

There is one major point that the MAAG senior advisor must instill in every member of the MAAG unit in regard to their assisting and advising of the host unit. The advisor is not a commander. He is none the less a leader; but, one who obtains his results through recommendation, advice, and persuasion—not through orders or directives. His counterpart may quickly perceive the giving of orders as being overbearing, disrespectful, and distasteful. Being unable to give direct orders can become very frustrating at times. Frustrating as it may be, the advisor must live with this frustration and obtain results through recommendation and persuasion. Whenever the MAAG advisor notes areas of weakness, mistakes, or programs that are not being implemented to the fullest, he must use the utmost tact in advising corrective measures to spur on the programs toward the eventual accomplishment of the mission. Otherwise, he may succeed only in antagonizing rather than helping the unit. Tactfulness in such corrections will also aid in the development of respect toward the MAAG personnel, which in turn is essential, since it represents a collateral objective for the MAAG unit.

RESERVE COMPONENT ADVISORS

Another area where the assistance and advice of the active service officer is necessary for national defense is in the maintenance of the combat readiness of the Reserve Component Forces. This category includes Army Reserve and Army National Guard units. The National Guard has a dual status. In addition to being a Reserve component of the U.S. Army, it is the organized militia of the several States and the District of Columbia. In this capacity, it is commanded by the State Governor. He exercises his command through the State Adjutant General. The U.S. Army Reserve is strictly a Federal force. Command of Reserve units and personnel not assigned to units is exercised by the Continental Armies. Benefits for reservists include pay for active duty for training and retirement pay at age 60 if qualified through adequate participation. Reserve and Guard forces stand ready to be called to active Federal service by the President to supplement the Active Army when it is deemed necessary to do so.

Active Army personnel assigned as advisors to Army Reserve and National Guard units assist in all phases of the unit's activities; however, they are not members of the units they advise. They neither command nor are commanded by individuals in the Reserve Components. Advisors are basically concerned with furthering the efficiency and mobilization readiness of units to which they are assigned. Unit advisors to Army National Guard and Army Reserve units generally have parallel functions. The primary functions of Reserve unit advisors are:

1. Inspection of training.
2. Maintenance of current information on status of training, efficiency, readiness of units.
3. Co-ordination of the use of facilities, equipment, and training aids provided by the Active Army.
4. Ensuring the prompt recording and reporting of attendance; preparation and prompt submission of payrolls.
5. Assisting in the activation, inactivation, organization, discontinuance, relocation, and reorganization of Reserve Component units as directed by higher authority.
6. Commenting on recommendations of the unit commander, as appropri-

ate, regarding promotions, schooling, transfers, reclassification, reassignment, and active duty training applications of personnel of the unit.

7. Attendance and rendering advice and assistance during all periods of reserve duty and annual active duty training periods.

8. Participating, as directed, as a member of an evaluation team.

Advisors of Reserve units must strive for the greatest degree of harmony and co-operation with the commanders and personnel of the Reserve units with which they are affiliated. They remember that they are dealing with citizen soldiers who have a primary obligation to their civilian occupation. It follows that professional motivation under such circumstances may not be as strong as that of an active duty military leader. Civilian occupational statuses tend to create informal power structures within the unit organization, and the advisor should seek to make these structures support rather than detract from the military organization. The advisor should never forget his advisory status, however, and deliberately or inadvertently assume responsibilities that rightfully belong to the unit commander. The advisor should recognize the unit's strengths and build upon them. Most Reserve Component units have a well established and honorable history. They are justifiably proud of what they are, how much they know, and how well they operate.

The advisor's personal example should be of the highest order. Since he is an advisor, he must be able to demonstrate a superior knowledge of his job. He should become thoroughly familiar with the Reserve Components, their organization, mission, history, and traditions. Exhibiting a high sense of duty and enthusiasm for his work favorably impresses the officers and men of the reserve unit. Avoiding critical remarks about the Reserve or Active Army is a must. This, of course, does not preclude the advisor from giving constructive criticism to the unit commander under appropriate circumstances.

Since the reservists are members of the civilian community, the advisor makes his task easier by associating with people of the community and joining in local social and civic organizations. Finally, the advisor must remember that his performance represents the Active Army. The people with whom he comes in contact will form their opinion of the Service on the basis of his performance.

RESERVE OFFICERS' TRAINING CORPS (ROTC)

The ROTC Program was established under the provisions of the National Defense Act of 1916. It is not a component of the Army, but is the principal source of officers for the Army in peacetime. At present, senior division ROTC units are established at over 200 colleges and universities throughout the country. In addition to the senior division ROTC, there are a number of military secondary schools and junior colleges which constitute a junior division of the ROTC. These latter units, while not directly producing officers, serve as feeder sources to the senior division units and help indoctrinate young men to the military.

Military personnel detailed as instructors with the ROTC are assigned to detachments, U.S. Army instructor group, ROTC, with duty station at the educational institutions. During summer vacation periods, most instructor personnel conduct field-type military training of the ROTC cadets (summer camp) at active military installations.

The professor of military science (PMS) and his assistants are assigned with the concurrence of the institution. They become members of the faculty and hold academic rank as determined by the institution. The department of military science is generally regarded as any other instructional department (e.g., History, English) and must adjust to the policies and procedures of the institution in such areas as academic credit, grades administration, class scheduling,

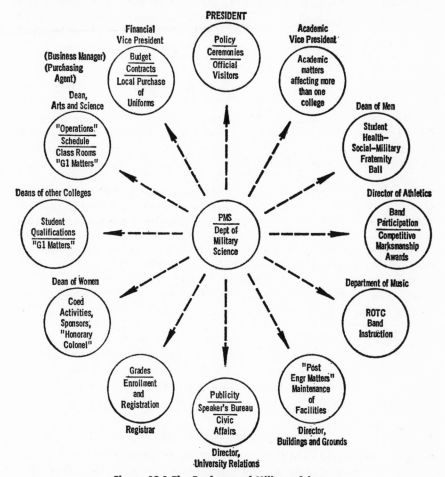

Figure 19.1 The Professor of Military Science

and other related regulations. Additionally, the PMS must adhere to his own military directives and protect the contractual interests of the Army. Co-ordination and close relations with all departments of the institution are essential in support of ROTC cadet activities and other college-sponsored programs. In essence, the PMS is both a member of the institutional staff and an Army officer, and, to be successful, he must learn to perform effectively in both roles.

As a member of the Army closely associated with civilian educators and students, the ROTC instructor has an unparalleled opportunity to demonstrate the qualities of the military leader. As with the Reserve Advisor and MAAG advisor, this leadership depends almost solely on the inspirational qualities of the individual. Enthusiasm for his assignment, setting an outstanding personal and professional example, competence as an instructor, and participation in student-faculty affairs all contribute to the goal of motivating these cadets toward successful military careers. It is of extreme importance to note that for most ROTC cadets their first and most lasting impression of the Army is gained by their impression of the officers and noncommissioned officers assigned to their university.

SUMMARY

Numerous assignments now exist for the military leader wherein the traditional tool of command authority is not present. The advisor faces a difficult leadership challenge in attempting to accomplish his objectives. Among such assignments are MAAG advisors, Reserve Component Advisors, and ROTC Instructors.

MAAG units exist to provide materiel support, advice, and training assistance to nations requesting such aid in order to resist communist aggression. This mission is accomplished by MAAG units that supply equipment, train and assist armies in developing their combat effectiveness. In accomplishing their mission, MAAG advisors do not command but develop their influence through good will, mutual respect, and respect for cultural differences.

Reserve advisors are primarily concerned with furthering the efficiency and mobilization readiness of units which they advise. They are not members of, nor do they command, the Reserve units. Reserve advisors seek their objectives by creating an atmosphere of harmony, co-operation and mutual respect. They must remember that Reservists are first civilians and secondly soldiers.

ROTC is a primary source of officers for the Active Army and Reserve Components. The PMS and his assistants share a dual role of faculty member and Army officer. As such, they are in a position to influence and mold the future officers of the Army.

Suggestions for Further Reading

Denno, B. F., "Advisor and Counterpart", *Army* 15:12, July 1965.
Hudlin, I. C., "Advising the Advisor", *Military Review* 45:2, November 1965.
Honigmann, J. J., *Understanding Culture*. New York: Harper & Row, 1963.
Lyons, G. M., and Masland, J. W., *Education and Military Leadership; A Study of the ROTC*. Princeton, N.J.: Princeton University Press, 1959.

XX

Situational Studies

THE PRECEDING chapters considered various aspects of the military situation in which the leader and his group must work. In the final analysis, all factors affecting the leader, group, and situation are focused in a specific situation in which you, the leader, face a particular problem with a specific group. To prepare for this eventuality, you can improve your exercise of leadership by mentally considering alternatives in hypothetical situations. Although it is impossible to derive fixed solutions to "type" situations, it is possible to improve analytical ability and gain confidence through such mental rehearsals. This prior consideration develops powers of analysis and decision-making ability. Thus, when you encounter a specific leadership situation, you have the necessary awareness of pertinent factors and the confidence to solve the problem.

Analyzing actual situations in which other leaders have faced specific problems can prove helpful. In this way, you are able to visualize different types of situations and, perhaps, leadership problems that might not otherwise occur to you. They also help you to expand your fund of experience as you analyze each problem and arrive at a solution. Each problem naturally includes many aspects of the leadership process and requires its own unique solution. The situations in this chapter are adapted from actual situations. Real leaders faced these problems with the people and in the situations described. In each case, the leader faced a problem that required some decision or action on his part. Put yourself in his position and determine how you would handle his problem.

At the end of the chapter is a brief outline of the outcome of each situation. These are not necessarily the only solutions. In some cases, they are far from the optimum or perfect solution. They are intended only to show what factors the actual leader, who had more complete information about the people and the situation, felt that he should consider. The outcomes also outline the actions that he felt would be most compatible with his personality for him to employ with the particular group of people he was leading in the situation as they saw it.

265

A GOOD APPLE ALMOST SPOILS THE BARREL

First Lieutenant Quinn was excited about going to the field. The 3d Platoon of "D" Company was preparing to take its Army Training Test. Quinn, new to the outfit, was being given an opportunity to train the platoon on his own, according to the company training schedule, of course, but on his own.

The glow was gone from the sky over the pine woods north of the Los Baños Drop Zone as the 3d Platoon settled in at the end of the first day's training. 1LT Quinn checked his security, then sat back against a stump in his platoon command post (CP) for a last cigarette and mental review of the day's training. Each of his squads had gone through the day's problems with good intentions and with enthusiasm, but it was evident that, except for the Second Squad, his leaders needed this training badly. Sergeant First Class Gomez, who had the Second Squad, was a confident, decisive leader with a great deal of experience. But because of the general low state of training, Quinn decided that for the next few days he had better issue very detailed instructions to his subordinate leaders. He also decided that he and PSG Thompson, his platoon sergeant, should supervise the squads very closely to ensure that they made the most of the week's training.

For the remainder of the training period, 1LT Quinn was very careful when he was issuing orders to be certain that the squad leaders understood exactly what was expected of them. Then he and PSG Thompson supervised them closely to see how well they carried out his directions and how well each leader handled his squad during the training problems. By the end of the week, there had been a great improvement in performance by the squad leaders and in the enthusiasm and *esprit* of the squads.

All, that is, except SFC Gomez's squad. Instead of showing the way with its usual spirit and drive, the Second Squad seemed to have lost its spark. Their hustle was gone and they made mistakes. They made careless mistakes such as being five minutes late crossing the line of departure (LD) in a squad attack problem. Whenever Quinn issued orders to his squad leaders, SFC Gomez seemed irritated and appeared to be only half-hearted in complying. Once Gomez started to object to a squad mission assigned him, but changed his mind and shuffled off towards his squad.

First Lieutenant Quinn returned to garrison on Thursday night with mixed feelings. On the one hand, the inexperienced squad leaders had improved noticeably in the four days they worked in the field. On the other hand, SFC Gomez and his squad had turned in a poor performance. He couldn't figure it out. When Quinn had taken over the platoon, PSG Thompson had described Gomez as the best squad leader in "D" Company, a very sincere individual who held the respect of all his squad members because of his experience, his initiative, and his excellent knowledge of squad tactics and weapons.

What had gone wrong?

If you were 1LT Quinn, how would you go about bringing Gomez and his squad to its former level of performance? What were the interpersonal communications aspects of this case?

THE CASE OF THE RELUCTANT RANGERS

It can be bitter cold in the mountains near Dahlonega, Georgia, in January. And when it rains, it is miserably uncomfortable. It was cold and rainy at three A.M. when a 35-man Ranger School patrol fell exhausted to the ground after hitting their objective on the third day of their final patrol. No one had eaten anything in the previous eleven hours and only a few of the recently commissioned second lieutenants who made up the class had slept since the second day of the patrol. Five-foot ten-inch, mild-mannered, Second Lieutenant Bill Dixon had slept less than most of the others. But at pick-up time minus three hours and with a rough march yet to go, Bill was designated patrol leader.

The extent of his new responsibility only gradually alerted Bill's numbed brain. The last patrol leader had strayed off course in the dark and the patrol had struggled one-and-a-half miles up a mountain trail before discovering the mistake. Now the condition of the men, the weight of their equipment, the rugged terrain, the darkness, and the problems of navigation made the four miles to the rendezvous point seem almost insurmountable. But this was a good class. They had had lots of spirit in all their patrols and exercises, and Bill Dixon figured that if they started right away there was a chance they could make it. So he struggled to his feet, and with all the assurance he could muster, gave his first order, "All right, let's saddle up."

The response was not impressive. There was bickering about who would carry the machine gun and a dejected voice from the dark spoke out, "Bill, the plan called for a half-hour's rest here; we gotta have it." Others muttered similar expressions of dissent. Of course, the wrong turn had negated that portion of the plan. But most of the men seemed too tired to care and those few who were on their feet slumped back to the wet ground.

If you were patrol leader, what courses of action would you consider now?

With men in this condition, what is most likely to motivate them to go on? Fear of punishment? Material reward? Other factors?

What are the sources of Dixon's authority? Which source should he rely on in this situation? What are the factors involved in determining the degree to which the leader in this case should be autocratic or democratic?

THE AWOL LIEUTENANT

Getting Headquarters Company through basic training had taken the full efforts of all the officers and the noncommissioned cadre. There appeared to be no let-up in sight as the company headed into the advanced individual training phase. If anything, Second Lieutenant Harris thought to himself, things were going to get tougher before they got better. The company commander had just received TDY orders to go to school, leaving Harris as the acting company commander. His pride in commanding a company only nine months after graduation was tempered by the sobering realization that he had only two other second lieutenants present to help him. One of these officers was kept busy full time in the supply room. The other was newly commissioned Second Lieutenant

George who had just been assigned to the company. Harris didn't know what he could do and doubted if George did himself. Things would be better when Second Lieutenant Stone, the fourth officer in the company, returned from his two weeks' honeymoon.

When Stone reported back in, Harris heaved a sigh of relief. After a week of working every night until ten o'clock and standing reveille every third morning, he was glad to see some help. But his sense of relief was blasted by Stone's immediate request for a three-day VOCO. Stone's new bride had decided their apartment was too small and they were going to have to find a larger one. Harris reflected momentarily on the long hours he and the other two officers had been putting in while 2LT Stone had been on leave. He also considered the effect of denying Stone's request and the strain it might put on a new marriage. Three more days? Oh well, might as well grant it and get it over with!

Just before the VOCO was over, 2LT Stone came in and said, "We're closing in on a place to stay, but we haven't completed the deal. How about letting me have a couple more days to secure the apartment and move?" Harris felt he could have been more sympathetic toward this request if he hadn't overheard comments at the Officer's Club to the effect that Stone had been "living it up" and not devoting his full efforts to house hunting. Secondly, it was the company's turn to furnish the Officer of the Guard, and guard mount was an hour away. Turning down the request, Harris told Stone to report to Battalion as OG, and then he drove home for his first evening meal with his wife that week.

About eleven o'clock the next morning, as he was working through a stack of papers brought in by the first Sergeant, 2LT George came in and asked to talk to him. At approximately 1900 hours the previous evening, 2LT Stone had come to George saying that his wife had called with a problem. He asked George to stand in as Officer of the Guard while he went to see about it. As the junior lieutenant in the company, George felt forced to oblige although he knew there was no authority for such an action. Besides, he expected him to be absent for only an hour or two. Stone, however, had not returned from town and George was still trying to find some of the guard property Stone must have signed for.

Second Lieutenant Harris told 2LT George to do the best he could as OG while he would try to locate 2LT Stone. After calling his home and several likely bars. Harris found Stone and told him to report to the company immediately. When 2LT Stone reported later that afternoon, he had obviously been drinking and was sullen and belligerent.

What actions should 2LT Harris take? He knew that if an enlisted man went AWOL or left his guard duty, the appropriate punishment would consist at least of an Article 15 or more likely a court-martial. It seemed to him that the circumstances were sufficiently aggravated to require some type of firm corrective action. The idea that Stone had pulled rank on a new second lieutenant struck Harris as particularly reprehensible. Of course, he could report Stone to the Battalion Commander for punishment. This, he knew would be the expected action. On the other hand, this would reflect on his own leadership and would probably put a permanent black mark on 2LT Stone's record.

How should 2LT Harris handle this problem?

What actions should Harris take or have taken in regard to 2LT George's problem?

"QUITTER" PLATOON

A "quitter" in an airborne outfit is an outcast, a coward, worse even than a "leg."

Newly arrived Platoon Sergeant G. H. Braxton had a platoon full of quitters —rejects from "The Division." In addition, no officer was assigned to the platoon. SFC Braxton commanded a Security Platoon attached to an Ordnance Company. His mission was to guard the restricted ammunition storage area that was the focus of the company's operations. Only twelve of his men were qualified to walk within this compound, and the highly sensitive nature of his assignment was demanding and nerve-racking. The guards were on duty for a twenty-four stretch and off for twenty-four hours. There was more rank among the specialists in the organic platoons of the Ordnance Company than in Braxton's outfit. It was obvious from other things, too, that the Security Platoon was a poor stepchild.

Onto the scene came Sp 4 Timothy Odey. "Sarge," said Odey, "I've been walking guard in the Restricted Area for the past two years and I'm beginning to feel as if I'm losing my mind. I'm so jumpy I'm ready to shoot at the slightest sound. It's just getting to be too much for me." Braxton was caught unprepared, so he told Odey to see him at 0800 the next morning.

As the Platoon Sergeant saw it, Odey was a conscientious type, very willing

to do his share of the work. He had always been quiet, reliable, and co-operative. Lately, however, Odey seemed to be brooding about something.

Braxton could see that the job of guarding the Restricted Area was not an appealing one, but it was vital and could not be relaxed for a minute. There wasn't much he could do to replace Odey or augment the existing guard detail —it took a long time to get a man cleared to permit him to walk within the compound—and, if he let Odey off, it would mean more work for the others and possibly would start a run of similar requests. On the other hand, could he allow a man who might be breaking down to walk guard with live ammo?

What action could you take with Odey?

Does there appear to be a greater problem confronting you as Platoon Leader? If so, what possible courses of action are open to you which might improve the situation as a whole?

FIRST READY COMPANY

"What a way to spend Saturday night!" said Second Lieutenant Short to no one in particular. At any rate that seemed to be the thing to say. Actually, it was a pretty exciting Saturday. At noon that day, after a full field inspection,

"C" Company had been designated "First Ready Company" for the Division. For the next seven days, Charlie Company was on the hot seat. If a crisis occured anywhere from Cuba to Iran, it would be the first U.S. force to go. The SOP called for the First Ready Company to be at the marshalling area with all of its equipment and ammunition in not more than one hour after being alerted. In order to be capable of meeting this requirement, every man in "C" Company was restricted to the barracks for the entire week.

In his office on the first floor of barracks, 2LT Short was reviewing his platoon's air loading manifest. The second name on the list was Williams, K. M., his Platoon Sergeant. Thinking back over the three weeks he had been the leader of the 2d Platoon, 2LT Short gratefully recalled all the help PSG Williams had given him. Williams was one of the older noncommissioned officers, had even been a platoon sergeant in combat, and though he had been the acting leader of the 2d Platoon for several months, he had shown no signs of resenting Short's presence. Yes, he was very fortunate in having a man like Williams to help him learn the ropes of his first command.

Looking further down the manifest, he noticed that his radio-telephone operator, PFC Sampson, had been omitted from the list. He glanced at his watch—it was 2010—and decided to go up to PSG Williams' room and ask him why Sampson was not on the manifest. He went up to the second floor, found PSG Williams' room, and knocked. When the door opened, a strong, unmistakable odor of liquor rushed over him. PSG Williams, looking a bit startled, said weakly, "Oh, hello, Lieutenant."

Second Lieutenant Short hesitated a moment before speaking, digesting what he saw and smelled. "Sergeant, you've been drinking," he said finally. "Just a little, sir—not enough to hurt anything," Williams replied. Short was stunned. He knew that Williams was aware of the regulation prohibiting alcohol in barracks—even "just a little." He was not prepared for this situation and had no idea what to do about it.

The two men stood there for a few short seconds without saying anything. 2LT Short's thoughts raced: This man isn't a problem drinker although I know he does drink some in his off-duty time. What shall I do? Should I see the Company Commander? Maybe I should handle it right now myself—maybe chew him out, restrict him, or something. I'd like to ignore it, just walk away and forget it.

Well, what would you do? Are there other alternatives?

What are the consequences of each of the above alternatives?

What are your obligations to PSG Williams? Yourself? Your company commander? Your platoon? How far do your responsibilities extend?

THE EIGHTBALL

Sometimes it is hard to tell, whether a man is an eightball because of inability or lack of motivation. If it is merely a problem of motivation, there is usually a solution.

Troop A had an eightball—he was Private Wakefield. Everyone said Wakefield had gotten off to a poor start. A "personality clash," they called it, between him and his squad leader, Sergeant First Class Bishop. Though he showed flashes of talent, Wakefield's performance was generally poor and he saw the company commander on a number of unhappy occasions.

First Lieutenant Hayes got Wakefield transferred to another platoon, but things there went from bad to worse. Wakefield had been assigned to Sergeant First Class Johnson's squad and Johnson had a reputation for "squaring away" deviant and recalcitrant soldiers. What is more, Johnson was a friend of SFC Bishop. By the end of his first week in Johnson's squad, Wakefield was AWOL.

A day later, when Wakefield returned from his first AWOL, he was given an Art. 15, and was subjected to even more intensive "shaping up" efforts by SFC Johnson and the rest of the noncommissioned officers in his platoon. Wakefield soon went AWOL again. This time he was picked up three weeks later 1,700 miles away. For this he went to the stockade.

When Wakefield left the stockade, he was sent right back to SFC Johnson's squad in spite of his request to be moved. None of the other platoons wanted him. SFC Johnson continued to work at shaping him up and Wakefield continued to get into trouble. This brought on further company punishment and finally a decision to put him before a 208 board (Discharge under AR 635-208). Before this action was completed, however, a new company commander took over and decided to try again to rehabilitate Wakefield.

What are some courses of action open to the new CO?

Where does the problem appear to lie? Is it a question of ability or motivation?

TOO BUSY TO LEAD

If you asked anyone in "B" Company, 1st Abn Battle Group, they would tell you that Platoon Sergeant Ignatz was the best platoon leader in the company and perhaps in the whole battle group.

Ignatz had been platoon leader or platoon sergeant for three of his 14 ½ years service. He was a forceful, physically powerful man, good natured, very enthusiastic, and serious about his work.

Private First Class Billy Cummings, an automatic rifle man in Ignatz' platoon, had been in the Army for a year and a half, had never been in trouble and had a high school diploma. Besides that, Cummings was willing and had plenty of hustle. The men in the platoon liked him because he always gave them a lift when things got tough in the field by making them see the humorous side of their situation. When the Company Commander asked for recommendations to fill a vacancy, PSG Ignatz put Cummings in for Specialist Fourth Class. The following Monday morning, just as the company was preparing to move to the field, the CO told PSG Ignatz that Cummings' promotion had come through and, according to company policy, the platoon leader could announce the promotion. When Cummings reported, PSG Ignatz began the traditional reprimand for a purported act of misconduct, but before he could finish, he was called to the phone in the orderly room. So the surprised Cummings was hurriedly congratulated and told that he had been promoted to Sp 4. Before Ignatz had time to say anything more to Cummings, the company was on its way to the field.

It was an exhausting, fast-moving, week-long exercise, and after it was over, Ignatz went to Fort Benning on a month's TDY.

Shortly after his return to "B" Company, Cummings' squad leader, Sergeant First Class McWaters, asked PSG Ignatz to have Cummings reduced in rank. Cummings had been found sleeping in the latrine while he was supposed to be in charge of the clean up detail. McWaters said it was the last straw. He said there had been other incidents since Cummings had been promoted which showed that he was not assuming the responsibilities of an Sp 4. Ignatz was shocked and disappointed. As he tried to collect his thoughts, his mind went back to the last real contact he had had with Cummings that Monday morning he had been promoted to Sp 4.

What had gone wrong? Since Cummings apparently had deserved the promotion, what possible explanation could there be for his behavior?

What steps might have been taken to prevent the necessity for the reduction?

Is there anything that can be done now to improve this soldier's performance to the point where he would warrant promotion again or at least not slide down further?

THE NEW PLATOON LEADER

Second Lieutenant Palmer was as eager to take over his first platoon as a bridegroom is to get started on his honeymoon. He had just seen the company commander and was certain he had impressed him. What is more, he had Jump Wings and a Ranger Tab to prove he had the stuff to be a leader. Palmer confidently headed for the billets of the 2d Platoon, "B" Company.

The first item of business was to talk with Platoon Sergeant Dillen. The new leader was short and to the point; he laid down his policies and the standards he expected the platoon to meet. Dillen, who had led the platoon well for eighteen months, flushed with resentment. The new lieutenant, concerned with his own image of military efficiency, did not notice.

After his first inspection, 2LT Palmer ordered a rearrangement of the partitions that originally were intended to break up the room and give the men a measure of privacy. The new arrangement, Palmer would have said if asked, made the room easier to clean, improved the ventilation and appearance, and tended to split up the informal cubicle groups that crossed platoon organizational lines. The real reason for the rearrangement was that Palmer felt that a leader should assume command in a forceful way through some kind of dramatic act.

Platoon Sergeant Dillen remained respectful and outwardly loyal, but within the two weeks after Palmer's arrival there was a noticeable drop in platoon *esprit*.

Second Lieutenant Palmer was aggressive and high-spirited. He wanted his platoon to do more and to do it better than the other platoons. In the third

week, he ordered the 2d Platoon to fall out with gas masks for the morning physical training run. PSG Dillen was obviously horrified. On order, the men donned their masks and, though the run was made at the "Airborne shuffle," more than three-fourths of them fell out before it was over. The 2d Platoon was strung out all along the route with their masks off, gasping for breath.

Platoon Sergeant Dillen, grim but respectful, stated his intent to see the company commander.

The Lieutenant and his Platoon Sergeant made it very clear to Captain Brooks as they stood before his desk at eight that morning that the 2d Platoon was not big enough for both of them.

What courses of action could you, as company commander, take? What is your decision?

What do you think of 2LT Palmer's sincere but aggressive methods?

DROWNING IN THE SEA OF INDEBTEDNESS

Sergeant First Class Smith had one of the best Forward Observer Sections in the whole battalion. In addition to doing a first-rate job as an FO, he looked after his men; and his section's equipment was always in top shape and ready to move out any time. He always had time to teach the men in his section and to help them with their problems. In fact, SFC Smith always had the solution to everyone's problems but his own. He took a deep interest in and liked people. He particularly enjoyed working after duty hours in a small musical combo he and a few of his friends had gotten together. They played at the officers' and noncommissioned officers' clubs and even had gotten a few engagements to play in some of the local German nightclubs.

A nicer guy you wouldn't want to meet. Consequently, the Battery Commander was surprised when the Battalion Commander handed him a copy of the Congressman's letter. It seemed that SFC Smith, in his good-hearted way, had run up a few debts. In fact, when they were all totaled up, it amounted to between two and three thousand dollars.

Sergeant First Class Smith acknowledged that he owed the debts and said he would take action to pay his creditors as much as he could each month. Everything went fine—for one week. The Battery Commander received a letter from a local merchant stating that SFC Smith had co-signed a note for $350.00 worth of musical instruments. The principal party to the note had defaulted on the first payment. When SFC Smith was asked about this, he stated that his friend in the combo had needed the instruments and he was sure his friend could pay for them. Besides, Smith hadn't bought the instruments himself; it was his friend who had, so he didn't see how this was his debt.

What can the Battery Commander do to develop a sense of financial responsibility in SFC Smith? What are the moral implications? How might this condition affect SFC Smith's performance of duty?

ONE FOR THE ROAD

"B" Company was making a road march from Ft. Campbell to Ft. Bragg, North Carolina, to participate in a large scale maneuver. The trip was to take three days and the Company planned to stop each night outside a small town. The idea was to let the troops, except those needed for guard, go into town in the evening to relieve the monotony of the trip.

Second Lieutenant Lew Dolan, recently assigned leader of a Forward Area Signal Center Platoon, was sweating out the trip. The "old man" had made it very clear what he expected of the company on the road, at halts, and overnight and the new lieutenant felt the briefing was primarily for his benefit. Dolan thought he had a pretty good platoon but there were many temptations on the long road to Bragg.

The first night of the march Dolan's anxieties were justified. The company had stopped about 1700 hours outside a little town in eastern Tennessee. The men were fed hot chow and turned loose at about 1830 to go into town. 2LT Dolan was making bed check of his march unit about 2230 hours that night when he came upon a small group of soldiers behind a van. The group was making considerable noise and showed no signs of breaking up and heading for their pup tents. It appeared to Dolan that most or all of the group had been drinking. He called the ranking man, Staff Sergeant Bosch, aside and, reminding him that it was past bedcheck time, told him to get the troops to bed. Bosch had been drinking himself and when he got the order, apparently became resentful and belligerent. 2LT Dolan, with voice rising, engaged briefly in a heated exchange with SSG Bosch. As a clincher he loudly proclaimed, "If you don't want to wear those stripes, take them off and give them to someone who does!" Bosch, after a short pause, ripped off his stripes and gave them to the Lieutenant. The startled group then headed for its pup tents and the Lieutenant hurried off to find the Company Commander.

What do you suppose the Lieutenant will say to the Company Commander?
What would you, as Company Commander, do when 2LT Dolan told you what has happened?

Does the Lieutenant have the authority to take the stripes and can you back him up?

How else might this situation have been handled by the Lieutenant?

THE MAYOR OF THE ORDNANCE COMPANY

During the Berlin Crisis of 1961, a number of reserve units were called to active duty to supplement the strength of the Active Army. One of these was an Ordnance Park Company from an Ohio town of about 20,000 people. Captain Stanbaugh, the company commander, a World War II veteran, very likeable and intelligent, was a career reservist who had commanded the company for over ten years.

First Lieutenant Ken Digby, a regular with 2½ years' service, reported to the company commander for duty not long after the unit had reached its mobilization station, Fort Campbell, Kentucky. While CPT Stanbaugh, and 1LT Digby were talking, a noncommissioned officer in the company, SGT Pratt, stuck his head in the door and said to the CO, "Say, Jim, I'm having trouble with this training schedule, how about giving me a hand." The CO replied, "Check with Frank (another officer) will you, Bill, I'm busy right now."

As Digby became more familiar with the unit and the men, he discovered that this informal atmosphere had always existed and the unit had operated on a first name basis while in a reserve status without apparent difficulty. Informal groups seemed to exist everywhere and they were the vehicle by which information and instruction were disseminated and things got done. The formal chain of command was seldom used and tasks were accepted and performed based on the mutual consent of the noncommissioned officer and his men. If the men accepted their noncommissioned officer as part of their group, he had their support and co-operation. Those noncommissioned officers without this affection had little or no co-operation. CPT Stanbaugh realized that the situation was not a healthy one for an active unit and he took steps to orient the officers and noncommissioned officers on effective senior-subordinate relations. This had some effect on relations between the noncommissioned officers and the lower grades, but little if any between noncommissioned officers and officers.

The first mission of the company, after being brought to TOE strength, was to pass its Army Training Test (ATT). In preparation for this, the company was scheduled to go to the field with the rest of the battalion. It was about this time that CPT Stanbaugh received word that he had been elected mayor of his hometown, and, reverting to inactive status, he returned home immediately. 1LT Digby being the next senior officer, assumed command and three days later moved the company to the training area for its first session of field work.

The first night in the field was utter chaos. It rained heavily and steadily all during the day and the rain turned to sleet by nightfall. Many vehicles became bogged in mud but the noncommissioned officers could not exert enough influence on the men to keep the unit vehicles moving toward their bivouac. As a result, by nightfall few of the organization's tents had been erected, individuals and small groups were concentrating on taking care of themselves, and subordinate leaders, when they could be found, were concerned about their own or their group's welfare. Some vehicles had not closed in, guards had not been posted and the unit was completely unprepared to perform its mission. At this point, as the company was totally ineffective, the Battalion Commander ordered 1LT Digby to take it back to garrison.

What are the probable causes of this situation?

Of these, what particular problem area must be attacked by the unit commander before any field training can be of maximum benefit?

How would you go about correcting the situation if you were 1LT Digby and the Battalion Commander said he would give you just two weeks to get that outfit ready to take the field?

A PROBLEM IN THE SUPPLY PLATOON

Paul Miller had been a first lieutenant for two years and had been the Supply Platoon Leader for four months. His platoon was part of the Supply and Transportation Company of the Support Group.

Miller was sitting alone that morning at the officers' table having a cup of coffee. His platoon sergeant came into the mess hall, obviously troubled, and Miller waved him to a chair. The sergeant wasted no time in telling 1LT Miller that he was disturbed about the harsh treatment one of the men was getting from Staff Sergeant Doaks, the Class II and IV Section Leader. At reveille, Doaks had given Private First Class Sam Turner, a Negro, a "royal chewing

out," apparently for being slow falling in. Doaks' yelling and profanity caused the entire company to witness the incident. After reveille, when the platoon sergeant questioned Doaks, the Section Leader replied that he felt extra harsh treatment was in order because Turner had become slovenly in appearance and had developed a very poor attitude. The platoon sergeant drained his coffee cup, set it down, and pointedly said that he thought the matter serious enough that the lieutenant should know about it. Miller dismissed him and began to ponder the problem.

First, Miller thought about Doaks. The Sergeant had a high school education, he had entered the Army from Georgia, he was known as a "hard" noncommissioned officer, but he performed his job in a very professional and efficient manner. Miller also recalled that he had heard SSG Doaks take a very positive position on the racial issue.

First Lieutenant Miller then mentally reviewed what he knew about PFC Turner. He recalled that Turner was married; above average in intelligence; had two years service; had been in the section for six months; had never been in trouble; was the only Negro in the section; appeared to be accepted by the other soldiers in the section and to have made friends among his associates. No report had come in on Turner's duty performance, but 1LT Miller had observed that Turner did not seem to have his heart in his job.

Later that morning, the Lieutenant had a chance to talk to SSG Doaks and he brought up the reveille incident. Doaks emotionally defended his actions to 1LT Miller by claiming that Turner was lazy, listless, and belligerent, just like the rest of "them," and that Turner was lowering the effectiveness of others in the section.

When the opportunity arose, 1LT Miller talked in general terms with other men in the section and found that most of them liked Turner and felt he was getting a raw deal from SSG Doaks. They cited instances where Turner had been assigned to unpleasant details out of turn and had been punished out of proportion to the offense when he made a mistake.

Finally, Miller talked to Turner, but all he got out of him was that he was dissatisfied with his present assignment and requested that he be allowed to transfer.

Are you satisfied that the problem stems from prejudice on Doaks' part?

Would you do anything further before taking action?

What courses of action are open to you?

What would you do?

What are the foundations of good senior-subordinate relations? Obviously there is no room for prejudice in the ideal relationship, but does it not exist to a degree in everyone?

How can it be reduced or eliminated?

THE ULTIMATUM

"Sir," said Platoon Sergeant Miller, "either Braun or I will have to leave this platoon."

The two men, Braun and Miller, stood before their surprised leader, First Lieutenant Harper, with very serious, set faces. Sergeant First Class Miller had been the platoon sergeant of the Battalion Reconnaissance Platoon for fifteen months. He was the senior E-7 in the battalion and was expected to become First Sergeant of Headquarters Company when the present first sergeant departed in about six weeks for reassignment to Seventh Army in Europe. Sergeant First Class Braun, the Scout Section Leader, would become the platoon sergeant when Miller moved up. The two sergeants had been close friends for as long as 1LT Harper could recall and spent a good deal of off-duty time together.

Harper told the two men to stand at ease and, after some prodding, pieced together the circumstances that had brought them before him.

Braun and Miller had gone to the Noncommissioned Officers' Club the night before and had had a few beers when they fell to arguing over the assignment of Private Nomura of the Support Squad. Braun had a vacancy in his own

section and knew that Nomura was an outstanding soldier. Braun argued that Nomura should be transferred to his section because he was being treated unfairly by the Support Squad Leader, and because Nomura had expressed a desire to be transferred to the Scout Section. SFC Miller had resented Braun's interference in what he considered to be the business of running the platoon and had told Braun so. They had argued all evening, each one becoming more entrenched in his position, until, finally, they had squared off. Braun apparently won the fight because there was not a mark on him, but Miller was sporting a beautiful shiner around his left eye. The fight resulted in an agreement: They would see 1LT Harper and request that one or the other be transferred out of the platoon.

Sergeant First Class Miller's ultimatum became 1LT Harper's dilemma. Harper promised the sergeants he would think it over and let them know what he had decided. With that he dismissed them both.

What would you do?

What other alternative does 1LT Harper have besides transferring one of the sergeants?

What are the considerations involved in transferring Miller? Braun?

Are you satisfied that the sergeants cannot effectively function together again?

Would you have talked to both noncommissioned officers at the same time?

ADVISOR'S DILEMMA

Major Richards was slowly learning the mores and customs of the country where he was assigned as an advisor. In the three months he had been there, he had come to respect his counterpart and felt that he had gained a measure of respect from him. Working together they had made good progress in suppressing the guerrillas in the province.

Therefore, they were glad to hear that they were to operate as a part of the division's next secure-and-hold operation in the province. The mission of the operation was first to clear the guerrillas from the area and then to secure the local inhabitants from exploitation by the guerrilla force until the local inhabitants could fortify, organize, and defend themselves. MAJ Richards' counterpart was responsible to the Division Commander for the co-ordination of the total effort and had both civil and military responsibilities.

The Commanding General (CG) of the Division was making a spot check of the conduct of the secure-and-hold operation. MAJ Richards and his counterpart were accompanying the General and the Regimental Commander. Upon

seeing a PRC-10 radio in the area, the CG asked to talk to the Commander of the 1st Battalion. The radio operator tried to contact the battalion but was unable to do so. Suddenly the Regimental Commander picked up the radio and stated, "I'll talk to them and make them answer!" The net control station had not opened the net, however, so no one was on the other set at the location of the 1st Battalion Headquarters. The CG became very disturbed and pointed to the Regimental Commander and announced, "You are under arrest," following this with instructions to disarm the Regimental Commander and to place him in jail for 20 days. The advisors were visibly concerned with the event and the Regimental Commander's Advisor was the first to speak. He explained that the net was not open and that this could not be construed as a deficiency on the part of the commander. Since this seemed logical to MAJ Richards, he attempted to intercede further in behalf of the Regimental Commander by asking his counterpart to ask the CG to reconsider his hasty action. The CG, who spoke enough English to understand this request, interrupted the conversation by pointing a finger at MAJ Richards' counterpart and announcing, "One word from you and you go to jail also." The guards took the side arms of the Regimental Commander and marched him off in front of his troops on the way to jail.

What should the U.S. Advisor to the Regimental Commander do?

What are some further facts which must be known before an attempt at a solution can be made?

Should advice be offered when it has not been solicited? How might such advice offered in this situation affect future advisor/counterpart relations?

WELFARE VS. MISSION

An apparently reliable defector not only provided intelligence on the location of the guerrilla regiment and its command post (CP) but offered to lead a force into their safe area to find it. This chance to reduce the guerrillas' operational capability in their own safe area could not be passed up even though it involved the risk of meeting them in their own backyard. The plan was for two columns of approximately two companies each to proceed to a rendezvous in the vicinity of the suspected CP. Here a link-up was to be made for a concerted attack, hopefully before the regiment could muster sufficient security to protect the CP. The operation was to be under the command of Major Oran, a rather weak executive officer to a strong commander.

The separate columns pushed through the jungle for two-and-a-half days. Fresh signs of activity were found such as hastily abandoned guerrilla camps and man-made trails, but there was no contact. On the third day, the column ambushed and killed what appeared to be the two lead scouts of a guerrilla force following the column. This action confirmed the Advisor's suspicions that their presence was known.

One platoon was dispatched quickly forward to locate the enemy CP in order to strike before the enemy could be alerted for counter-measures. The decision was to attack with the two companies rather than to wait for the other column and risk giving the guerrilla regiment time to form.

The main force moved up to the river bank and crossed under sporadic and ineffective automatic weapons fire from a guerrilla delaying force on the far bank. The enemy CP had been located. The camp was assaulted with the enemy offering only scattered resistance, leaving cooking fires and personal possessions behind in their hasty evacuation into the jungle. The huts were burned and what equipment could not be destroyed was captured. The column recrossed the river and moved right back to where contact had first been made and set up the bivouac for the night. The guerrillas probed the perimeter with small arms fire all night, harassing and trying to locate accurately the perimeter in the dark jungle. The hunters had become the hunted.

As the column prepared to move out, it had to fight its way out of the perimeter. A body count of three Killed in Actions (KIAs) and blood trails where they had dragged their wounded off into the jungle indicated that the enemy had gotten the worst of the short exchange. The hammock-slung litter for the wounded slowed the column, however, and made it easier for the guerrillas to follow and harass. By now there was no doubt the enemy regiment was alerted and probably knew the approximate size of the invading government force.

The column commander's malaria was getting the better of him so the force moved slowly and wandered about continually losing its way and being fired upon by harassing elements. Although MAJ Oran would speak to his advisors, he appeared politely preoccupied when they offered any advice concerning direction or security for the force.

When the acting senior advisor and his counterpart found the force and arrived for a visit by helicopter, the ranking advisor with the column handed him a hastily scribbled note: "Oran is going to get us annihilated! He won't listen to us, and refuses to provide proper security. The men have lost confidence in him. GET US OUT OF HERE!"

The acting senior advisor knew that MAJ Oran had been considered the "weak sister" in the organization all along. What was he to do now when the lives of his advisors were being threatened by this lack of initiative and aggressiveness on Oran's part? What are the factors he must consider in arriving at a decision?

OUTCOMES

A Good Apple Almost Spoils the Barrel

In thinking the problem over, 1LT Quinn remembered what now appeared to be a key point in this situation. PSG Thompson had overheard Gomez tell another squad leader that 1LT Quinn was "leading him by the hand" and that he (Gomez) already knew "how to run a squad." Thompson had passed this comment along to Quinn during a discussion of the platoon's performance one day at lunch in the field.

First Lieutenant Quinn concluded he had not sufficiently explained to Gomez why he had supervised the platoon's training so closely, and for the same reason had probably hurt his subordinate leader's position in the eyes of his squad. Quinn realized he had been so intent on bringing along his weaker squads that he had not publicly credited nor adequately challenged his best squad.

From that time on, 1LT Quinn was careful to give SFC Gomez only mission type orders, at the same time approaching that point gradually with the other squad leaders. In addition, Quinn made it a point occasionally to ask Gomez for his opinion on weapons or tactical matters in front of the Second Squad. He also worked out ways of communicating to the platoon the reasons behind his orders when this was appropriate, and he established an atmosphere that encouraged the upward flow of communications from his subordinates. The result was a renewed enthusiasm on SFC Gomez's part and a quick return to an outstanding level of performance on the part of his squad. SFC Gomez now prides himself on his ability to help the Platoon Leader solve problems and to accomplish the tasks and missions given to him by 1LT Quinn.

The Case of the Reluctant Rangers

What happened? Well, Bill Dixon, considering the group's feelings and the realities of the situation, decided not to attempt to force the issue. Instead, he explained the need to get moving. Then, in a rising voice that showed both excitement and displeasure, he told them he was as tired as any of them but he certainly wasn't going to quit with the end in sight. He stopped talking abruptly, picked up the light machine gun, and announced, "I'm heading for the pick-up point" as he moved out. Very shortly the patrol was on his heels and someone relieved him of the machine gun. Moving at a good clip and with noticeable cooperation, the entire patrol arrived at the pick-up point on time.

The AWOL Lieutenant

Second Lieutenant Harris, in trying to be fair, decided to offer 2LT Stone a choice. Stone could either voluntarily restrict himself to the post for a week, in which case the offense would be overlooked, or Harris would officially report the incident to the Battalion Commander. Stone was initially abusive and profane, but at length agreed that he preferred the restriction to being reported to the Battalion Commander. He was then told to apologize to 2LT George and to get with him to straighten out the guard property.

All went well for two days until 2LT Stone was reported as absent from the post. When Harris questioned him about this, Stone readily admitted going home for the evening. With some heat, he stated that 2LT Harris didn't have the authority to confine him to the post. He called Harris a stupid, autocratic martinet, and defied Harris to do anything about it.

Lt. Harris was now in a bad position. He had, in fact, exceeded his authority by what amounted to restricting an officer to the post. He felt he had no alternative now, if he were to retain any authority in the company. Harris went to his Battalion Commander and reported all the facts, withholding none of the details. The Battalion Commander, an officer of considerable experience, admonished him for not reporting the incident as soon as it happened. He also reassigned Stone from the company and designated an investigating officer to inquire into court-martial charges against 2LT Stone.

"Quitter" Platoon

Sergeant First Class Braxton decided for the time being to counsel Odey until he could work out a broader, more lasting solution to the bigger problem involving the *esprit* of the platoon and the morale of the individual soldiers in it.

Part of the counseling included suggestions as to how to vary Odey's activity during his off-duty time, encouragement to take part in company and battalion sports events, and a push to contact his chaplain to seek help available there.

But Braxton knew that this was only a partial solution to a symptom of the real problem. Thus, he determined to get help from the Company Commander to obtain greater recognition for the platoon and a more equitable share of promotions. In addition, he asked to billet his men in one barracks, which was not now the case; to permit the wearing of some type of distinctive item as part of the uniform; and to initiate platoon competition within the company in sports, inspections, and possibly drill. Braxton decided that the platoon should be constantly aware of the mission it had to perform and its importance. He further resolved to talk to the platoon as a unit at least once a week and to attempt to involve the platoon in activities as a unit whenever possible.

To improve individual morale, he looked into the possibility of arranging for and encouraging attendance at high school and college level extension courses. In addition, he proposed a plan to the Company Commander that would enable the men in his platoon to get the training necessary to allow them to compete for the positions of higher level skill and pay that were frequently opening up in the technical platoons of the company.

Sp 4 Odey? Apparently he got some good advice from the Platoon Sergeant and followed it. In fact, he re-enlisted and decided to make the Army a career.

First Ready Company

Right or wrong, or perhaps neither completely right nor completely wrong, 2LT Short decided to restrict PSG Williams to his room so that the other men would not see him. Inside the room, Short talked to PSG Williams about his responsibility to enforce the "no alcohol" regulation. "How can you expect compliance when you break the regulation yourself?" he asked. "Besides," Short added, "in the company's critical status an even mildly intoxicated sergeant would be a serious liability." Because of PSG Williams' past record and the fact that this was a first offense, Short decided not to report the incident. He did, however, promise a visibly relieved platoon sergeant that he would recommend a one-grade reduction if it ever happened again. It never did.

The Eightball

The new company commander reviewed Wakefield's personnel file and found that he had had experience as a typist and had been a warehouse attendant. On this basis, he asked the Squadron Commander to reassign the man to the S-4 Section (Supply). The request was approved.

Wakefield was as happy as a clam in deep water. He was soon promoted to private first class and was doing an outstanding job as a typist. In two months he rose to clerk in charge of a storeroom. In time, he was promoted to Sp 4 and completed the remainder of his tour in the Army with a clean record.

Too Busy to Lead

Platoon Sergeant Ignatz had no choice; he had Cummings reduced in grade to PFC. But, in talking with him, PSG Ignatz discovered that Cummings had had no notion of the additional responsibilities expected of an Sp 4.

Then Ignatz realized where the major part of the fault lay—in himself. He had failed, because of his haste and preoccupation, to counsel Cummings as to just what was expected of a Specialist Fourth Class. As a result, Cummings continued to be responsible solely for his own actions.

Within 7½ months, PSG Ignatz again promoted Cummings to Sp 4, this time being sure to counsel him and to take time for occasional subsequent guidance counseling.

Platoon Sergeant Ignatz admitted readily that his failure to counsel Cummings when he was originally promoted was an exception to his normal practice. He further stated that he felt Cummings' current good performance was due to his increased maturity as well as to proper performance counseling.

The New Platoon Leader

Captain Brooks decided that his best course lay in asking the Battalion CO to transfer 2LT Palmer. He was probably influenced by these two considerations. First, in his opinion, PSG Dillen was the best noncommissioned officer in the battalion, and certainly the most effective and aggressive in the company. To lose him would be losing a key man, hard to replace.

The second factor was the possibility of transferring 2LT Palmer without much fanfare. It was a policy in this signal battalion to transfer junior officers every few months to give them experience at running different kinds of platoons.

Although this solution solves the immediate problem as far as the unit is concerned, it does not satisfy the company commander's responsibilities for 2LT Palmer's leadership development. Both PSG Dillen and 2LT Palmer should realize they are working toward the same goal. CPT Brooks needs to emphasize to 2LT Palmer that he has accomplished his purpose of assuming command in a forceful manner and that the time has come to foster sustaining motivation in the platoon members. His greatest aid here is the experience and influence of his competent platoon sergeant. CPT Brooks needs to explain to 2LT Palmer the role and authority relationship of the platoon leader and the platoon sergeant. CPT Brooks has a real leadership opportunity to develop 2LT Palmer's commendable enthusiasm and desire into productive and rewarding leadership.

Drowning in the Sea of Indebtedness

Sergeant First Class Smith needed help in arranging his finances. He had apparently not been a very good manager. Not only was he unable to forecast financial obligations, but also, he did not plan ahead to take care of unforeseeable eventualities. The Battery Commander and the Forward Observer, Lieutenant Zilenski, worked out a budget for SFC Smith. As a further aid, LT Zilenski would sit down with SFC Smith every pay day and plan the next month's expenses. He also accompanied SFC Smith to the American Express office where Smith made out and mailed checks and money orders to his various creditors. The Battery Commander got in touch with the Commanding Officer of Smith's buddy who had signed the note for the musical instruments. His friend then assumed his own debt. Thus, SFC Smith was able to reduce his debts and keep the finance company from repossessing his car.

Smith was better able to resist the temptations of "easy" installment buying. In fact, he started taking even better care of the men in the FO section by advising them of the dangers of "getting in over your head."

One for the Road

Second Lieutenant Dolan realized almost immediately that he had acted rashly and had need of some advice from the "old man" as to what to do. The "help" from the CO was in the form of a reprimand in which 2LT Dolan was told that he had no authority to take the stripes and must return them to SSG Bosch immediately. The lieutenant did so, explaining his lack of authority to take the stripes, but reminding SSG Bosch that he would be under observation during the upcoming exercise and that any further misconduct would call for consideration of his reduction for inefficiency.

With the advantage of hindsight, 2LT Dolan might have reached a better solution. The chief point in his favor was that he took immediate leadership action when the situation demanded it. Even in a situation such as this, however, the dignity of the noncommissioned officer must be respected and orders given to him should be given in such a manner and tone of voice as to inspire compliance rather than resentment. This is especially important when the subordinate's judgment is impaired by alcohol. Another important point illustrated by this incident is the admonition in Chapter XIII that "the extent of promised punishment should not exceed the leader's authority."

The Mayor of the Ordnance Company

First Lieutenant Digby felt that, while a lack of experience and inadequate training were contributing factors, the key to the situation was the unwillingness on the part of the men and noncommissioned officers to give and take orders stemming from the close personal relationships among the members of the unit.

To remedy this, 1LT Digby began a series of classes to the noncommissioned officers on proper noncommissioned officer-enlisted men relationships and customs and courtesies of the service. In addition, he undertook a series of individual counseling sessions with his noncommissioned officers which covered a period of two weeks.

Gradually the noncommissioned officers began to assert themselves and the formal chain of command within the company was exercised. This appeared to have a favorable effect and the men's morale and efficiency improved steadily.

The Ordnance Company went to the field twice after this and received satisfactory ratings on their performance. In the end, the company passed its ATT and reverted to an inactive status.

A Problem in the Supply Platoon

Miller concluded that Turner was being treated unfairly. He assumed the reason was racial prejudice on the part of SSG Doaks. He felt he could do one of four things:

1. Leave Turner in the job and try to eliminate Doaks' prejudice.
2. Transfer Turner to another section in the platoon.
3. Recommend that Turner be transferred to another platoon in the company or to another company.
4. Transfer Doaks.

Miller chose to reassign Turner within the platoon as platoon driver. This got him away from Doaks and gave him a chance to show his stuff. Within two months of his reassignment Turner had been promoted to Specialist Fourth Class. Turner's performance improved radically and within three months he was named Support Group "Soldier of the Month." He later graduated as honor student from the Division Radio Telephone Operator's School and much later applied for and attended the Officer Candidate School at Fort Benning.

SSG Doaks' attitude changed, too, after he observed that Turner could do a good job when he was respected and trusted. Also, he realized his prejudice had cost him a good man in the Class II and IV Section.

The Ultimatum

First Lieutenant Harper decided he could do one of three things: (1) transfer Braun; (2) transfer Miller; (3) keep both and try to work out a solution.

If he transferred Braun, he would be backing up his platoon sergeant; however, he would then be without a platoon sergeant when Miller moved to First Sergeant.

He could release Miller, since he would leave the platoon soon anyway, and Braun would get his platoon sergeant's job sooner than expected. Of course, this would seem to degrade Miller whose authority should be upheld. Besides, there would be the problem of Miller's assignment while waiting for the First Sergeant's job—and perhaps this would affect his chance for the job.

He could let it ride for awhile and see if a little time and talk would solve it.

First Lieutenant Harper called the two sergeants in and asked them to put their differences aside until after the platoon test the following month, since he needed them both and wanted to keep them at least until then.

There was a long silence after the platoon leader had explained his position. Miller finally broke it by saying, "I think I can still work with Braun. I'm willing to give it a try." Braun grunted out about the same sentiments.

Harper felt relieved that he would have both men for the platoon test. By the time they had taken the test, though, the two sergeants were friends again. The way Harper assessed it, both men apparently had regretted their actions and words while drinking, but were too proud to back down from their decision that one of them must leave. 1LT Harper's appeal had given each of them a chance to escape gracefully and the incident was soon forgotten by everyone.

Advisor's Dilemma

Something further should be known about the relationships between the Division Advisor and the Division Commander and between the Division Commander and the Regimental Commander. How good is the Regimental Commander? It is possible that the Division Commander had already made up his mind to relieve the Regimental Commander and that such an incident was inevitable.

At this point, irrevocable public action has been taken by the Division Commander. Nevertheless, the Division Advisor should discuss the matter with his counterpart and impress him with the implications and serious effect that the relief of a commander in combat has upon his followers. Some of the difficulties involved were pointed out when the Advisor to the Regimental Commander asked, "Who is the Commander now?"

Major Richards has a responsibility to his counterpart not to undermine his loyalty to the Division Commander. He might, however, offer assurance that he personally would not condemn or report minor mistakes made in the name of aggressiveness.

Welfare vs. Mission

The acting senior advisor quickly analyzed the situation. Drawing his counterpart aside, he prevailed upon him to plan an operation for the assembled companies. His counterpart then conferred with MAJ Oran and his officers and planned an offensive sweep back to the government secured village on the west edge of the guerrillas' safe area. With a stated positive mission, initiative and aggressiveness were restored and the *esprit* of the column went up again. They once again became an effective fighting force and completed the mission without further incident.

Factors which the senior advisor considered were concerned with restoring an aggressive spirit in the command, looking after the welfare of his advisors, not embarrassing MAJ Oran in front of his command, saving face for his counterpart so he did not appear to be a puppet, and obtaining the most effectiveness from a combat unit committed to action on the guerrilla's own terrain.

Bibliography

Albers, H. H., *Principles of Organization and Management.* New York: John Wiley & Sons, 1965.

Allen, L. A., *Management and Organization.* New York: McGraw-Hill, 1958.

Allport, G. W., *The Nature of Prejudice.* Garden City, N.Y.: Doubleday & Company, Inc., 1958.

Allport, G. W., and Postman, L., *The Psychology of Rumor.* New York: Henry Holt & Co., 1947.

Almond, G. A., and Verba, S., *The Civic Culture.* Boston, Mass.: Little-Brown, 1965.

Anderson, L. R., "Initiation of structure, consideration, and the task performance in intercultural discussion groups," Technical Report No. 30, Group Effectiveness Research Laboratory, University of Illinois, 1966.

Anderson, L. R., and Fiedler, F. E., "The Effect of Participatory and Supervisory Leadership on Group Creativity," *Journal of Applied Psychology,* 48, 1964, pp. 227-236.

Arbuckle, D. S., *Counseling: An Introduction.* Boston, Mass.: Allyn & Bacon, 1961.

Argyris, C., *Interpersonal Competence and Organizational Effectiveness.* Homewood, Ill.: Richard D. Irwin, Inc., 1962.

Army Regulations 40-4, *Army Medical Service Facilities.* Washington: U.S. Government Printing Office, 1964.

Army Regulations 165-20, *Duties of Chaplains and Commanders' Responsibilities.* Washington: U.S. Government Printing Office, 1966.

Army Regulations 350-30, *Code of Conduct.* Washington: U.S. Government Printing Office, 1964.

Army Regulations 608-50, *Legal Assistance.* Washington: U.S. Government Printing Office, 1965.

Army Regulations 623-105, *Officer Efficiency Reports.* Washington: U.S. Government Printing Office, 1966.

Army Regulations 910-10, *Army Emergency Relief.* Washington: U.S. Government Printing Office, 1961.

293

Army Regulations 940-10, *National Red Cross Service Program and Army Utilization*. Washington: U.S. Government Printing Office, 1955.

Aronson, E., and Worchel, P., "Similarity Versus Liking as Determinants of Interpersonal Attractiveness," *Psychonomic Science*, 5, 1966, pp. 157-8.

Babbage, C., *On the Economy of Machinery and Manufacturers*. Philadelphia: Carey & Lea, 1832.

Baritz, L., *The Servants of Power*. Middletown, Conn.: Wesleyan University Press, 1960.

Bass, B. M., *Leadership, Psychology and Organizational Behavior*. New York: Harper & Bros., 1960.

Bavelas, A., "Communication Patterns in Task-oriented Groups," in Lerner, D. and Lasswell, H. D. (eds.), *The Policy Sciences*. Stanford, Calif.: Stanford University Press, 1951, pp. 193-202.

Beishline, J. R., *Military Management for National Defense*. New York: Prentice-Hall, Inc., 1950.

Berelson, B., and Steiner, G. A., *Human Behavior*. New York: Harcourt, Brace & World, Inc., 1964.

Berlo, D. K., *The Process of Communication*. New York: Holt, Rinehart & Winston, Inc., 1960.

Berne, E., *Games People Play*. New York: Grove Press, Inc., 1964.

Benét, S. V., *John Brown's Body*. New York: Holt, Rinehart & Winston, Inc., 1927.

Blake, R. R., and Mouton, J. S., *The Managerial Grid*. Houston, Tex.: Gulf Press, 1964.

Blau, P. M., and Scott, R. W., *Formal Organizations*. San Francisco: Chandler Publishing Co., 1962.

Borg, W. R., and Tupes, E. C., "Personality Characteristics Related to Leadership Behavior in Two Types of Small Group Situation Problems," *Journal of Applied Psychology*, 42, 1958, pp. 252-6.

Borgatta, E. F., Bales, R. F., and Couch, A. S., "Some Factors Relevant to the Great Man Theory of Leadership," *American Sociological Review*, 19, 1954, pp. 755-9.

Bowers, D. G., and Seashore, S. E., "Predicting Organizational Effectiveness With a Four-Factor Theory of Leadership," *Administrative Science Quarterly*, 2, September 1966, pp. 238-263.

Bradley, O. N., *A Soldier's Story*. New York: Henry Holt & Co., 1951.

Bradley, O. N., "Leadership," *Military Review*, 46, September 1966, pp. 48-53.

Brennan, L. D., *Modern Communication Effectiveness*. Englewood Cliffs, N.J.: Prentice-Hall, Inc., 1963.

Brown, R. W., *Social Psychology*. New York: Free Press, 1965.

Browne, C. G., and Cohn, T. S. (eds.), *The Study of Leadership*. Danville, Ill.: The Interstate Printers & Publishers, Inc., 1958.

Burke, P. J., "Authority Relations and Disruptive Behavior in Small Discussion Groups," *Sociometry*, 29, 1966, pp. 237-250.

Burke, R. J., "Are Herzberg's Motivators and Hygienes Unidimensional?" *Journal of Applied Psychology*, 50, 1966, pp. 317-321.

Campbell, J. P., "Management Training: The Development of Managerial

Effectiveness," in *Identification and Enhancement of Managerial Effectiveness*, Richardson Foundation Survey Report, 1966.

Carlyle, T., MacMechan (ed.), *On Heroes, Hero-Worship and the Heroic in History*. Boston, Mass.: Ginn, 1901.

Carter, L. F., Haythorn, W., Shriver, B., and Lanzetta, J., "The Behavior of Leaders and Other Group Members," *Journal of Abnormal and Social Psychology*, 46, 1951, pp. 589-595.

Cartwright, D., and Zander, A. (eds.), *Group Dynamics: Research and Theory*. 2d ed.; New York: Harper & Row, Publishers, Inc., 1960.

Chemers, M. M., Fiedler, F. E., Lekhyananda, D., and Stolurow, L. M., "Some Effects of Cultural Training on Leadership in Heterocultural Task Groups," Technical Report No. 31, Group Effectiveness Research Laboratory. Urbana, Ill.: University of Illinois Press, April 1966.

Cherry, C., *On Human Communication*. New York: John Wiley & Sons, Inc., 1957.

Clarke, B. C., *Guidelines for the Leader and Commander*. Harrisburg, Pa.: The Stackpole Co., 1963.

Cleland, D. I., "Project Management," *Air University Review*, 16, January/February 1965, pp. 13-22.

Coch, L. R., and French, J. R. P., Jr., "Overcoming Resistance to Change," *Human Relations*, 1, 1948, pp. 512-532.

Cohen, A. R., "Upward Communication in Experimentally Created Hierarchies," *Human Relations*, 11, 1958, pp. 41-53.

Cooley, C. H., *Social Organization*. New York: Charles Scribner's Sons, 1924.

Coleman, J. C., *Abnormal Psychology and Modern Life*, 3rd ed., Chicago: Scott, Foresman & Co., 1964.

Cooper, J. B., and McGaugh, J. L., *Integrating Principles of Social Psychology*. Cambridge, Mass.: Schenkman Publishing Co., Inc., 1963.

Costello, T. W., and Zalkind, S. S., *Psychology in Administration*. Englewood Cliffs, N.J.: Prentice-Hall, Inc., 1963.

Crane, S., *The Red Badge of Courage*. New York: Appleton, 1895.

Daniel, D. R., "Reorganizing for Results," *Harvard Business Review*, 44, November/December 1966, pp. 96-104.

Davis, K., *Human Relations at Work*. New York: McGraw-Hill Book Co., Inc., 1962.

Dearden, J., and McFarlan, F. W., *Management Information Systems*. Homewood, Ill.: Irwin Publishing Co., 1966.

Denno, B. F., "Advisor and Counterpart," *Army*, 15, July 1965, pp. 25-30.

Deutsch, M., "An Experimental Study of the Effects of Cooperation and Competition Upon Group Process," *Human Relations*, 2, 1949, pp. 199-231.

Drucker, P. F., *The New Society: The Anatomy of Industrial Order*. New York: Harper & Row Publishers, Inc., 1962.

Dubin, R., Homans, G. C., Mann, F. C., and Miller, D. C., *Leadership and Productivity*. San Francisco: Chandler Publishing Co., 1965.

Duke, M. L., "The Lawful Order," *Proceedings*. U.S. Naval Institute, 92, July 1966, pp. 82-90.

Eachus, H. T., "Comparison of Various Approaches to Training for Culture-contact," Air Force Systems Command, Wright Patterson Air Force Base, March 1966.

Eisenhower, D. D., *Crusade in Europe*. New York: Doubleday & Co., Inc., 1948.

Eisenhower, D. D., *Report by the Supreme Commander to the Combined Chiefs of Staff on the Operation in Europe of the AEF, June 6, 1944-May 8, 1945*.

Emerson, R. M., "Mount Everest: A Case Study of Communication Feedback and Sustained Group Goal-Striving," *Sociometry*, 29, 1966, pp. 213-227.

Etzioni, A., "Dual Leadership in Complex Organizations," *American Sociological Review*, 30, 1965, pp. 688-698.

Farnsworth, P. R., McNemar, O., and McNemar, Q. (eds.), *Annual Review of Psychology*. Palo Alto, Calif.: Annual Reviews, Inc., 1966.

Fayol, H., *General and Industrial Management*. New York: Pitman Publishing Corporation, 1949.

Fenalson, A. F., Ferguson, G. B., and Abrahamson, A. C., *Essentials in Interviewing*. New York: Harper & Row Publishers, Inc., 1962.

Fergusson, B. E., *The Black Watch and the King's Enemies*. London: Crowell, 1950.

Festinger, L., *A Theory of Cognitive Dissonance*. Evanston, Ill.: Row, Peterson & Co., 1957.

Fiedler, F. E., "A Contingency Model for the Prediction of Leadership Effectiveness," Technical Report No. 10, Group Effectiveness Research Laboratory, University of Illinois, 1963.

Fiedler, F. E., "A Note on Leadership Theory: The Effect of Social Barriers Between Leaders and Followers," *Sociometry*, 20, 1957, pp. 87-94.

Fiedler, F. E., *Leader Attitudes and Group Effectiveness*. Urbana, Ill.: University of Illinois Press, 1958.

Fiedler, F. E., "Leader Attitudes, Group Climate, and Group Creativity," *Journal of Abnormal and Social Psychology*, 65, 1962, pp. 308-318.

Fiedler, F. E., "The Effect of Leadership and Cultural Heterogeneity on Group Performance: A Test of the Contingency Model," *Journal of Experimental Social Psychology*, 2, 1966, pp. 237-264.

Field Manual 21-5, *Military Training Management*. Washington: U.S. Government Printing Office, December 1964.

Field Manual 22-100, *Military Leadership*. Washington: U.S. Government Printing Office, November 1965.

Field Manual 101-5, *Staff Officer's Field Manual: Staff Organization and Procedure*. Washington: U.S. Government Printing Office, July 1960.

Flesch, R., *The Art of Plain Talk*. New York: Harper & Row, 1946.

Frederick the Great, *Instructions for His Generals*, translated by T. R. Phillips. Harrisburg, Pa.: Military Service Publishing Co., 1951.

Freeman, G. L., and Taylor, E. K., *How to Pick Leaders*. New York: Funk & Wagnalls, 1950.

French, J. R. P., "The Disruption and Cohesion of Groups," *Journal of Abnormal and Social Psychology*, 36, 1949, pp. 361-377.

French, W., *The Personnel Management Process: Human Resources Administration*. Boston, Mass.: Houghton-Mifflin, 1964.

Friedlander, F., "Underlying Sources of Job Satisfaction," *Journal of Applied Psychology*, 47, 1963, pp. 256-260.

Fromm, E., *Man For Himself*. New York: Holt, Rinehart & Winston, 1964.

Gerard, H., and Mathewson, G. C., "The Effect of Severity of Initiation on Liking for a Group: A Replication," *Journal of Experimental Social Psychology*, 2, 1966, pp. 278-287.

Gerth, H. H., and Mills, C. W. (eds), *From Max Weber*. New York: Galaxy, Oxford University Press, 1958.

Ginzburg, E., *The Ineffective Soldier: The Lost Division*. New York: Columbia University Press, 1959.

Ginzberg, E., *The Ineffective Soldier: Patterns of Performance*. New York: Columbia University Press, 1959.

Glass, A., in *Symposium on Preventive and Social Psychiatry, 15-17 April 1957*, Walter Reed Institute of Research. Washington: U.S. Government Printing Office, 1957.

Gordon, T., *Group-Centered Leadership*. Boston, Mass.: Houghton-Mifflin Co., 1955.

Gouldner, A. W., *Studies in Leadership*. New York: Harper, 1950.

Gruen, W., "A Contribution Toward Understanding of Cohesiveness in Small Groups," *Psychological Reports*, 17, 1965, pp. 311-322.

Guion, R. M., "Some Definitions of Morale," in *Studies in Personnel and Industrial Psychology*, Fleishman, E. A. (ed.). Homewood, Ill.: The Dorsey Press, Inc., 1961.

Hackett, J. W., *The Profession of Arms*. London: Times Publishing Co., 1963.

Haimann, T., *Professional Management*. Boston, Mass.: Houghton-Mifflin Co., 1962.

Halpin, A. W., "The Leadership Behavior and Combat Performance of Airplane Commanders," *Journal of Abnormal and Social Psychology*, 49, January 1954, pp. 19-22.

Hare, A. P., *Handbook of Small Group Research*. New York: Free Press of Glencoe, 1962.

Hare, A. P., Borgatta, E. F., Bales, R. F. (eds.), *Small Groups: Studies in Social Interaction*. New York: Alfred A. Knopf, 1955.

Harms, E., and Schreiber, P. (eds.), *Handbook of Counseling Techniques*. New York: Pergamon Press, 1963.

Hatch, K. M., "Creative Thinking and the Military Profession," *Military Review*, 46, August 1966, pp. 78-86.

Hayes, J. H., "Systems Analysis," *Army*, 14, February 1964, pp. 41-5.

Haylitt, H., *The Foundations of Morality*. Princeton, N.J.: Van Nostrand, 1964.

Heckman, I. L., Jr., and Huneryager, S. G., *Human Relations in Management*. Cincinnati, Ohio: South-Western Publishing Co., 1960.

Heider, F., *The Psychology of Interpersonal Relations*. New York: John Wiley Co., 1958.

Hemphill, J. K., "Situation Factors in Leadership," *Ohio State University*

Educational Research Monograph No. 32, Columbus, Ohio: Ohio State University Press, 1949.

Herzberg, F., Mausner, B., and Snyderman, B. B., *The Motivation to Work.* 2d ed.: New York: John Wiley & Sons, Inc., 1959.

Heslin, R., and Dunphy, D., "Three Dimensions of Member Satisfaction in Small Groups," *Human Relations,* 17, 1964, pp. 99-112.

Hodge, R. W., Siegel, P. M., and Rossi, P. H., "Occupational Prestige in the United States," *American Journal of Sociology,* 70, May 1964, pp. 286-302.

Hoffman, I. R., Burke, R. J., and Maier, N. R. F., "Participation, Influence, and Satisfaction Among Members of Problem Solving Groups," *Psychological Reports,* 16, 1955, pp. 661-7.

Hollander, E. P., *Leaders, Groups, and Influence.* New York: Oxford University Press, 1964.

Hollander, E. P., and Hunt, R. G. (eds.), *Current Perspectives in Social Psychology.* New York: Oxford Press, 1967.

Hollander, E. P., and Julian, J. W., "Leadership," in Borgatta, E. F., and Lambert W., *Handbook of Personality Theory and Research* (not yet published).

Hollander, E. P., Julian, J. W., and Perry, F. A., "Leader Style, Competence, and Source of Authority as Determinants of Actual and Perceived Influence," Technical Report No. 5, State University of New York at Buffalo, 1966.

Hollingsworth, H. L., *Psychology and Ethics.* New York: The Ronald Press Co., 1949.

Homans, G. C., *The Human Group.* New York: Harcourt, Brace & World, Inc., 1950.

Honigmann, J. J., *Understanding Culture.* New York: Harper & Row, 1963.

Hovland, C. I., Janis, I. L., and Kelley, H. H., *Communication and Persuasion.* New Haven, Conn.: Yale University Press, 1953.

Hq., Sixth U.S. Army, General Court-Martial Order No. 14, 21 February 1956.

Hudlin, I. C., "Advising the Advisor," *Military Review,* 45, November 1965, pp. 94-6.

Huntington, S. P., *The Soldier and the State.* New York: Random House, 1957.

Jackson, Robert H., *The Nürnberg Case.* New York: Alfred A. Knopf, 1947.

Janowitz, M., *Sociology and the Military Establishment.* New York: Russell Sage Foundation, 1959.

Janowitz, M. (ed.), *The New Military.* New York: Russell Sage Foundation, 1964.

Janowitz, M., *The Professional Soldier.* Glencoe, Ill.: Free Press of Glencoe, 1960.

Jenkins, W. O., and Stanley, J. C., Jr., "Partial Reinforcement: A Review and Critique," *Psychological Bulletin,* 47, 1950, pp. 193-234.

Jennings, E. E., *An Anatomy of Leadership.* New York: Harper & Bros., 1960.

Johnson, R. A., Kast, F. E., and Rosenzweig, J. E., *The Theory and Management of Systems.* New York: McGraw-Hill Book Co., Inc., 1963.

Kardiner, A., and Spiegel, H., *War Stress and Neurotic Illness,* New York: Paul B. Hoeber, Inc., 1947.

Katz, D., and Kahn, R. L., "Human Organization and Worker Motivation," *Industrial Productivity.* Madison, Wis.: Industrial Relations Research Assoc., 1951.

Kelman, H. C., "Processes of Opinion Change," *Public Opinion Quarterly,* 25, 1961, pp. 57-78.

Kipling, R., *Rudyard Kipling's Verse.* Garden City, N.Y.: Doubleday Doran & Co., Inc., 1934.

Koontz, H. (ed.), *Toward a Unified Theory of Management.* New York: McGraw-Hill, 1964.

Koontz, H., and O'Donnell, C., *Principles of Management.* New York: McGraw-Hill, 1959.

Kornhauser, W., *The Politics of Mass Society.* New York: Free Press, 1959.

Krech, D., Crutchfield, R. S., and Ballachey, E. L., *Individual in Society.* New York: McGraw-Hill, 1962.

Ladd, J., *The Structure of a Moral Code.* Cambridge, Mass.: Harvard University Press, 1957.

Laird, D. A., and Laird, E. C., *The New Psychology for Leadership.* New York: McGraw-Hill Book Co., Inc., 1956.

Lange, C. J., Campbell, V., Katter, R. V., and Shanley, F. J., *A Study of Leadership in Army Infantry Platoons (OFFTRAIN II),* HumRRO Research Report 1, U.S. Army Leadership Human Research Unit, Presidio of Monterey, Calif., November 1958.

Lange, C. J., and Jacobs, T. O., *Leadership in Army Infantry Platoons: Study II (OFFTRAIN III),* HumRRO Research Report 5, U.S. Army Infantry Human Research Unit, Ft. Benning, Ga., July 1960.

LaPierre, R. T., *A Theory of Social Control.* New York: McGraw-Hill Book Co., Inc., 1954.

Leeds, H. D., and Weinberg, G. M., *Computer Programming Fundamentals.* New York: McGraw-Hill, 1961.

Letter, Office of the Secretary of Defense, *Defense Advisory Committee on Prisoners of War,* July 29, 1955.

Lewin, K., *Field Theory in Social Science,* D. Cartwright (ed.). New York: Harper & Row, 1951.

Lewin, K., Lippitt, R., and White, R. K., "Patterns of Aggressive Behavior in Experimentally Created 'Social Climates,'" *Journal of Social Psychology,* 10, 1939, pp. 271-299.

Little, R. W., "Buddy Relations and Combat Performance," in *The New Military,* M. Janowitz (ed.), New York: Russell Sage Foundation, 1964.

Lyons, G. M., and Masland, J. W., *Education and Military Leadership: A Study of the ROTC.* Princeton, N.J.: Princeton University Press, 1959.

McClelland, D. C., *The Achieving Society.* Princeton, N.J.: Van Nostrand, 1961.

McCloskey, J. F., and Trefethen, F. N., *Operations Research for Management.* Vols. I and II; Baltimore: The Johns Hopkins Press, 1954.

McGrath, J. E., *Social Psychology, A Brief Introduction*. New York: Holt, Rinehart & Winston, 1964.

McGrath, J. E., and Altman, I., *Small Group Research: A Synthesis and Critique of the Field*. New York: Holt, Rinehart & Winston, Inc., 1966.

McGregor, D., *The Human Side of Enterprise*. New York: McGraw-Hill, 1960.

McGregor, D., *Leadership and Motivation*. New Rochelle, N.Y.: Cambridge Press, 1966.

McMillan C., and Gonzalez, R. F., *Systems Analysis*. Homewood, Ill.: Richard D. Irwin, Inc., 1965.

MacArthur, D. Annual Report, Chief of Staff, U.S. Army, 1933.

Maier, N. R. F., *Psychology in Industry*. 3rd ed.; Boston: Houghton-Mifflin, 1965.

Maier, N. R. F., *The Appraisal Interview*. New York: John Wiley & Sons, 1958.

Maier, N. R. F., and Hayes, J. J., *Creative Management*. New York: John Wiley & Sons, Inc., 1962.

Malinovsky, M. R., and Barry, J. R., "Determinants of Work Attitudes," *Journal of Applied Psychology*, 49, 1965, pp. 446-451.

Marshall, S. L. A., *Men Against Fire*. Washington: Infantry Journal, 1947.

Marshall, S. L. A., *The Officer as a Leader*. Harrisburg, Pa.: Stackpole Company, 1966.

Marting, E., Finley, R. E., and Ward, A., *Effective Communication on the Job*. New York: American Management Association, Inc., 1963.

Maslow, A. H., "A Theory of Human Motivation," *Psychological Review*, 50, 1943, pp. 370-396.

Masson, D. J., "Judgments of Leadership Based Upon Physiognomic Cues," *Journal of Abnormal and Social Psychology*, 54, 1957, pp. 273-4.

Mathewson, R. H., *Guidance Policy and Practice*. New York: Harper & Row, 1962.

Mayo, E., *The Human Problems of an Industrial Civilization*. New York: Macmillan, 1933.

Mayo, E., *The Social Problems of an Industrial Civilization*. Boston: Harvard University, 1945.

Mellinger, G. D., "Interpersonal Trust as a Factor in Communication," *Journal of Abnormal and Social Psychology*, 52, 1956, pp. 304-9.

Metcalfe, H., *The Cost of Manufacturers and Administration of Workshops, Public and Private*. New York: Wiley & Son, 1885.

Miller, D. W., and Starr, M. K., *Executive Decisions and Operations Research*. Englewood Cliffs, N.J.: Prentice-Hall, Inc., 1960.

Moder, J. J., and Philips, C. R., *Project Management with CPM and PERT*. New York: Reinhold Publishing Corp., 1964.

Mooney, J. D., *The Principles of Organization*. New York: Harper, 1947.

Moore, B. V., "The May Conference on Leadership," *Personnel Journal*, 6, 1927, pp. 124-8.

Moser, L. E., and Moser, R. S., *Counseling and Guidance: An Exploration*. Englewood Cliffs, N.J.: Prentice-Hall, 1963.

Murray, H. A., "Explorations in Personality," in Hall and Lindzey, *Theories of Personality*. New York: John Wiley & Sons, Inc., 1963.

Myers, A. E., *Team Competition, Success, and the Adjustment of Group Members*, Technical Report No. 12, Group Effectiveness Research Laboratory, University of Illinois, Urbana, Ill., June 1961.

Myers, M. S., "Who Are Your Motivated Workers?" *Harvard Business Review*, 42, 1964, pp. 73-88.

Newcomb, T. M., Turner, R. H., and Converse, P. E., *Social Psychology*. New York: Holt, Rinehart & Winston, Inc., 1965.

Newman, W. H., and Summer, C. E., Jr., *The Process of Management*. Englewood Cliffs, N.J.: Prentice-Hall, Inc., 1961.

Office of Armed Forces Information and Education, Department of Defense, DOD Pamphlet 1-16, *The U.S. Fighting Man's Code*, Washington: U.S. Government Printing Office, 1959.

Office of Strategic Services Assessment Staff, *The Assessment of Men—Selection of Men for the Office of Strategic Services*. New York: Holt, Rinehart & Winston, 1948.

Oliver, R. T., *Culture and Communication*. Springfield, Ill.: Charles C. Thomas, 1962.

Osborn, A. F., *Applied Imagination*. New York: Scribner's, 1957.

Osgood, C. E., Suci, G. J., and Tannenbaum, P. H., *The Measurement of Meaning*. Urbana, Ill.: The University of Illinois Press, 1957.

Pamphlet, Civilian Personnel, 41-D, *Principles of Work Management*, Washington: U.S. Government Printing Office, 1957.

Pamphlet 611-1, *The Army Interview*. Washington: U.S. Government Printing Office, 1965.

Pareto, V., *The Mind and Society*, Livingston, A. (ed.), New York: Harcourt Brace, 1935.

Patterson, C. H., *Moral Standards*. New York: The Ronald Press Co., 1949.

Patton, G. S., Jr., *War As I Knew It*. Boston: Houghton-Mifflin, 1947.

Payne, S. L., *The Art of Asking Questions*. Princeton, N.J.: Princeton University Press, 1951.

Pelz, D. C., "Influence: A key to Effective Leadership in the First Line Supervisor," *Personnel*, 29, November 1952, pp. 209-217.

Petrullo, L., and Bass, B. M. (eds.), *Leadership and Interpersonal Behavior*. New York: Holt, Rinehart & Winston, Inc., 1961.

Porter, L. W., "Personnel Management," *Annual Review of Psychology*, 17, 1966, pp. 395-422.

Raube, S. A., "Principles of Good Organization," in Richards, M. D., and Nielander, W. A. (eds.), *Readings in Management*. Cincinnati, Ohio: South-Western Publishing Co., 1958, pp. 536-547.

Read, W., "Upward Communications in Industrial Hierarchies," *Human Relations*, 15, February 1962, pp. 3-15.

Reese, T. H., "An Officer's Oath," Department of the Army Pamphlet 27-100-25, *Military Law Review*. Washington: U.S. Government Printing Office, July 1964.

Richards, M. D., and Nielander, W. A., (eds.), *Readings in Management*. Cincinnati, Ohio: South-Western Publishing Co., 1959.

Roethlisberger, F. J., and Dickson, W. J., *Management and the Worker*. Cambridge, Mass.: Harvard University Press, 1956.

Rogers, C. R., *On Becoming a Person*. Boston, Mass.: Houghton-Mifflin, 1961.

Rogers, C. R., *Client-Centered Therapy*. Boston: Houghton-Mifflin, 1951.

Roskill, S. W., *The Art of Leadership*. Hamden, Conn.: Archon Books, 1965.

Sarason, I. G., and Sarason, B., "Effects of Motivating Instructions and Reports of Failure on Verbal Learning," *American Journal of Psychology*, 70, 1957, pp. 92-6.

Sayles, L. R., and Strauss, G., *Human Behavior in Organizations*. Englewood Cliffs, N.J.: Prentice-Hall, Inc., 1966.

Schein, E. H., *Organizational Psychology*. Englewood Cliffs, N.J., Prentice-Hall, Inc., 1965.

Schofield, J. M., Address to the Corps of Cadets, USMA, 11 August 1879.

Secord, P. F., and Backman, C. W., *Social Psychology*. New York: McGraw-Hill, 1964.

Senate Document 221, 56th Congress, 1st Session. *Report of the Commission Appointed by the President to Investigate the Conduct of the War Department in the War with Spain*. Washington: U.S. Government Printing Office, 1899.

Shannon, C. E., and Weaver, W., *The Mathematical Theory of Communication*. Urbana, Ill.: University of Illinois Press, 1949.

Shartle, C. L., *Executive Performance and Leadership*. Englewood Cliffs, N.J.: Prentice-Hall, 1956.

Shepherd, C. R., *Small Groups*. San Francisco: Chandler Publishing Co., 1964.

Shibutani, T., "Reference Groups as Perspectives," in Hollander, E. P. and Hunt, R. G. (eds.), *Current Perspectives in Social Psychology*. 2d ed.; New York: Oxford University Press, 1967, pp. 74-82.

Shils, E. A., and Janowitz, M., "Primary Groups in the German Army," in Broom, L., and Selznick, P., *Sociology*. New York: Harper & Row, 1963, pp. 156-163.

Sobel, R., "Anxiety-Depressive Reactions After Prolonged Combat Experience —The Old Sergeant Syndrome," Bulletin, U.S. Army Medical Dept., *Combat Psychiatric Supplement*, November 1949, pp. 137-146.

Steffere, B. (ed.), *Theories of Counseling*. New York: McGraw-Hill, 1965.

Stewart, E. C., "American Advisors Overseas," *Military Review*, 45, February 1965, pp. 3-9.

Stewart, M. B., *Military Character, Habit, Deportment, Courtesy and Discipline*. Menasha, Wis.: George Banta Publishing Co., 1913.

Stogdill, R. M., *Individual Behavior and Group Achievement*. New York: Oxford University Press, 1959.

Stogdill, R. M., "Personal Factors Associated With Leadership: A Survey of the Literature," *Journal of Psychology*, 25, 1948, pp. 35-71.

Stogdill, R. M., and Coons, A. E. (eds.), *Leader Behavior: Its Description and Measurement*. Columbus, Ohio: Ohio State University, 1957.

Stouffer, S. A., Suchman, E. A., DeVinney, L. C., Star, S. A., and Williams,

R. M., Jr., *The American Soldier*, Vol. I, *Adjustment During Army Life*, (a) Vol. II, *Combat and Its Aftermath*, (b) Princeton, N.J.: Princeton University Press, 1949.

Suojanen, W. W., "The Span of Control—Fact or Fable?" in Richards, M. D., and Nielander, W. A. (eds.), *Readings in Management*. Cincinnati, Ohio: South-Western Publishing Co., 1958, pp. 548-564.

Tannenbaum, R., and Schmidt, W. H., "How to Choose a Leadership Pattern," *Harvard Business Review*, 36, March-April 1958, pp. 95-101.

Tannenbaum, R., Weschler, I. R., and Massarik, F., *Leadership and Organization: A Behavioral Science Approach*. New York: McGraw-Hill, 1961.

Taylor, D. W., Berry, P. C., and Block, C. H., "Group Participation, Brainstorming, and Creative Thinking," *Administrative Science Quarterly*, 3, 1958, pp. 23-47.

Taylor, F. W., *Principles of Scientific Management*. New York: Harper & Bros., 1919.

Taylor, F. W., *Shop Management*. New York: Harper & Bros., 1911.

Taylor, Jack W., *How to Select and Develop Leaders*. New York: McGraw-Hill, 1962.

Technical Manual 8-244, *Military Psychiatry*. Washington: U.S. Government Printing Office, 1957.

Terry, G. R., *Principles of Management*. Rev. ed.; Homewood, Ill.: Richard D. Irwin, Inc., 1956.

Thibaut, J. W., and Kelley, H. H., *The Social Psychology of Groups*. New York: John Wiley & Sons, Inc., 1959.

Tiffin, J., and McCormick, E. J., *Industrial Psychology*. Englewood Cliffs, N.J.: Prentice-Hall, 1965.

Toynbee, A. J., *A Study of History*. Vols. I, II, III, and IV; New York: Oxford University Press, 1947.

Tyler, L., *The Work of the Counselor*. 2d ed.; New York: Appleton-Century-Crofts, 1961.

United States Army Command and General Staff College, *Leadership: Reference Book 22-1*, Fort Leavenworth, Kansas: USAC&GSC, July 1964.

United States Army Command and General Staff College, "The Reserve Components," *Subject A399*. Fort Leavenworth, Kan.: USAC&GSC, 1964.

United States Army Management School, *Army Management*. Fort Belvoir, Va.: 1963.

U.S. Congress Section 1757, Revised Statutes, As Amended, 5 U.S.C. S16, 1958.

USCONARC Pamphlet No. 350-11, *Training: Guide for Commanders of Company Size Units*. Fort Monroe, Va.: Headquarters, United States Continental Army Command, November 1966.

Van Dersal, W. R., *The Successful Supervisor in Government and Business*. New York: Harper & Bros., 1962.

Vroom, V. H., *Work and Motivation*. New York: John Wiley & Sons, Inc., 1964.

Wager, L. W., "Leadership Style, Hierarchical Influence, and Supervisory Role Obligations," *Administrative Science Quarterly*, 4, 1965, pp. 391-420.

Walton, E., "How Efficient Is The Grapevine?" *Personnel*, 38, March/April 1961, pp. 47-51.

Ward, C., *The War of the Revolution*. Vol. I; New York: The Macmillan Co., 1952.

Warters, J., *Techniques of Counseling*. New York: McGraw-Hill, 1964.

Weitz, H., *Behavior Change Through Guidance*. New York: John Wiley & Sons, 1964.

Wetzel, R. K., *The Nürnberg Trials in International Law*. New York: Frederick A. Praeger, 1962.

Whyte, W. H., Jr., *The Organization Man*. New York: Simon & Schuster, 1956.

Williams, R. H. (ed.), *Human Factors in Military Operations—Some Applications of the Social Sciences to Operations Research*, Technical Memorandum ORO-T-259. Washington: Operations Research Office, The Johns Hopkins University, 1954. Operating under contract with the Department of the Army.

Wolf, W. B., *The Management of Personnel*. San Francisco, Calif.: Wadsworth Publishing Co., Inc., 1961.

Worthy, J. C., "Organizational Structure and Employee Morale," *American Sociological Review*, 15, April 1950, pp. 169-179.

Yamashita, K. S., "Problems of Cross-cultural Communication and Culture Shock in Stabilization Operations," presented at Eleventh Army Human Factors Research and Development Conference, U.S. Army Special Warfare School, Fort Bragg, N.C.: July 1965.

Zagona, S. V., and Zurcher, L. A., Jr., "Participation, Interaction and Role Behavior in Groups Selected from the Extremes of the Open-Closed Cognitive Continuum," *Journal of Psychology*, 2, 1964, pp. 255-264.

Zaleznik, A., *Human Dilemmas of Leadership*. New York: Harper & Row, Publishers, 1966.

Zaleznik, A., and Moment, D., *The Dynamics of Interpersonal Behavior*. New York: John Wiley & Sons, Inc., 1964.

Zander, A. and Curtis, T., "Social Support and Rejection of Organizational Standards," *Journal of Educational Psychology*, 56:2, 1965, pp. 87-95.

Zurcher, L. A., Jr., "The Sailor Aboard Ship: A Study of Role Behavior in a Total Institution," *Social Forces*, 43, 1965, pp. 389-400.

Glossary

Affiliative Needs—The desire to belong to a group.

Appointed Leadership—Leadership within a formal group wherein the leader has been granted his authority from above rather than by the members of the group.

Aptitude—The potentiality of acquiring proficiency in a skill or ability. Differentiated from actual ability.

Assignment—The placing of an individual in a specific organization or a specific job.

Attitude—A readiness to become motivated favorably or unfavorably toward a person, policy or other object; a motivational state which accounts for a certain amount of consistency in behavior relative to an object.

Authority—The power to direct the activities of others.

Autocratic Leadership—A pattern of authority relationships within a group wherein the leader retains most power for himself; absolute; despotic.

Authoritarian—When applied to leadership style, synonymous with autocratic. When applied to personality of an individual, refers to a pattern of personality traits marked by inflexibility and an overconcern with authority relationships.

Chain of Command—The vertical hierarchy of commanders from the highest to the lowest echelon.

Charismatic Leader—One who is endowed, according to his followers, with infallibility, great wisdom, and a divine or mystical quality.

Classification—A process in which personnel are evaluated to determine which tasks they have the potential or proficiency to perform. Used extensively in military personnel management, particularly in personnel assignment.

Collateral Objective—A goal which provides a social or economic benefit to the members of an organization, supporting organizations, or the general public.

Command—The lawful authority which an individual in the military service exercises over subordinates by virtue of his rank and assignment.

Communication—The process of transmission and receipt of information between two or more individuals.

Continuum—A one-dimension scale along which an indeterminate number of

305

variations may occur. Examples: height and weight. Often described in terms of the two extremes, such as autocratic-democratic continuum.

Controlling—The action taken by a leader to ensure that plans, orders, directives, and policies are being accomplished in such a manner that the objectives will be attained.

Co-ordinating—The integration of all details necessary for the accomplishment of a mission.

Critical Control Point—A specific activity of an organization which is selected by the leader for observation in the hope that it will provide an evaluation of the manner in which many other activities are progressing. Also extended to include the geographical location at which the observed activity is supposed to take place, such as a Line of Departure.

Culture—The principal ways of behaving; the values, and the material possessions of a people.

Cybernetics—A science relating electrical and mechanical systems to human functioning to include decision-making and control.

Democratic Leadership—A pattern of authority relationships within a group wherein power is retained by the members of the group.

Directing—The issuance by the leader of an oral or written communication which establishes a certain policy or order for action.

Discipline—The individual or group attitude that ensures prompt obedience to orders and initiation of appropriate action in the absence of orders.

Dual Subordination—The placing of an individual under two different commanders for two different jobs, where the delineation of responsibilities of the individual toward each commander for each job is clearly defined. This can be an acceptable way of organizing.

Efficiency Rating—A systematic means of recording evaluations of the performance of military personnel. Usually rendered on an individual by his commander or supervisor.

Elected Leadership—Leadership conferred upon a member of a group as a result of voting by the group members.

Emergent Leadership—Leadership conferred upon a member of the group without formal election or appointment, or seized by a member and accepted by the group.

Empirical—Refers to the process of gaining knowledge by experiment and observation.

Esprit de Corps—The loyalty to, pride in, and enthusiasm for a unit shown by its members. Involves both group solidarity and identification with the formal organization.

Esteem—Respect accorded an individual because of his worth (as perceived by others) as a member of the organization, whether the organization be formal or informal.

Exception Principle—Routine matters are handled without requiring action on the part of the leader. Only those matters which vary from established policy are brought to his attention.

Factor Analysis—A statistical method for identifying and measuring the relative importance of common factors or variables underlying a complex trait or ability. Frequently used in attempts to isolate personality traits associated with leadership ability.

Feedback—A process by which an individual receives some indication of the effect that his action has had on other people. In communication this consists of some return information from the receiver to the originator indicating the degree to which the receiver understands the original message.

Forecasting—That phase of planning which occurs before the receipt of a mission or the formulation of an objective by the commander. Chiefly concerned with the gathering of information which may influence operations.

Formal Organizations—A group wherein there exists a formally designated differentiation between members in terms of function (job) and/or status (position).

Frame of Reference—A system of standards for comparison, derived from past experience, by which the individual evaluates objects and events in his environment.

Functional—In leadership, the face-to-face relationships maintained between leader and group as a whole and between leader and individual members as they pursue a common goal. Also used to refer to activity expected of a person in the performance of his role. Example: The function of a platoon leader is to accomplish his unit mission. A third definition refers to an organizational concept advocated by F. W. Taylor. (See Chapter VIII).

Generalization—A general conclusion based on a specific event or the interpretation of data gained through experimental observation. Also used to describe the thought process at the conceptual level through which a concept is formed.

Grapevine—Informal communication channel through which information is transmitted. Normally oral. It is differentiated from official communication transmitted through the chain of command.

Great Man Theory—A theory of history espoused by Thomas Carlyle which views human progress in terms of the acts of outstanding individuals.

Group—A collection of two or more interacting individuals with a common purpose.

Group Dynamics—The study of group behavior in terms of the interaction between members of the group. As an approach to leadership, the theory that leadership is a social role derived from this interaction among group members. Major emphasis is placed upon the needs of the followers rather than the personality of the leader or the situation in which the group exists.

Group Solidarity—The sense of unity and integration within a group.

Group Structure—The pattern of formal or informal interpersonal relationships within a group. Generally synonymous with organization.

Homeostasis—The maintenance of constancy of relations or equilibrium in the bodily processes.

Homogeneity of Tasks—The grouping together of similar or related jobs in an organization.

Human Relations—The application of group dynamics theory to the work situation.

Identification—The psychological process of expanding the self through making external things a part of the self.

Induction—A procedure for procuring personnel through involuntary entry into the service.

Informal Group—A group organized on the basis of social and personal relationships not prescribed by a formal organization.

Institutional Leadership—Leadership within a formal group wherein the leader has been granted his authority from above rather than by the members of the group. Also known as appointed leadership.

Interaction—A process in face-to-face groups wherein an action initiated by one member is reacted to by other members, in turn leading to other reactions. Conversation and teamwork are two examples of interaction.

Intermediate Objective—A goal short of the final goal which serves either to accomplish partially the final goal or to provide direction or guidance to the final goal.

Interpersonal Relations—The interaction of persons in a social or work situation. The response of one person to another, and the perception that a person has of the other's response to him. Human relations studies variables in this area such as communication processes, formal and informal groups, and interactional quality of group members.

Leadership—The art of influencing human behavior so as to accomplish a mission in the manner desired by the leader.

Management—The science of employing men and material in the economical and effective accomplishment of a mission. A component of leadership.

Manpower Management—That aspect of military personnel management concerned with manpower resources in terms of numbers of people and dealing with the bulk procurement, allocation and use of manpower.

Materialism—The tendency to value material worth more than social or spiritual values.

Military Occupational Speciality (MOS)—A job description identifying a grouping of duty tasks possessing such close relationships as to warrant the same classification.

Morale—The mental and emotional state of the individual resulting from the various attitudes he has toward all things that affect him.

Motive—A complex state within an organism that directs behavior toward a goal or incentive. A goad to action.

Multiple Command—The placing of an individual under two or more commanders for the same job.

Operations Research—The analytical study of military problems, undertaken to provide commanders and staff agencies with a scientific basis for decisions.

Organizing—Providing a structure that establishes relationships between men and material grouped together for a common purpose.

Perception—The process of interpreting objects or events in the environment so as to make them meaningful.

Performance Counseling—A face-to-face session wherein a senior advises a subordinate of strengths and weaknesses in the latter's performance of duty. Together they devise means for improving the subordinate's performance.

Personality—The sum total of the unique dynamic organization of characteristics within the individual that determines his behavior patterns as he reacts to his environment.

Personnel Management—That component of leadership which is concerned with the employment and treatment of personnel in an organization in such a way as to balance individual needs and job requirements while motivating individuals to maximum effective productivity in the accomplishment of the organization's objective.

Persuasive Leadership—A style of leadership wherein the leader exercises his authority by motivating his subordinates to carry out his decisions. Emphasis is placed on the leader's understanding of the needs of his subordinates and on the example that he personally sets.

Planning—Deciding in advance what is to be done. It includes the who, what, where, when, how, and sometimes the why of a projected course of action.

Policy—A considered decision made by a commander for the purpose of setting guidelines for future action.

Pragmatism—A system of, or tendency in, philosophy that tests the validity of all concepts by their practical results.

Prestige—Respect accorded an individual because of the position held in the formal organization.

Primary Objective—The principal goal toward which a unit's activities are directed.

Problem Counseling—The process whereby one individual assists another to solve a problem of a personal nature that is interfering with the latter's effectiveness.

Proficiency—The skill or knowledge of an individual or ability of a unit.

Reliability—The consistency of a measurement instrument. Fairly consistent results are obtained each time the instrument is administered if the instrument is reliable.

Role—Behavior expected of an individual in a particular position.

Scientific Method—A method of objective investigation of natural phenomena which depends on observation and on careful interpretation of these observations. Makes use of experimental observation whenever variables can be controlled and naturalistic observation when such control of variables is impossible.

Secondary Objective—A goal designed to contribute to the efficiency and/or effectiveness with which primary objectives can be obtained.

Situational Approach—A theory of leadership that proposes that leadership is a function of the skills of the individual members of the group to deal with the demands of the environment in which the group finds itself. The individual most skilled to meet the situational demands is the leader.

Social Distance—The degree of intimacy or closeness of association between individuals occupying positions at different hierarchial levels in the organization structure.

Social Needs—Needs arising out of relationships with other people. Include affiliative, status, and security needs.

Staff—The principal assistants to the line commanders in the execution of their duties. The staff provides advice, prepares plans, accomplishes coordination, and exercises control in the name of the commander.

Staff Parallelism—A practice whereby staff members at different echelons of command complete required actions wholly within staff channels, without the personal attention of the commander. This expedites administration and relieves the commander of burdensome details.

Standing Operating Procedure (SOP)—A set of instructions prescribing specific methods to be used by personnel of a particular unit to perform those tactical and administrative features of operations which the commander desires to make routine.

Status—A position occupied or attributed in relation to other members of a group.

Status Needs—Desire for an established and respected relationship with others in a group.

Subculture—The culture of a definable part of a people; for example, the military.

Suboptimization—Obtaining less than optimum performance in some area of a unit's operations, usually due to the presence of other objectives that preclude maximum effectiveness in all areas.

Systems Analysis—An orderly study of the integrated relationship of objects and their attributes to establish proper functional continuity toward the successful performance of a defined task or tasks.

Theory—A formulation of apparent relationships or underlying principles of certain observed phenomena which has been supported to some degree.

Trait—A characteristic of an individual, either physical or psychological. Physical traits include bodily factors such as height, weight, hair color, etc. Psychological traits are consistent patterns of behavior and include such factors as intelligence, initiative, honesty, etc.

Trait Approach—A theory of leadership that sees the leader as an individual possessed of personality traits that permit him to attract the members of the group to him and set them in motion toward the goal.

Validity—Extent to which a measuring instrument measures what it is supposed to measure.

Index

311